First and Second Corinthians
A Study of Paul's Letters

First and Second Corinthians
A Study of Paul's Letters

Barbara Pappas

Regina Orthodox Press

Salisbury, Massachusetts

1-928653-25-1

Regina Orthodox Press
PO Box 5288
Salisbury MA 01952

800 636 2470
Non-USA 978 463 0730
FAX 978 462 5079

www.reginaorthodoxpress.com

Paul of Tarsus
(circa A.D. 3–67)

A Fond Remembrance

Having one's words in print can bring unique experiences. One of my most memorable has to do with two chance encounters with Bishop Gerasimos Papadopoulos of Abydos, which took place shortly after the first edition of this work was published.

Rev. William Chiganos, Chairman of the Religious Education Commission of the Greek Orthodox Diocese of Chicago and Pastor of the Holy Apostles Church in Westchester, Illinois, introduced me to His Grace when he spoke at the Celebration of Books at Holy Apostles in 1990. At that time, Bishop Gerasimos graciously indicated that he had read my then new book on Paul's *First Epistle to the Corinthians* and offered warm congratulations. Knowing that the province of Corinth was the place of his birth and that he was considered an authority on Paul's writings to that early church, I said that if he ever found the time to read my work completely, I would appreciate any constructive criticism he might offer. "I have read every word," he responded immediately, "it is perfect." Too much in awe to think of anything else to say, I thanked him and our conversation ended. Upon his departure that day, however, he said, "Carry on the work." "We will try to follow your lead, your grace," I responded. "My time on earth will soon be over," he replied, "you must carry on."

The following year, Bishop Gerasimos was the featured speaker at Sts. Peter & Paul Greek Orthodox Church in Glenview, Il. I was anxious to sit at his feet again, to try to absorb some of his wisdom. When Rev. George Scoulas escorted him into the room to take his place at the podium, they passed the chair on the aisle where I was seated. He offered no sign of recognition, but later Fr. George hurried over to tell me that His Grace had recognized me as the author of "the book on Corinthians" and had indicated his hearty approval of it.

Thus emboldened, I approached His Grace after his presentation. He immediately spoke of my text again, so I took the opportunity to ask if he would put his comments in writing, to be included if there were ever to be a second edition. "Take this down," he said:

> *I find this work well prepared and supported by the proper sources. It is a trustworthy guide to help everyone understand the life of the early Church and, thus, to help us know how to live our faith. Practical, yet based on solid Orthodox theology. The text is perfectly right!*
>
> +Bishop Gerasimos of Abydos

I wrote out his words and he signed the paper. To be sure I quoted him correctly, I typed the short paragraph and mailed it to him at his residence on the campus of Holy Cross Seminary in Brookline, Ma. He added a few thoughts, signed the sheet, and returned it to me with his personal greetings.

Bishop Gerasimos fell asleep in the Lord on the Feast of the Holy Spirit, 1995. He has been called a scholar, a true spiritual father, and a leader of the Church. To me he is all that and more. When I get tired or discouraged, his is the loving face I see, and his the voice I hear: "Carry on the work." If loving-kindness, humility, commitment to Christ, and the ability to encourage emulation in others are attributes of holiness—I had the privilege of meeting a living Saint.

While I know that no book written by merely human hands is "perfect," and certainly not this one, Bishop Gerasimos' generous endorsement has encouraged me to offer this new edition.

Contents

Preface

Jesus Christ taught His Apostles orally. They passed on His revelations orally. Before He ascended into Heaven to take His place at the right-hand of God, He told them He would return one day. At first they thought this would take place in their lifetimes. As time went on, however, they began to realize that this was not to be, so some began to preserve, in writing, the great truths He had entrusted to them. Others, like Paul, obeyed His Commission to "make disciples of all the nations" (Mt. 28:20), establishing arms of the original, undivided Church wherever they went and following up visits with letters when teachings had to be strengthened or clarified or abuses corrected.

Thus the individual books of the New Testament were born, written approximately between the years A.D. 50 and 100. The early Christians who had access to these writings treasured them and shared what they had. By the end of the first century, they began to gather all that were in existence. Then a sorting process began: which writings, of all that had been gathered, were inspired by God? To be considered canonical, a document had to pass three tests: it had to have been written by an Apostle or an immediate disciple of an Apostle; it had to be recognized as authentic by at least one leading ecclesiastical community in the ancient Church; and it had to be consistent with Apostolic doctrine—faith preserved in the living tradition of the Church.

There was much contention. Some wanted to exclude books that were finally included: Hebrews, James, 1 Peter, 1 & 3 John, Jude, and Revelation. Others that were finally excluded were considered canonical by some, such as the Shepherd of Hermas or the Epistle of Barnabas. By the fourth century, however, the Church had resolved the disputes with a list of books of the New Testament as we now know it, which was compiled by Athanasius, Bishop of Alexandria, and revealed in his 39th Letter to the churches of his diocese, on the occasion of the Paschal Feast, A.D.367. These 27 books were decreed canonical by Canon XXIV at the Synod of Africa of A.D. 419.[1] Thus it is clear that the Bible came to be through the historical Church, which, when acting as a whole, has the guidance of the Holy Spirit.

From the beginning, heresies were a problem. It was easy to misconstrue scripture and, therefore, necessary that the full intent of Christ's teachings be safeguarded. Enter those whom we now call the Fathers of the Church—those who taught and wrote in the early years of its existence, shedding light on the issues of Scripture as delivered by Christ and as lived and preserved by the early Christians. The present work is a study of Paul's epistles to the Christians at Corinth, based primarily on the Homilies of John Chrysostom (the golden-mouthed), who received his name because of his inspired oratorical and teaching skills. Excerpts from his writings and those of other Church Fathers, as follows, are sprinkled liberally throughout this study (with words in brackets added by the author), because they vividly convey Orthodox theology with ageless clarity and beauty, and because they are just as beneficial today as when they were written:

Andrew of Caesarea (c. A.D. 600)

Aphraates of Alexandria (280–345)

Athanasius of Alexandria (c.298–373)

Augustine of Hippo (354–430)

Barnabas[2]

Basil the Great, of Caesarea (330–379)

Cassian, John (360–435)

Chrysostom, John (347–407)

Clement of Alexandria (150–215)

Clement of Rome (c.30–101)

Climacus, John (570–649)

Cyprian of Carthage (200–258)

Cyril of Alexandria (373–444)

Cyril of Jerusalem (318–386)

Ephraem the Syrian (306–373)

Evagrios the Solitary (c.345)

Gregory the Great (of Rome) (540–603)

Gregory of Nazianzus (329–390)

Gregory of Nyssa (332–394)

Gregory Palamas (1296–1359)

Ignatius of Antioch (c.69)

Irenaeus of Lyons (120–202)

Isaac the Syrian (c. late seventh century)

Isaias of Sketis (d.489)

Justin the Martyr (100–165)

Leo the Great (of Rome) (440–461)

Makarios of Egypt (300–390)

Mathetes[3]

Maximus the Confessor (580–662)

Peter of Damaskos (12th century)

Philotheos of Sinai (9th to 10th century)

Polycarp of Smyrna (c.69–155)

Symeon the New Theologian (949–1022)

Tertullian (160–220)

It is hoped that this taste will inspire some to delve deeper into these spiritual treasures. Quotes are exact from the sources cited, except for minor updating of language form to make reading easier. Where appropriate, quotes from contemporary authors and theologians have been included, to develop a tool useful for teaching the fullness of the truth of Scripture as taught by the early Church and as applicable to contemporary everyday Christian lives—for God's word is never out of date.

"Food for Thought" questions are included at appropriate points within each chapter, with corresponding comments at the end of each chapter, to encourage meditation and discussion. Scripture quoted is from the *New King James Version of the Holy Bible.*

Foreword

When we study Holy Scripture, so we are told by the Early Fathers, we should give a personal application to everything we read. We should regard the words as addressed to each of us, individually, and not to someone else. We should ask not merely, "What does it mean?," but, "What does it mean *for me*, here and now?" The message of Scripture is to become an integral part of our daily life. "In everything that you do or say," St. Anthony of Egypt tells us, "take always as your guide the witness of the Holy Scriptures."

This is exactly what Barbara Pappas helps us to do, in this very welcome introduction to St. Paul's *Second Epistle to the Corinthians*. As in her commentary on the *First Epistle*, she seeks to relate the words of the Bible to our present-day concerns. She is faithful to the Orthodox principle that our understanding of Scripture should be Patristic; so at every point she quotes the Fathers, especially St. John Chrysostom, who more than any other author has shaped the "Scriptural mind" of Orthodoxy. But at the same time, she indicates the practical relevance of Scripture to every one of us at this present moment; she makes Paul and Chrysostom speak to us as our contemporaries. Her words are simple but not superficial, and in the sections titled "Food for Thought," she poses searching questions. All of this makes her book suitable for use equally by individuals and by study circles.

For many of us, I suspect, the *Second Epistle to the Corinthians* is not our favorite epistle. Probably we quote far more often from the *First Epistle*, with its precious references to the Eucharist (1 Cor. 10:16–17, 11:23–29), its image of the Church as a single body formed from many members united in love (12:12–13:13), and its vision of the final resurrection (15:12–

58).   By contrast, when reading the *Second Epistle to the Corinthians* we may easily grow restless when Paul insists at such length on the importance of fundraising (chapters 8–9), while his repeated warnings and rebukes in the final section (chapters 10–13) may leave us discouraged.   Yet, it would be greatly to our loss if, on these grounds, we were to neglect the *Second Epistle*, for it contains some of the Apostle's deepest teaching.   In any case, is not Paul's insistence on almsgiving and mutual responsibility as timely today as ever it was in the past, and should not his warnings lead each of us to examine our own conscience?

For myself, I treasure the *Second Epistle to the Corinthians* more particularly because of four "great moments" that it contains:

First, there is the Trinitarian blessing with which Paul's letter concludes: "The grace of the Lord Jesus Christ, and the love of God, and the communion of the Holy Spirit be with you all" (13:14). This, along with the baptismal command at the end of St. Matthew's Gospel (28:19), is the most definite and explicit affirmation of the doctrine of the Trinity in the whole of the New Testament.

Second, the epistle includes one of Paul's clearest statements about our salvation in Christ: "God was in Christ reconciling the world to Himself" (5:19).   Christ Jesus is our Savior, our "reconciler," because He is one with God the Father: He is the second person of the Holy Trinity, "true God from true God."

Third, Paul indicates not only *that* Christ saves us but also *how* He does so.   He who is true God reconciles us to the Father by sharing totally in our humanness: "For you know the grace of our Lord Jesus Christ, that though He was rich, yet for your sakes He became poor, that you through His poverty might become rich" (8:9). It is typical of Paul that, in the middle of a passage of practical advice concerned with almsgiving, he includes—almost in passing—a concise phrase that sums up the whole meaning of the Incarnation. The "riches" of Christ are His divine glory; His "poverty" signifies His total solidarity with us in our alienated and fallen condition. There is a two-way exchange: Christ shares in our "poverty" and we in His "riches."

Fourth, in memorable words Paul sets before us our future hope, which is nothing less than an unending transfiguration and *Theosis* (deification): "But we all, with unveiled face, beholding as in a mirror the glory of the Lord, are being transformed into the same image from glory to glory" (3:18). "From glory to glory," says the Apostle: there is no limit or final end to our journey through eternity, for however great the "glory" to which we have attained, there is always a greater glory that still awaits us.

These four texts from the *Second Epistle to the Corinthians* have for many years helped me to set my compass as I pursue the spiritual journey. Other readers, with the help of this book, will discover their own personal guidelines or "great moments" in the epistle.

"Christ is not a text but a living Person," says Father Georges Florovsky; and he also states that none of us will profit from reading Scripture unless at the same time we are "in love with Christ." May Barbara's book help us, as we study Scripture, to discover in and through the text the living Person of our Lord. May her words make us more "in love with Christ."

+BISHOP KALLISTOS OF DIOKLEIA

Introduction

Paul was born a Jew and a Roman citizen in Tarsus, Cilicia (now in Turkey), about A.D. 3 and given the name "Saul." Educated as a Pharisee under the renowned rabbinical tutor Gamaliel in Jerusalem (Acts 22:3), he was very devout. Though Jesus' life, Crucifixion, and Resurrection took place while Saul was pursuing his studies, there is no indication he ever saw Jesus. When the young Church began to grow, however, under the guidance of the Apostles and zealous teachers such as Stephen (Acts 6), Saul's opposition was aroused. He stood by and watched, giving tacit approval, while Stephen was stoned to death (Acts 7). Determined to stamp out those who called Jesus the Son of God (Acts 8:3), he received authority from the high priest to travel to Damascus to arrest those who belonged to "the Way" (Acts 9:1–2). On the road to that city, however, he encountered the wonder and power of Christ (Acts 9:3–6). Thoroughly transformed by the events that took place during and after this meeting, he became the "Apostle to the Gentiles," completely devoted to proclaiming Jesus as the Messiah of prophecy. He ceased using the name Saul, taking instead its equivalent in Greek (the common language of the day): Paul.

Paul's turnabout angered the Jews he tried to enlighten. Forced to flee Damascus (Acts 9:23–25), he spent about three years alone in Arabia, where he sought direction from God. He then returned to Jerusalem to confer with Peter (Gal. 1:16–18) and began a life of preaching and organizing the early Church, mainly through writings addressed to churches founded during his three great missionary journeys: from Antioch (now Antakya, Turkey) to Cyprus and several cities in Galatia (now also part of Turkey); from Jerusalem through cities in Syria and Asia Minor to Macedonia (now part of Greece), where he visited Philippi, Thessalonica, Athens, and Corinth; then to many of these cities again and to Ephesus, where he spent two years. Because of his persuasive and relentless style, Paul was constantly beleaguered by adversaries of the Gospel and spent much time in bonds during these years. He was brought to trial in Rome and, because he was a Roman citizen, afforded the "privilege" of being beheaded rather than subjected to the more torturous crucifixion. Thus he became a martyr of the Church in about A.D. 67.

Ancient tradition describes Paul as "small in size, baldheaded, bow-legged, well-built, with eyebrows meeting, rather long-nosed, and full of grace; for sometimes he seemed like a man and sometimes he had the countenance of an angel."[1] His detractors looked with contempt upon his appearance and his speech (2 Cor. 10:10), but no one could deny the power of his written word. He ministered to Corinth under direct instruction from the Lord (Acts 18:1–11). Through Paul, less than 25 years after the Crucifixion of Jesus Christ, His Gospel was preached in the first and worst city in Greece.

Corinth, a city of ancient Greece near the southern extremity of the Isthmus of Corinth, was a very wealthy, worldly city because of its strategic location on the land-bridge linking northern Greece with Peloponnesus and with sea routes to the east and west. It boasted almost half a million people: Greeks, Romans, and Jews. Splendidly placed for commerce and communication, anything preached there would quickly be disseminated in all directions and among all sorts and conditions of people.

The infant Corinthian Church was in a remarkably foul place, for Corinth had a notorious reputation for the love of pleasure and the lax morals of its people. The temple of Aphrodite, the pagan goddess of love, beauty, and fruitfulness, Greek counterpart to the Roman Venus, perched about 1500 feet above the town on the Corinthian acropolis, provided an excuse for sexual license.

> The devil, therefore, seeing that a great and populous city had laid hold of the truth, a city admired for wealth and wisdom and the head of Greece (for Athens and Lacedaemon were then and since in a miserable state, the dominion having long ago fallen away from them) and seeing that with great readiness they had received the word of God, what does he? He divides them. For he knew that even the strongest kingdom of all, divided against itself, shall not stand.
>
> CHRYSOSTOM[2]

Aspects of St. Paul's relationship with the Christians of Corinth have become the subject of modern contention (the dates of his visits, the number of letters he wrote to them, and the order in which they received his various letters). This study presumes the following traditional viewpoint:

The date of Paul's initial visit to Corinth is unknown. He followed up on that visit with a letter (referred to in 1 Cor. 5:9) that has been lost. Returning around A.D. 50, he stayed for 18 months to establish a church there. Then he went to Ephesus, where he was visited by a delegation from Corinth, sent to apprise him of the problems that had developed in the community after his departure. His response was a letter to his errant charges that has become known as his *First Epistle to the Corinthians*, written about A.D. 55. Soon after, he sent Timothy to give them additional guidance (1 Cor. 4:17). Timothy returned to Paul (1 Cor. 16:11) and informed him that the spiritual condition of the church in Corinth was still not good. Paul gave the Corinthians more time, then sent Titus to see how they were doing. Titus met up with Paul again in Macedonia. He brought the good news that, although the

Corinthians had at first resented the harsh words of his epistle, their hearts had softened as they realized his and Christ's love for them. They were now repentant and eager to see Paul again (2 Cor. 7:6–9). Paul then wrote what we know as his *Second Epistle to the Corinthians* (c. A.D. 56) to tell them he had not yet returned as promised because he did not want to be among them until they corrected their ways (2 Cor. 1:23). Now, however, he hoped to come soon. He sent Titus back to Corinth with his latest letter (2 Cor. 8:16–24, 9:1–5) to guide them in the merits of almsgiving and to be sure their collection for the church in Jerusalem would be ready when he arrived—his third visit.

The First Letter of Paul
to the Corinthians

CHAPTER ONE

A Call to Unity in Jesus Christ

After bringing the Gospel to Corinth and establishing a church there, Paul went on to Ephesus. While there, a delegation from Corinth visited him (16:17) and others wrote (7:1) telling him of serious problems, divisions, and disorders that had arisen in their community (1:11). Those who had become leaders of the Christian community in Corinth were focusing their efforts on maintaining their popularity rather than on directing and strengthening the Church. Sexual sins were taking place, pagan rites were being indulged in, Christ's teachings were being misconstrued, and His work was not being done.

Paul considered the Christians of Corinth his spiritual children since he was the first to introduce them to the Gospel. He, therefore, loved them, prayed for their progress and perfection, and tried diligently to help them. Upon hearing of the dissension in the church, he wrote this epistle, around A.D. 55. It seems that he had written them an earlier letter (5:9), which has been lost.

1:1. Paul, called to be an apostle of Jesus Christ through the will of God, and Sosthenes our brother ... Paul establishes his credentials as an Apostle and speaks of himself as having been called—referring to his encounter with Jesus on the road to Damascus, where he had intended to continue his persecution of Christians (Acts 6:8–15, 7:54–60, 8:1–3, 9:1–22). He refers to having been called, not out of pride but to remind the Corinthians that he had been headed in the wrong direction until God redirected his life. This is a significant point because the Corinthian Christians have gone astray, and Paul will now tell them how they must correct their ways.

FOOD FOR THOUGHT: (a). Why would God *call* Paul, who was a known persecutor of Christians, and who had watched while Stephen (one of the first seven deacons of the Church, and the first Christian martyr) was stoned to death? (b). What does this indicate with regard to our lives?

1:2. To the Church of God which is at Corinth ... It was Paul's custom to begin his epistles in this manner, but this verse is also an effort to remind the Corinthians that they are a part of the Church as a whole and are to be united in thought and action, not divided by factions and heresies.

to those who are sanctified in Christ Jesus ... To sanctify is to make holy, to purify, to consecrate. Everyone who is Baptized becomes a part of the Church, the Body of Christ (1 Cor. 12:27), which is holy. The Sacraments are outer visible signs of inner spiritual grace. Through Baptism, we undergo an outer washing in water, symbolizing inner cleansing from sins (the original sin of Adam and Eve and our own personal sin). We retain, however, the consequences of Adam and Eve's disobedience: life in our world of many temptations, where it is easy to sin and difficult to pursue righteousness. Thus we must continually struggle against contamination of the holy state to which we are introduced at Baptism. We are offered assistance in that endeavor by the Sacrament of Eucharist, as part of a lifestyle committed to trying to live according to God's will. "Each one of us receives, through the Sacraments, a seed of sanctity, but it is up to us to make it bear fruit."[1]

called to be saints ... In this world, a saint is a person who is taking part in the struggle toward growth in holiness, while calling upon the Holy Spirit for guidance and power. Man can never totally succeed in this endeavor because of his tendency

to sin, but a sincere attempt shows faith in and love for God—
the basis for salvation (Jas. 1:12).

> FOOD FOR THOUGHT: (c). How does the Church
> help us to become saints?

With all who in every place call on the name of Jesus Christ our Lord, both theirs and ours. The Church throughout the world must be one, involved in the same struggle and bound together by a common faith in Christ. Each of us is a member of His Body. His eyes, ears, and heart are those who are aware of that which needs to be done; His hands, feet, and mouth are those who follow through accordingly. He is the Head. Each member of His Body is called to try to do that which is necessary in the Church and in the world so that His work, the salvation of mankind, will be accomplished.

1:3. Grace to you and peace from God our Father and Lord Jesus Christ. Paul's prayer is that the Corinthian Christians open themselves to grace and peace, gifts from God which have the power to resolve the differences between them.

Grace is a gift from God that enables man to take part in the struggle to grow in holiness, striving against his tendency to sin. The peace that Paul refers to is not the fragile peace of this world, where trying to live by Christian standards often brings turmoil (Mt. 10:34–42) but the inner peace that comes from true communion with God (Jn. 14:27, 16:33). In the Divine Liturgy we consistently pray for peace from above and are asked to pray in peace.

1:4. I thank my God always concerning you for the grace of God which was given to you by Christ Jesus ... Paul practices what he preaches (Eph. 5:20; Phil. 4:4–7)—thanking

God in all situations. Almost all of his epistles begin in this manner.

> **FOOD FOR THOUGHT:** (d). How is it possible to be thankful in all situations—times of tribulation, persecution, illness, death? (Read Rom. 8:28–39.)

1:5–8. that you were enriched in every thing by Him in all utterance and all knowledge, even as the testimony of Christ was confirmed in you, so that you came short in no gift, eagerly waiting for the revelation of our Lord Jesus Christ, who will also confirm you to the end, that you may be blameless in the day of our Lord Jesus Christ. Armed with Christ's teachings and the power of the Holy Spirit, the Corinthians had all they needed to try to live Christ-like lives to demonstrate faith. Paul's hope is that on the Day of Judgment, at Christ's Second Coming, it will be revealed that they (and we) zealously persisted in this effort (Phil. 3:12–14). A person who professes belief in Christ but does not try to grow in obedience to Him is not really a Christian.

1:9. God is faithful, by whom you were called ... We are called by God to become a part of His eternal Kingdom through Christ (see Jn. 15:16). Those who respond to this call will be beneficiaries of all of His promises.

> God, wishing men and angels to follow His will, resolved to create them free to do righteousness; possessing reason, that they may know by whom they are created, and through whom they, not existing formerly, do now exist; and with a law that they should be judged by Him, if they do anything contrary to right reason: and of ourselves we, men and angels, shall be convicted of having acted sinfully, unless we

repent beforehand. But if the word of God foretells that some angels and men shall be certainly punished, it did so because it foreknew that they would be unchangeably wicked—but not because God had created them so.

JUSTIN[2]

God calls those who seek Him, following the inner yearning He creates in man (Acts 17:26–27). Man perceives this inherent yearning as an emptiness—a need—and strives to fill it. Fortunate are those who fill it with love for God. Those who, instead, pursue false gods such as money, power, fame, pleasure, a person (whatever takes first place in our lives and distracts or diverts us from union with the Creator) never find true peace.

> **FOOD FOR THOUGHT:** (e). Who does God want to be saved? (Read 2 Peter 3:9.) (f). Will there be universal salvation? (Read Mt. 22:14, Rom. 2:5–10.) (g). What is the criteria for salvation? (Read Mt. 7:21–27.)

into the fellowship of His Son, Jesus Christ our Lord. This fellowship is described by 2 Tim. 2:11–13:

> *If we died with Him, we shall also live with Him.* If we have died with Christ symbolically through Baptism and lived a life of trying to do His will, not our own, we will live with Him in His Kingdom—forever.

> *If we endure, we shall also reign with Him.* If we continue, throughout our lives, to try to be Christ-like, to show our love for and faith in Him in spite of difficulties, God will call each of us by

name and give us the Crown of Life (Jas. 1:12, Rev. 3:5).

If we deny Him, He also will deny us. If we spurn this fellowship, and deny through our words or actions that He is the Lord of our lives, He will deny (on Judgment Day) that we belong to Him (Mk. 8:38).

If we are faithless, He remains faithful. He is always there for us. As long as we have life, it is never too late to turn to Him (Mt. 20:1–16), but sooner is better (Mk. 10:13–16).

1:10–13. Now I plead with you brethren, by the name of our Lord Jesus Christ, that you all speak the same thing, and that there be no divisions among you, but that you be perfectly joined together in the same mind and in the same judgment. For it has been declared to me concerning you, my brethren, by those of Chloe's household, that there are contentions among you. Now I say this, that each of you says, "I am of Paul," or "I am of Apollos," or "I am of Cephas," or "I am of Christ." Is Christ divided? Was Paul crucified for you? Or were you baptized in the name of Paul? Through Baptism we are united with Christ—not the person who introduced us to Him. Thus all Christians are connected through Him and should be of one mind on matters having to do with the Christian life.

FOOD FOR THOUGHT: (h). What do verses 10–13 say about divisions in the Church (among all who call themselves Christians)? (i). There are hundreds of Christian denominations. Is this acceptable to God? (Read Eph. 4:4–6.) (j). What is the criteria for unity? (See 2 Thess. 2:15.)

1:14–16. I thank God that I baptized none of you except Crispus and Gaius, lest anyone should say that I baptized in my own name. Yes, I also baptized the household of Stephanas. Besides, I do not know whether I baptized any other. Paul's calling was to teach the Gospel—he usually left to others the easier task of administering the rite of Baptism. Note that Stephanas' entire family was Baptized at one time, which was the custom in the early Church, upon conversion of the parents to Christianity (see also Acts 16:15). This must, in many cases, have included infants and children, a practice that corresponds with the Orthodox tradition of Baptizing infants when they are brought to the Church by believing parents and/or godparents. Being a part of the Church from a very young age, with continual access to the Sacraments, allows for early and continual spiritual nourishment. As we do not refrain from giving our children food until they understand the need of their bodies for vitamins and minerals, neither do we refrain from providing spiritual nourishment to them until they understand Christian theology. This, of course, presupposes that parents and/or godparents will teach their children about God, His love, and His promises as they are able to absorb the knowledge. Infants and children learn in mysterious ways, using all of their senses. The faith is best taught through experience and by example, with explanations offered at appropriate times.

> You have seen how numerous are the gifts of Baptism. Although many think that the only gift it confers is the remission of sins, we have counted its honors to the number of ten. It is on this account that we baptize even infants, although they are sinless, that they may be given the further gifts of sanctification, justice, filial adoption, and inheritance, that they may

be brothers and members of Christ, and become dwelling places for the Spirit.

CHRYSOSTOM[3]

Besides the gifts of Baptism outlined above, Chrysostom elsewhere lists pardon from punishment, justification, and redemption.

1:17–19. For Christ did not send me to baptize, but to preach the gospel, not with wisdom of words, lest the cross of Christ should be made of no effect. For the message of the cross is foolishness to those who are perishing, but to us who are being saved it is the power of God. For it is written: "I will destroy the wisdom of the wise, and bring to nothing the understanding of the prudent." Under God's divine plan, sin had to be atoned for, but this required a perfect life. No mere man could accomplish this on his own—he needed a savior. Jesus lived a perfect life, then accepted death, the consequence of man's sin. Since then, under the final Blood Covenant between God and man, those who are a part of Christ through Baptism and a life of faith will share that which He earned—eternal life with God in His Kingdom—which begins in this life but will reach its fullness after Christ's Second Coming. This is the message of the Cross. This knowledge is power because it enables us to live joyously, with freedom from fear of death, and to pass this confidence on to others. No matter what happens to us or to those we love in this life, no one can rob us of this power. To those who do not believe this saving truth, however, or are indifferent to it, the message of the Cross is foolishness.

> FOOD FOR THOUGHT: (k). To whom was "paid"
> the price of death for sin? ... to God? ... to Satan?

1:20–21. Where is the wise? Where is the scribe? Where is the disputer of this age? Has not God made foolish

the wisdom of this world? For since, in the wisdom of God, the world through wisdom did not know God, it pleased God through the foolishness of the message preached to save those who believe.** Man, through his own efforts, can never fully comprehend God. Only He, Who accomplishes His purposes in wondrous ways, possesses perfect wisdom, of which we partake when we accept, by faith, the Gospel of salvation through His Son. Living a sacramental life is the natural and necessary outcome of true faith. Through the Sacraments which God offers His people through the Church, man is the recipient of divine grace, power, and wisdom. These gifts enable him to try to live a Christ-like life, the indicator of true faith.

1:22–24. For Jews request a sign, and Greeks seek after wisdom; but we preach Christ crucified, to the Jews a stumbling block and to the Greeks foolishness, but to those who are called, both Jews and Greeks, Christ the power of God and the wisdom of God. Crucifixion was the Roman method of executing slaves. It was an agonizing, degrading death, which usually took four to six days. (In Jesus' case it took only six hours because God shortened His agony, see Mk. 13:20.) To the Jews, a crucified Messiah was unthinkable, a curse (Deut. 21:23; Gal. 3:13). They felt that if Jesus was really the Son of God, He would not have allowed Himself to hang on the Cross (Mt. 27:41–42). To the Greeks (pagans), who prized worldly "wisdom" and intellectual debate, and among whom the study of philosophy was popular, for God to take human form and then allow Himself to be put to death made no sense. The Apostles were ordinary men who relied not on dazzling others with philosophical thought but on the simple truth of salvation through Christ.

1:25. Because the foolishness of God is wiser than men, and the weakness of God is stronger than men. God's all-encompassing strength and wisdom make Him unafraid to appear weak and foolish to the unenlightened.

1:26–29. For you see your calling, brethren, that not many wise according to the flesh, not many mighty, not many noble, are called. But God has chosen the foolish things of the world to put to shame the wise, and God has chosen the weak things of the world to put to shame the things that are mighty; and the base things of the world and the things that are despised God has chosen, and the things which are not, to bring to nothing the things that are, that no flesh should glory in His presence. The Gospel was and is offered to all people, but most of the first Christians belonged to the common class of people, fishermen and manual laborers, for two reasons:

First, because those who are wise, successful, and influential in worldly matters are often too distracted by their pursuits to consider spiritual matters.

> The unlearned were more open to conviction, for they were free from the extreme madness of accounting themselves wise. ... Nothing is so useless towards an accurate knowledge of God as arrogance and being nailed down to wealth; for these dispose a man to admire things present, and make no account of the future; and they stop up the ears through the multitude of cares.
>
> CHRYSOSTOM[4]

Second, so that those who did God's work could boast, not of their own abilities, but only of the power of God.

> And when they say that the Apostles were rude, let us say that they were also untaught, and unlettered, poor, vile, stupid, and obscure. It is not a slander on

the Apostles to say so but even a glory that, being such, they should have outshone the whole world.

For those untrained, rude, illiterate men completely vanquished the wise, the powerful, the tyrants, and those who flourished in wealth and glory and all outward good things: which makes it abundantly clear that great is the power of the Cross and that these things were done by no human strength.

CHRYSOSTOM[5]

God used the inglorious elements of the Crucifixion of His Son on a cross to bring about the most glorious gift of salvation for mankind. He accomplished this through those who were considered insignificant in the eyes of the world.

1:30–31. But of Him you are in Christ Jesus, who became for us wisdom from God—and righteousness and sanctification and redemption—that is, as it is written, "He who glories, let him glory in the Lord." The Son of God took on flesh and became man to bring man to God.

For in no other way could we have learned the things of God, unless our Master, existing as the Word, had become man. For no other being had the power of revealing to us the things of the Father, except His own proper Word. For what other person *knew the mind of the Lord,* or who else *has become His counselor?* (Rom. 11:34). Again, we could have learned in no other way than by seeing our Teacher and hearing His voice with our own ears, that, having become imitators of His works as well as doers of His words, we may have communion with Him.

IRENAEUS[6]

Think what this means: God loved man so much that He sent His Son, Who willingly took on the condition of fallen humanity with its frustrations, pain, sorrow, loneliness, danger, and death. Like a lifeguard who enters a turbulent ocean to lead a struggling swimmer to shore, Jesus Christ entered the world to help those who, recognizing that He can save them, reach out for His helping hand (Jn. 1:1–14). Through the Holy Spirit, they gradually take on His qualities to prepare for life in His Kingdom. Those who understand this realize that everything they have that is worthwhile comes from God—therefore all glory belongs to Him.

FOOD FOR THOUGHT COMMENTS

(a). Why would God *call* Paul, who was a known persecutor of Christians, and who had watched while Stephen (one of the first seven deacons of the Church, and the first Christian martyr) was stoned to death? God called Paul because, while his actions were wrong, his motives were pure. He loved God and thought he was doing His work—routing those who were, in his opinion, blaspheming by calling Jesus the Son of God.

(b). What does this indicate with regard to our lives? If we act out of sincere belief, while asking for and being open to guidance from God, He will direct or redirect our paths as necessary. Working with God is always synergistic—His will and our cooperation with it are required.

(c). How does the Church help us to become saints? The Church offers Sacraments, guidance, and prayer. It has also preserved the stories of the lives of many who have struggled throughout their days on earth to become holy in imitation of Christ and who have been recognized as having endured to the end, thus showing themselves, after death, to be members of the

Church Triumphant, the Kingdom of Heaven (Jn. 12:26 and Phil. 3:17). The stories of their lives can inspire us to dedicate our lives to Christ in like manner, which is the reason we find icons of these Saints in every Orthodox Church. There are also countless numbers of unknown Saints in Heaven and on earth—known only to God and perhaps those around them in their quiet, dedicated lives.

> It's a wonderful thought that at this moment friends of ours, people we have known and loved, are at the side of the Lord in Heaven, sharing His joy as once they shared his pains. Their hearts were never wedded to this world and its values, but were focused on Him who died for us, and was raised from the dead for us by God.
>
> So copy them, as they copied Christ. Hold the faith firmly, join together to defend the truth, and love one another as brothers. Indeed, make a habit of giving way to one another, not regarding anyone as inferior or beneath your attention. In that way you will have the spirit of Christ, who never treated any person with anything less than courtesy and love, however poor, or sinful, or outcast they were.
>
> POLYCARP[7]

(d). How is it possible to be thankful in all situations— times of tribulation, persecution, illness, death? (Read Rom. 8:28–39.) Nothing can happen without God's knowledge to those who belong to Him—He knows even the exact number of hairs each of us has on our head (Lk. 12:7). He is in control but sometimes allows (does not cause) difficulties to enter our lives for good reason (1 Pet. 1:6–7): to *test* us, for a person's true faith and character (or lack of) are revealed under stress; to *purify* us, as gold is refined by fire; to *strengthen* us, because each hurdle we overcome makes us better able to confront the next obstacle in our lives; to *awaken* us to those things that are of eternal value; to *call us to repentance*, and/or to *remind us of our need for Him.* God also sometimes allows the righteous to suffer to *serve as examples of faith* to others. (See this study and "Food for Thought Comment" for 2 Cor. 12:7–10.)

God never promised that the Christian life would be free from pain. Suffering is a part of being human and living in this imperfect world, where evil exists. It would be the cruelest of hoaxes for God to step in to right every wrong, for then each of us would waste our lives without realizing that the barrier of sin between God and man has been removed only by Jesus Christ, to Whom those who desire union with God must attach themselves.

> How could the Lord Jesus bring himself to suffer at the hands of men? After all, He is the Lord of all the earth, the one through whom men themselves were made in God's image. Even if He was willing to suffer as a mark of His love for us, how could it happen? Would this not detract from his power and dignity?
>
> The answer, as one would expect, is to be found in the Scriptures. The prophets, inspired by the Lord Himself, foretold His coming as a man, since if He were to destroy death and bring in eternal life it was essential that He should take upon Himself human flesh. And to take on human flesh involves suffering: the two are virtually indistinguishable. Has there ever been a human being who went through life without suffering?
>
> BARNABAS[8]

What God *has* promised is that He will help us through every difficulty we encounter in life (Mt. 28:20) *if* we ask for His help—because doing so shows faith in His existence, His omnipotence, and His Love (Mt. 7:7). Whatever enters into our lives becomes a part of the total picture of who we are and what we are becoming. If we invite Him to direct our lives according to His will and accept the outcome, whatever it might be, we will continue to grow in His image. In this regard it can be said that "all things work together for good for those who love God" (Rom. 8:28).

> It is impossible to escape tribulation in this world, but the man who is given over to the will of God bears tribulation easily, seeing it but putting his trust in the Lord, and so his tribulations pass![9]

These are the basic truths to remember when trouble strikes. They enable us to be thankful in every situation: that God is in control and that everything fits somehow into His divine plan.

> Always to give thanks, this is a mark of a philosophic soul. Have you suffered any evil? But if you will, it is no evil. Give thanks to God, and the evil is changed into good. Say as Job said, *Blessed be the name of the Lord forever* (Job 1:21). For tell me, what such great thing have you suffered? Has disease befallen you? Yet it is nothing strange. For our body is mortal, and liable to suffer. Has a want of possessions overtaken you? But these also are things to be acquired, and again to be lost, and that abide here. But is it plots and false accusations of enemies? But it is not we that are injured by these, but they who are the authors of them. *For the soul,* he says, *that sins, itself shall also die* (Ezek. 18:4). And he has not sinned who suffers the evil, but he who has done the evil.
>
> CHRYSOSTOM[10]

(e). Who does God want to be saved? (Read 2 Peter 3:9.) God loves all His creations and wants everyone to be saved from damnation (eternity separated from Him and His goodness), and gives everyone this opportunity.

As you may learn by examining our writings, the chief of the wicked demons we call the serpent, Satan, the Devil, and Christ foretold that he with his army of demons, and the men who follow him, will be cast into the fire [of Hell—the burning agony of having denied oneself eternal blessedness] to be punished for endless ages. The cause of God's delay in doing this is His regard for mankind, for in His foreknowledge He sees that some will be saved by repentance, some who are, perhaps, not yet in existence.

JUSTIN[11]

(f). Will there be universal salvation? (Read Mt. 22:14, Rom. 2:5–10.) There will not be universal salvation. God offers salvation to everyone, through His Son, but not all avail themselves of it.

> Indeed, in the beginning when He created man, He endowed him with the power of understanding, of choosing the truth, and of doing right; consequently, before God no man has an excuse if he does evil, for all men have been created with the power to reason and to reflect. If anyone does not believe that God takes an interest in these things, he will by some artifice imply either that God does not exist, or that though He does exist, He takes delight in evil, or that He is (as unmoved) as stone, and that neither virtue nor vice is a reality, but that things are considered good or bad only in the opinion of men: this indeed would be the height of blasphemy and injustice.

JUSTIN[12]

(g). What is the criteria for salvation? (Read Mt. 7:21–27.) Only those whose lives demonstrate faith (that God exists and that His Son Jesus Christ is the Messiah of prophecy) will be a part of God's eternal Kingdom (Jn. 14:6).

Perhaps each of you will say to himself: "I have believed, I shall be saved." He speaks what is true if to faith he joins good works. That is indeed true faith which does not deny in work what it professes in word. For this Paul says of certain false faithful: *They profess that they know God; but in their works they deny Him* (Tit. 1:16). For this John also says: *He who says that he knows God, and keeps not His Commandments is a liar, and the truth is not in him* (1 Jn. 2:4).

GREGORY THE GREAT[13]

(h). What do verses 10–13 say about divisions in the Church (among all who call themselves Christians) Since there is only one Savior of mankind—Jesus Christ, the Son of God—all Christians should be living and teaching the same truths, for "God is not the author of confusion" (1 Cor. 14:33).

> The emphatic force of the word "schisms," [shown in Scripture text as "divisions"] was a sufficient accusation. For it was not that they had become many parts, each entire within itself, but rather the One [Body which originally existed] had perished. For had they been entire churches, there might be many of them; but if they were divisions, then that first One was gone. For that which is entire within itself not only does not become many by division into many parts, but even the original one is lost. Such is the nature of divisions.

CHRYSOSTOM[14]

The beliefs and practices that were contrary to the teachings of the Gospel would destroy the church of Corinth if they were not corrected, because they would cause permanent divisions. Some believed one thing, some another. Some followed one leader, some another. The unity that comes from a common faith in one Lord would no longer be the binding element it is intended to be. Thus there would be no continuity of the Church that Christ had founded through Paul in existence in Corinth—each group would be only somewhat like the original. The same would hold true in our day. There can be many "entire churches," each containing the fullness of the truth about Jesus Christ, but there should not be divisions, with each containing only parts of the truth.

> Although the Church of Jesus Christ is found in many different places, she is one Church, not many. After all, there are many rays of sunlight, but only one sun. A tree has many boughs, each slightly different from the others, but all drawing their strength from one source. Many streams may flow down a hillside, but they all originate from the same spring. In exactly the same way, each local congregation belongs to the one Church.
>
> If you put a solid object across a ray of the sun it disappears, cut off from its source of light. If you break a branch off a tree, it dies and can never bud again. And if you dam up a stream, the course will soon dry up.
>
> The Church offers the light of Christ to the world, flooding out from Him who is the source of all light. Cut off that light, and the darkness is total. To cut oneself off from the Body of Christ, where the light shines, is to choose darkness.
>
> The Church stretches out her branches all over the earth, offering shelter and refreshment to the weary. And she also pours out the living water, which we can drink and never thirst again.

At all costs, let's make sure that we are not guilty, by
our divisions, of cutting off from men and women that
light, that shelter and that water of life.

CYPRIAN[15]

**(i). There are hundreds of Christian denominations. Is
this acceptable to God?** Jesus said, "If a Kingdom is divided
against itself: that Kingdom cannot stand. And if a house is
divided against itself: that house cannot stand" (Mk. 3:24–25).
The many Christian denominations in existence serve to
weaken the Church, robbing her of the power she would have if
all were united in "one Lord, one Faith, one Baptism" (Eph.
4:5).

All who profess to be followers of Christ should be united in the
fullness of the truth of His Gospel. Divisions do harm to the
entire Body. All Christians have an obligation to seek the
fullness of the truth and to share it. It is logical to seek this
truth in the life and teachings of the early Church, as
contained in writings which have been preserved from those
times: Scripture and the teachings of the Fathers of the
Church, who sought to safeguard the true meanings of God's
word, and in the Holy Tradition of the Church, which at first
was not written but taught by one Christian to another.

> Concerning the teachings of the Church, whether
> publicly proclaimed (kerygma) or reserved to mem-
> bers of the household of faith (dogmata), we have
> received some from written sources, while others have
> been given to us secretly, through apostolic tradition.
> Both sources have equal force in true religion. No one
> would deny either source—no one, at any rate, who is
> even slightly familiar with the ordinances of the
> Church. If we attacked unwritten customs, claiming
> them to be of little importance, we would fatally
> mutilate the Gospel, no matter what our intentions—
> or rather, we would reduce the Gospel teachings to

25

bare words. For instance ... which book teaches us to pray facing the East? Have any saints left for us in writing the words to be used in the invocation over the Eucharistic bread and the cup of blessing? As everyone knows, we are not content in the liturgy simply to recite the words recorded by St. Paul or the Gospels, but we add other words both before and after, words of great importance for this mystery. We have received these words from unwritten teaching. We bless Baptismal water and the oil for Chrismation as well as the candidate approaching the font. By what written authority do we do this, if not from secret and mystical tradition? Even beyond blessing the oil, what written command do we have to anoint with it? What about Baptizing a man with three immersions, or other Baptismal rites, such as the renunciation of Satan and his angels? Are not all these things found in unpublished and unwritten teachings, which our fathers guarded in silence, safe from meddling and petty curiosity? They had learned their lesson well; reverence for the mysteries is best encouraged by silence. The uninitiated were not even allowed to be present at the mysteries; how would you expect these teachings to be paraded about in public documents? ...

Dogma is one thing, kerygma another; the first is observed in silence, while the latter is proclaimed to the world. One form of silence is the obscurity found in certain passages of Scripture, which makes the meaning of some dogmas difficult to perceive for the reader's own advantage. For instance, we all pray facing East, but few realize that we do this because we are seeking Paradise, our old fatherland, which God planted in the East in Eden. We all stand for prayer on Sunday, but not everyone knows why. We stand for prayer on the day of the Resurrection to remind ourselves of the graces we have been given: not only because we have been raised with Christ and are obliged to seek the things that are above, but also because Sunday seems to be an image of the age to come. ... This day [which is called, theologically, the first and the eighth day] foreshadows the state which is to follow the present age: a day without sunset, nightfall, or successor, an age which does not grow old or come to an end. It is therefore necessary for the Church to teach her newborn children to stand for prayer on this day, so that they will always be reminded of eternal life, and not neglect preparations for their journey.

BASIL[16]

(j). What is the criteria for unity? (See 2 Thess. 2:15.) Truth cannot be compromised. Orthodoxy holds that true unity (inter-communion) among Christians can come only from full agreement in matters of faith: the fullness of the teachings that Jesus handed down to the Apostles, which the Orthodox Church considers itself to have "been enabled to preserve." For a full discussion of this topic read "The Orthodox Church and the Reunion of Christians," *The Orthodox Church*, Chapter 16, by Bishop Kallistos Ware.

(k). To whom was "paid" the price of death for sin? ... to God? ... to Satan? Jesus' death for sin is not to be understood in the literal sense as being exacted "by" and paid "to" someone, but more in the sense of a substitute accepting the painful consequences for the wrongful actions of others.

To whom was that Blood offered which was shed for us, and for what purpose was it shed; this great and precious Blood of our God Who was both Priest and Victim? For we were held in bondage by the Wicked One, sold under the dominion of sin, receiving instead the pleasure of wickedness. But if the price of redemption is paid to the one who holds the bond, to whom, I ask, was it offered here, and why? If to the

Wicked One: then alas for the loss of it! If the thief receives, not alone from God, but also God Himself as ransom, it would have been more equitable to have saved the payment of so great a price in exchange for his tyranny. But if it was paid to the Father first, how was this done? For we were not held in bondage by Him. And again, why should the Blood of His only-Begotten Son be acceptable to the Father, Who would not accept Isaac when he was offered by his father, but instead changed the sacrifice, substituting a ram in place of the rational victim? (Gen. 22:11.)

Is it not plain that the Father accepted It, but that He neither demanded It, nor had need of It; but because of the plan of the redemption, and because it was required that man be restored to sanctity by means of the humanity assumed by God, so that, tyranny being overcome by a man's strength, He might deliver us, and bring us back to Himself by means of His Son, Who did all this for the honor of the Father Whom in all things He obeys?

GREGORY OF NAZIANZUS[17]

In the beginning, after God created the heavens and the earth and everything visible and invisible, He looked at what He had created and saw that it was good (Gen. 1). Then, out of love, in order to share His handiwork, God fashioned man: His masterpiece. He put man in a perfect place, where there was no sickness, no sorrow, no death. In return for eternal blessedness, growing in union with Him, God asked only that man return this love and that he demonstrate it by obeying one commandment. The condition of love was also necessary if man were to live in Eden: where anything less than love is allowed, perfection ceases to exist.

Disobedience would bring eviction from paradise to a place where there would be danger, suffering, and death: a steep price, but one commensurate with the potential good. Because love must include choice, man was given the gift of free will. Because of this gift, God *allowed* Satan to tempt Adam and Eve, and He *allowed* Adam and Eve to disobey, as a means of testing their love for Him. Thus through Satan's influence, suffering and death came to mankind. God did not assign this role to Satan, he chose it for himself.

Jesus' perfect life satisfied God's condition of obedience. Yet because Satan's chief concern is to make war with those "who keep the commandments of God" (Rev. 12:17), he conspired to bring about Jesus' death (Jn. 13:26–27), which was unwarranted, illegal. He had been completely obedient, yet He suffered the consequences of disobedience. Thus Satan's hold over man was broken.

> Irenaeus, Origen, and Gregory of Nyssa all show how Satan, wishing to take into his power the only being over whom he had none, is justly dispossessed. Certain Fathers, especially Gregory of Nyssa, propose the symbol of a divine ruse: on the hook of His divinity, the humanity of Christ is the bait; the devil throws himself on the prey, but the hook pierces Him—he cannot swallow God, and dies.[18]

God accepted the sacrifice of His Son, by economia, on behalf of those who are united with Him through Baptism and a life of faith. As part of Him (His Body, the Church) they share His inheritance: the fullness of the Kingdom.

CHAPTER TWO

The Power of the Gospel

Chapter One closes with the reminder that God often chooses a common person to be an instrument of His will, to make it clear that the work accomplished takes place through divine—not human—power. Paul stresses that this is so in his case.

2:1–2. And I, brethren, when I came to you, did not come with excellence of speech or of wisdom declaring to you the testimony of God. For I determined not to know anything among you except Jesus Christ and Him crucified. Paul writes in a humble tone, reminding the Corinthians that he came to them without any power or glory of his own but with the simple truth about Christ: He accepted death to atone for the sins of mankind, then rose from the grave, proving that He is the Messiah of Old Testament prophecy (Isa. 53:1–12, Rom. 5:6,8).

2:3. I was with you in weakness, in fear, and in much trembling. The message Paul brought was powerful, staggering, and dangerous. It put him and those who listened to it at risk of angering the Jews, many of whom were as zealously anti-Christian as Paul had been. To be a Christian was to live in danger of persecution and death. Paul had no illusions about himself and the difficult job he had to do. He felt ill-equipped for his mission and had the same fears anyone would, dreading suffering and death, but did not flee from his calling or its consequences.

> So that they who assert that he had no fear ... not
> only do not honor him, but rather deprive him of his

due praises. For if he feared not, what endurance or self-restraint was there in bearing the danger?

CHRYSOSTOM[1]

FOOD FOR THOUGHT: (a) What fears does a modern Christian face? Using Paul as an example, how can we best deal with these fears?

2:4. And my speech and my preaching were not with persuasive words of human wisdom, but in demonstration of the Spirit and of power ... Paul was learned, but he had no worldly power. He was a common person bringing a dangerous message to common people, yet he was believed and lives were changed. This clearly points to heavenly assistance.

2:5. that your faith should not be in the wisdom of men but in the power of God. The Apostles developed no new theories of their own. They just preached the Gospel and lived their lives by it as Christ had taught them. Yet, through the grace of God, they changed the course of the world.

FOOD FOR THOUGHT: (b). What is the message of this verse for us?

2:6–8. However, we speak wisdom among those who are mature, yet not the wisdom of this age, nor of the rulers of this age, who are coming to nothing. But we speak the wisdom of God in a mystery, the hidden wisdom which God ordained before the ages for our glory, which none of the rulers of this age knew; for had they known, they would not have crucified the Lord of glory. To those who cannot read, the knowledge imparted in a book is hidden, the words being to them meaningless hieroglyphics, though they hold the open book in their hands. Likewise, when unbelievers encounter the word of God, its power eludes them.

They hear not and see not because their hearts and minds are closed (Mt. 11:15). Believers hear God's truths and see evidence of Him everywhere. It is for them that the Apostles unfolded God's plan for the salvation of all mankind.

God is all-wise, all-knowing. From the beginning, He gave man, His most beloved creation, the gift of free will (the ability to choose). Without free will, man would have been like a robot, able to do only that for which he had been programmed. With this gift, man is able to become like God, through love demonstrated by obedience (Gen. 2), not for God's sake but for his own. However, with this gift comes the right to turn from God, in disobedience. God could foresee that man would not use the gift of free will wisely; he would succumb to Satan's deceptions and would disobey, making it necessary that God follow through with the stated consequences of sin: eviction from Paradise.

The perils outside the Garden of Eden were great: sorrow, sickness, tragedy. But for the ultimate good of man, it was necessary that he experience them, in much the same way a child must be allowed, in a controlled manner, to experience the consequences of his actions, so that he learns to make wise choices. Thus God gave mankind the painful but invaluable opportunity to see for himself that which is wrought by disobedience. It was part of His divine plan though, from the very beginning, to send His Son when the time was right, to offer man a chance to return to a state of grace. God revealed this divine plan to Adam and Eve in the first prophecy, after they had disobeyed, before He drove them out of Eden (Gen. 3:24).

> **FOOD FOR THOUGHT:** (c). What were the specifics of the first prophecy (Gen. 3:15)?

2:9. But as it is written: "Eye has not seen, nor ear heard, nor have entered into the heart of man the things which God has prepared for those who love Him." It is beyond man's ability to fathom the fullness of God's Kingdom. The grandest earthly experience in combination with the most fertile imagination can provide only hints as to the wonder and beauty that await God's people.

> FOOD FOR THOUGHT: (d). What does Scripture indicate about the conditions that will prevail in Heaven?

2:10–13. But God has revealed them to us through His Spirit. For the Spirit searches all things, yes, the deep things of God. For what man knows the things of a man except the spirit of the man which is in him? Even so no one knows the things of God except the Spirit of God. Now we have received, not the spirit of the world, but the Spirit who is from God, that we might know the things that have been freely given to us by God. These things we also speak, not in words which man's wisdom teaches, but which the Holy Spirit teaches, comparing spiritual things with spiritual. God is Spirit ... (Read Jn. 4:24). In order to understand Him we must be filled with His Holy Spirit, which is available to us through the Sacrament of Chrismation, our own personal Pentecost.

> Only the Holy Spirit will transmit to us that which
> the Son and Word of God has offered to us.[2]

The grace that the Holy Spirit manifests in each person is commensurate with the extent to which, by faith, s/he invites and cooperates with that power.

> When we hear of the Spirit, the mind may not
> imagine to itself an image of some limited circum-

scribed nature, liable to change, or alteration, or at all like a created thing, but must go on in its conception to the very highest notions, and form to itself an idea of an intelligent Being, infinite in power, of greatness without measure, bounded neither by time nor by ages, bountiful of its own goodness, to whom all turn who need sanctification, to whom all aspire who live in holiness, as though watered and assisted by Its breath to arrive at their due perfection. A Being who perfects others, Itself needing nothing; existing as not needing to be renewed, yet giving life abundantly; enlarging through no addition, but at once complete; at rest within itself, yet in all places; the source of holiness, the light of the mind, and *providing light from Itself to every faculty of the soul that searches for truth*; by nature inaccessible, yet yielding to goodness; filling every need by Its power, but *given only to those who are worthy of It, to whom It is not given in the same measure, but in the measure of each man's faith (Rom. 12:6).*

Simple in nature, manifold in powers, wholly present in each single one, and whole and entire in all places. Impassively divided, yet wholly bestowed, like the rays of the sun whose favor each enjoys as though it shone for him alone; yet it shines on land and sea and fills the air. So the Spirit, to each one who receives It, as though given to him alone, pours forth sufficient and perfect grace to each one, is *enjoyed by each one, not in the measure of Its power, but of their capacity.*

Now the Spirit is not united to the soul by drawing near to it in place (for how may what is corporeal draw near to what is incorporeal?) but through the withdrawal of the passions, which, drawing close to the soul through its affection for the flesh, have drawn it away from its friendship with God. When a man becomes clean of the stain he received through sin, and has returned to his natural beauty, restoring to

its former resemblance the royal image within him,
only then may he draw near to the Paraclete. And
He, like the sun, will show you, your eye now made
pure, the Image of the Invisible in Himself. And in
the blessed contemplation of this Image you shall see
the unspeakable beauty of the Archetype.

Through His aid hearts are lifted up, the weak led by
the hand, those going forward are perfected. Shining
upon those who have been purified of every stain, He
makes them spiritual in heart, through union with
Himself. For just as when the sunlight falls on clear
transparent bodies, they too become resplendent and
begin to shine from another light within themselves,
so the souls that contain the Spirit within them
become themselves spiritual, and their brightness
shines forth on others.

From this comes knowledge of the future, the
understanding of mysteries, the seeing of things
hidden, the apportioning of gifts, heavenly association
with the angelic choirs, joy without end, abiding with
God, being made like to God, and highest of all, that
you are made God [partaker of the divine nature,
2 Pet. 1:4].

BASIL[3]

"that you are made God" is to be understood as ultimate union
with our Creator in that we become one with Him but are still
what we are—and not God. At the Second Coming of Christ
and Judgment, those whose lives on earth showed love and
faith will live on in the fullness of the Kingdom (which begins
in this life) where they will continue to grow in His image.

If it is true of our experience in this life that holiness
is not monotonous but always different, must this not
be true also, and to an incomparably higher degree, of
the future life? *To him that overcomes will I give ... a*

35

white stone, and on the stone a new name written, which no man knows except the one who receives it (Rev. 2:17). Even in the age to come, the inner meaning of my unique personhood will continue to be eternally a secret between God and me. In God's Kingdom each is one with all the others, yet each is distinctively himself, bearing the same delineaments as he had in this life, yet with these characteristics healed, renewed and glorified. ... We move constantly onwards. And it is forward that we go, not back. The Age to come is not simply a return to the beginning, a restoration of the original state of perfection in Paradise, but it is a fresh departure. There is to be a *new* heaven and a *new* earth; and the last things will be greater than the first ... *Gregory of Nyssa* believed that even in Heaven perfection is growth. In a fine paradox he says that the essence of perfection consists precisely in never becoming perfect, but in always reaching forward to some higher perfection that lies beyond. Because God is infinite, this constant "reaching forward" or *epektasis*, as the Greek Fathers termed it, proves limitless. The soul possesses God, and yet still seeks Him; her joy is full, and yet grows always more intense. God grows ever nearer to us, yet He still remains the Other; we behold Him face to face, yet we still continue to advance further and further into the divine mystery. Although strangers no longer, we do not cease to be pilgrims. We go forward *from glory to glory* (2 Cor. 3:18), and then to a glory that is greater still. Never in all eternity, shall we reach a point where we have accomplished all that there is to do, or discovered all that there is to know.[4]

2:14. But the natural man does not receive the things of the Spirit of God, for they are foolishness to him; nor can he know them, because they are spiritually discerned. A person who is led to the road to the Kingdom through the Sacraments of Baptism and Chrismation, then begins spiritual growth by receiving regular spiritual nourishment as he is able (Eucharist, Scripture reading, prayer, fasting, etc.), and tries concurrently to become Christ-like as a result of love and faith, sincerely repenting when he falls short, will begin to understand spiritual things. The Holy Spirit will remain active and growing in influence within him. But this is not automatic. The person who never begins—or at a point ceases—upward movement toward God remains a natural man, a man of the world, with no capacity to understand spiritual things.

> When the upward movement toward God—which is activated by repentance—ceases, it reveals the insensitivity of a hardened heart. This is the chief symptom of spiritual death. It is at this point that there is no spiritual life. Death reigns. Truly, sin deadens the life of the spirit. That is why St. John of the Ladder says that repentance is a renewal of our Baptism, a new birth, that is, a new resurrection.[5]

The Holy Spirit received through Baptism and Chrismation does not depart in the absence of spiritual striving, but neither does He force Himself upon anyone. With the great gift of free will God has given man, each of us have the privilege and the power to cooperate with, or to refuse to cooperate with the Spirit of God. Indifference is the same as refusal (Mt. 12:30).

> However careless and indifferent the baptized may be in their subsequent life, this indwelling presence of the Spirit is never totally withdrawn. But unless we cooperate with God's grace—unless, through the exercise of our free will, we struggle to perform the commandments—it is likely that the Spirit's presence within us will remain hidden and unconscious. As pilgrims on the Way, then, it is our purpose to advance from the stage where the grace of the Spirit is present and active within us in a hidden way, to the

point of conscious awareness, when we know the Spirit's power openly, directly, with the full perception of our heart. *I am come to cast fire on the earth,* Christ said, *and how I wish it were already kindled!* (Lk. 12:49). The Pentecostal spark of the Spirit, existing in each one of us from Baptism, is to be kindled into a living flame. We are to become what we are.[6]

Some Church Fathers have taught, however, that under instances of grave sin, the Holy Spirit *may* depart.

> For now oftentimes the abundant grace of the Holy Ghost flies away when men commit great sins; and even when the Spirit does not leave them, vitality leaves the body.
>
> CHRYSOSTOM[7]

> When a man falls from the Spirit for any wickedness, if he repents, the grace remains irrevocably; otherwise he who has fallen is no longer in God (because that Holy Spirit and Paraclete which is in God has deserted him), but the sinner shall be in him to whom he has subjected himself, as took place in Saul's instance; for the Spirit of God departed from him and an evil spirit was afflicting him (1 Sam. 16:14).
>
> ATHANASIUS[8]

2:15–16. But he who is spiritual judges all things, yet he himself is rightly judged by no one. For "who has known the mind of the Lord that he may instruct Him?" But we have the mind of Christ. As man progresses spiritually, God gives him the gift of discernment (1 Cor. 12:4–11). This gift enables him to correctly evaluate the things of the world because he sees them as Christ did. The worldly man, however, has no means by which to judge the spiritual man and cannot correctly evaluate the things of the world.

One must be growing "in the grace and knowledge of our Lord and Savior, Jesus Christ" (2 Peter 3:18) to truly understand life's purpose.

FOOD FOR THOUGHT: (e) What is life's purpose? (Read Acts 17:26–27.)

FOOD FOR THOUGHT COMMENTS

(a). What fears does a modern Christian face? Using Paul as an example, how can we best deal with these fears? Most people fear the unknown: those things that might unexpectedly present themselves, like difficulties, illness, pain, death. It is easy also, in this world, to fear being seen as different from those around us. People of all ages seek comfort in numbers and often succumb to peer pressure to conform to the norms of the world rather than to the Christ-like lifestyle to which we are called. If we learn to turn to God with these fears, He will comfort us (Ps. 34:4) and help us to understand that if we put our trust in Him and His promises we will live with Him eternally in a place where there will be nothing to fear. Those who press on in every circumstance, even though they may be trembling inside, demonstrate the power that comes from God.

(b). What is the significance of putting our faith in "the power of God" rather than in the "wisdom of men" (2:5)? The only real and enduring power in this world comes from making God's truths the center and backbone of our existence, because when we do so, He responds with His grace.

(c). What were the specifics of the first prophecy (Gen. 3:15)? Speaking to the Devil in the serpent, God foretold that Satan and his seed (his followers) and the Woman (the Church and/or the Theotokos) and her seed (Jesus Christ and His followers) would be enemies. The Devil would wage war against Jesus to try to prevent Him from fulfilling His mission to save mankind but would succeed only in slowing Him down through Crucifixion (the bruise to the heel, which is annoying but not life-threatening). Jesus would win with a devastating blow to the head of Satan (with His Resurrection, which trampled down death, wresting the adversary's original victory from him).

This prophecy also speaks to the existence of evil in a world created by God. God created everything, visible and invisible, and everything He created was "good" (Gen. 1:31). He also decreed that which is necessary to maintain that state of goodness. Evil comes about when and to the degree that the gift of free will is used to ignore, thwart, or flout (scornfully disobey) those decrees.

God also continually works toward turning everything back to "good," as in using the death of Christ (a consequence of sin, brought about by Satan's influence) to return eternal life to man.

Satan does just the opposite. He uses that which was created good to bring about evil, as he did in tempting man to eat of the tree of the knowledge of good and evil. The fruit of that tree was good—evil came about when man disobeyed God's decree by eating it.

(d). What does Scripture indicate about the conditions that will prevail in Heaven? Life in God's Eternal Kingdom will consist of:

Fellowship with Christ (1 Cor. 13:12, 1 Jn. 3:2, Jn. 14:3, Rev. 22:4).

Rest (Rev. 14:13).

Holiness (Rev. 21:27).

Joy (Rev. 21:4).

Service (Rev. 22:3).

Abundance (Rev. 21:6).

Glory (2 Cor. 4:17, Col. 3:4).

Worship (Rev. 5:13, 19:1).

Community of Saints (Rev. 7:9–17).

(e). What is life's purpose? Life on earth affords each of us the opportunity to return to the assurance of union with God, in His eternal Kingdom. This is possible only through the Holy Spirit (Acts 17:26–27).

> The true purpose of the Christian life is that we receive the Holy Spirit as our own, which in turn divinizes our existence.[9]

CHAPTER THREE

Spiritual Growth Required

After describing the difference between a spiritual and a worldly person, Paul continues that he cannot speak to the Corinthians as he would to those more spiritually inclined.

3:1–4. And I, brethren, could not speak to you as to spiritual people but as to carnal, as to babes in Christ. I fed you with milk and not with solid food; for until now you were not able to receive it, and even now you are still not able; for you are still carnal. For where there are envy, strife, and divisions among you, are you not carnal and behaving like mere men? For when one says, "I am of Paul," and another, "I am of Apollos," are you not carnal? When Paul first visited the Corinthians to teach them about Jesus Christ, he found that their concerns were more worldly than spiritual; therefore, he could not teach them deep spiritual truths—only introduce them to basic facts. He is distressed to discover that they still have not gone beyond that point. Proof of their spiritual immaturity is the fact that there is jealousy and strife among them. Some brag that they were taught by Paul, others by Apollos or Cephas, as if the distinction of one's teacher gave certain rights and was more important than the Gospel that was conveyed to them.

> Jealousy and envy have often caused havoc, even in the Church, and some of our most godly leaders have suffered because of it. Look at the Apostles. Peter was the object of sinful jealousy on several occasions. So was Paul, who because of the jealousy and envy of others was arrested several times, imprisoned, stoned, exiled. He did not let this distract him from his ministry. Disregarding the envy of lesser people, he preached the Gospel all over the world, made his

testimony in front of kings and rulers, and in the end silenced the critics by his faith, his patience and his endurance.

But it's not only the famous who suffer through envy. Plenty of ordinary Christians have gone through agony because others have envied their courage and confidence. For example, there were those brave Christian women, here in Rome, who were hounded by unbelievers who resented their peace and joy in believing. Out of sheer envy, their enemies tried to make them act the parts of pagan goddesses in heathen rituals; and when they refused, they were shamefully put to death.

Jealousy has divided homes. It has come between husbands and wives, contradicting the Bible's claim that a wife is bone of her husband's bone and flesh of his flesh. Envy and jealousy have brought ruin to prosperous cities and overthrown great nations.

So let's remind ourselves that envy and jealousy are nothing but tricks of the mind, attitudes, self-induced fantasies; and let us put them from us.

CLEMENT[1]

FOOD FOR THOUGHT: (a). Why will there be no envy or jealousy in Heaven?

3:5–7. Who then is Paul, and who is Apollos, but ministers through whom you believed, as the Lord gave to each one? I planted, Apollos watered, but God gave the increase. So then neither he who plants is anything, nor he who waters, but God who gives the increase. Paul and Apollos are both servants of the Lord, doing that which He directed. While, perhaps, one of them introduced a person to the Gospel and the other guided that person to a deeper understanding of it, the efforts of each would be futile without

God, Who alone makes it possible for the seeds of faith and love to grow in accepting hearts. The power of the Gospel comes not from the messenger but from the message.

3:8. Now he who plants and he who waters are one, and each one will receive his own reward according to his own labor. All aspects of God's work are of equal value toward salvation because anything done with love shows faith in Him. He expects each of us to use the gifts we have been given to do the work at hand (Lk. 12:48).

> Judgment is in accord with grace; and as you have used what was given you, so shall the Judge judge you.
>
> BASIL[2]

The level of enthusiasm and dedication with which a person uses his talents in God's service is rewarded accordingly.

> The Lord Jesus in His mercy grants rest to each according to his works—to the great according to his greatness and to the little according to his littleness, for He said, *In my Father's house there are many mansions* (Jn. 14:2). Though the Kingdom is one, yet in the Kingdom each finds his own special place and his own special work.
>
> ISAIAS OF SKETIS[3]

3:9. For we are God's fellow workers; you are God's field, you are God's building. Those who pass on Christ's teachings help God build His Church, which is made up of those who believe the Gospel and try to live by it.

3:10. According to the grace of God which was given to me, as a wise master builder I have laid the foundation, and another builds upon it. But let each one take heed

how he builds on it. When Paul was among the Corinthians, he taught them the basic truths about salvation through Christ. Another of God's workers followed to add to that knowledge—a process which continues in each generation. Each of God's workers is answerable to Him and must be sure that he is teaching and guiding according to the truth, so that the resulting Church will be strong. Clergy, laity, parents—all Christians who witness—must not teach what they "think" is so, but only that given to us through the Apostles and preserved by the Church through Holy Scripture, writings of the Church Fathers, Liturgics, Hymnology, Iconography, etc., where they agree and speak as a whole.

3:11. For no other foundation can anyone lay than that which is laid, which is Jesus Christ. The Church can stand only on the truths that He taught.

> FOOD FOR THOUGHT: (b). What does this verse say about groups that point to the teachings of specific individuals as their foundation?

3:12–13. Now if anyone builds on this foundation with gold, silver, precious stones, wood, hay, straw, each one's work will become manifest; for the Day will declare it, because it will be revealed by fire; and the fire will test each one's work, of what sort it is. Gold and silver soften in great heat. They become malleable but are not destroyed. Fire also purifies and strengthens them, revealing their glory. These precious metals represent those whose faith is based solidly on truth, allowing God to mold them in His image and to stand firm in good times and in bad. In the same fire, however, wood, hay, and straw burn, and are easily consumed (Heb. 12:29). They represent those whose faith is vulnerable to destruction by life's difficult moments.

FOOD FOR THOUGHT: (c). Does questioning God during the difficult times of life indicate flimsy faith?

God is love. The icon of the Last Judgment depicts the truth that on Judgment Day, love will pour forth from His throne like a river of fire. It will illuminate everything, disclosing the quality of each person's faith or lack thereof as well as the faith of those s/he brought to the Kingdom. By it, the righteous will be enlightened, soothed, and healed. But by it also, sinners will be "scourged."[4] They will know they do not belong to God but it will be too late to change (where there can be no corruption, there can be no change).

> It is totally false to think that the sinners in Hell are deprived of God's love. Love is a child of the knowledge of truth, and is unquestionably given commonly to all. But love's power acts in two ways: it torments sinners while at the same time it delights those who have lived in accord with it.
>
> ISAAC THE SYRIAN[5]

Of his own volition, the sinner will try to flee from God's presence (Mt. 25:41). This is the concept illustrated by Rom. 12:20: showing kindness to enemies is like heaping coals of fire on their heads. But God's love follows, the fire that is never quenched (Mk. 9:43). In the wake of this eternal fire, sinners will find themselves:

(1). separated from God:

> Nothing is more grievous than the wretchedness of being deprived of God's good things.
>
> CHRYSOSTOM[6]

(2). bearing eternal shame:

> ... before God the Father and His Anointed, before angels, archangels, principalities and all mankind.
> EVAGRIOS THE SOLITARY[7]

(3). alone in a crowd:

> ... neither seeing nor being seen, but in so vast a multitude, thinking that we are alone because of the darkness [absence of God's light].
> CHRYSOSTOM[8]

The worm that does not die (Mk. 9:44) may describe the sinner's unending despair at seeing others (like the rich man's Lazarus, Lk. 16:25–6) enjoying eternal happiness, which they have denied themselves.

3:14–15. If anyone's work which he has built on it endures, he will receive a reward. If anyone's work is burned, he will suffer loss; but he himself will be saved, yet so as through fire. Judgment, characterized as "fire" in its effects, will reveal the total effect of each person's life to see if faith in and love for Christ were evident. Beyond that basic criterion for salvation, however, the question of the quality of our work for God has to do with our relationship with Him, our "reward," which is unlimited in its potential.

> If there is a reward and a punishment in this revelation—and there really is—it does not come from God but from the love or hate which reigns in our heart.[9]

FOOD FOR THOUGHT: (d). Can anyone be "saved" (from exclusion from God's Kingdom), without trying to bring others to Christ?

3:16–17. Do you not know that you are the temple of God and that the Spirit of God dwells in you? If anyone defiles the temple of God, God will destroy him. For the temple of God is holy, which temple you are. A Baptized, Chrismated believer who is making the effort to live his faith and grow spiritually is a part of the Church, the "temple of God," in which the Holy Spirit dwells. God does not look kindly upon those who weaken this holy temple by causing divisions.

3:18–20. Let no one deceive himself. If anyone among you seems to be wise in this age, let him become a fool that he may become wise. For the wisdom of this world is foolishness with God. For it is written, "He catches the wise in their own craftiness," and again, "The Lord knows the thoughts of the wise, that they are futile." He who focuses entirely on the wisdom of this world courts disaster because of its fickle and temporary nature. Conversely, he who concentrates on knowledge of the Kingdom of God may be considered a fool in this world but is the possessor of true wisdom, which will lead to eternal life with God.

3:21–23. Therefore let no one glory in men. For all things are yours: whether Paul or Apollos or Cephas, or the world or life or death, or things present or things to come—all are yours. And you are Christ's, and Christ is God's. No one should impoverish his/her spiritual growth by focusing on a person, whether parent, teacher, leader, or Saint, other than as examples to follow. Those who have responded to and live by the Gospel of Jesus Christ naturally love, respect, and perhaps even revere their spiritual fathers and others who have lived with and before them and have guided them in their spiritual growth. However, a true teacher of the Gospel will always point to Jesus Christ as the only vehicle through whom one can possess all the glories of the Kingdom (Jn. 14:6). All good things belong to those who belong to Christ because Christ belongs to God—is God—part of the Holy Trinity.

FOOD FOR THOUGHT COMMENTS

(a). Why will there be no envy or jealousy in Heaven? Because there will be no competition in that perfect place. Each person in God's Kingdom develops a unique personal relationship with Him that begins during one's days on earth and continues eternally. The special qualities of this relationship are known only to Him and to us. Just as Christ gave Simon the new name of Peter—from the Greek word *petros,* meaning *stone* (Jn. 1:42)—symbolizing the rock-like faith that he demonstrated in proclaiming that Jesus was Christ, the Anointed One (Mt. 16:16), God has a name for each of us symbolizing that which has developed between us and Him (Rev. 2:17).

(b). What does the fact that the Church is built on the truths of Christ (3:11) say about groups that point to the teachings of specific individuals as their foundation? Any group founded upon the teachings of someone other than Christ (like Joseph Smith's Mormons, Charles T. Russell's Jehovah's Witnesses, and Mary Baker Eddy's Christian Scientists) does not have Christ as the Head, and therefore is not the Church (the Body of Christ). In Orthodoxy, only the Church as a whole, acting in accordance with the truths taught by Christ, which it has preserved, has the authority of Christ and is infallible, as when it comes together in an Ecumenical Synod representing all the people.

> The Apostles, like a rich man depositing his money in
> a bank, lodged the truth in the hands of the Church:

so that every man, whosoever will, can draw from her the water of life. For she is the entrance to life; all others are thieves and robbers. On this account we are obligated to avoid them, to choose those things pertaining to the Church with the utmost diligence, and to lay hold of the tradition of the truth. For how stands the case? Suppose there arises a dispute relative to some important question among us. Would we not desire recourse to the most ancient churches with which the Apostles held constant intercourse and to learn from them what is certain and clear in regard to the question?

IRENAEUS[10]

(c). Is the questioning of God during difficult times an indication of flimsy faith? To question God in times of duress or to temporarily waver when tempted to disobey is not a sign of flimsy faith. What matters is that if we make a mistake we repent, confess, and begin again, and that, to the end, we continue the struggle.

(d). Can anyone be "saved" (from exclusion from God's Kingdom), without trying to bring others to Christ? If we really believe that Jesus Christ is the Savior of mankind, we will try to live a Christ-like life, which must include bringing the truth of His Gospel to others, because that is what He did. To know what He was like, we must study His word and live a prayerful, sacramental life, as He did.

> Each of you, if he will, is a teacher, although not of another, yet of himself. Teach yourself first. If you teach yourself to observe all things He commanded ... you will have many emulating you. For as a lamp, when it is shining, is able to light ten thousand others but being extinguished will not give light even to itself ... so also in the case of a pure life, if the light that is

in us is shining, we shall make both disciples and teachers numberless, being set before them as a pattern to copy.   CHRYSOSTOM[11]

52

CHAPTER FOUR

Being Stewards of the Mysteries of God

Chapter Three closes with the reminder that though he who strives for knowledge of God's Kingdom may be considered a fool by the world, he is the possessor of true wisdom. This chapter begins with the responsibilities of those who, knowing this, have glimpsed the mysteries of God.

4:1–2. Let a man so consider us, as servants of Christ and stewards of the mysteries of God. Moreover it is required in stewards that one be found faithful. A steward is responsible for overseeing his master's household. A Christian's Master is God. God's household is the Church, which is made up of those who are true followers of Jesus Christ. Paul's emphasis here is that all Christians are charged with teaching the truth about the Gospel of Jesus Christ, the "mysteries of God" (1 Cor. 2:6–9), and with building up the Church (1 Cor. 3:9).

> FOOD FOR THOUGHT: (a). How can we be "stewards of the mysteries of God"?

4:3–5. But with me it is a very small thing that I should be judged by you or by a human court. In fact, I do not even judge myself. For I know nothing against myself, yet I am not justified by this; but He who judges me is the Lord. Therefore, judge nothing before the time, until the Lord comes, who will both bring to light the hidden things of darkness and reveal the counsels of the hearts; and then each one's praise will come from God. As a steward of the mysteries of God, Paul is answerable to Him, not to the self-proclaimed authorities in Corinth, where:

Religious men and dear to God were ridiculed and cast out for their want of learning; while others, brimful of evils innumerable, were classed highly because of their fluent speech. Then like persons sitting in public to try causes, these were the sort of votes they kept rashly passing: "this one is worthy; this one is better than that one; this man is inferior to that; that better than this." And, forgetting to mourn for their own bad ways, they had become judges of others; and in this way again were kindling grievous warfare.

CHRYSOSTOM[1]

In other words, those who lived in an ungodly manner but spoke eloquently were held in higher regard than those who used more ordinary speech but were trying to live Christ-like lives and to bring others to Him. Paul reminds them that no one has the right to judge individuals and to class them according to false worldly standards. We should not judge ourselves because to do so could bring undue pride or despondency. We should not judge others because only God knows the secrets of each heart and the hidden circumstances of each life. When Christ returns to earth, He will judge each person according to His standards.

> **FOOD FOR THOUGHT:** (b). If we are not to judge, should we be unconcerned as to what is right and what is wrong in the world in which we live?

4:6–7. Now these things, brethren, I have figuratively transferred to myself and to Apollos for your sakes, that you may learn in us not to think beyond what is written, that none of you may be puffed up on behalf of one against the other. For who makes you differ from another? And what do you have that you did not receive? Now if you did indeed receive it, why do you glory as if you had not received it? Everything good that anyone has or is comes from God, so no one has the right to boast, to feel superior to another, or to give to any person the honor that belongs to God alone.

> **FOOD FOR THOUGHT:** (c). Why is it said that we have achieved nothing of value solely of our own accord?

If we receive praise and glory for our good deeds on earth, we have been recompensed—God owes us nothing. If, however, we devote ourselves to Christ unselfishly, our reward will come from Him, Who alone knows the secrets of our heart and our unpublicized deeds. He has ordained that this be so in order to discourage competition, envy, and pride among His people (Mt. 6:1–6, 16–18). Several times in this letter, Paul mentions that conceit and arrogance are to be guarded against (1 Cor. 4:18, 5:2, 8:1, 13:4).

> **FOOD FOR THOUGHT:** (d). Why are conceit and arrogance so detrimental in our relationship with Christ?

4:8. You are already full! You are already rich! You have reigned as kings without us and indeed I could wish you did reign, that we also might reign with you. Paul admonishes the Corinthians for considering themselves worthy of praise, as if becoming a Christian was the end rather than the beginning of the spiritual struggle. If this were so, Paul says, the Apostles could be enjoying glory with them, instead of struggling and suffering as they were.

4:9. For I think that God has displayed us, the apostles, last, as men condemned to death; for we have been made a spectacle to the world, both to angels and to men. Jesus said: "If anyone desires to be first, he shall be last of all and servant of all" (Mk. 9:35). The Apostles, in worldly terms, appeared to be held in very low esteem. They were paraded and ridiculed in public, imprisoned, put to death. Their sufferings were witnessed by everyone. This was the cross that Jesus said one who follows Him must bear (Mt. 16:24), which differs for each person. Those who accept this fact, however, will be first in the Kingdom of Heaven, unlike those who take the path of ease and comfort in this life.

4:10–13. We are fools for Christ's sake, but you are wise in Christ! We are weak, but you are strong! You are distinguished but we are dishonored! Even to the present hour we both hunger and thirst, and we are poorly clothed, and beaten, and homeless. And we labor, working with our own hands. Being reviled, we bless; being persecuted, we endure it; being defamed, we entreat. We have been made as the filth of the world, the off-scouring of all things until now. Unlike the teachers, the students were experiencing none of the difficulties of the Christian life because they have been more concerned with pleasing the world than with pleasing God.

> This puts the whole world into confusion, that we do all things with an eye to men, and even for our good things, we esteem it nothing to have God as an admirer but seek the approval that comes from our fellowmen ... yet surely they shall stand with us before that tribunal, doing us no good ... yet, though we know these things, we still gape after men, which is the first of sins. Thus were a man looking on, no-one would choose to commit fornication; but even though he be ten thousand times on fire with that plague, the tyranny of the passion is conquered by his reverence for men. But in God's sight men not only commit adultery and fornication; but other things also much more dreadful many have dared and still dare to do. Is this alone not enough to bring down from above ten thousand thunderbolts? Adulteries, did I

say, and fornications? Things even far less than these we fear to do before men: but in God's sight we fear no longer. From this, in fact, all the world's evils have originated; because in things really bad we reverence not God but men.

CHRYSOSTOM[2]

Chrysostom's point, of course, is that most of us worry about the impression we make on those around us. We don't want to be seen doing anything that will lessen their esteem for us, yet we seem to forget that God is all-seeing, all-knowing. He knows everything we do, say, think—everything we are.

> If you wish to sin, seek a place where He cannot see you, and then do what you will.

AUGUSTINE[3]

4:14–15. I do not write these things to shame you, but as my beloved children I warn you. For though you might have ten thousand instructors in Christ, yet you do not have many fathers; for in Christ Jesus I have begotten you through the Gospel. As the spiritual father of the Christians of Corinth, Paul's intention is not to shame them but to lovingly yet firmly correct and direct them, as a parent should.

4:16. Therefore I urge you, imitate me. He urges them to imitate him, because he imitates Christ, not man (see 1 Cor. 11:1).

4:17. For this reason I have sent Timothy to you, who is my beloved and faithful son in the Lord, who will remind you of my ways in Christ, as I teach everywhere in every church. The truths Paul brought the Corinthians, which Timothy reinforced, are the same for everyone everywhere.

4:18–20. Now some are puffed up, as though I were not coming to you. But I will come to you shortly, if the Lord wills, and I will know, not the word of those who are puffed up, but the power. For the kingdom of God is not in word but in power. In Paul's absence from Corinth, leaders had arisen who, through conceit and pride, brought divisions to the Church there. These false leaders had boasted of their eloquence and wisdom. Paul wrote that when he arrived he would be able to discern whether they truly possessed power from God or merely spoke empty words. (Read 2 Peter 2.)

> FOOD FOR THOUGHT: (e). To what power is Paul referring? What power did the Apostles exhibit (Mt. 10:8)? What power do Christ's disciples have today (Acts 1:8, Eph. 3:7–21, 1 Thess. 1:5)?

4:21. What do you want? Shall I come to you with a rod, or in love and a spirit of gentleness? The spirit of Paul's next visit to the Corinthian Christians will be determined by whether or not they amend their ways. The conduct of children determines their father's demeanor toward them. Though he loves them "unconditionally," if they disobey he must use stern measures to correct their behavior for their own good. If they are obedient, he may be able to relax and be gentle with them.

FOOD FOR THOUGHT COMMENTS

(a). How can we be "stewards of the mysteries of God"? To be faithful stewards, His Kingdom has to be our priority. We must grow in knowledge of God's word and teach it to those around us whenever and wherever possible.

God's gifts are marvelous, aren't they? Some of them we know and enjoy already: the experience of life that knows no death; the splendor of His sheer goodness; the truth that is honest and complete; faith that gives assurance and confidence in God; a purity that is infinitely better than self-indulgence.

But there are other gifts of God which by their very nature we cannot know yet. They can only be revealed by the Creator and Father of eternity, and only He knows how magnificent they are. But if they are better than the gifts we know already, how wonderful, how utterly desirable they must be!

For such gifts it is worth waiting patiently. But it is also worth straining every nerve to achieve them, by fixing our minds on the Giver, by seeking to discover His will for us and then doing it; by renouncing deceit and pursuing truth. And—most of all—by coming to Jesus Christ, the High Priest who is the appointed way to Heaven and our Protector on earth. Through Him alone can our eyes look up to the highest Heaven, even to the face of God. Through Him alone the Father allows us to taste those wonderful joys of eternity, all of which are "in Him."

CLEMENT[4]

(b). If we are not to judge, should we be unconcerned as to what is right and what is wrong in the world in which we live? If the Kingdom of God is to be our priority, we must make judgments as to what is true about God and His word and what is not, and to distinguish right actions from wrong, good from bad. To do so, we must know God's word (Acts 17:11) and the fullness of the truth about its interpretation, which the Church has preserved. We must also examine our own lives regularly to be sure we are really trying to grow in the image of Christ (1 Cor. 11:27–31), according to Scripture.

(c). Why is it said that we have achieved nothing of value solely of our own accord? God is the Creator of everything that is good (Jas. 1:17). If we achieve anything of merit, we do so in cooperation with Him (as His "fellow-workers"), through the capabilities He has given us. The composer creates beautiful music with God-given talents and with the sounds God has put in the world, which man-made instruments can only try to capture. The sun, the moon, the stars, our loved ones—all good things—come from Him. The ultimate good, eternal life with Him in His Kingdom, comes to us only though His beneficence.

(d). Why are conceit and arrogance so detrimental in our relationship with Christ? Conceit and arrogance indicate a love of oneself over and above anyone or anything else, including God. To love anyone or anything more than God is to love the creation rather than the Creator and is a violation of the first Commandment (Ex. 20:3).

(e). To what power is Paul referring? What power did the Apostles exhibit (Mt. 10:8)? What power do Christ's disciples have today (Acts 1:8, Eph. 3:7–21, 1 Thess. 1:5)? Paul is referring to the power of the Holy Spirit, to which a person who has strong faith in and love for God and an understanding of His will for man has access.

The Apostles had power to "heal the sick, cleanse the lepers, raise the dead, cast out demons," and rightly discern the word of God (2 Pet. 3:15–16). The ability to affect the lives of man physically pointed to the more important power to effect change spiritually. All true Christians have power to be used as vehicles to direct and redirect lives and souls by witnessing to the truth about Jesus, with their words and with their lives.

Thus the power to heal, cleanse, bring sinners back from spiritual death (to eternal life) and to cast out demons (of sin) continues.

CHAPTER FIVE

Christian Morality

To this point, Paul has been speaking rather gently about the divisions in the Church. Now he becomes more indignant, speaking vehemently against the immorality that he has heard is taking place among them.

5:1. It is actually reported that there is sexual immorality among you, and such sexual immorality as is not even named among the Gentiles—that a man has his father's wife! One of the Christians and his stepmother have been involved in an illicit relationship (see Lev. 18:8, Deut. 22:30, 27:20). The woman must not have been a Christian, or Paul would have admonished her also. Corinth was notorious for its sexual freedom, but this particular sin shocked even the pagans.

5:2. And you are puffed up, and have not rather mourned, that he who has done this deed might be taken away from you. This situation was apparently being condoned because the Corinthians were mistakenly convinced that as Christians they were free from the moral code of the Old Testament (the Mosaic Law) given by God, through Moses, to His people (see Books of Exodus, Leviticus, and Numbers). This "Law" had been given to the people of Israel for many reasons:

(1). *as types, symbols, and prophesies* of the coming of the Messiah, Who would rescue mankind from the effects of sin (Lev. 16:20–22, 1 Jn. 2:2), and of the events of His life; for example, the Passover Lamb (Ex. 12) prefigured His Crucifixion (1 Cor. 5:7).

(2). *to teach them to be holy (set apart from others)*; in the world, not of it; good and just, showing love through obedience.

(3). *to protect them in some way.* For example, the Jews were not allowed to eat pork in the days when cooking and storage methods were inadequate. Thus God's law safeguarded their physical as well as their spiritual well-being.

(4). *to define sin* (Rom. 3;19–20; 5:13), allowing them to realize that they could never earn salvation through their own efforts, and so needed a Savior.

(5). *because of the hardness of their hearts* (Ezek. 20:22–26).

> At first God deemed it sufficient to inscribe the natural law, or the Decalogue, upon the hearts of men; but afterwards He found it necessary to bridle, with the yoke of the Mosaic Law, the desires of the Jews, who were abusing their liberty; and even to add some special commands, because of the hardness of their hearts.
>
> They therefore had a law, a course of discipline, and a prophecy of future things. For God at first warned them by means of natural precepts, which from the beginning He had implanted in mankind, that is, by means of the Decalogue (which, if anyone does not observe, he has no salvation), did then demand nothing more of them. As Moses says in Deuteronomy, *These are all the words which the Lord spoke to the whole assembly of the sons of Israel on the mount, and He added no more. And He wrote them on two tablets of stone, and gave them to me* (Deut. 5:22), so *that they who are willing to follow Him might keep these commandments.* But when they turned themselves to make a calf, and had gone back in their minds to Egypt, desiring to be slaves instead of free men, they were placed for the future in a state of

servitude suited to their wish—(a slavery) which did
not indeed cut them off from God but subjected them
to the yoke of bondage; as Ezekiel the prophet, when
stating the reasons for the giving of such a law,
declares: *And their eyes were after the desire of their
heart; and I gave them statutes that were not good,
and judgments in which they shall not live* (Ezek.
20:24).

IRENAEUS[1]

FOOD FOR THOUGHT: (a). How does Orthopraxia
(Orthodox Practice) reflect items (2) and (3)
above?

The Mosaic Law (the Written Covenant between God and man)
contained 613 rules (as well as the Ten Commandments), each
of which had to be followed precisely. To break one was to be
guilty of breaking them all (Jas. 2: 10). This was the bondage
of the Law from which Jesus saved His people.

Under the new and final Blood Covenant through Jesus Christ,
those who acknowledge Him as their Savior are no longer
under the Law as far as having to *be* perfect to earn salvation—
Jesus did that for us (Rom. 3:16–21). Death came to the world
as a consequence of sin. Christ lived a perfect life, so did not
deserve death, yet He willingly accepted its ravages for our
sake (Jn. 10:17–18). Then He rose from the dead to show us
there is life beyond the grave. Those who are a part of the
Body of Christ (the Church) through Baptism and who try to
live a Christ-like life to remain so will naturally be with Him
eternally, in this life and the next.

While Christians no longer have to follow the laws of the old
covenant perfectly in order to earn salvation (an impossibility),
we are still required to try to follow its moral order (basically
the Ten Commandments as summarized by Jesus in Mark

12:29–31). As Jesus said, He came not to abolish the Law, but to fulfill it (Mt. 5:17), a truth that Paul continually emphasizes (Rom. 3:31). Accepting this discipline demonstrates faith and, at the same time, it molds us in His (holy) image.

The mistaken notion that Jesus did everything for us, so all we have to do is say we believe then continue to live in any manner we choose is a heresy which, as this Chapter shows, arose very early in the Church. The Book of James was written to refute this heresy, the danger of which is obvious. Many in every segment of Christianity have been led astray by it.

5:3–5. For I indeed, as absent in body but present in spirit, have already judged, as though I were present, concerning him who has so done this deed. In the name of our Lord Jesus Christ, when you are gathered together, along with my spirit, with the power of our Lord Jesus Christ, deliver such a one to Satan for the destruction of the flesh, that his spirit may be saved in the day of the Lord Jesus. Since the Corinthians have not taken the proper action with regard to the sin taking place, Paul tells them what they must do: gather in a meeting of the entire Church at Corinth and cast out of their midst—excommunicate—the offending member "in the name of" and "with the power of … Jesus Christ." To be a part of the Church is to be a part of the Body of Christ, with Him as the Head. To be cast out of the Church is to become a member of the society ruled over by Satan, the prince of this world (Jn. 12:31, 14:30), who boasts of having all the Kingdoms of the earth at his disposal (Mt. 4:8–9). The Corinthians are to take this action in the hope that the severity of it will shock the offender and bring him to repentance.

FOOD FOR THOUGHT: (b). Why is excommunication not practiced in the Church today as a means of trying to correct sinful conduct and bring an offender to repentance?

When Jesus chose the Apostles to act *in His Name,* He was continuing the Jewish tradition of sending, when necessary, someone to act in one's stead. The person fulfilling this role was called a "shaliach." Any action taken by the shaliach when acting in this capacity, if taken according to the instructions of the principal, was binding on the one by whom he was sent. Thus, when Abraham sent his servant to choose a wife for his son Isaac, the servant's choice was honored (Gen. 24). This is the authority Jesus gave the Apostles (Jn. 20:21), which Paul is citing in this chapter, and which Orthodox Christian ordained clergy have possessed ever since, through Apostolic succession (Acts 20:28), by means of the Holy Spirit.[2]

Jesus gave the Apostles authority to bind and to loose sins on earth, with such decisions accepted in Heaven (Jn. 20:23). This action of excommunication from the Church that Paul is advising would also extend to Heaven, as would any resultant repentance and reinstatement to the Church through the Apostles or their successors. Always though, any such actions taken are valid only to the extent that they follow the truths Christ passed on to the Apostles, and final judgment belongs to God.

"For the destruction of the flesh" implies that Satan would be allowed to inflict some physical difficulty upon the offender to bring him to his senses. Suffering is a blessing if, through it, a person is awakened to the need to examine his spiritual life. Thus, even if he loses his life, he may regain his soul.

> **FOOD FOR THOUGHT:** (c). How would suffering a physical ailment bring a sinner to his senses?

5:6. Your glorying is not good. Do you not know that a little leaven leavens the whole lump? Paul continues his analogy (see 5:2) regarding boasting and the swelling of dough containing leaven (colloquially known as being filled with "hot air"). He charges that their self-righteousness in the midst of gross disobedience has caused immorality to be condoned among the people. Beyond the spiritual danger to those involved, Paul warns that if this activity is allowed, others may assume that such conduct is acceptable for Christians and may indulge in further immorality. Just as a little yeast in a much larger amount of flour affects the whole mixture, sin among a group of Christians affects the whole community.

> The devil does his part, and never ceases to whisper in the heart of those he holds fast in bonds. I know that to fornicators, to adulterers who are not content with their own wives, he says that the sins of the flesh are not grievous. Against such whispering we must hold before our minds the Incarnation of Christ. It is through the enticements of the flesh that the enemy deceives the Christian; making light of what is grave sin, mild what is fierce, sweet what is bitter.
>
> AUGUSTINE[3]

FOOD FOR THOUGHT: (d). How does the sexual climate in ancient Corinth compare with the state of the world today, when many who call themselves Christians think premarital sex is not only acceptable but even expected?

5:7. Therefore purge out the old leaven, that you may be a new lump, since you truly are unleavened. For indeed Christ, our Passover, was sacrificed for us. *Leaven* refers to sinfulness. The Corinthians had been spiritually cleansed through Baptism, but the unquestioned sin in their midst posed a spiritual danger to all of them. By association with it they could slip back to what they had been.

Under the Old Testament, to give His people a way of escape from 400 years of slavery in Egypt, God told them to sacrifice young perfect male lambs and to spread the blood of those lambs around the doors of their homes (read Ex. 12:3–7). On the appointed night, death came upon the first-born in every home not so marked (12:23). The resulting trauma and chaos in the unmarked homes of the Egyptians gave the Hebrew people the opportunity to escape. This event came to be called the Jewish *Passover* because the destroyer "passed over" every marked home, sparing those inside from death.

This was a pre-figuration of Christ's sacrifice for us under the New Testament. He is called the new Passover, the Lamb of God, the last living sacrifice, because He died to save us (to atone for our sins). Those marked with His blood (through receiving Holy Communion as part of living in a Christ-like manner) will be rescued from death, having only to pass through it to eternal life with God in His Kingdom.

> The mystery of the lamb which God ordered you to sacrifice as the Passover was truly a type of Christ, with whose Blood the believers, in proportion to the strength of their faith, anoint their homes, that is, themselves. ... Moreover, that lamb which you were ordered to roast whole was a symbol of Christ's Passion on the Cross. Indeed, the lamb, while being roasted, resembles the figure of the cross, for one spit transfixes it horizontally from the lower parts up to the head, and another pierces it across the back, and holds up its forelegs.
>
> JUSTIN[4]

5:8. Therefore, let us keep the feast, not with old leaven, nor with the leaven of malice and wickedness, but with

the unleavened bread of sincerity and truth. The Jews of the Old Testament were told to keep the Feast of the Passover every year forever (Ex. 12:14, 13:3–10). Christ was crucified on the eve of the Feast of Passover (Jn. 19:14)[5] because He was to be the new Passover. His sacrifice superseded the Exodus sacrifice.

> In the following fashion I can show that God's precept concerning the paschal lamb was only temporary. God does not allow the paschal lamb to be sacrificed in any other place than where His name is invoked (that is, in the Temple at Jerusalem), for He knew that there would come a time, after Christ's Passion, when the place in Jerusalem [where ... the paschal lamb was sacrificed] would be no more ... and then all sacrifices would be stopped.
>
> JUSTIN[6]

FOOD FOR THOUGHT: (e). What event in history caused the Temple at Jerusalem to "be no more"?

We remember Christ's sacrifice (Crucifixion) and celebrate the festival (His Resurrection) at Pascha (Greek for Passover—called Easter in the West) every year in obedience to the Lord's instruction to observe it forever.

Paul reminds the Corinthians that the best remembrance or celebration of Pascha is to continually try to cleanse ourselves from sinfulness and to follow Christ according to the fullness of the truth. The new Passover is also celebrated every Sunday (the Lord's Day), when we gather together in remembrance of the Resurrection of Christ, to receive His Body and Blood.

5:9–10. I wrote to you in my epistle not to keep company with sexually immoral people. Yet I certainly did not mean with the sexually immoral people of this world, or

with the covetous, or extortioners, or idolaters, since then you would need to go out of the world. Christians are expected to follow biblical standards of sexual morality because God's word to His people never changes (Heb 13:7–8). For a sincere Christian to identify closely with a professed Christian who acts in ways that flout those standards would give the erroneous impression that those things no longer matter. It would be impossible, however, to avoid interaction with sexually immoral non-Christians because they are so prevalent in our world. Rather, we must try always, in their presence, to exemplify the Christian way of life. It has always been said that one good example is worth a thousand sermons.

> **FOOD FOR THOUGHT:** (f). Christ sat with sinners to try to bring them into the fold (Mt. 9:10–13). Can we have similar associations with that motive?

5:11. But now I have written to you not to keep company with anyone named a brother, who is a fornicator, or covetous, or an idolater, or a reviler, or a drunkard, or an extortioner—not even to eat with such a person. The word Christian means "Christ-like," or "belonging to Christ." A Christian does not have to *be* perfect like Christ but must always be *trying to become* like Him (Mt. 5:48) and not be blatantly sinful. We cannot judge the person—that is God's job—but we can judge activity that is not Christ-like and refuse to be a part of it, so as not to seem to condone it.

To encourage Christians to judge the actions of other Christians is very delicate ground, but we cannot just say: "live and let live" because this prevailing attitude has produced too many "name-only" Christians, a fact that non-Christians are quick to point out.

> When one who has sinned sees that all turn away from him, he will then come to see that his sin is something evil and reprehensible. But should he see that others do not consider his conduct to be unworthy, and accept him without complaint, and even encourage and abet him, then will the approval of others, abetting his own corrupt soul corrupt also the judgment of his conscience.
>
> CHRYSOSTOM[7]

We must also take care to not become self-righteous and hypocritical, condemning the faults of others and excusing our own (Lk. 6:41–42). Mahatma Gandhi once said, "I like your Christ. I do not like your Christians. Your Christians are so unlike your Christ."[8]

5:12–13. For what have I to do with judging those also who are outside? Do you not judge those who are inside? But those who are outside God judges. Therefore "put away from yourselves that wicked person." God will judge non-Christians. We as a Church (not as individuals) must determine what is proper conduct for Christians according to Scripture and the truths preserved by the Church, and must try to redirect each other with love when necessary in order to help one another stay on the road to the Kingdom.

FOOD FOR THOUGHT COMMENTS

(a). How does Orthopraxia reflect the precept that God's people should be holy, in the world, not of it? One example is fasting, a spiritual discipline that helps us learn to suppress worldly elements in our lives in order to elevate the spiritual. Fasting also teaches us to have the courage to be "different" than others around us, set apart for God (the definition of holiness). If we learn to fast regularly in a world where most do not, we may also develop what it takes to separate ourselves from the pack as we try to become Christ-like in morals, behavior, etc.

When we teach our children to fast, even under rather trying circumstances (as in school when no one around them is doing likewise) we are teaching them to have the courage to say "no" to the ways of the world when necessary. This discipline can be taught as a way to express love for and dedication to Christ and the way He asks us to live, with appropriate flexibility in consideration of physical and spiritual maturity and strength, and as a growing personal response to God through obedience.

Modern understanding of nutrition with regard to the reduction of red meat and harmful fats in our diet make it clear that the principles of fasting, if followed throughout the Church year, also promote physical well being. Traditional Christian discipline is good for the body and for the soul.

(b). How would suffering a physical ailment bring a sinner to his senses? Suffering can teach valuable lessons, awaken a person from a spirit of apathy, bring about reflection (Ps. 46:10), and/or test and strengthen faith (read the Old Testament story of Job and 1 Pet. 1:6-9). A physical affliction can make one realize which things in this life have real value. When our health is threatened, we may pay more attention to our spiritual life—which endures forever. Also, God may sometimes allow the righteous to suffer so that they may provide examples of faith under difficult circumstances, to the end that the faith of those looking on might be strengthened. (See this study for 2 Cor. 12.)

(c). Why is excommunication not practiced in the Church today as a means of trying to correct sinful conduct and bring an offender to repentance? This chapter is not about excommunication, but about the fact that being a Christian incurs the responsibility to try to live a Christ-like lifestyle to demonstrate faith and to be a good example for others.

While still possible by Church Court—usually a synodical court—excommunication is almost never imposed today. It was probably necessary in the early Church because a firm foundation, built on the truths Christ taught, was still being laid down. The living Church had to be kept as pure as possible in practice to preserve these truths. When, with the passage of time, they were put into writings which were later compiled by the Church into what we now call the New Testament, and when the Fathers of the early Church clarified and interpreted the New Testament with their writings, according to the Holy Traditions that had been preserved intact by the living Church, these harsh practices could be relaxed. The Sacrament of Repentance (Confession) is the vehicle that the priest, who has the authority not only to bind and loose sins (Jn. 20:22–23) but also to prescribe penance, can use today to try to bring about realization of sin, repentance, and re-instatement to the sacramental life of the Church.

(d). How does the sexual climate of ancient Corinth compare with the state of the world today, when many who call themselves Christians think premarital sex is not only acceptable but even expected? The devil has succeeded in deluding the masses to such an extent that even some Christians in today's world—in every age category and from all walks of life—feel that while certain actions like stealing and murder are wrong, sexual activity between unmarried "consenting adults" is natural, pleasurable, and hurts no one. The New Testament and the writings of the early Church Fathers are very clear: any sexual relationship outside of marriage is immoral and not befitting a Christian (read 1 Thess. 4:1–8, 1 Cor. 6:9–10, Gal. 5:19–21, Heb. 13:4, 1 Cor. 7:2, 7–9). What sometimes causes confusion is a difference between the way the world defines the words adultery and fornication and biblical usage of these words. Even a worldly source[9] recognizes the difference:

> *adultery* (1) defiling of marriage bed; (2) in scripture, all manner of lewdness or unchastity.

> *fornication* (1) act of voluntary sexual intercourse in single persons; if either party married, it is adultery; (2) in the Bible, any unlawful sexual intercourse, including adultery.

In other words, adultery and fornication are used interchangeably in Scripture to express any sexual activity outside of marriage. (As examples read Mt. 5:27–28, which calls looking lustfully at any woman [other than one's wife] adultery and applies it to the unmarried as well as the married, and 1 Cor. 5:9–11, which cautions that Christians are not to associate with sexually immoral people but mentions only fornicators and not adulterers specifically.)

> What is adultery? What sort of necessity is there to bring us to this? Doubtless, it will be said, the tyranny of lust. But why, tell me, should this be? Is it not in everyone's power to have his own wife, and thus to put a stop to this tyranny? True, he will say, but a sort of passion for my neighbor's wife seizes hold on me. Here the question is no longer one of necessity. Passion is not a matter of necessity. No one loves of necessity, but of deliberate choice and free will. Indulgence of nature, indeed, is perhaps a

74

matter of necessity, but to love one woman rather than another is no matter of necessity. Nor is the point with you natural desire, but vanity, wantonness, and unbounded licentiousness. For which is according to reason, that a man should have an espoused wife, and her the mother of his children, or one not acknowledged? Do you not know that it is intimacy that breeds attachment? This, therefore, is not the fault of nature. Blame not natural desire. Natural desire was bestowed with a view to marriage; it was given with a view to the procreation of children, not with a view to adultery and corruption. The laws, too, know how to make allowance for those sins which are of necessity—or rather nothing is sin when it arises from necessity but all sin rises from wantonness. God has not so framed man's nature that he should have any necessity to sin, since were this the case, there would be no such thing as punishment. We ourselves exact no account of things done of necessity and by constraint, much less would God, so full of mercy and loving-kindness ... it is virtue which is according to nature, and vice which is against nature.

CHRYSOSTOM[10]

(e). What event in history caused the Temple at Jerusalem to "be no more"? Because He is omniscient, God foreknew that the Temple in Jerusalem would be destroyed (by the Roman Army in A.D. 70). Orthodox Jews would like to rebuild the Temple to reinstate the sacrifices (which makes Muslims nervous, because one of their most treasured sites, the Dome of the Rock, sits on the land previously occupied by the Temple). Christians have no interest in having the Temple rebuilt because they know Christ was the last living sacrifice required by God according to the Law.

(f). Christ sat with sinners to try to bring them into the fold (Mt. 9:10–13). Can we have similar associations with that motive? If our lifestyles are guided by Christian teachings, we are careful to reflect this in our conversations whenever possible, and we are able to answer questions with regard to God's word fully and correctly, we can be very powerful in outreach to those outside the Church. We must be very careful, however, not to let such associations endanger our spiritual condition. If there is any doubt as to whether we can withstand such temptation, we should flee from it. (Read 1 Thess. 4:10–12). It is also important that such associations do not mislead others (see Chapter 8, Food For Thought (c).)

CHAPTER SIX

Settling Differences Within the Church

When the Corinthian Christians had serious differences among themselves, they would take the matter into the prevailing courts of law, the ruling members of which were not Christian. Thus those who should have been trying to live according to God's law were being judged by those who did not rule on that basis. In this chapter, Paul expresses shock at this practice, since even Jews living in heathen cities did not take such cases before Gentile courts.

6:1. Dare any of you, having a matter against another, go to law before the unrighteous, and not before the saints? Paul implores the Corinthian Christians to settle differences between themselves by appointing judges from among their members, rather than turn to non-Christians to decide matters of contention.

6:2–3. Do you not know that the saints will judge the world? And if the world will be judged by you, are you unworthy to judge the smallest matters? Do you not know that we shall judge angels? How much more, things that pertain to this life? The lives of the saints, those who are members of the Body of Christ and trying to grow in holiness, set the standard for judgment in that God will use the life of a believer as an indictment against an unbeliever of like circumstances.

> For when beholding the same sun and sharing all the same things, we shall be found believers but they unbelievers, they will not be able to take refuge in ignorance. For we shall accuse them, simply by the

things which we have done. And many such ways of judgment one will find there.

CHRYSOSTOM[1]

This is so, not because God needs such a tool to judge by, but so everyone will readily see that His judgment is fair.

> In short, on the awesome Day of Judgment every sinful man will see one who is like him opposite to him in eternal life, in that unutterable light, and will be judged by him. What do I mean? As every sinner looks on him who is like him, the king upon the king, the ruler upon the ruler, the impenitent whoremonger on the whoremonger who repented, the poor man on the poor man, and the slave on the slave, he will remember that the other was also a man, with the same soul, the same hands, the same eyes, in short with all other things in common, the same kind of life, and the same rank, the same occupation, the same resources. Yet, since he was unwilling to imitate Him, his mouth will at once be stopped (Ps. 107:42) and he will remain without excuse (Rom. 1:20), without a word to speak!
>
> SYMEON THE NEW THEOLOGIAN[2]

Before God created man, He created angels—and endowed them with the gift of free will. Lucifer, an angel so named because it meant "bearer of light," was next to God in power and glory, but that was not enough for him. Envy and pride grew in Lucifer to the extent that he rebelled against God. Together with other angels with that same rebellious spirit, he tried to unseat God from His throne—an impossibility (Isa. 14:12–15). So Lucifer (the serpent of Eden—called the dragon, Satan—after his rebellion) was thrown from Heaven with his cohorts, one-third of the angels of Heaven (Rev. 12:3–4, 8–9). Thus the angels had their opportunity to choose between being with God or against Him, which is the opportunity each person has during his/her lifetime. The lives of believers and the extent to which they remain obedient to God will also be used as indictments against the fallen angels, who will receive final judgment at Christ's Second Coming along with man (Jude 6).

> **FOOD FOR THOUGHT:** (a). In what way does man, like Satan, sometimes try to unseat God from His throne?

6:4–5. If then you have judgments concerning things pertaining to this life, do you appoint those who are least esteemed by the church to judge? I say this to your shame. Is it so, that there is not a wise man among you, not even one, who will be able to judge between his brethren? The argument put forth by the Corinthians was that there was no one wise enough in the Church to judge their disputes. Chrysostom's comment is that even if this were so, which is doubtful, it would be better to have these matters judged by the least esteemed Christians than by non-Christians, who live by different standards.

6:6–8. But brother goes to law against brother, and that before unbelievers! Now brethren, it is already an utter failure for you that you go to law against one another. Why do you not rather accept wrong? Why do you not rather let yourselves be defrauded? No, you yourselves do wrong and defraud, and you do these things to your brethren! To have disputes among themselves that need to be settled by non-Christians is an admission that they are not living according to Christian guidelines, under which it is better to be sinned against than to sin, better to be defrauded than to defraud. This lack of fairness, honesty, and love is a more serious matter than determining who is right or wrong among them.

6:9–10. Do you not know that the unrighteous will not inherit the kingdom of God? Do not be deceived. Neither fornicators, nor idolaters, nor adulterers, nor homosexuals, nor sodomites, nor thieves, nor covetous, nor drunkards, nor revilers, nor extortioners will inherit the kingdom of God. Those who live unrighteously will deny themselves the blessings of God's Kingdom. Those who are wronged in this life yet continue trying to live the life of Christ as a product of their faith will enjoy God's promises forever, more than compensating for all injustices suffered in this world.

Notice the different types of sin mentioned:

idolaters: <u>sin against God</u> by giving to someone or something, worship that is due to God. One can "idolize" anyone or anything. Whatever comes first in our life is what we worship, be it self, spouse, children, friends, hobby, money, fame, power, etc. God must be our priority. If we give Him the worship that is His due, all other elements in our lives will take their proper places. We will be at peace, with joy in our hearts.

thieves, covetous, revilers, extortioners: <u>sin against their neighbor</u> by taking or desiring that which belongs to another. To help us not to sin against our neighbor, Jesus said: "whatever you wish that men would do to you, do so to them" (Mt. 7:12).

fornicators, adulterers, homosexuals, sodomites, drunkards: <u>sin against themselves</u> by corrupting that which was formed in the image of God and destined to become as much like Him as possible, according to each individual's abilities and opportunities (read Luke 12:48).

These sins pointed out by Paul, therefore, violate Jesus' new commandment to love God first, then neighbor as self (Mt. 22:36–39). To avoid sinning against God, neighbor, and self would be to obey the spirit of all of the Commandments. Conversely, to sin against neighbor and self is also to sin against God, in whose image neighbor and self were created.

6:11. And such were some of you. But you were washed, but you were sanctified, but you were justified in the name of the Lord Jesus and by the Spirit of our God. They who are baptized in the name of the Trinity are *washed* of all sin and become a part of the Body of Christ. Christ is holy, so they, too, are made holy, *sanctified*, through the Holy Spirit. As part of the Blood Covenant, they are *justified* (qualified for salvation) through His perfect obedience.

> FOOD FOR THOUGHT: (b). We are cleansed of sin at Baptism and are sanctified and justified by becoming a part of the Body of Christ. Do we automatically remain in that purified state? How does the Church help us to do so?

6:12–13. All things are lawful for me, but all things are not helpful. All things are lawful for me, but I will not be brought under the power of any. Foods for the stomach and the stomach for foods, but God will destroy both it and them. Now the body is not for sexual immorality, but for the Lord, and the Lord for the body. Certain behavior is expected of Christians. A specific type of immorality was mentioned in Chapter Five, but now Paul speaks in general terms.

Even though Christians are no longer under the Old Testament Law as far as having to be perfect to earn salvation (see this study for 1 Cor. 5:2), they should not be ruled by their passions.

Food is an example. The Old Testament law required that the Jews eat only certain "clean" animals (Lev. 11). This requirement was abolished by Christ, Who cleansed all creation with His atoning sacrifice (read Acts 10:9–16). But even though Christians can now eat anything they wish, they should not abuse this freedom by becoming slaves to the stomach, giving it anything it wants and becoming gluttonous. The stomach and food are perishable and meant to serve man. We should be in control of them, not allow them to control us. The spiritual discipline of fasting is a tool to help us learn to control our passions.

6:14. And God both raised up the Lord and will also raise us up by His power. The same power that raised Christ from the dead will, if we call upon it and cooperate with it, help us control our worldly passions and raise us to new life now and on the last day.

6:15–18. Do you not know that your bodies are members of Christ? Shall I then take the members of Christ and make them members of a harlot? Certainly not! Or do you not know that he who is joined to a harlot is one body with her? For "The two," He says, "shall become one flesh." But he who is joined to the Lord is one spirit with Him. Flee sexual immorality. Every sin that a man does is outside the body, but he who commits sexual immorality sins against his own body. Through the Sacrament of Marriage, "two become one flesh" (Gen. 2:24), with Christ involved in the relationship, rendering it holy. A Christian, however, who is involved in an illicit sexual relationship creates an unholy alliance, which brings shame to the Church, as well as to him/herself.

FOOD FOR THOUGHT: (c). Is sexual immorality more or less harmful spiritually to a Christian than other activities that are harmful to the body, such as using recreational drugs or excessive alcohol?

6:19–20. Or do you not know that your body is the temple of the Holy Spirit, who is in you, whom you have from God, and you are not your own? For you were bought at a price; therefore glorify God in your body and in your spirit, which is God's. Christ's sacrifice on the Cross atoned for the sins of mankind. Those who become a part of Him through Baptism avail themselves of this saving grace. The Holy Spirit dwells in them through Chrismation. Having provided for us in such a grand fashion, unworthy though we are, God expects us, by our intentions and by our actions, to bring glory (not shame) to Him.

FOOD FOR THOUGHT COMMENTS

(a). In what way does man, like Satan, sometimes try to unseat God from His throne? God has set forth guidelines which, to the extent they are followed, will prepare us to share eternity with Him. Those who insist, rather, upon making their own rules as they go through life—on doing things "their way"—are, in essence, trying to unseat God from His throne and put themselves in His place. They are doomed to failure.

(b). We are cleansed of sin at Baptism and are sanctified and justified by becoming a part of the Body of Christ. Do we automatically remain in that purified state? How does the Church help us to do so? We are sanctified and justified through Christ as long as we remain a part of His Body by trying to grow in holiness. This process can be compared to a difficult uphill climb, but the Holy Spirit helps us as long as we invite and cooperate with Him. Unfortunately, as human beings living in a world where it is easy to sin and difficult to pursue righteousness, we tend to stray from this path. Sin erects barriers between us and God. If we sincerely regret such a lapse, the Church offers restoration through the Sacrament of Repentance (Confession), which, if participated in sincerely, removes any barriers and returns us to the sin-free state of the newly Baptized, free to continue the struggle (Mt. 10:22). The Sacrament of Eucharist offers the opportunity to continually renew our union with Christ.

(c). Is sexual immorality more or less harmful spiritually to a Christian than other activities that are harmful to the body, such as using recreational drugs or excessive alcohol? Any voluntary activity which is harmful to a body in which the Holy Spirit dwells is sinful.

> For it is not your body which is insulted; since it is not
> your body at all, but Christ's.
>
> CHRYSOSTOM[3]

Sexual immorality, however, involves the union of sinful persons who live in rebellion against God's word. Therefore, the sin is compounded.

CHAPTER SEVEN

Marriage or Celibacy?

Some of the questions the Corinthian Christians posed in their letter to Paul dealt with the proper Christian attitude toward sexuality and marriage.

7:1. Now concerning the things of which you wrote me: It is good for a man not to touch a woman. Paul's advice is that virginity and celibacy are preferable for Christians, if these states allow a life that is more fully dedicated to Christ in a particular ministry.

> If you abstain from marriage that you may have leisure for the service of God and yet do not so employ that leisure, it is of no advantage to you.
>
> CHRYSOSTOM[1]

7:2. Nevertheless, because of sexual immorality, let each man have his own wife, and let each woman have her own husband. According to Chrysostom, "There is no relationship between man and man so close as that between man and wife, if they are joined together as they should be."[2] The power of the love between a man and a woman is "truly stronger than any passion" because it (eros) is "planted within our inmost being." Without their even being aware of it, the bodies of men and women are attracted to each other because "in the beginning woman came forth from man and from man and woman other men and women proceed." From one "point of origin" (Adam), he said, came the entire human race. Woman came from man so man would "not think of her as essentially different from himself," and woman cannot bear children without man, so they would be dependent upon each other.[3]

> Just as the branches of a tree proceed from a single
> trunk, He made the one man Adam to be the origin of
> all mankind, both male and female, and made it
> impossible for men and women to be self-sufficient."
> CHRYSOSTOM[4]

7:3–4. Let the husband render to his wife the affection due her, and likewise also the wife to her husband. The wife does not have authority over her own body, but the husband does. And likewise the husband does not have authority over his body, but the wife does. A man and woman united in marriage become one body, "one flesh" (Gen. 2:24), a fact that is clearly symbolized by the sexual union but applicable to all aspects of human life. In a good marriage, that which one partner lacks is provided by the other. They become whole in a way not possible for either alone. When one feels fear, the other provides hope; when one is short on patience, the other ameliorates with love; where one is weak, the other tries to be strong. Through this union, one is not master of the other, they become servants to each other. Each should concern himself with the happiness of his partner. The husband's body belongs to his wife, so he cannot offer it to another. Likewise, the wife's body is not her own, but her husband's. Notice the equality of the sexes in these verses, unusual for the time in which this epistle was written.

7:5–6. Do not deprive one another except with consent for a time, that you may give yourselves to fasting and prayer; and come together again so that Satan does not tempt you because of your lack of self-control. But I say this as a concession, not as a commandment. A husband and wife may agree at certain times to abstain from sexual activities in order to give themselves more fully to prayer, fasting, meditation, and almsgiving for the purpose of spiritual growth in the image of Christ. Though one can and should pray at all times as Paul taught (1 Thess. 5:17), a couple that is growing together spiritually can find such a time of more intense spiritual focus very rewarding. This type of mutual spiritual discipline encourages a deeper marital intimacy and is appropriate before receiving Holy Communion and during the Lenten periods prescribed by the Church.[5]

Concurrence in this matter, however, is not always possible. If one partner desires abstinence for a time but the other does not, the non-concurring partner may become angry and quarrelsome or restless, and in the extreme, could become involved in adultery. If this were to happen, any potential spiritual advancement on the part of the individual who desires to abstain would be negated by the unrest caused by and to the unwilling party. The non-concurring partner should sincerely try to understand the spiritual concerns of his/her mate, and the partner desiring a time of abstinence should try to understand the physical and emotional needs of the other, always for the purpose of strengthening their union and their mutual commitment to Christ. It is incumbent upon the individual more understanding of God's ways to have more patience in this and every area of the human struggle for spiritual growth.

7:7–9. For I wish that all men were even as I myself. But each one has his own gift from God, one in this manner and another in that. But I say to the unmarried and to the widows: It is good for them if they remain even as I am; but if they cannot exercise self-control, let them marry. For it is better to marry than to burn with passion. Both celibacy, for the purpose of dedicating oneself more fully to Christ, and marriage are holy states—each given to some.

> Marital sexuality has been elevated to a Sacrament
> and it must be treated as a precious, beautiful and

holy gift that God gives as a reward to two hetero-
sexual beings who place themselves under God's law
in order to procreate and continue God's creativity.[6]

Through the Sacrament of marriage, God invites man to cooperate with Him in creating new human life (Gen. 1:27–28, 2:21–24, Mt. 19:4–6), one aspect of man having been created in the image of God. Angels do not procreate. Animals procreate without responsibility and without, for the most part, the creation of a family unit.

Other purposes of marriage are to "provide physical and moral assistance to two individuals who have placed themselves willingly under the same yoke,"[7] and to provide for fulfillment of sexual desire for those not given the gift of celibacy, in order to prevent the sin of fornication (1 Cor. 6:9).

7:10–11. Now to the married I command, yet not I but the Lord: A wife is not to depart from her husband. But even if she does depart, let her remain unmarried or be reconciled to her husband. And a husband is not to divorce his wife. Whether to marry or not is a matter of personal choice. But once married, Christ instructed, there is no divorce, except in the case of "sexual immorality" on the part of one of the partners (Mt. 19:8–9; Mk. 10:12; Lk. 16:18).

Accordingly, "the Orthodox Church opposes the dissolution of marriage except for the cause of fornication, because one of the two partners has become one flesh with another individual."[8] However, in the role of a wise, caring, loving mother, the Church, in order to prevent further sin, "has modified her teachings and divorce is granted today on several other grounds such as desertion, extreme cruelty and incompatibility, inability on the part of either partner to consummate the physical union, or incurable mental illness."[9] This is a serious step with far-reaching effects, and should be taken only after the parish priest, the Bishop, and his Diocesan spiritual court have attempted to assist in the reconciliation of the couple. These situations are private matters between the parties involved and their Father Confessor, and are separate from civil procedures.

After such an unavoidable divorce, neither spouse, if they are able, should remarry, but should with fervor dedicate themselves to Christ or work to reconcile differences, if possible, in order to reunite. The Church, however, again to avoid further sin, allows remarriage in the Lord (in the Church), within its guidelines. The original Greek word used in Scripture in place of the word "divorce" is actually closer in meaning to the term "separation." Separation also more appropriately describes the Church's dissolution of a marriage. The ties that bind can be loosed but are never completely eliminated—consequences linger.

The Church's reluctant but realistic conclusion that some marriages should be dissolved is in keeping with the fullness of God's revelation. Scripture continually gives glimpses of the ideal—the goal to strive for. Always, however, we are reminded of the love of Christ and the fact that He accepts us as we are as long as we keep trying to do our best to follow His example (like a good parent who wants his children to live up to their potential for their own good, but loves them no matter what).

> The Lord showed that certain precepts were enacted for (the Jews) by Moses, on account of their hardness (of heart), and because of their unwillingness to be obedient, when, on their saying to Him, *Why then did Moses command to give a certificate of divorce, and to put [a wife] away?* He said to them, *Moses, because of the hardness of your hearts, permitted you to divorce your wives, but from the beginning it was not so.* (Mt.

19:7–8); thus exonerating Moses as a faithful servant, but acknowledging one God, who from the beginning made male and female, and reproving them as hard-hearted and disobedient. And therefore it was that they received from Moses this law of divorcement, adapted to their hard nature. But why do I say these things concerning the Old Testament: For in the New also are the Apostles found doing this very thing, on the ground which has been mentioned, Paul plainly declaring, *I, not the Lord, say* (1 Cor. 7:12). And again: *But this I say as a concession, not as a commandment* (1 Cor. 7:6). And again: *Now, concerning virgins: I have no commandment from the Lord, yet I give judgment, as one whom the Lord in His mercy has made trustworthy* (1 Cor. 7:25). But further, in another place he says: *so that Satan does not tempt you because of your lack of self-control* (1 Cor. 7:5) ... the apostles are found granting certain precepts in consideration of human infirmity, because of the incontinence of some, lest such persons, having grown obdurate and despairing altogether of their salvation, should become apostates from God.

IRENAEUS[10]

When we find ourselves at the point where we really understand how far short we fall from Christ's perfection, we begin to understand the message of salvation: that we are saved not through merit (by our works) but by faith (through His grace). However, our works—the fact that we sincerely and doggedly keep trying to grow in holiness—are necessary to demonstrate and strengthen our faith. This is also the way God's work is accomplished. Some may progress in this more than others because each person enters the struggle with different talents, handicaps, and opportunities. The gap between Christ's perfection (the legalistic requirement for salvation), which is our goal (Mt. 5:48), and the degree of holiness each of us attains with the guidance and power of the Holy Spirit is filled by God's grace.

Our involvement, then, in the spiritual life should not be half-hearted, while relying on the thinking that because God is loving, everyone will get into Heaven. Rather, each of us must struggle as if trying to win the most important race of our lives (see 1 Cor. 9:24). But there is no need to despair. God's grace will bring us over the finish line if a review of our life shows we really tried. Of this we can be confident!

7:12–13. But to the rest I, not the Lord, say: If any brother has a wife who does not believe, and she is willing to live with him, let him not divorce her. And a woman who has a husband who does not believe, if he is willing to live with her, let her not divorce him. In the era in which Paul wrote, Christianity was brand new. Everyone who came to it was a convert. Often one partner in a marriage would convert and the other would not. The question here was, should the Christian partner continue in the marriage with the non-Christian partner? Paul's opinion is that the Christian partner should not be the one to call an end to the marriage.

7:14,16. For the unbelieving husband is sanctified by the wife, and the unbelieving wife is sanctified by the husband; otherwise your children would be unclean, but now they are holy. For how do you know, O wife, whether you will save your husband? Or how do you know, O husband, whether you will save your wife? Divine blessings, to a certain extent, extend to a Christian's family and sphere of life (see Gen. 17:7, 26:3–5, 39:5), the hope always being to eventually bring spouse, children, and other relatives and friends within the fold of believers.

FOOD FOR THOUGHT: (a). Do Paul's instructions
that the "unbelieving husband is sanctified by

the wife" and vice versa apply to any situation common in our times?

7:15. But if the unbeliever departs, let him depart; a brother or a sister is not under bondage in such cases. But God has called us to peace. If the unbelieving partner insists on divorce, the Christian partner should grant it, rather than reject Christ in order to follow one's spouse or live in a home of constant turmoil. Note the use of the terms *brother* and *sister* to denote fellow Christians.

7:17–24. But as God has distributed to each one, as the Lord has called each one, so let him walk. And so I ordain in all churches. Was anyone called while circumcised? Let him not become uncircumcised. Was anyone called while uncircumcised? Let him not be circumcised. Circumcision is nothing and uncircumcision is nothing, but keeping the commandments of God is what matters. Let each one remain in the same calling in which he was called. Were you called while a slave? Do not be concerned about it; but if you can be made free, rather use it. For he who is called in the Lord while a slave is the Lord's freedman. Likewise he who is called while free is Christ's slave. You were bought at a price; do not become slaves of men. Brethren, let each one remain with God in that calling in which he was called. A person need not alter his/her status or condition of life in order to be a Christian, only follow Christ within those circumstances. Like flowers, we are expected to bloom where we are planted.

Circumcision and slavery were issues during the time in which Paul wrote. Circumcision was the symbol or seal of inclusion under the Written Covenant of the Old Testament (Rom. 4:11). Circumcision was superseded by Baptism as the symbol of faith under the new and final Blood Covenant through Jesus Christ, so whether or not one was circumcised no longer mattered.

The condition of slavery would not preclude one's becoming a Christian. If freedom from slavery could be gained—great! If not, this fact was no impediment—it too could provide opportunities for witness. A Christian belongs to Christ, and can and must serve Him no matter what the outward circumstances of life. One can obey an earthly master as long as s/he does not in so doing disobey God. To allow an earthly master to induce us to disobey God would make us *slaves of men,* but we are called to be *slaves of Christ.*

We were *bought* with the *price* of Christ's precious blood. All who believe that His sacrifice atoned for sin will share in the reward He earned: eternal life with God in His Kingdom. We are *slaves of Christ* to the extent that our obedience is demanded in order to prove our faith. Each of us though is a *freedman,* in that we are no longer under obligation to actually be perfect according to the Mosaic Law in order to earn salvation. We have the freedom to operate within the limitations of our individual abilities and opportunities, as long as we continually and whole-heartedly strive toward Christ's perfection.

> **FOOD FOR THOUGHT:** (b). Slaves had to obey their earthly masters. They could find themselves in situations where they were forced to choose to either disobey God or to die, as when they were told to publicly denounce Christ. In our modern world, in what spiritual dangers do we find ourselves where we might have to choose between being *slaves of men and slaves of Christ?*

7:25–38. Now concerning virgins: I have no commandment from the Lord; yet I give judgment as one whom the Lord in His mercy has made trustworthy. I suppose therefore that this is good because of the present distress—that it is good for a man to remain as he is: Are you bound to a wife? Do not seek to be loosed. Are you loosed from a wife? Do not seek a wife. But even if you do marry, you have not sinned; and if a virgin marries, she has not sinned. Nevertheless such will have trouble in the flesh, but I would spare you. But this I say, brethren, the time is short, so that from now on even those who have wives should be as though they had none, those who weep as though they did not weep, those who rejoice as though they did not rejoice, those who buy as though they did not possess, and those who use this world as not misusing it. For the form of this world is passing away. But I want you to be without care. He who is unmarried cares for the things that belong to the Lord—how he may please the Lord. But he who is married cares about the things of the world—how he may please his wife. There is a difference between a wife and a virgin. The unmarried woman cares about the things of the Lord, that she may be holy both in body and spirit. But she who is married cares about the things of the world—how she may please her husband. And this I say for your own profit, not that I may put a leash on you but for what is proper, and that you may serve the Lord without distraction. But if any man thinks he is behaving improperly toward his virgin, if she is past the flower of her youth, and thus it must be, let him do what he wishes; he does not sin; let them marry. Nevertheless he who stands steadfast in his heart, having no necessity, but has power over his own will, and has so determined in his heart that he will keep his virgin, does well. So then he who gives her in

marriage does well, but he who does not give her in marriage does better. In view of the difficulties of the Christian life, the amount of work to be done to teach the Gospel fully, and the shortness of time remaining because of the limits of life and the Second Coming of Christ, which each generation of Christians has thought was imminent,[11] Paul's opinion is that married or unmarried, Christians should focus on serving Christ:

> *if married*: remain married and serve the Lord together.

> *if single*: do not seek a spouse because being unmarried allows a closer walk with Christ, with fewer worldly distractions. If unable to remain celibate and chaste for that purpose, then marry.

> *if engaged*: if breaking one's promise to one's betrothed would cause lasting distress, then marry—it is no sin.

> FOOD FOR THOUGHT: (c). What is the message in this for our time?

7:39–40. A wife is bound to her husband as long as her husband lives; but if her husband dies, she is at liberty to be married to whom she wishes, only in the Lord. But she is happier if she remains as she is, according to my judgment—and I think I also have the Spirit of God. One who marries is bound to his/her spouse as long as the partner lives. If one partner dies, the remaining partner is allowed to remarry (in the Church), but in Paul's opinion should remain unmarried in order to more fully serve the Lord, with fewer divided loyalties. "In the Lord" refers to the fact that a Christian must not marry a non-Christian and points to the sacramental nature of marriage from the beginning of the Church.

FOOD FOR THOUGHT COMMENTS

(a). Do Paul's instructions that the "unbelieving husband is sanctified by the wife" and vice versa (7:14, 16) apply to any situation common in our times? Partners in marriage often are not at the same spiritual level. One may come to an awakening apart from the other—or to a deeper commitment to Christ than the other. It is incumbent upon the one more spiritually mature to try to bring the other along, for if anyone does not provide for his own, and especially for those of his household, he has denied the faith and is worse than an unbeliever (1Tim. 5:8).

(b). Slaves had to obey their earthly masters. They could find themselves in situations where they were being forced either to disobey God or to die, as when they were told to publicly denounce Christ. In our modern world, in what spiritual dangers do we find ourselves where we might have to choose between being *slaves of men and slaves of Christ?* In our modern society, we are sometimes almost slaves to our employers. We may also find ourselves in the position of being slaves to society and its norms and fads. Christians should obey their employers as long as doing so does not diminish or contradict their following of Christ. The same holds true in following social dictates. The first commandment (Ex. 20:3) prescribes that God must come first, and all must be brought under subjection to Him, not vice versa.

(c). As in the ancient Church, the Christian life is still difficult, there is still a lot of work to be done, and the time that remains to us is short. What does this mean with regard to our commitment to Christ? Each of us must assess our lives to determine how, given our own individual gifts, strengths, abilities, opportunities, and circumstances of life, we can best serve the Lord. This is a question to be addressed continually when considering the direction our lives should take from any point.

CHAPTER EIGHT

Take Care Not to Mislead

The Christians of Corinth were living in the midst of the pagan world, where much of the meat offered for sale in public marketplaces had first been offered in sacrifice to an idol. This practice prompted questions: Was it fitting for Christians to buy and eat this meat? Was it appropriate for them to participate in the social functions of the city, many of which revolved around gathering for meals in a pagan temple?

8:1. Now concerning things offered to idols: We know that we all have knowledge. Knowledge puffs up, but love edifies. He who concentrates on gathering knowledge without growing in the practice of love becomes concerned only with himself and his importance. Such an isolated focus on facts can, therefore, be destructive. One who loves is aware of the needs of others and uses his knowledge on their behalf.

8:2. And if anyone thinks that he knows anything, he knows nothing yet as he ought to know. The Christian life should include growth in knowledge of God but it is important to remember that no matter how much we know, God always has something more to teach us. If we think that we have perfect knowledge, we only advertise our ignorance and arrogance.

> FOOD FOR THOUGHT: (a). What does this verse say to those who feel that since they have already "read" the Bible, there is no further need for them to study it?

8:3. But if anyone loves God, this one is known by Him. The person who has attained knowledge of what really matters shows his love for God through his concern for others, which Jesus said is one of the two greatest commandments (Mk. 12:30–31). All those who live by these commandments are known by God (Jn. 14:21).

8:4–6. Therefore concerning the eating of things offered to idols, we know that an idol is nothing in the world, and that there is no other God but one. For even if there are so-called gods, whether in heaven or on earth (as there are many gods and many lords), yet for us there is only one God, the Father, of whom are all things, and we for Him; and one Lord Jesus Christ, through whom are all things, and through whom we live. Idols have no spiritual reality. They are called gods only by the foolish. There are entities in the heavens that some have called gods (the sun, moon, and stars, which pagans worshiped), and there are those on earth to whom some look as gods and lords of a sort because they have much earthly power and authority. All these, however, are but creations of the one true God, Who alone is uncreated and eternal. We call His Son Lord because through Him, God created everything that exists in Heaven and on earth.

> FOOD FOR THOUGHT: (b). Who are they who might be considered "gods" by some in the times in which we live? What is the danger in this?

8:7. However, there is not in everyone that knowledge; for some, with consciousness of the idol, until now eat it as a thing offered to an idol; and their conscience, being weak, is defiled. But food does not commend us to God; for neither if we eat are we the better, nor if we do not eat are we the worse. But beware lest somehow this

liberty of yours become a stumbling block to those who are weak. For if anyone sees you who have knowledge eating in an idol's temple, will not the conscience of him who is weak be emboldened to eat those things offered to idols?** To a Christian who has knowledge of God's truths, it does not matter whether food he is about to eat has first been offered to an idol. To him, it is just food. A new Christian, however, might not yet have this proper understanding. He might be a former pagan, still not thoroughly convinced that an idol has no real existence. If such a person ate this type of food while thinking of it as something offered to an idol which had validity and power, and that this must be acceptable because he saw a knowledgeable Christian do it, his worship of idols could continue.

8:11–12. And because of your knowledge shall the weak brother perish, for whom Christ died? But when you thus sin against the brethren, and wound their weak conscience, you sin against Christ. The freedom of the knowledgeable Christian could be confusing to the new or less well-grounded Christian and cause him/her to go astray.

8:13. Therefore, if food makes my brother stumble, I will never again eat meat, lest I make my brother stumble. Paul's declaration that he would rather not eat meat again than do so under conditions that might lead another Christian to sin is the type of love Christ expects of all of His people.

> **FOOD FOR THOUGHT:** (c). What are some modern examples of actions by which a knowledgeable Orthodox Christian may cause a new or newly awakened Orthodox Christian to falter? What about converts to Orthodoxy from another faith? Might they hear or see certain things that might offend them or hamper their

growth? What can more knowledgeable Orthodox Christians do to prevent such situations?

FOOD FOR THOUGHT COMMENTS

(a). Paul said, "If anyone thinks that he knows anything, he knows nothing yet as he ought to know" (8:2). What does this say to those who feel that since they have already "read" the Bible, there is no further need for them to study it? The Bible contains the word of God as given to man by inspiration, through prophecy, and through the coming to earth of the Son of God, the Logos, the Word of God. It contains the fullness of the truth about God's divine plan for the salvation of man. As such it represents truth, beauty, and mystery to such a degree that ordinary man, at whatever spiritual level he might be, can only begin to understand its magnitude and wonder. The Holy Spirit, however, blesses every effort at spiritual growth. So as we study Scripture with the guidance of the Church (through the writings of the Fathers), we receive enlightenment commensurate with our level of spiritual maturity. Each time we read God's word, if we continue at the same time to put what we learn into practice, we come to it at a new level, as a different person, and our progress continues from there. Thus, no matter how many times we have read the Bible, or to what degree we have studied it, through the grace of God it will always have something new and exciting to offer. We are taught and understand at our own level, grasping that for which we are ready. To say, at any juncture, that we "know" the Bible is to show the inadequacy of our knowledge. We should, therefore, consider ourselves, throughout our lives, to be students of the Bible and pilgrims on the road to holiness.

Sacred Scripture is our food and drink. ... We ... open our mouths when we prepare our minds to understand His sacred word. ... But even this is not within our power, unless He feeds us Who has commanded us to eat (Ezek. 3:1–3). For he is given food, who of himself is unable to eat. And since our human infirmity is unable to grasp heavenly words, He feeds us, Who in due season gives us our measure of wheat (Lk. 12:42), in that while today we understand in the sacred word what yesterday we could not, and when tomorrow likewise we understand what today we cannot grasp, we are through the grace of divine providence being nourished with daily bread. For as often as Almighty God opens our understanding and places in our minds the food of His sacred words, so often does He stretch forth His hand to the mouth of our heart.

GREGORY THE GREAT[1]

(b). Who are they who might be considered "gods" by some in the times in which we live? What is the danger in this? Rock (music) and movie stars, political and national leaders—even religious leaders—are looked upon as "gods" of a sort by some in our modern society. A Christian must remember always to put God the Father first in his love and allegiance, and to follow no worldly leader in any manner that would hamper his endeavor to grow in holiness. We must pray for and use great discernment as to whom we (and especially our children) will follow. No one can take God's place.

(c). What are some modern examples of actions by which a knowledgeable Orthodox Christian may cause a new or newly awakened Orthodox Christian to falter? What about converts to Orthodoxy from another faith? Might they hear or see certain things that might offend them or hamper their growth? What can more knowledgeable Orthodox Christians do to prevent such situations?

Those who are knowledgeable about the teachings of Christ must be careful that their actions are not misunderstood by those around them who may still be struggling to understand how these truths affect their everyday lives. One example might be the knowledgeable Christian who tries to emulate Jesus' habit of keeping company with "sinners" in order to teach them (Mt. 9:10–13), which could be confusing to someone new to the faith. The more knowledgeable Christian also must be careful not to overestimate his/her spiritual strength.

The tendency among Orthodox Christians to lean toward ethnocentrism, produced by immigration to America from Greece, Russia, etc., with resettlement in groups according to these origins, presents another example. This ethnic atmosphere can have many positive aspects, but in the Church, it can also take the focus away from God and might leave those with different backgrounds feeling like outsiders. When that happens, the Church loses the force and all-inclusive dimension it is meant to have. In the fullness of the truth that Orthodoxy claims, it is important to reach out to and to welcome all of God's people, taking care not to offend with thoughts or actions that could be construed as feelings of ethnic superiority. Most offenses in these areas are caused by a lack of awareness rather than a lack of love—but those looking on don't necessarily know that.

CHAPTER NINE

The Extra Mile

Paul's critics in Corinth were suspicious of the fact that he accepted no compensation for his work there (see 2 Cor. 11:7–12, 12:11–13). They implied that perhaps his refusal to do so indicated that he was not really authorized to teach the Gospel. He now answers the questions thus raised: (1) Did he have a right, according to scriptural criterion, to be paid for the work he did in the course of his ministry? (2) If so, why would he refuse it?

9:1–2. Am I not an apostle? Am I not free ? Have I not seen Jesus Christ our Lord? Are you not my work in the Lord? If I am not an apostle to others, yet doubtless I am to you. For you are the seal of my apostleship in the Lord. Paul was not one of the original twelve apostles, but he was called by Christ, Who appeared to him while he was on the road to Damascus (Acts 9:10–16, 1 Cor. 15:8). He had proved himself capable of teaching and bringing others to the Lord by those he had converted in Corinth, truly accomplishing the work of an Apostle among them.

9:3–4. My defense to those who examine me is this: Do we have no right to eat and drink? Since he fulfilled the essential qualifications of and was doing the work of an Apostle (Acts 1:21–22), he was entitled to be supported by the Christian community.

9:5–6. Do we have no right to take along a believing wife, as do also the other apostles, the brothers of the Lord, and Cephas? Or is it only Barnabas and I who have no right to refrain from working? Paul and Barnabas were not married, but if they were, or if (as the original Greek text can be translated) a sister-in-the-Lord were to accompany them, to help with the ministry, they were entitled to her support also. (Peter [see Mt. 8:14] and at least some of the other Apostles were married. Clement of Alexandria wrote that Philip was married, and Eusebius intimated that they were all married[1]) "Brothers of the Lord" refers to Joseph's children by his wife who had died (Mt. 13:55), not by Mary, the Theotokos (Mother of God), who gave birth to no child other than Jesus.

9:7. Who ever goes to war at his own expense? Who plants a vineyard and does not eat of its fruit? Or who tends a flock and does not drink of the milk of the flock? Paul offers some examples to illustrate the point: a soldier's needs are provided for by those he serves; a farmer receives some of the harvest; and a shepherd receives some of the milk of the flock. Note the inference: an Apostle (Bishop, Priest) is like a soldier in that he is a part of the Lord's army to fight evil, like a farmer in that he plants churches, and like a shepherd in that he guides and guards his congregation.

9:8–12. Do I say these things as a mere man? Or does not the law say the same also? For it is written in the law of Moses, "You shall not muzzle an ox while it treads out the grain." Is it oxen God is concerned about? Or does He say it altogether for our sakes? For our sakes, no doubt, this is written, that he who plows should plow in hope, and he who threshes in hope should be partaker of his hope. If we have sown spiritual things for you, is it a great thing if we reap your material things? If others are partakers of this right over you, are we not even more? Nevertheless we have not used this right, but endure all things lest we hinder the gospel of Christ. As it would be unfair to muzzle a threshing ox, not allowing it to eat of the grain it treads (Deut. 25:4), it is unfair to deprive a hard-working man of his just wages. Likewise, the needs of those who do the work of the Lord should be recognized and their work recompensed. A plowman begins the cycle of work (with planting); a thresher completes the harvest (with gathering). Both have a right to expect to profit from their work. Both he who first plants the seed of faith in the Lord in a man's heart and he who guides him to a more mature faith deserve to have their efforts rewarded (Mt. 10:10, Lk. 10:7).

> The teacher ought to enjoy the returns of his labors.
> CHRYSOSTOM[2]

9:13–15. Do you not know that those who minister the holy things eat of the things of the temple, and those who serve at the altar partake of the offerings of the altar? Even so the Lord has commanded that those who preach the gospel should live from the gospel. But I have used none of these things, nor have I written these things that it should be done so to me; for it would be better for me to die than that anyone should make my boasting void. Just as the priests of the Jewish temple and their families were allowed to take of the offerings brought to the temple for their personal use (see Numbers 18:21), Paul was entitled to have his needs provided for. Because his love for Jesus Christ was so great, however, he declined that support so as not to hinder the Gospel in any way—he did not want anyone to be able to say that the work he did was just a job to him.

9:16–18. For if I preach the gospel, I have nothing to boast of, for necessity is laid upon me; yes, woe is me if I do not preach the gospel. For if I do this willingly, I have a reward; but if against my will, I have been entrusted with a stewardship. What is my reward then? That when I preach the gospel, I may present the gospel of Christ without charge, that I may not abuse my authority in the gospel. Having been commissioned by

106

Christ, Paul must preach the Gospel (Mt. 28:19–20). He is also compelled to do so by an inner zeal that pushes him constantly onward. He goes further, however, in laboring without pay, for the satisfaction of knowing that he did more than just what was expected. He also wanted to set a good example in order to prevent false teachers from pretending to do God's work for material gain.

> **FOOD FOR THOUGHT:** (a). How can we go "the extra mile" in our walk with God?

9:19. For though I am free from all men, I have made myself a servant to all, that I might win the more; ... Paul was a tentmaker, so was able to support himself (Acts 18:3). He was also willing to live in a very simple manner (1 Cor. 4:10–13). Therefore, he was obligated to no one. But he willingly made himself a servant to all in order to bring souls to Christ.

> **FOOD FOR THOUGHT:** (b). Paul truly tried to follow Christ's example in this and other precepts. Is it possible to pursue this lifestyle today?

9:20–22. and to the Jews I became as a Jew, that I might win Jews; to those who are under the law, as under the law, that I might win those who are under the law; to those who are without law, as without law (not being without law toward God, but under law toward Christ), that I might win those who are without law; to the weak I became as weak, that I might win the weak. I have become all things to all men, that I might by all means save some. Paul was born a Jew, but as a Christian he was no longer bound by the legalisms of the Mosaic Law. However, he made good use of his heritage, following Jewish teachings and customs insofar as they did not conflict with the Gospel in order to maintain his relationship with Jews, to put himself in a position from which he might lead them to Christ. He also followed the customs of the Gentiles that did not conflict with the Christ-like life for the same reason. Further, with those still immature in faith he was tolerant while trying to nurture them. He thus used every means available to him to bring as many people as possible from all walks of life to Christ.

Note the words: "that I might by all means save some." Those who take biblical verses out of context might misinterpret this verse to mean that Paul taught that people could find salvation through him. Nothing is farther from the truth. He claimed to "save" only by bringing souls to Christ. In like manner, all Biblical verses, prayers, and hymns of the Church must be understood in the context in which they were written. When we pray to those whom, we have good reason to believe, have gone beyond this life to God's Kingdom (including the Theotokos and the Saints—the Church Triumphant), we ask only, but importantly, that they pray with us and for us to God for His mercy, as we ask for prayers from our friends around us in this life (the Church Militant—those still struggling through this life trying to live by faith).

> The Saints take part in the governing of the Church of Christ on earth, and therefore it is natural and proper to appeal to them with prayers, asking their intercession before Christ, with Whom they reign.[3] (See 1 Cor. 6:2–3, Rev. 20:4.)

We know, however, that only God (through His Son) can save us.

9:23. Now this I do for the gospel's sake, that I may be a partaker of it with you. Those who believe the Gospel of Jesus Christ and live accordingly will share eternity with God

in His Kingdom. Paul does the work of the Lord with that goal
in mind.

**9:24. Do you not know that those who run in a race all
run, but one receives the prize? Run in such a way that
you may obtain it.** This does not mean that only he who has
surpassed all others in spiritual accomplishments will enter
the Kingdom, but that the Christ-like life should be pursued
with the fervor that would be required if that were the case.
These words paint a picture far different from that painted by
those who take Paul's words (in Rom. 10:9) out of context,
teaching that one's works have nothing to with salvation, that
all one need do to be "saved" is profess belief, with absolute
assurance of eternity with God from that point on.

**9:25. And everyone who competes for the prize is
temperate in all things. Now they do it to obtain a
perishable crown, but we for an imperishable crown.**
When an athlete is in training in preparation for the running of
an important race, he withdraws from the world to concentrate
on his goal. He is taught to use moderation in his eating,
drinking, and social activities in order to funnel all of his
energies into the task at hand and to train with all his might.
He goes to these great lengths to win a crown that is perishable. This was a very apt analogy for the Corinthians because
of their familiarity with the Isthmian games, held every three
years in Corinth, which were considered second only to the
Olympics and drew immense crowds. "To win was to be
immortalized by the Greek public."[4]

We who call ourselves Christians are participating in a race in
which those who cross the finish line (Mk. 13:13) will receive
an imperishable crown from God. We must therefore prepare
ourselves and concentrate on our goal with even greater fervor

than the most ambitious athlete. (Read Heb. 12:1–4; 2 Tim. 4:6–8; Jas. 1:12, 2:14–17; 1 Pet. 5:1–4; Rev. 2:10–11.)

> **FOOD FOR THOUGHT:** (c). What would a review of our life indicate as to where we expend the greater effort: in our worldly affairs or in our spiritual walk with Christ?

9:26–27. Therefore I run thus: not with uncertainty. Thus I fight: not as one who beats the air. But I discipline my body and bring it into subjection, lest, when I have preached to others, I myself should become disqualified. Paul practiced what he preached. He was very actively involved in the struggle himself, fighting against the devil, who tries to dissuade every Christian from the goal.

A Protestant interpretation of these verses, reflecting the theology of "salvation by faith alone," says: "His own salvation is not in question but his reward for acceptable service."[5] The Orthodox interpretation is that every person's faith in Christ as Savior, or lack thereof, as shown by his works (the overall picture of his life) will be revealed on Judgment Day. (See this study for 1 Cor. 3:12–15, 10:6–10).

If Paul felt absolutely confident of his salvation at the moment, he would not sound so adamant about the need to press on to win the race, nor would he be so concerned about his reward. Wouldn't being in Heaven be glorious enough in itself (Ps. 84:10)? Why would he struggle so and refer to the "terror of the Lord" (2 Cor. 5:11) with regard to getting a higher reward? Why would he write about being "disqualified" if he did not know that there is always an element of doubt about our salvation until our lives are over and it is certain that we have endured to the end (Mt. 24:13)?

110

There *are* levels of union with God (see this study for 1 Cor. 2:10–13;3:8,12–15; and 15:39–41). But here Paul was talking about the need to continue throughout life to do God's work, because that is what one who has true faith would do, as opposed to one who thinks he need only profess belief in Jesus Christ but continue to live the type of life he likes, or as opposed to one who takes part in the struggle to a certain point and then rests on his laurels, thinking he has "done enough." No one can ever do enough to earn salvation. Salvation cannot be earned or purchased but comes through demonstrated faith that Jesus Christ is the promised Messiah, Lord of our lives. In the end, we will see that we have judged ourselves by the way we lived (see this study for 1 Cor. 6:2–3).

> Just as tools without the workman and the workman without tools are unable to do anything ... neither is faith without the commandments, nor the fulfillment of the commandments without faith able to renew and re-create us.
>
> SYMEON THE NEW THEOLOGIAN[6]

In his First Apology to the Emperor Titus Aelius Adrianus Antonius Pius Augustus Caesar, on behalf of those who were being unjustly persecuted merely because they called themselves Christians, Justin wrote the following in explaining why they would not deny their Christianity to avoid punishment:

> It is in our power, when we are examined, to deny that we are Christians; but we would not live by telling a lie. For, impelled by the desire of the eternal and pure life, we seek the abode that is with God, the Father and Creator of all, and hasten to confess our faith, *persuaded and convinced as we are that they who have proved to God by their works that they followed Him, and loved to abide with Him where there is no sin to cause disturbance, can obtain these*

things. This then, to speak briefly, is what we expect and have learned from Christ, and teach. ...

And we have been taught, and are convinced, and do believe, that He accepts those only who imitate the excellences which reside in Him, temperance, and justice, and philanthropy, and as many virtues as are peculiar to a God who is called by no proper name. ...

. And when you hear that we look for a kingdom, you suppose, without making any inquiry, that we speak of a human kingdom; whereas we speak of that which is with God, as appears also from the confession of their faith made by those who are charged with being Christians, though they know that death is the punishment awarded to him who so confesses. For if we looked for a human kingdom, we should also deny our Christ, that we might not be slain; and we should strive to escape detection, that we might obtain what we expect. But since our thoughts are not fixed on the present, we are not concerned when men cut us off. ...

And more than all other men are we your helpers and allies in promoting peace, seeing that we hold this view, that it is alike impossible for the wicked, the covetous, the conspirator, and for the virtuous, to escape the notice of God, and that each man goes to everlasting punishment or salvation according to the value of his actions.[7]

Only when Paul saw the end of his life at hand did he display confidence in his own salvation, because he knew his struggle was almost over (2 Tim. 4:6–8).

FOOD FOR THOUGHT COMMENTS

(a). How can we go "the extra mile" in our walk with God? Mt. 5:38–48 offers examples. Willingness to do more than just what is necessary to achieve one's goal in any area shows love, which is the goal of the Christian life (Jn. 15:9–12). God is love (1 Jn. 4:8). He created man out of His love and desire to share with him the wonders of Creation. In return, He asks only love, which we extend to Him in outreach to others (Mt. 25:31–46). To do only that which one thinks he must do for salvation is legalistic and devoid of love.

(b). Paul truly tried to follow Christ's example in this and other precepts. Is it possible to pursue this lifestyle today? Everyone in every age is called to try to follow Christ's example in all things (read Phil. 2:5–8). Our modern world presents unique challenges to the Christ-like lifestyle, but so has every age. Each of us has different strengths, talents, opportunities, and responsibilities. God asks only that we do the best we can in the circumstances in which we find ourselves—but with Him, "all things are possible" (Mt. 19:26).

(c). What would a review of our life indicate as to where we expend the greater effort: in our worldly affairs or in our spiritual walk with Christ? All that is required for salvation is to continually try to show God we believe that He exists and that we have faith in His promises, by trying to live a Christ-like life. But trying means making a sincere effort— with all our might. The greater effort should of course be for that which is eternal, rather than for that which is passing.

CHAPTER TEN

Obedience: An Indicator of Love

Paul's recurring theme, mimicking that throughout the Bible from the Old Testament to the New, is that of the salvation of mankind through faith in Christ as Savior. Further, this faith is subject to times of testing during one's lifetime and to Judgment as to its validity. In this chapter, Paul gives examples of this truth.

10:1–5. Moreover, brethren, I do not want you to be unaware that all our fathers were under the cloud, all passed through the sea, all were baptized into Moses in the cloud and in the sea, all ate the same spiritual food, and all drank the same spiritual drink. For they drank of that spiritual Rock that followed them, and that Rock was Christ. But with most of them God was not well pleased, for their bodies were scattered in the wilderness. The Book of Exodus tells the story of the Hebrew people, God's chosen, who were led by Moses out of the Land of Egypt after 430 years of slavery (12:40). God's Hand delivered them from captivity (chaps. 3–14) and guided them with a pillar of cloud by day and of fire by night (13:21). When they reached the sea with Pharaoh's army behind them, Moses lifted his hand and God divided the waters so they could reach the other side unharmed (14:21). When the Egyptians followed into the dry seabed, Moses again lifted his hand and the waters returned to their normal level, drowning Pharaoh's army (14:27). When they were hungry, God provided quail and manna from heaven (16:11–15), and when they were thirsty, Moses struck a rock with his rod as God directed, and water poured forth (17:6). God asked in return only that they obey Him, as a sign of their love for Him (19:3–6), which would also serve to shape them spiritually into what He wanted them to

114

be: His people—for their own benefit, not His. But in spite of the many miracles surrounding them, they continually complained (Num. 11:1, 14:11) and rebelled, so God refused to allow most of them to reach the promised land (Num. 14:22–23,29,43).

10:6–10. Now these things became our examples, to the intent that we should not lust after evil things as they also lusted. And do not become idolaters as were some of them. As it is written, "The people sat down to eat and drink, and rose up to play." Nor let us commit sexual immorality, as some of them did, and in one day twenty-three thousand fell; nor let us tempt Christ, as some of them also tempted, and were destroyed by serpents; nor complain, as some of them also complained, and were destroyed by the destroyer. This story is told to remind us that God showers us with blessings because He loves us, but He expects our love (demonstrated by obedience) in return, because His Kingdom consists of love. Those who, like the Hebrews of old, are indifferent or rebellious will suffer the consequences as they did. Those who allow God to continually mold them in holiness will be blessed, in this life and the next.

> In the beginning, therefore, did God form Adam, not as if He stood in need of man, but that He might have [someone] upon whom to confer His benefits. ... Nor did He stand in need of our service when He ordered us to follow Him; but He thus bestowed salvation upon us. For to follow the Savior is to be a partaker of salvation, and to follow light is to receive light. But those who are in light do not themselves illumine the light, but are illumined and revealed by it: they do certainly contribute nothing to it, but, receiving the benefit, they are illumined by the light. Thus, also, service (rendered) to God does indeed profit God nothing, nor has God need of human obedience; but

He grants to those who follow and serve Him life and incorruption and eternal glory, bestowing benefit upon those who serve (Him), because they do serve Him, and on His followers, because they do follow Him but does not receive any benefit from them: for He is rich, perfect, and in need of nothing. But for this reason does God demand service from men, in order that, since He is good and merciful, He may benefit those who continue in His service. For, as much as God is in want of nothing, so much does man stand in need of fellowship with God. For this is the glory of man, to continue and remain permanently in God's service.

IRENAEUS[1]

These verses also dramatically illustrate the fact that Old Testament events prefigured New Testament truths:

> For as the gifts are figures, even so are the punishments figures: and as Baptism and the Table were sketched out prophetically, so also by what ensued, the certainty of punishment coming on those who are unworthy of this gift was proclaimed beforehand for our sake that we by these examples might learn soberness.

CHRYSOSTOM[2]

Old Testament Event	Prefigured New Testament Truth
Moses and the Hebrew people (God's chosen)	Christ and His people (the Church)
guided by pillar of cloud by day, fire by night	Jesus, the Good Shepherd leads his sheep (Jn 10:2-4, 9, 11)
passed through sea (which opened for them opportunity for new life)	Baptism (in water): cleansing and entrance into new Life-in-Christ

116

<u>Old Testament Event</u>	<u>Prefigured New Testament Truth</u>
freedom from Egyptian slavery	freedom from slavery to sin
ate spiritual food: manna provided by God	The Lord's Body (Jn 6:48-58)
drank spiritual drink: water from Rock (Ex 17:6)	The Lord's Blood
spiritual Rock followed them (Christ's presence)	Christ with us always through the Church
with most of them God was not well-pleased (Num 14:19-24)	Judgment
their bodies scattered in the wilderness (Num 14:29)	reward or punishment (inclusion or exclusion) (Mt 25:34, 41)
they lusted after forbidden things (Num 11:4-34)	
they became idolators (Ex 32:4, 6)	
they committed sexual immorality ... 23,000 fell (idol worship was accompanied by or led to sexual immorality) (Num 25:1-9)	certainly analogous to our times
they spoke against God and were destroyed (Ex 16:2, Num 21:4-6)	

Verses 1–10 illustrate dramatically the fact that the Exodus story of the Hebrew people was a prefiguration of the struggle required to enter fully into the Kingdom of God (Mt. 11:12). They also outline the four steps in the process of salvation.[3]

<u>One</u>: we are called to *believe* in God and His Son Jesus Christ, our Savior, through the blessings God bestows upon us.

<u>Two</u>: we must *prove our belief* by trying to become Christ-like throughout our lives through obedience, because it is not enough to just say we believe. Faith is tested continually throughout our daily lives, as we respond to difficulties and temptations. When the going gets rough, and it does, we must not complain, just keep going, keeping our focus on the goal.

<u>Three</u>: we must *face judgment*. God will judge, through His Son, whether our lives showed faith (Rev. 20:11–12).

<u>Four</u>: we will *receive* (our) *reward*, that for which we have prepared—eternity with God for those whose lives demonstrated true faith (Mt. 25:34), and for those who did not, eternity in the agony of knowing they forever denied themselves His blessings (Mt. 25:41).

> God searches the intention of everything that we do, whether we do it for Him or for any other motive ... He will reward good works but not those done apart from a right intention even if they appear good. ... For God's judgment looks not on what is done but to the intention behind it.
>
> MAXIMUS THE CONFESSOR[4]

No matter how much struggle our life in Christ entails, however, we do not despair because we have the hope of salvation (Rom. 8:18–25). We know that God keeps His promises, so if we truly love Him, the Holy Spirit will dwell in us, sanctify us, and help us grow in His image; thus we "shall be saved" (Mk. 13:13, Mt. 24:13). This is what fills us with deep, inner joy, no matter what ups and downs our earthly life brings.

> In man's nature pleasure is of two kinds: one has place in the soul through calm, and one in the body through passion. Whichever of the two the will may choose, this has dominion over the other. For if one turns towards the senses, choosing the pleasure that has its root in the body itself, such a one will pass through life without tasting of the divine delights: for the more perfect joys will have been shut out by the baser. But to those in whom the desire for God is strong, from these the True God does not remain hidden, provided that they shun whatever is wont to bewitch the senses.
>
> GREGORY OF NYSSA[5]

10:11. Now all these things happened to them as examples, and they were written for our admonition, upon whom the ends of the ages have come. These events took place in the Old Testament to serve as examples to mankind through the centuries. Paul calls attention to them:

> … to point out that as they were not profited by the enjoyment of so great a gift, so neither (we) by obtaining Baptism and partaking of spiritual Mysteries, except (we) go on and show forth a life worthy of this grace.
>
> CHRYSOSTOM[6]

10:12. Therefore let him who thinks he stands take heed lest he fall. We of the New Blood Covenant are saved, by our Messiah, from having to be completely perfect to earn salvation. But we must remember the need to continually try to follow in His footsteps to prove our faith in what He did for us and in love for Him because of it (Jude 5, 14–15). Those who have an aversion to the idea that we are required to "prove" our faith should read 2 Cor. 13:5 and Jas. 1:12.

> For our standing here is not secure until we are delivered out of the waves of this present life and have sailed into the tranquil haven. Be not therefore high-minded at thy standing, but guard against thy falling; for if Paul feared who was firmer than all, much more ought we to fear.
>
> CHRYSOSTOM[7]

We have no right to judge our own salvation or that of others. Orthodox theology remains true to the teachings of the Apostles and the early Church: we are saved by grace, through faith which is demonstrated by works, the genuineness of which will be revealed at the Second Coming of Christ. This is in stark contrast to the teachings of various other groups that advocate either salvation based on "works," on "faith alone," or on "grace alone." It is very important to understand this theological distinction, because it shapes our relationship with Christ.

10:13. No temptation has overtaken you except such as is common to man; but God is faithful, who will not allow you to be tempted beyond what you are able, but with the temptation will also make the way of escape, that you may be able to bear it. A Christian is not exempt from temptations. S/he is subject to the same difficulties in life that all human beings have faced through the ages. God does allow the Devil to tempt us. He does not, however, allow him to tempt us beyond our capacity to endure, and He will help us through any difficulty, if we turn to Him for strength and direction.

FOOD FOR THOUGHT: (a).This is a good verse to remember. However, if God does not allow us to be tempted beyond what we can endure, and if He always gives us a way out of our difficulties, why are some people embittered or destroyed by the hardships in their lives?

10:14–20. Therefore, my beloved, flee from idolatry. I speak as to wise men; judge for yourselves what I say. The cup of blessing which we bless, is it not the communion of the blood of Christ? The bread which we break, is it not the communion of the body of Christ? For we, though many, are one bread and one body; for we all partake of that one bread. Observe Israel after the flesh: Are not those who eat of the sacrifices partakers of the altar? What am I saying then? That an idol is anything, or what is offered to idols is anything? Rather, that the things which the Gentiles sacrifice they sacrifice to demons and not to God, and I do not want you to have fellowship with demons. Paul has already told the Corinthian Christians that by eating meat that had been sacrificed to idols they might mislead others (1 Cor. 8). Now he warns them not to participate in pagan festivities in general. Just as we, through partaking of the Body and Blood of Christ through Eucharist become one with Christ and with each other, so too, those who participate in the worship of idols have fellowship with demons. An idol has no spiritual reality, but demons do. Worship of an idol is inspired by demons, who use any means to try to steal our worship away from God.

10:21–22. You cannot drink the cup of the Lord and the cup of demons; you cannot partake of the Lord's table and of the table of demons. Or do we provoke the Lord to jealousy? Are we stronger than He? Those who have fellowship with demons are utterly incompatible with those who have fellowship with the Lord. If we think we can keep company with both without negative effects, we are sadly mistaken (see Deut. 32:21–22). God is omnipotent. No one can pit himself against God and win, as Lucifer found out (Isa. 14:12–17). God is jealous (Ex. 20:5) in that He wants our total allegiance (for our own good). He does not want to lose us to Satan.

> **FOOD FOR THOUGHT:** (b). What is a contemporary equivalent of a demonic activity?

10:23–28. All things are lawful for me, but all things are not helpful; all things are lawful for me, but all things do not edify. Let no one seek his own, but each one the other's well-being. Eat whatever is sold in the meat market, asking no questions for conscience' sake; for "the earth is the LORD's, and all its fullness." If any of those who do not believe invites you to dinner, and you desire to go, eat whatever is set before you, asking no question for conscience sake. But if anyone says to you, "This was offered to idols," do not eat it for the sake of the one who told you, and for conscience' sake, for "The earth is the Lord's, and all its fullness." Paul's advice is that meat bought in the marketplace should be eaten with thanksgiving to God, from Whom it came, with no questions asked. But if a Christian were told that the meat s/he is being offered for dinner had first been offered in sacrifice to the pagan gods, it should not be partaken of because of the spiritual danger involved to others.

Although it is not unlawful for a knowledgeable Christian to eat meat that has been sacrificed to idols, because he knows that idols have no reality, to do so can be confusing and therefore harmful to others in their struggle to follow Christ (see this study for 1 Cor. 8:7–10).

FOOD FOR THOUGHT: (c). How might this concept apply to a modern situation?

10:29–33. "Conscience," I say, not your own, but that of the other. For why is my liberty judged by another man's conscience? But if I partake with thanks, why am I evil spoken of for the food over which I give thanks? Therefore, whether you eat or drink, or whatever you do, do all to the glory of God. Give no offense, either to the Jews or to the Greeks or to the church of God, just as I also please all men in all things, not seeking my own profit, but the profit of many, that they may be saved. This advice is not designed to inhibit our personal freedom as Christians but as an example of the fact that we must do nothing to hinder, and all in our power to spread, the truth about salvation through Jesus Christ. The goal is that everyone has an opportunity to learn about Christ, to make the choice for which they have been given life: whether they are with or against Him (Acts 17:26–27; Mt. 12:30).

FOOD FOR THOUGHT COMMENTS

(a). If God does not allow us to be tempted beyond what we can endure, and if He always gives us a way out of our difficulties, why are some people embittered or destroyed by the hardships in their lives? The negative events of life can adversely affect those:

> (1). who have not developed an understanding of God's divine plan for His people, including why suffering is a part of it (see 1 Cor. 1, Food for Thought Comment (d)).

(2). who do not turn to God for help (Mt. 7:7–8; Jas. 4:2–3).

(3). who want to continue to follow their own will instead of His (Num. 14:43).

When we face tribulation, it is very important to resist the temptation to blame God. Evil is in the world because of rebelliousness, the source of which is Satan—not God. God allows rebelliousness as a by-product of the gift of free will and as part of the testing process. As the Hebrew people, in order to enter the promised land, had to endure the difficult years in the desert without turning against God, we must endure the suffering of this life with faith and hope in order to enter God's eternal Kingdom.

> What is required is not only to suffer for Christ but also to nobly bear the things that come on us, and with all gladness: since this is the nature of every crown. And unless this be so, punishment will instead attend those who take calamity with a bad grace. The Apostles, when they were beaten, rejoiced, and Paul gloried in his sufferings.
>
> CHRYSOSTOM[8]

(b). What is a contemporary equivalent of a demonic activity? Astrology, which is popular among some in our society, is a good example. Though many look upon astrology as harmless fun, it is actually "a denial of the Christ-like way of living; something to be rejected as unchristian."[9] It is dangerous because of the fact that it looks for guidance to the sun, moon, and stars: to creations rather than to the Creator. Followers of astrology surrender their God-given gift of free will to supposed powers created by the alignment of the planets at the time of their birth. To open oneself to this nonsense is to invite Satan to control our lives through his workers, who have the ability to use such tools to mislead us. God does not want us to be overly concerned about what might happen in the future (Mt. 6:28–34) but rather to keep our focus on our daily walk with Him.

(c). Activities that are not unlawful for Christians might still be misleading to others, and should thus be avoided. How might this concept apply to a modern situation? Using the example of astrology, almost every local and national newspaper publishes horoscopes or astrological predictions daily. Christians buy and read those newspapers regularly with no danger, typically ignoring that section. They might glance at it occasionally, knowing that it is nonsense, perhaps just to keep apprised of ways in which the unenlightened can be misled. However, with any such activity, it is important to steer clear of any actions or conversations that onlookers could interpret as giving credence to astrology.

On the other hand, a Christian who is asked a question like, "What sign are you?" is presented with an opportunity to share the Christian message.

CHAPTER ELEVEN

Relationships in Heaven and on Earth

During his visit to the Corinthian Christians, Paul instructed them as to proper dress in church, as we will see in verses 1-16 below. Both men and women used to prophesy at that time (Joel 2:28, Acts 2:17, 21:9). Women were to pray and prophesy with their heads covered, men, uncovered. It came to Paul's attention that some had reversed these traditions.

11:1. Imitate me, just as I also imitate Christ. Paul counsels the Corinthians to do as he does, because he, in turn, follows Christ's example (1 Cor. 4:16).

11:2. Now I praise you, brethren, that you remember me in all things and keep the traditions just as I delivered them to you. It was Paul's custom to offer praise wherever circumstances allowed in order to keep their morale up, a good point for all who are trying to teach God's word to remember. As flowers need sunshine to flourish, man thrives on praise honestly but generously bestowed.

11:3. But I want you to know that the head of every man is Christ, the head of woman is man, and the head of Christ is God. God's divine plan for man includes a sort of organizational order of authority: a hierarchal interdependence of woman upon man, man upon Christ, and Christ upon God.

> *God*: Creator and Ruler of all. Only He is ruled by no one.

> *Christ*: Obedient to the Father, "as the Son of God ... as God ... not as a slave under command, but as free, yielding obedience and giving

126

counsel. For the counselor is no slave. ... Do not understand it (counselor) as though the Father were in need, but that the Son has the same honor with Him that begat Him."[1]

Man: Under subjection to Christ and the "head of woman" in the same sense that God is the head of Christ, with equal but different roles.

Woman: Under subjection to man, but "as free and equal in honor," not as a slave to her master.

11:4. Every man praying or prophesying, having his head covered, dishonors his head. In the times in which Paul lived, wearing a head covering was a sign of subjection to another human being (see Gen. 24:65). Since the head of man is Christ, for a male to wear a head-covering in church would take honor away from his Master, Christ, the only one to whom he owes total submission.

11:5–6. But every woman who prays or prophesies with her head uncovered dishonors her head, for that is one and the same as if her head were shaved. For if a woman is not covered, let her also be shorn. But if it is shameful for a woman to be shorn or shaved, let her be covered. Since woman is under subjection to man under God's hierarchy, it was the custom in Paul's time for her head to be covered in public, the sign of human authority over her. The respectable woman covered her head at all times, not just during prayer—only women of ill repute appeared outside of their homes bareheaded. Thus a woman who appeared in church without her head covered would bring shame to her head (if married, her husband; if unmarried, her father or other male) for the implication was that she did not accept her position in God's hierarchy—or that she was immoral. Also, then as now, there were those who had fallen into sexual perversions of homosexuality or trans-sexuality and who dressed in such a way as to obliterate the God-given distinctions of male and female, and some false teachings asserted that there were no gender distinctions for Christians.

> What has been annihilated and destroyed *in Christ* is not the natural distinction between women and men, but all division between them, with the enmity and hostility which comes from domination, subservience and tyranny which derives not from God but from the devil and sin.[2]

Among the Jews at that time, prostitutes were punished by having their heads shaved, thus Paul's reference that it was just as shameful for a woman's head to be uncovered as it was to have a shaved head.

Having been told of their new freedom in Christ (Gal 3:28) referring to freedom from the divisions between male and female outlined above and from bondage to the Mosaic Law (see this study of 1 Cor. 5:2), some women misinterpreted this and began to appear in church with their heads uncovered, thus scandalizing the congregation. Paul's message is that they should not defy that which is considered proper feminine decorum.

11:7–9. For a man indeed ought not to cover his head, since he is the image and glory of God; but woman is the glory of man. For man is not from woman, but woman from man. Nor was man created for the woman, but woman for the man.

(1). Christ is the head of man and man the head of woman, but only to the extent that man subjects himself to Christ. Male and female have different, yet fundamentally equal roles given to them by God, so that all facets of His work may be accomplished.

> It is one of the chief glories of human nature that men and women, although equal, are not interchangeable. Together they exercise a common ministry that neither could exercise alone; for within that shared ministry each has a particular role ... with man as the head and woman as the partner or *helper* (Gen. 2:18).[3]

In marriage, as Christ is Head, Savior, Lover, and Defender of the Church, so also ought the man to be of his wife (see Eph. 5:22–33). A man who loves his wife as Christ loves the Church does not try to dominate or enslave her. He cherishes her, and she responds in kind. They work together to create a strong family unit—a haven from the chaos of the world. If a man "revolts against Christ, he loses his privilege of ruling his own wife. ... The extent to which the husband disobeys Christ is equal to that in which a wife is justified in disobeying her husband. ... Every woman treated unjustly by her husband seeks from Christ the restoration of her rights; for Christ allows no man to abuse his wife."[4]

> The partner of one's life, the mother of one's children, the foundation of one's every joy, one ought never to chain down by fear and menaces, but with love and good temper. For what sort of union is that, where the wife trembles at her husband? And what sort of pleasure will the husband himself enjoy, if he dwells with his wife as with a slave, and not as with a free-woman? Though you should suffer anything on her account, do not upbraid her; for neither did Christ do this.
>
> CHRYSOSTOM[5]

(2). Man is the glory of God and woman the glory of man. That is, God made man, His ultimate creation, and took pride in him, and then made woman from man, so man could be comforted by, helped by, and take pride in her. Each completes the other. Together they are more than either can be alone. Man and woman brought together by God in Holy Matrimony form a triad, reflecting the Trinity in Heaven. Thus, Christ is (or should be) the head of every Christian home. If family members understand this, they will look to Christ and His teachings for guidance in all things, and there will be harmony, not resentment of roles. The relationships of a husband and wife to each other do not (and should not be allowed to) interfere with the personal, individual relationships of man and woman separately to Christ. (See Gal. 3:28, which speaks of all, male and female, being "one in Christ," and 1 Peter 3:7, which speaks of husband and wife "being heirs together of the grace of life".)

(3). Woman is from man, not man from woman. However, woman was made from man's "side" (Gen. 2:21, translation from the Greek), which includes flesh, tissue, and blood as well as bone; so they are of the same substance, equal but different human beings.

> For they were joined to each other from the sides, they
> who walk side by side, they who together look where
> it is they walk.
>
> AUGUSTINE[6]

(4). Woman was made for man, not man for woman (Gen. 2:18), but all men are born through woman, including Christ, sanctifying womanhood (1 Tim. 2:15).

(5). Chrysostom adds that an additional reason for woman's position in this hierarchy is that she yielded to the temptation of the serpent in the Garden of Eden (1 Tim. 2:14).

You see, she was not subjected as soon as she was made; nor, when He brought her to the man, did she hear any such thing from God; nor did the man say any such word to her. He said indeed that she was *bone of his bone, and flesh of his flesh* (Gen. 2:23), but of rule or subjection he nowhere made mention to her. But when she made an ill use of her privilege and she who had been made a helper was found to be an ensnarer and ruined all, then she is justly told for the future, *your desire shall be for your husband, and he shall rule over you* (Gen. 3:16).[7]

FOOD FOR THOUGHT: (a). How can Biblical teachings be used to promote healthy relationships in a marriage?

This hierarchal order is necessary because "equality of honor causes contention."[8] In order to insure peaceful relationships, an order of authority must be in force, as it is in any organization. There are even hierarchies of equal but different roles in Heaven, as reflected in the Holy Trinity and among the spirits.

These holy spirits of our heavenly fatherland are indeed always spirits but cannot always be called angels; for then only are they angels when by means of them certain things are announced. Accordingly, through the Psalmist it is said: *Who makes His spirits angels* (Ps. 104:4), as though saying: Who when He wills makes angels (messengers) of those spirits who stand forever in His Presence.

GREGORY THE GREAT[9]

There are nine orders (Dionysius the Areopagite called them choirs) of spirits (celestial beings) who, like us, were created by God. They are divided into three hierarchies.

Seraphim, Cherubim, and Thrones: These are "councilors." They have "no direct dealings with man but are absorbed in unending love and adoration of God. No other creature is so intensely capable of loving God,"[10] except perhaps she who is "queen" (Ps. 45:9), the Theotokos, who, in her role as Mother of God, is called "more honorable than the Cherubim, and incomparably more glorious than the Seraphim."[11]

Dominions, Virtues, and Powers: "These are understood to be the governors of space and the stars. Our orb, consequently, as part of the galaxy, is under their dominion; otherwise, we have no direct contact with the second choir."[12]

Principalities, Archangels, and Angels: "These have this earth of ours in their special charge. They are the executors of God's will, the perpetual guardians of the children of men, and the messengers of God." They who announce things of lesser significance are called angels; they who make announcements of greater significance are called archangels.

11:10. For this reason the woman ought to have a symbol of authority on her head, because of the angels. Chrysostom explains that during the Divine Liturgy, "the whole sanctuary and the space before the altar are filled with the heavenly Powers come to honor Him who is present upon the altar."[13] Paul writes here that because of the presence of these angels, women were to cover their heads in church, in acknowledgment of and submission to God's order of things.

> For although you despise your husband [or any particular male, who may in fact, be disobedient to Christ], yet reverence the angels.
>
> CHRYSOSTOM[14]

FOOD FOR THOUGHT: (b). Jesus said, "Where two or three are gathered together in my name, I am there in the midst of them" (Mt. 18:20). If then, when we gather to celebrate the Divine Liturgy, Jesus is among us in that sense and also through the Eucharist, if the Holy Spirit is among us in response to our prayers inviting Him to bless us and to change our gifts of bread and wine into the very Body and very Blood of Christ, and if angels are among us to honor Christ, how can there be inattentiveness and lack of participation in the Liturgy?

11:11–12. Nevertheless, neither is man independent of woman, nor woman independent of man, in the Lord. For as the woman was from the man, even so the man is also through the woman; but all things are from God. The hierarchal order notwithstanding, male and female are both from God and are dependent upon each other, for woman was made from man (Gen. 2:22), and man is born through woman. Male and female each have their distinctive, irreplaceable, and important roles in the order of creation. Jesus Christ entered the world as a male, exalting the male role and rendering the eternal Priesthood of Christ a male prerogative; but He was born through Woman, redeeming and exalting the female role and rendering "the woman of whom He was born the most highly honored of all creatures."[15] Only woman has the awesome privilege of being the bearer of children, with the ability to nourish them from her body (a fact not lost on pagans, who often worshiped the female).

A woman does disservice to herself if she covets the male role rather than taking pride and joy in her own God-given role and trying to be the best woman she can be; and a man distorts the beauty of God's creation if he fails to give the female role the respect it deserves. A true understanding of the different but equal roles God has given to man and woman includes honor, glory, and respect for each, as well as great opportunities for service.

> But if any say, "How can this be a shame to the woman, if she ascends to the glory of the man?" we might make this answer: "She does not ascend, but rather falls from her own proper honor."
>
> CHRYSOSTOM[16]

11:13–16. Judge among yourselves. Is it proper for a woman to pray to God with her head uncovered? Does not even nature itself teach you that if a man has long hair, it is a dishonor to him? But if a woman has long hair, it is a glory to her; for her hair is given to her for a covering. But if anyone seems to be contentious, we have no such custom, nor do the churches of God. That a woman's hair is her glory was especially true in Paul's day, when women were traditionally completely covered in public. To allow herself to be seen with her hair uncovered in church would bring attention to her and be a distraction to the worship of God.

The length of a man's hair has carried various connotations throughout history. In Old Testament times, keeping one's hair long was a sign of holiness (Num. 6:5). In the fourth and fifth centuries, shearing or even shaving of the head was practiced by monastics of both sexes as "an outward sign of forsaking worldly appearance and love of the body."[17] In the 11th and 12th centuries, man's hair and beard at "full natural length became the sign of monasticism and asceticism in the East in the place of the original practice of shearing." At the time Paul wrote this epistle, however, for a man to let his hair and beard grow to full length was a symbol of his devotion to a worldly study such as philosophy, poetry, etc. It was also the pagan custom at the time for men to cover their heads when praying, and long hair on a male was considered the same as covering his head. Among early Christians, therefore, perhaps in an attempt to counteract pagan symbolism, women were to have their heads covered in church and men's heads were to be uncovered.

> **FOOD FOR THOUGHT:** (c). Does woman's position
> in God's hierarchy mean that women of our time
> should cover their heads in church?

In verses 17-34, we read about the practice of the early Christians to gather together for the Sacrament of Eucharist as part of a common meal (Jude 12, Acts 2:46), in imitation of the Mystical Supper of our Lord (Mt. 26:26–29). The forerunner of this meal that Jesus ate with His Apostles was not the Passover meal[18] but most likely the Jewish religious supper called the Chaburah, which included the ceremonies of bread breaking and the cup of the blessing. During the meal, the host broke a loaf of bread in pieces while pronouncing a blessing and gave a fragment to each person at the table, as a sign of unity among them. At the end of the meal, the host similarly pronounced a blessing over a special cup of wine, and after sipping a little from it, passed it around to each of those present. Again, the common cup symbolized unity among the group.

At the Mystical Supper, Jesus repeated this ritual but with an added dimension. That which, "among the Jews had been a mere sign of unity and fellowship, was transformed into real union and oneness by sharing in the one Body and Blood of Christ."[19]

The common meal was a way for wealthier Christians to share what they had with the poor, who had little or nothing to bring. It became known as the Feast of Love (Agape), which took place every evening. Because of abuses, some of which Paul mentions here, this meal was gradually separated from the Eucharist, which came to be celebrated in the morning, with the Agape meal in the evening.

11:17. Now in giving these instructions I do not praise you, since you come together not for the better but for the worse. Paul admonishes the Corinthian Christians because their coming together for the common meal and the Eucharist was not producing the love and fellowship that was its intent.

11:18–19. For first of all, when you come together as a church, I hear that there are divisions among you, and in part I believe it. For there must also be factions among you, that those who are approved may be recognized among you. It was impossible for the Christians of Corinth to partake of the Lord's Supper with the proper feeling and meaning because there were many disagreements among them. However, God allowed discord in the Church because the various matters of contention that arose served to reveal the true nature of each of them (another test) and to separate heresy from truth.

> **FOOD FOR THOUGHT:** (d). How did disagreements among the early Christians help to separate heresy from truth?

11:20–22. Therefore when you come together in one place, it is not to eat the Lord's Supper. For in eating, each one takes his own supper ahead of others; and one is hungry and another is drunk. What! Do you not have houses to eat and drink in? Or do you despise the church of God and shame those who have nothing? What shall I say to you? Shall I praise you in this? I do not praise you. In general, they were not being considerate of each other. They were not waiting for latecomers (possibly servants, who had to discharge their various duties before being free to attend), some were just plain gluttonous, and those who had plenty were not sharing with those who had little to offer, thereby bringing shame to the Church and neglecting as well as insulting the poor.

11:23–25. For I received from the Lord that which I also delivered to you: that the Lord Jesus on the same night in which He was betrayed took bread; and when He had given thanks, He broke it and said, "Take, eat; this is My body which is broken for you; do this in remembrance of Me." In the same manner He also took the cup after supper, saying, "This cup is the new covenant in My blood. This do, as often as you drink it, in remembrance of Me." To induce them to repent, Paul recounts the events of the Mystical Supper, when Christ instituted the Sacrament of Eucharist, the means by which Christians receive His Body and His Blood and continually become one with Him.

11:26. For as often as you eat this bread and drink this cup, you proclaim the Lord's death till He comes. Eucharist is also a reminder of His sacrifice for us. The implication is that it is unthinkable that anyone would dare to receive this awesome Mystery, which anticipates the Second Coming of Christ, while being part of dishonoring his brother and neglecting the poor.

11:27. Therefore whoever eats this bread or drinks this cup of the Lord in an unworthy manner will be guilty of the body and blood of the Lord. He who receives the Body and Blood of Christ without trying to become Christ-like in his actions not only receives no profit from the Sacrament but is considered just as guilty of the Crucifixion of Christ as those who participated in it:

Those who distribute or receive the Eucharist unworthily wound His Body every day.

TERTULLIAN[20]

That is, they shall have the same guilt, and the same punishment, as those who crucified Christ. For as those butchers became guilty of His Blood, so likewise are they who partake unworthily of the Eucharist.

CHRYSOSTOM[21]

FOOD FOR THOUGHT: (e). If there are those who distribute the Eucharist or administer any other Sacrament or blessing from the Church while being themselves unworthy, what is the result to those to whom they distribute these gifts? Does the validity of the gifts depend upon the worthiness of the celebrant?

11:28. But let a man examine himself, and so let him eat of that bread and drink of that cup. A Christian must always evaluate his actions and motives to be sure he is really trying to do all things in the manner Christ would. This type of introspection is at the root of the Sacrament of Confession, which is available in the Church to remove any barriers of sin between man and God, enabling him to go forward with confidence to receive Holy Communion.

11:29. For he who eats and drinks in an unworthy manner eats and drinks judgment to himself, not discerning the Lord's body. He who receives Holy Communion without making a sincere effort to live in a Christlike manner does not realize the danger in which he puts himself.

But why does he eat judgment to himself? "Not discerning the Lord's Body": i.e., not searching, not bearing in mind, as he ought, the greatness of the things set before him; not estimating the weight of the gift. For if you should come to know accurately Who it is that lies before you, and Who He is that gives Himself, and to whom, you will need no other argument, but this is enough for you to use all vigilance, unless you are altogether fallen.

CHRYSOSTOM[22]

11:30. For this reason many are weak and sick among you, and many sleep. During the Divine Liturgy, the priest invites all to receive the Body and Blood of Christ with the words: "With fear of God, with faith and with love, draw near." Prayers at that moment exclaim:

> Behold, I approach for Holy Communion, O Creator,
> burn me not as I partake,
> For you are Fire which burns the unworthy ... do cleanse me from every stain.[23]

This reminds us dramatically that those who receive the Body and Blood of Christ hypocritically succeed in excluding themselves from the Kingdom of God and, therefore, from His promises.

> Has this Table which is the cause of so many blessings and teeming with life, become judgment? Not from its own nature ... but from the will of him that approaches. For as Christ's presence, which conveyed to us those great and unutterable blessings, condemned the more those who did not receive Him: so also the Mysteries become provisions of greater punishment to such as partake unworthily.

CHRYSOSTOM[24]

FOOD FOR THOUGHT: (f). What is the meaning of Chrysostom's words above?

On the other hand, Holy Communion is the greatest of all blessings for those who understand its power and wonder:

> Holy Communion, being divine food and medicine, affords our souls nourishment, growth, strength, health, and even more importantly, eternal life. It is also a safeguard and cure for the ills of our bodies, because the abundance of grace with which Holy Communion enriches the soul is also communicated by it to the body, which is so intimately united with the soul. The grace that the soul receives exercises wholesome influence on the body, whose sensual nature is consequently weakened.[25]

11:31–32. For if we would judge ourselves, we would not be judged. But when we are judged, we are chastened by the Lord, that we may not be condemned with the world. God sometimes allows difficulties to befall us to teach us something, to awaken us from our indifference to Him, to test our faith, or to show us the error of our ways while we still have time to repent, which includes change (see this study for 1 Cor. 10:1–13). If we would assess ourselves and honestly strive to grow in those areas in which we fall short of Christ's example, we would not have to suffer the consequences.

11:33–34. Therefore, my brethren, when you come together to eat, wait for one another. But if anyone is hungry, let him eat at home, lest you come together for judgment. And the rest I will set in order when I come. Paul encourages them to show consideration to one another, and to remember the purpose and value of fellowship with one another—the reason for the Agape Feast. It always boils down to love: the ultimate goal.

FOOD FOR THOUGHT COMMENTS

(a). How can biblical teachings be used to promote healthy relationships in a marriage? It is easy for husband and wife to begin to take each other for granted and neglect to extend to one another the niceties that are often offered rather easily to strangers or casual acquaintances. Paul wrote that "marriage is honorable" (Heb. 13:4). Husband and wife should remember to honor each other and each other's role in their partnership. Each should do those little things that encourage love to grow, be patient and forgiving with the other (Col. 3:13), not let anger carry over to a new day (Eph. 4:26), and continually work at their relationship, as they would work at anything that is very important (1 Cor. 13:4–7).

(b). Jesus said, "Where two or three are gathered together in my name, I am there in the midst of them" (Mt. 18:20). If then, when we gather to celebrate the Divine Liturgy, Jesus is among us in that sense and also through the Eucharist, if the Holy Spirit is among us in response to our prayers inviting Him to bless us and to change our gifts of bread and wine into the very Body and very Blood of Christ, and if angels are among us to honor Christ, how can there be inattentiveness and lack of participation in the Liturgy? The answer can only be lack of awareness. Many people do not know what the Divine Liturgy is all about and the ways in which worshipers are invited to participate. Fr. Stanley Harakas' classic book, *Living the Liturgy,* uncovers the secrets of that service. It is a wonderful tool for learning to make the Liturgy the "work of the people" that it is meant to be. The ride to and from church (with a captive audience) is a good time for parents (grandparents, etc.) to teach children about the spiritual world and matters of faith. Often the best teaching takes place not from the pulpit or in the classroom but as the everyday events of life provide opportunities. Every Christian should continually grow in knowledge of the faith for his/her own spiritual well-being and to be ready and able to pass it on.

(c). Does woman's position in God's hierarchy mean that women of our time should cover their heads in church? Women (as well as men) should not defy current thinking as to what is considered proper dress in church, for to do so would call attention to themselves and be a distraction to others in their worship of God. Neither should men or women dress in such a way as to obliterate the God-given distinctions of male and female. There is no gender-identity crisis in the Church. Men and women are distinct, with equal but different roles.

One school of thought says that women should still wear head coverings in church—and some do, as an act of reverence and obedience. Another says that they need not, else we would also have to revert to the other modes of dress of Paul's time (as well as to the social norms of the day, such as the custom of shaving the head of a woman considered immoral). It might also be considered that wearing a head covering when most do not could have the undesirable affect of bringing attention to the wearer.

The important point is that Christians, men as well as women, should always dress respectably, especially in church. The outward appearance of a person reflects his inner attitude. Hence an outward appearance of respect in church reflects an inner awareness of the presence of God in His house and consideration of all that is taking place there. No one should come to the house of God to worship and to receive the Body and Blood of Christ dressed in poor taste, or ostentatiously, in clothes and jewels that would call attention to him/herself, possibly causing feelings of pride in oneself and envy in those looking on. Neither, however, should a person have less concern for what is worn to church than would be the case if s/he were meeting with someone considered by the world to be very important. When we gather together in church, the heavenly hierarchy is among us.

(d). How did disagreements among the early Christians help to separate heresy from truth? Disagreements among the early Christians prompted the Apostles and those who had learned from them and traveled with them to clarify, in writing, points of disagreement. Thus the truth, as Christ delivered it to His Apostles and disciples, was sorted out and preserved.

(e). If there are those who distribute the Eucharist or administer any other Sacrament or blessing from the Church while being themselves unworthy, what is the result to those to whom they distribute these gifts? Does the validity of the gifts depend upon the worthiness of the celebrant? As is the case with everyone who calls himself a Christian, an ordained priest of the Church must strive throughout his life to grow in holiness, as a reflection of his faith and to provide a good example. The question of whether a priest really had faith in Christ and became a priest for the right reasons, and whether he did his best to fulfill his calling are matters that Christ will judge. However, if it were to happen that one who is blatantly sinful continues to function as a priest, he would do so and distribute the Body and Blood of Christ and other blessings of the Church without loss of benefit to the recipient. God's grace is transmitted through the ordained priest and is valid regardless of the sanctity of the instrument through whom it is given.

> I am saying this to you, not as excusing those who may exercise the priesthood unworthily: for such as these I weep and sorrow exceedingly. Nevertheless, I declare that it is not fitting that they be judged by those they rule; especially by the ruder kind. Though their conduct may be greatly criticized, you, if you pay heed to yourself, will suffer no harm from them in regard to the things entrusted to them by God. For if He made use of the voice of an ass to speak [Num. 22:22–34], and bestowed spiritual blessings by means of a soothsayer; because of the Jews, working by the mouth of a dumb beast, and by the unclean tongue of Balaam, how much more for you who are worthy, even though the priests be wholly unworthy, will He do all things, and send His Holy Spirit upon you?

> And neither does a mind that is pure draw down grace because of its purity; it is the divine favor that does all: For all things, it says, are yours, whether it be Paul, or Apollo, or Cephas (1 Cor. 3:22). For what the priest has had entrusted to him, it is God alone who bestows; and however much human wisdom may help us, it will ever appear less than grace. ...

> But why do I say priests? For neither an angel nor an archangel can do anything in regard to what is given us by God. It is the Father, Son, and Holy Ghost Who disposes of all things: the priest but lends his tongue and puts forth his hand. For it would not be just that because of the wickedness of another they should

suffer injury who draw near in faith to the symbols of
our salvation.   CHRYSOSTOM[26]

The valid officiation of the sacraments does not
depend upon the moral character of the officiator, for
if the validity of the mysteria depended upon the
officiator's personal character, justification and
sanctification would be doubtful and uncertain.
Scripture does not touch directly on this question, but
the influence on the sacraments of the personal faith
and piety of the officiator has always been rejected. ...
The officiator of the sacraments of the Church, as the
indispensable organ, has been ordained by God
Himself for the sanctification of the members of the
Mystical Body of Jesus Christ ... [he] utters the
pronouncement of the sacraments in the passive voice
or in the third person, saying, "The servant of God is
...," not "I," etc.[27]

**(f). What is the meaning conveyed by Chrysostom's
words, the "Table which is the cause of so many
blessings and teeming with life become(s) judgment"?**
Just as Jesus' presence in the world brought blessings to
those who received Him as the prophesied Messiah and
condemned those who rejected Him, the Body and Blood of
Christ, which is continually offered through the Church,
brings blessings to those who partake worthily and condemnation to those who partake unworthily, as well as to those
who reject the opportunity.

CHAPTER TWELVE

Gifts of the Holy Spirit

God showered the early Church with many miracles and manifestations of the Holy Spirit because they were needed. Jesus chose only twelve Apostles, yet he commissioned this small group to bring the Gospel to all of the then known world (Mt. 28:19–20), a formidable task. Communities were far apart and there was no reliable means of communication between them. They did not have the New Testament to use as a tool as we do; teaching had to be done in person, or by means of a letter (epistle) sent with a traveler. False teachers and teachings were rampant. So God provided supernatural assistance!

> Whoever was baptized immediately spoke with tongues ... many also prophesied, and some also performed many other wonderful works. For since on their coming over from idols, without any clear knowledge or training in the ancient Scriptures, they at once on their baptism received the Spirit, yet the Spirit they saw not, for It is invisible; therefore God's grace bestowed some sensible proof of that energy. And one immediately spoke in the Persian, another in the Roman, another in the Indian, another in some other such tongue: and this made it clear to everyone that it was the Spirit speaking in the person.
>
> CHRYSOSTOM[1]

This abundance of gifts among the Christians of Corinth was causing much jealousy and division among them:

> ... inasmuch as many used even to raise the dead and to cast out devils and to perform many other such wonders. And they had gifts too, some less, and some

more. But more abundant than all was the gift of tongues among them. However, this became a cause of division, not from the nature of the gift but from the perversity of those who had received it: on the one hand, the possessors of the greater gifts were lifted up against those who had the lesser: and these were grieved and envied the owners of the greater.

CHRYSOSTOM[2]

12:1–2. Now concerning spiritual gifts, brethren, I do not want you to be ignorant. You know that you were Gentiles, carried away to these dumb idols, however you were led. The Corinthians were accustomed to the worship of idols. Paul warns them not to allow the spiritual gifts they have received to become idols themselves, by putting their emphasis on the gifts rather than on the One who had bestowed them. Worship belongs to God alone.

12:3. Therefore I make known to you that no one speaking by the Spirit of God calls Jesus accursed, and no one can say that Jesus is Lord except by the Holy Spirit. The proliferation of spiritual gifts among them created a supernatural atmosphere and gave magicians and soothsayers, who were very common among eastern nations, an opportunity to try to capitalize on the frenzy (Acts 8:9–24). This verse focuses on how to know the difference between prophecy, which is a gift from God, and soothsaying, which is the equivalent of fortune telling/witchcraft and has always been against God's law (Lev. 20:6). It is important to be able to distinguish between the two, so as not to be led astray. It was for this reason that the gift of discernment was given. (For more on this gift, see this study for 2 Cor. 10.)

Prophets teach, counsel, and comfort God's people in the name of Jesus Christ. A prophet also occasionally discloses what is going to take place in the future (see this study for 1 Cor. 14:1–

4). However, true prophecy cannot be proved at the time it is given when it foretells future events, so it is easy to be fooled by a false prophet. Soothsayers are filled with "lying spirits" (1 Kings 22:22) because they are tools of the Devil. They curse (Greek: anathematize) the name of Jesus by denying that He is the Son of God, the promised Messiah.

> To cause distraction and madness and great darkness is the proper work of a demon: but it is God's work to illuminate and with consideration to teach things needful. This then is the *first difference* between a soothsayer and a prophet.
>
> CHRYSOSTOM[3]

> A *second difference* is what Paul states in verse 3: "no one speaking by the Spirit of God calls Jesus accursed and no one can say that Jesus is Lord except by the Holy Spirit." *Chrysostom* adds: "without being scourged."[4]

In other words: (1). God's prophets only foretell and teach those things that are necessary for living the life of holiness in preparation for entrance into the Kingdom, ultimately the only thing in this life that really matters. (2). God's prophets would not denounce Jesus or pronounce prophecy without using His Name. Anyone who dared to use Jesus' Name insincerely, without being guided by the Holy Spirit, would sooner or later reveal his true nature—and will receive due justice, in this life and/or the next.

In order to discern the difference between fortune tellers and prophets, it is necessary to grow in understanding of God's divine plan, as revealed in Scripture. We know He does not want us to know the future (Mt. 24:36, 1 Thess. 5:1–2, Rev. 3:3) because He wants us to live in readiness for Christ's Second Coming at all times. Thus we should have no dealings with those who claim to have knowledge of coming events. Also, those who truly have power from God to enlighten as to the work of God in the future would not do so for money, power, or fame.

12:4–6. Now there are diversities of gifts, but the same Spirit. There are differences of ministries, but the same Lord. And there are diversities of activities, but it is the same God who works all in all. Ministries and activities of God all come from the same Godhead, the Holy Trinity. He who thinks that the gift he has received is of lesser value than those received by others must remember that a gift is something that is given—not owed. He who has received what he thinks is a highly valued gift must remember the giver of the gift and the fact that "for everyone to whom much is given, from him much will be required" (Lk. 12:48). Serious contemplation of these truths will prevent both envy and conceit.

12:7. But the manifestation of the Spirit is given to each one for the profit of all: God gives His gifts to individuals not for their personal gain but for the good of the whole Body of Christ, the Church.

12:8–10. ... for to one is given the word of wisdom through the Spirit, to another the word of knowledge through the same Spirit, to another faith by the same Spirit, to another gifts of healings by the same Spirit, to another the workings of miracles, to another prophecy, to another discerning of spirits, to another different kinds of tongues, to another the interpretation of tongues. The person who has the gift of wisdom is able to grow in understanding of the ways of God and to explain them to others. S/he who has the gift of knowledge can pass on facts about the life of Christ, His teachings, etc. He with the gift of rock-like faith is so certain that God is in control, loves us, and has prepared a place for us in His Kingdom that he bases his decisions and his life on those truths and inspires faith in those around him. Those with the gift of healing diseases through Christ—like many of the Saints (and the modern-day St. Nectarios)—can ease much suffering. Others can perform miracles (they do happen!), others can prophesy or discern spirits (be able to know the difference between the work of God's Holy Spirit and evil spirits). Others may speak in tongues, heavenly and earthly; while still others can interpret those languages, to make that which they impart meaningful (see this study for 1 Cor. 14).

12:11. But the one and the same Spirit works all these things, distributing to each one individually as He wills. The Holy Spirit distributes spiritual gifts according to God's will in the same manner as physical gifts are distributed to the human body.

12:12–13. For as the body is one and has many members, but all the members of that one body, being many, are one body, so also is Christ. For by one Spirit we were all baptized into one body—whether Jews or Greeks, whether slaves or free—and have all been made to drink into one Spirit. It was a fact of the early Church that everyone who was baptized in the name of the Father, Son, and Holy Spirit (Mt. 28:19) was thus a part of the Church—there was only one. Then through the laying on of hands (Acts 8:14–17), the baptized received the one Holy Spirit (Chrismation). Thus, just as the human body is made up of many individual parts, the Body of Christ is made up of many individual Christians, no matter to which local church they belong.

12:14–20. For in fact, the body is not one member but many. If the foot should say, "Because I am not a hand, I

am not of the body," is it therefore not of the body? And if the ear should say, "Because I am not an eye, I am not of the body," is it therefore not of the body? If the whole body were an eye, where would be the hearing? If the whole were hearing, where would be the smelling? But now God has set the members, each one of them, in the body just as He pleased. And if they were all one member, where would the body be? But now indeed there are many members, yet one body. As each part of the human body has a different gift or function as designed by God, for the purpose of doing all the things that a whole body can do, so too each Christian is given different gifts or functions by God, for the purpose of doing all the things that the Church as a whole can do and be. The Holy Spirit brings all of these elements together as the Body of Christ.

> **FOOD FOR THOUGHT:** (a). God reaches out to teach great truths by hiding important lessons in the events of our lives. When do we most fully realize the lesson of the importance of each part of the body?

12:21–25. And the eye cannot say to the hand, "I have no need of you"; nor again the head to the feet, "I have no need of you." No, much rather, those members of the body which seem to be weaker are necessary. And those members of the body which we think to be less honorable, on these we bestow greater honor; and our unpresentable parts have greater modesty, but our presentable parts have no need. But God composed the body, having given greater honor to that part which lacks it, that there should be no schism in the body, but that the members should have the same care for one another. What one part of the body lacks in strength or comeliness is balanced by its indispensable qualities. The hands and the feet rush to protect the eyes and ears from danger because of their importance to the quality of life. The inner organs are generally not even visible but they are more essential than the parts that are more evident and more beautiful.

> God distributed among the members of the body advantages and drawbacks, so that neither the inferior would hate the superior nor the superior spurn the inferior but rather take care of them than their own selves. [5]

FOOD FOR THOUGHT: (b). How do these verses apply to the Church?

12:26–27. And if one member suffers, all the members suffer with it; or if one member is honored, all the members rejoice with it. Now you are the body of Christ, and members individually. Following the example of the physical body, the individual members of the spiritual Body of Christ, the Church, should be neither conceited about nor embarrassed by their individual functions but should use their gifts from God with love, working always for the good of the entire Church.

Just as the entire physical body suffers if one of its parts is in pain, and rejoices if one of its members has occasion, as through healing or accomplishment, so too, the entire Body of Christ should share the sufferings and the joys of each of its individual members.

FOOD FOR THOUGHT: (c). How can we share the joys and sorrows of fellow Christians?

12:28–30. And God has appointed these in the Church: first Apostles, second prophets, third teachers, after

that miracles, then gifts of healings, helps, administrations, varieties of tongues. Are all Apostles? Are all prophets? Are all teachers? Are all workers of miracles? Do all have gifts of healings? Do all speak with tongues? Do all interpret? All spiritual gifts contribute to the quality of life and work of the Church, but some are more crucial to its existence than others. Just as the physical body cannot function at all without vital organs such as the heart and brain, the Church cannot function at all without Apostles (Bishops, Priests), who provide access to the Sacraments, the tools that help us begin and continue our walk with Christ. Next in order of importance because of their vital functions are prophets who proclaim the message of God, then teachers who pass on an understanding of the will and word of God. Only then come workers of miracles, then those who have the gifts of healing, then those who help others, then administrators, and finally, those who speak in tongues.

Notice that while all gifts from God are valuable to the Church, those that top the list are the ones having to do with helping others in their spiritual life, which is eternal, rather than those having to do with the physical aspects of life.

12:31. But earnestly desire the best gifts. And yet I show you a more excellent way. Just as physical exercise can expand the capacity and endurance of the human body, spiritual exercise such as prayer, fasting, participation in the Sacraments, study of Scripture, and practice in living a Christ-like life can expand a person's spiritual qualities. Each of us should pray for the guidance of the Holy Spirit and try to "stretch" ourselves to acquire the higher gifts. As with all aspects of God's divine plan, He works in cooperation with man. The Parable of the Talents teaches that if we make good use of God's gifts, He showers us with more (Mt. 25:14–30).

FOOD FOR THOUGHT: (d). Have you developed your gift(s) from God and determined how to use them in His service?

Paul's next topic is God's greatest gift: love.

FOOD FOR THOUGHT COMMENTS

(a). God reaches out to teach great truths by hiding important lessons in the events of our lives. When do we most fully realize the lesson of the importance of each part of the body? Byproducts of life in this imperfect world to which Adam and Eve were exiled after their disobedience are the possibilities of illness, accidents, injury from others, and of being born with imperfections. These occurrences can cause much physical, emotional, and psychological pain, but God allows us to experience them so we can get a taste of that to which estrangement from Him (expulsion from the Garden of Eden—that perfect place) leads. The physical difficulties that are a part of the human experience also teach us to appreciate the wonder and amazing intricacy of God's ultimate creation: man.

If we injure our little finger, we realize how often we require the use of that member of our body. When we suffer impairment to a vital body part, we realize that we had taken many blessings for granted. Who among us has seen a person handicapped in some way and not been reminded of many personal blessings, which would probably escape our notice if some were not allowed to bear the burden of being living lessons of the miracle of life in a marvelously complex, fully-functioning body. When those who serve this special purpose in the world turn to God for strength, we see another phenomenon: He fills their hearts with such love and inner joy, in spite of their outward circumstances, that that too becomes a lesson, for "the Lord is near to the broken-hearted" (Ps. 34:18).

(b). How does the precept of the importance of each part of the body apply to the Church? As the hand cannot cut off the foot without causing pain, suffering, and loss of fullness of life to the entire body, the Church needs each of its members. To lose one is to lose fullness of function and should cause pain. A Priest is necessary to celebrate the Divine Liturgy but so is the person who bakes the prosphora and brings the wine, the altar boy and parish council member who assist, and each member of the congregation who brings a different urgent prayer and a different emphasis on thanksgiving and worship to God. Each Christian who reaches out with love and concern to those within and without the Church does important work for the Kingdom.

Just as there should be no war among the parts of the physical body, there also should be no antagonism in the Church. He who would ignore all parts of his body except one or two would be extremely foolish. If he were to spend his life, for instance, concentrating only on being an eye, and doing and appreciating only what an eye can do, imagine the great tragedy—the waste—of not doing all that he could do or being all that he could be if he appreciated and cooperated with all parts of his body. As the physical body would be commensurately deprived without the diversity of gifts each of its members possesses, so too would the Church be deprived without the diversity of gifts at hand through each of its members. This is according to God's design, so that we may learn to depend upon and to have love and concern for each other.

Great also is the tragedy of a fragmented Church, one that does not live, teach, and embody the fullness of Christ's teachings as a whole but instead emphasizes only one or two of them. A divided Church delights Satan because it dilutes the great power she would have if all her members, all Christians, were united. (See this study for 1 Cor. 1:10–13 and Food For Thought questions (i).–(j).)

(c). How can we share the joys and sorrows of fellow Christians? Joys shared are multiplied and sorrows shared are divided. When we show fellow Christians that we care about the things that are happening in their lives, we help them celebrate their joys and carry their burdens.

We can pray for help in overcoming any jealousy we might feel so that we can sincerely rejoice with those who have made advancement of any sort, and we can pray for and reach out to help those who are in need. Sometimes just a note showing concern can remind the receiver of God's love and can give that little extra strength needed to surmount the insurmountable. God has promised to be with His people to help them through the difficulties of life, but most often His presence is manifested through one of us.

(d). Have you developed your gift(s) from God and determined how to use them in His service? Everyone has a gift or gifts from God that can be used for the good of the universal Church. In fact, every situation in which we find ourselves should be considered a gift from God that we can use for His glory. Those who have yet to discover what their individual special gifts are and how they may be used should ask, in prayer, for His help (Lk. 11:9) and should remain open to and excited about possibilities.

> All of us ought always to give thanks to God for both
> the *universal* and the particular gifts of soul and body
> that He bestows on us. The universal gifts consist of
> the four elements and all that comes into being

through them, as well as all the marvelous works of God mentioned in the divine Scriptures. The *particular* gifts consist of all that God has given to each individual. These include wealth, so that one can perform acts of charity; poverty, so that one can endure it with patience and gratitude; authority, so that one can exercise righteous judgment and establish virtue; obedience and service, so that one can more readily attain salvation of soul; health, so that one can assist those in need and undertake work worthy of God; sickness, so that one may earn the crown of patience; spiritual knowledge and strength, so that one may acquire virtue; weakness and ignorance, so that, turning one's back on worldly things, one may be under obedience in stillness and humility; unsought loss of goods and possessions, so that one may deliberately seek to be saved and may be helped when incapable of shedding all one's possessions or even of giving alms; ease and prosperity, so that one may voluntarily struggle and suffer to attain the virtues and thus become dispassionate and fit to save other souls; trials and hardship, so that those who cannot eradicate their own will may be saved in spite of themselves, and those capable of joyful endurance may attain perfection. All these things, even if they are opposed to each other, are nevertheless good when used correctly; but when misused they are not good, but are harmful for both soul and body.

Better than them all, however, is the patient endurance of afflictions. He who has been found worthy of this great gift should give thanks to God in that he has been all the more blessed, for he has become an imitator of Christ, of His holy Apostles, and of the martyrs and saints. He has received from God great strength and spiritual knowledge, so that he may voluntarily abstain from pleasure and may readily embrace hardship through the eradication of his own will and his rejection of unholy thoughts and may thus always do and think that which is in accordance with God's will. Those who have been found worthy of using things as they ought to be used should in all humility give heartfelt thanks to God, for by His grace they have been freed from what is contrary to nature and from the transgression of the commandments. We, however, who are still subject to the passions and who still misuse things, and who, therefore, act in a manner that is contrary to nature, should tremble and in all gratitude should give heartfelt thanks to our Benefactor, astonished at His unutterable forbearance, in that though we have disobeyed His commandments, misused His creation, and rejected His gifts, He endures our ingratitude and does not cease to confer His blessings on us, waiting until our last breath for our conversion and repentance.

PETER OF DAMASKOS[6]

CHAPTER THIRTEEN

The Greatest Gift

Having expounded upon the various gifts of the Holy Spirit, their relative importance, and their role in the Church, Paul turns to the gift of love: the one that tops them all.

13:1. Though I speak with the tongues of men and of angels, but have not love, I have become as sounding brass or a clanging cymbal. Love is the best of God's many gifts; the ability to speak in tongues is considered the least important (see 1 Cor. 12:28). If he who can speak in all the languages of Heaven and earth does not also love God and his neighbor (Mk. 12:30–31), his linguistic abilities are as useless as "sounding brass or a clanging cymbal," instruments which produce dull, empty sounds and can be disturbing when not accompanied by other more melodious tones.

> FOOD FOR THOUGHT: (a). What is the best way to express love to "God and neighbor"? Who is our neighbor?

13:2. And though I have the gift of prophecy, and understand all mysteries and all knowledge, and though I have all faith, so that I could remove mountains, but have not love, I am nothing. Even if he possessed to a high degree those gifts considered superior to speaking in tongues—prophecy, knowledge, and faith—if he did not in addition possess love, it would be as if he had nothing.

> Have faith with love, for love without faith you cannot have. I warn you ... have faith with love; for it is possible to have faith without love. I am not exhorting you to have faith, but to have charity. For

you cannot have charity without faith: I mean the love of God and your neighbor: where can these come from without faith? How does anyone love God, who does not believe in God? How does the fool love God who says in his heart: "There is no God" (Ps. 14:1)? It could be that you believe Christ has come, yet not love Christ. But it cannot be that you love Christ, yet affirm that Christ has not come.

AUGUSTINE[1]

Faith that expresses itself in an attempt to be Christ-like leads to love, which leads to the Kingdom. Faith that does not lead to love, as demonstrated by good works, is useless for the Kingdom, as the Book of James makes clear (Jas. 2:14–26). Satan has faith (knowledge) that God is the Creator and that Jesus is His Son and the Savior of mankind (Jas. 2:19). Yet his faith led not to love but to rebellion and to a continued all-out effort to cause as many as possible to fall from grace with him (Rev. 12:17).

This verse brings to mind the words of invitation to participate in Divine Eucharist: "With the fear of God, with faith and with love draw near." It often happens that one initially turns to God through fear—fear of events in life, of the unknown, of death and judgment. This is an example of how God can turn even the negative to good. If because of fear one begins to search for answers to life's complexities and finds the meaningful answers that can only be found with God, fear will produce faith, because only through the light of God's divine plan do life and death make sense and become purposeful. Through continual spiritual growth in the image of Christ, with the grace of the Holy Spirit, faith then progresses to love. Hence the invitation to step forward to receive the Body and Blood of Christ hints at the natural progression of spiritual growth, if it is continually nurtured: from fear to faith to the epitome—love, the last step in the *Ladder of Divine Ascent* described by John Climacus.

> Fear shows up if ever love departs, for the man with
> no fear is either filled with love or is dead in spirit.[2]

FOOD FOR THOUGHT: (b). God is love (1 Jn. 4:8).
He loves us all! In what sense, then, is He to be
feared? (Read Jude 20–23.)

13.3. And though I bestow all my goods to feed the poor, and though I give my body to be burned but have not love, it profits me nothing. It is possible for a person to give all that he has to the poor and even to give his life for motives other than love. One may desire, for instance, to be well thought of by family and friends, or by the world, or to be remembered in history. Another may be motivated by fear of Hell or may think that he can buy Heaven. These sacrifices are useless and empty gestures, which will not be recognized by God if they are devoid of love. Chrysostom explains that God commands not merely the deed but wants the heart of the giver to be entwined with his gift:

> God wants us not merely to give without sympathy,
> but to ... grieve with the needy. This is why God
> invites almsgiving. He could have nourished the poor
> Himself ... but that He might bind us together unto
> charity and that we might be thoroughly fervent
> toward each other, He commanded them to be
> nourished by us.[3] (Read Jn. 13:34–35.)

13:4–7. Love suffers long and is kind; love does not envy; love does not parade itself, is not puffed up; does not behave rudely, does not seek its own, is not provoked, thinks no evil; does not rejoice in iniquity, but rejoices in the truth; bears all things, believes all things, hopes

all things, endures all things. Paul offers a definition of love that causes all others to pale by comparison. He who loves …

… *is long-suffering*: does not strike back in anger when insulted or treated unjustly; love returns good for evil, time after time. (How many times should we forgive? "until seventy times seven" [Mt. 18:22]).

… *is kind*: treats his beloved (every human being—even his enemies [Mt. 5:44]) as he would like to be treated.

… *does not envy*: resists bad feelings about someone who possesses something he does not.

… *is humble*: does not look for glory for himself but for his beloved. (To put another ahead of oneself is impossible without the gift of humility.)

… *is not puffed up*: not egotistical, but modest and level-headed, knowing that all the good things about himself and his life are gifts from God.

… *does not behave rudely*: is considerate of others, behaves properly, so as not to offend his beloved.

… *is not selfish*: puts the interests of his beloved ahead of his own.

… *is not provoked*: not easily irritated or ready to take offense.

… *thinks no evil*: since he who loves does not readily take offense, he neither allows resentment to build up, nor plans revenge, nor is quick to think evil of his beloved.

... does not rejoice in iniquity, but rejoices in truth: hates evil and takes no joy in recognizing another's evil deeds in order to elevate his own standing but rejoices whenever God's good shines forth.

... bears all things, believes all things, hopes all things, endures all things: accepts difficulties good-naturedly, always believes the best of his beloved, always has high hopes, but realistically presses on in whatever situation he finds himself.

> **FOOD FOR THOUGHT:** (c). The word "love" is often used very loosely. How can Paul's definition of love be helpful to a couple attracted to each other? ... in any relationship? ... in our relationship with God? ... in interaction with our "enemy" (Mt. 5:44)?

13:8. Love never fails. But whether there are prophecies, they will fail; whether there are tongues, they will cease; whether there is knowledge, it will vanish away. True love embraces all these qualities unendingly. Though everything comes to an end, including prophecies, tongues, and the imperfect knowledge of the world, which will not be necessary in the fullness of God's Kingdom of Heaven, true love continues eternally.

13:9–10. For we know in part and we prophesy in part. But when that which is perfect has come, then that which is in part will be done away. Whatever spiritual understanding we are able to develop in our lifetime is only partial as compared to the perfect, total knowledge possible in the Kingdom of Heaven:

> Now we know that God is everywhere, but how, we know not. That He made out of things that are not

the things that are we know; but of the manner we are ignorant. That He was born of a virgin, we know; but how, we know not yet. But then we shall know somewhat more and clearer concerning these things.
CHRYSOSTOM[4]

13:11. When I was a child, I spoke as a child, I understood as a child, I thought as a child; but when I became a man, I put away childish things. Just as an adult normally has greater understanding than a child, one who has entered into the eternal Kingdom of Heaven will have a fuller understanding of God's ways than he did when he was bound by the earthly life. However, even this knowledge will not be the perfect knowledge that God has but one that will continue to grow as we advance in perfection in His image (Gen. 1:26), "from glory to glory" (see this study for 1 Cor. 2:10–13).

13:12. For now we see in a mirror, dimly, but then face to face. Now I know in part, but then I shall know just as I also am known. Our present knowledge is partial because of our imperfections, as though we were observing God and His plan for us through a faulty mirror, which reflects a combination of what we want to see and what we have been taught to see. When we enter the fullness of the Kingdom, we will have clear vision, with no obstacles separating us from God. We shall know Him as He knows us.

> Not that we shall know Him as He is, but that even as He hastened toward us now, so also shall we cling unto Him then, and shall know many of the things which are now secret and shall enjoy that most blessed society and wisdom.
> CHRYSOSTOM[5]

God does all He can, without taking away our gift of free will, to bring us to Him. We shall, with that same fervor, cling to Him then.

13:13. And now abide faith, hope, love, these three; but the greatest of these is love. Love is greater than faith and hope, because the need for them will cease with the Second Coming of Christ, when the fullness of God's eternal Kingdom has been established. But love will continue.

> FOOD FOR THOUGHT: (d). Why will faith and hope no longer be necessary after the Second Coming of Christ? Why will love continue?

FOOD FOR THOUGHT COMMENTS

(a). What is the best way to express love to "God and neighbor"? Who is our neighbor? The first four of the Ten Commandments God gave to Moses deal with man's relationship with God. The last six deal with man's relationship with man. When asked which was the most important of these Commandments, Jesus said that the first is to love God and the second is to love our neighbor as we love ourselves (Mk. 12:30). Called the new commandments, these two actually summarize all ten of the Old Testament Commandments, which, in turn, really boil down to one: loving God. If we love our neighbor who is made in the image of God, we love God. To "love God and neighbor" means to truly consider God first in all things. It means to ask, when we are confronted with a decision, "How does God want me to proceed?" or "How would Jesus respond in this situation?" In so doing, we would be trying to live a Christ-like life in all situations, which would include treating everyone we meet in our daily walk through life (our neighbor) as we would want them to treat us.

Loving everyone, however, does not mean giving in to them in all situations and at all costs—even to keep peace. Love means wanting the best (salvation) for everyone, and thus doing our best to put them and keep them on the road to God. Sometimes love has to be tough!

(b). God is love (1 Jn. 4:8). He loves us all! In what sense, then, is He to be feared? (Read Jude 20–23.) To be indifferent to God is to have no awareness of the need for spiritual growth, which can lead to permanent estrangement from Him. To have faith that there is indeed a Creator, and to realize that He naturally expects a commitment from His people will produce fear in the mind of a rational person as to the consequences of following his own will rather than God's. This type of fear has the potential of developing into love. Scripture says that "fear of the Lord is the beginning of wisdom" (Ps. 111:10), and that fear is the only way to reach some (Jude 23). According to the Philokalia:

> If you have faith in the Lord you will fear punishment, and this fear will lead you to control the passions. Once you control the passions you will accept affliction patiently, and through such acceptance you will acquire hope in God. Hope in God separates the intellect from every worldly attachment, and when the intellect is detached in this way it will acquire love for God.

> Fear of God is of two kinds. The first is generated in us by the threat of punishment. It is through such fear that we develop in due order self-control, patience, hope in God, and dispassion; and it is from dispassion that love comes. The second kind of fear is linked with love and constantly produces reverence in

166

the soul, so that it does not grow indifferent to God because of the intimate communion of its love.

The first kind of fear is expelled by perfect love when the soul has acquired this and is no longer afraid of punishment (1 Jn. 4:18). The second kind, as we have already said, is always found united with perfect love. The first kind of fear is referred to in the following two verses: *Out of fear of the Lord men shun evil* (Prov. 16:6), and *Fear of the Lord is the beginning of wisdom* (Ps. 111:10). The second kind is mentioned in the following verses: *Fear of the Lord is pure, and endures forever* (Ps. 19:9), and *Those who fear the Lord will not want for anything* (Ps. 34:10).

MAXIMUS THE CONFESSOR[6]

(c). The word "love" is often used very loosely. How can Paul's definition of love be helpful to a couple attracted to each other? ... in any relationship? ... in our relationship with God? ... in interaction with our "enemy" (Mt. 5:44)? A couple attracted to each other can use Paul's definition of love as a guide by which to evaluate their relationship. If they do not, and cannot, at least work toward treating each other in the manner indicated, perhaps what they feel for each other is not really love at all. This definition can be used as a pattern for continual growth in any relationship, for a love that will never fade but rather continue to bloom.

If we love God, we will use the gifts He has given us to do His work. We will not look for glory for ourselves but rather reflect it where it belongs—toward Him—knowing that if we do receive tribute from the world, we have received our reward and can expect none from Him (Mt. 6:1–4). We will not give up when the work becomes too difficult or put our own comfort or pleasure first at all times. Our spiritual accomplishments will not engender arrogance, because we know that without Him we can do nothing. We will not envy those who seem to have an easier time or what we may consider a better role. We will be considerate, even when we are tired and hassled. We will not take offense easily, or blame God when something goes wrong in our lives.

Paul's definition of love calls for us to be kind to those with whom we interact, even if they are unkind to us, in keeping with Christ's instruction to love even our enemy. To the extent that we succeed, we may find that we lose an enemy and gain a friend!

To *rejoice in truth* is to love Christ's teachings, teach them to others, and try to live by them as best we can. But we rejoice especially when we remember that salvation through Jesus Christ does not depend on our perfection—only upon the fact that if we really have love-producing faith, we will keep trying to follow this pattern (Mt. 5:48).

(d). Why will faith and hope no longer be necessary after the Second Coming of Christ? Why will love continue? The ultimate goal of the qualities of faith and hope that we strive for is eternal life with God. The Second Coming of Christ will bring Judgment of everyone. Those whose lives are judged to have demonstrated faith in and love for Jesus Christ will see their hopes realized (Mt. 25:34–40). Faith will be replaced by perfect knowledge of God and His Kingdom and hope by promises fulfilled.

Love, however, is the stuff of which the Kingdom is made, so it will continue. Thus our daily goal should be to grow in love—to practice love—to be ready for and suitable residents of that perfect place. If we routinely try to just "do," to the best of our ability, what is required by love, even when we don't feel like it, our capacity for love will increase accordingly. Love has no limits!

CHAPTER FOURTEEN

Peace and Order in Worship

The Corinthian Christians were focusing on the gift of tongues more than the other gifts from God, creating a spiritual imbalance and the danger of pursuing this gift, or a simulation of it, for its emotional effects.

14:1. Pursue love, and desire spiritual gifts, but especially that you may prophesy. Love for God and all of His creations is the highest gift, thus should be pursued aggressively. One who pursues something does not give up. He persists, no matter what, in striving for that which he seeks. Love is attained through obedience. If we show God our love for Him by obeying His word, even when our own will may lean in another direction, He will bless our efforts and His love will flourish in us. (Read Phil. 2:5–11, which indicates that God exalted Jesus because of His obedience.)

> Spread wide your love, and not only to your wives and children. Love such as that we find also in sheep and sparrows. You know how sparrows and swallows love their mates, how both will hatch their eggs, and both feed the young with a certain sweet and natural goodness, without thought of recompense. The sparrow will not say: "I feed my young, so that when I am old, they will feed me." It bestows the love of a parent, looking for no return. ... Spread wide your love ... let it grow. To love your wives and children is not yet the Wedding Garment. Have faith in God. First love God. Extend your love to God; and seize whomsoever you can for God. You have an enemy. Seize him for God. A wife, a son, a slave. Bring them to God. Here comes a stranger. Bring him to God.

An enemy; seize him for God. Bring him; bring your enemy. Bring him; he is no longer your enemy.
AUGUSTINE[1]

FOOD FOR THOUGHT: (a).What is the "Wedding Garment?" How can it be acquired? Can it be purchased? Stolen? (See Mt. 22:12, Col. 3:1–17, 2 Peter 1:1–11.)   (b). Why is bringing family, friends, and enemies to God an indicator of love?

In addition to striving always to grow in love, we should desire, pray to be given, and work toward acquiring the higher gifts, especially the gift of prophesy.

> The prophet is essentially a person called by God to proclaim His message to men. Through the prophet, God makes known his secrets, warns of punishment, encourages through exhortations and promises of grace, and occasionally discloses what is going to take place in the future.[2]

If it is God's will that we receive the gift(s) we desire, the Holy Spirit will work in us toward that end (1 Cor. 12:11). As with the whole of God's divine plan, a synergistic cooperation between God and man is required. (See this study for 1 Cor. 12:31.)

14:2–4. For he who speaks in a tongue does not speak to men but to God, for no one understands him; however, in the spirit he speaks mysteries. But he who prophesies speaks edification and exhortation and comfort to men. He who speaks in a tongue edifies himself, but he who prophesies edifies the church. The value of a spiritual gift is measured by its usefulness to the Church. 1 Cor. 12:28 establishes the order of importance of the various gifts. "Speaking in tongues" (Corinthian Glossolalia) is listed last because this gift is for personal benefit. Prophecy is listed second because through this gift the Church is enlightened and strengthened.

There are two types of speaking in tongues (Glossolalia):

(1). Pentecostal Glossolalia: This is the type that occurred 50 days after the Resurrection of Jesus Christ. On that day the Apostles received from the Holy Spirit the ability to speak in many different languages in order to preach the Gospel to all who had gathered in Jerusalem to celebrate the Hebrew Pentecost (referred to by Acts 2:1).

> **FOOD FOR THOUGHT:** (c). Christian Pentecost (Acts 2:2–4) occurred on the day commemorating the Hebrew Pentecost of old (Lev. 23:15–22; Acts 2:1). Was this a coincidence? Of what was it an indication?

(2). Corinthian Glossolalia: the type the Corinthian Christians were experiencing. Corinthian Glossolalia was an activity of the Holy Spirit coming upon a person and compelling him to external expressions directed to God but not understood by others. In Pentecostal Glossolalia, while speaking in several different tongues, both the speaker and the listener understood what was uttered. The Glossolalia manifested in Corinth was the utterance of words, phrases, sentences, etc., intelligible to God but not to the person uttering them. What was uttered needed to be interpreted by another who had the gift of interpretation.

> When the person spoke, his soul became passive and his understanding became inactive. He was in a state of ecstasy. While the words or sounds were prayer and praise, they were not clear in meaning and gave the impression of something mysterious. The phe-

nomenon included sighs, groanings, shoutings, cries and utterances of disconnected speech, sometimes jubilant and sometimes ecstatic.[3]

14:5. I wish you all spoke with tongues, but even more that you prophesied; for he who prophesies is greater than he who speaks with tongues, unless indeed he interprets, that the Church may receive edification. For the Corinthians to get carried away with the gift of tongues, emphasizing it more than the other gifts, was a natural danger because of their pagan background.

> Greek paganism ... included demonstrations, frenzies and orgies all intricately interwoven into their religious practices. In post Homeric times the cult of the Dionysiac orgies made ... [its] entrance into the Greek world. According to this, music, the whirling dance, intoxication and utterances had the power to make men divine; to produce a condition in which the normal state was left behind and the inspired person perceived what was external to himself and the senses.[4]

On the other hand, he who is able to interpret an episode of Corinthian tongues is equal to a prophet, for through the interpretation, the entire Church is edified.

14:6–11. But now, brethren, if I come to you speaking with tongues, what shall I profit you unless I speak to you either by revelation, by knowledge, by prophesying, or by teaching? Even things without life, whether flute or harp, when they make a sound, unless they make a distinction in the sounds, how will it be known what is piped or played? For if the trumpet makes an uncertain sound, who will prepare for battle? So likewise you, unless you utter by the tongue words easy to understand, how will it be known what is spoken? For

you will be speaking into the air. There are, it may be, so many kinds of languages in the world, and none of them is without significance. Therefore, if I do not know the meaning of the language, I shall be a foreigner to him who speaks, and he who speaks will be a foreigner to me. In order for sounds and languages to be effective as a means of communication, they must have clear and consistent meanings. In order for speaking in tongues (Corinthian Glossolalia) to have value to the Church, it must be accompanied by the gift of interpretation.

> For excellent indeed and necessary is the gift, but it is so when there is someone to explain what is spoken. Since the finger too is a necessary thing, but when you separate it from the other members, it will not be equally useful; and the trumpet is necessary, but when it sounds at random, it is rather an annoyance. Yea, neither shall any art come to light without matter subject to it; nor is matter put into shape, if no form be assigned to it. Suppose then the voice to be as the subject matter, if it can take no shape and form it is of no use.
>
> CHRYSOSTOM[5]

14:12. Even so you, since you are zealous for spiritual gifts, let it be for the edification of the church that you seek to excel. The gifts that should be sought after are the ones that benefit the Church (all of God's people). To put the Church ahead of oneself in this manner is to practice the love that Paul calls God's greatest gift.

14:13–17. Therefore, let him who speaks in a tongue pray that he may interpret. For if I pray in a tongue, my spirit prays, but my understanding is unfruitful. What is the result then? I will pray with the spirit, and I will also pray with the understanding. I will sing with the spirit, and I will also sing with the understanding.
174

Otherwise, if you bless with the spirit, how will he who occupies the place of the uninformed say "Amen" at your giving of thanks, since he does not understand what you say? For you indeed give thanks well, but the other is not edified. He who has the gift of tongues should seek the gift of interpretation also, so that he can understand what is spoken in tongues and can teach others with the fruit of his gift. Paul gave these instructions to the people of Corinth at a time when the gift of speaking in tongues and many other wonderful supernatural manifestations of the Holy Spirit were abundantly in evidence in the Church. This was necessary at the time so that the Gospel would be accepted as being from God. Workers were few, conditions were poor, and there was much work to be done—so God stepped in to help.

Contemporary Pentecostal and Charismatic groups repeat the Corinthian mistake of putting undue focus on the gift of speaking in tongues, thereby creating imbalance in the spiritual lives of their followers. These groups refer to the phenomenon of Glossolalia as being evidence of having been "born again," defined as having received the Holy Spirit and been spiritually awakened.

> The Greek Orthodox Church does not preclude the use of Glossolalia, but regards it as one of the minor gifts of the Holy Spirit. If Glossolalia has fallen out of use, it is because it served its purpose in New Testament times and is no longer necessary. However, even when used, it is a private and personal gift, a lower form of prayer. The Orthodox Church differs with those Pentecostal and Charismatic groups which regard Glossolalia as a prerequisite to being a Christian and to having received the Holy Spirit.[6]

Orthodox theology holds that through the Sacraments of Baptism and Chrismation we are "born again" (Jn. 3:3) "of water and the spirit" (Jn. 3:5). From that point on, gradual spiritual growth should take place through the combined influences of the home and the Church. If this does not happen, or if at some point it ceases or is abandoned, there may come about, sooner or later, a falling away from the spiritual life. If such a person, at any point, comes to regret the absence of God in his/her life, repents, and seeks reconciliation with God through the Sacrament of Confession, this too may be called a spiritual rebirth. Sincere repentance, which includes the desire for change, returns the penitent to the sin-free state of the newly baptized.

14:18–20. I thank my God I speak with tongues more than you all; yet in the church I would rather speak five words with my understanding, that I may teach others also, than ten thousand words in a tongue. Brethren, do not be children in understanding; however, in malice be babes, but in understanding be mature. Paul had the gift of tongues but knew that it was better for the Church if he spoke five words he could understand and explain to others than if he spoke ten thousand words in an indiscernible language. The Corinthians were condoning immorality on one hand (1 Cor. 5) and immaturely flaunting a lower spiritual gift on the other, like children. He warns that we are to be infant-like only when it comes to malice (of which they are incapable) but mature in our understanding of spiritual matters.

Just as in Corinth during Paul's time there was a danger of being carried away by the idea of the gift of tongues, this danger exists for us. Zeal for evidence of God working in one's life can cause conscious or subconscious imitation of someone heard speaking in tongues. A study done by researchers at Carleton University in Ottawa, Ontario, results of which were published in the Journal of Abnormal Psychology, reports that it is easy to mimic those who profess to speak in tongues and

176

that while "it is impossible to test whether any of the religious glossolalics were actually divinely inspired … their research suggests that speaking in tongues can be taught by one religious person to another and is not always evidence of holy presence."[7]

14:21. In the law it is written: With men of other tongues and other lips I will speak to this people; and yet, for all that, they will not hear Me, says the Lord. Paul quotes the prophecy of Isaiah 28:11–12, which refers to the fact that God uses all means to reach all people, including giving His workers (Acts 2) the ability to speak in the tongues of the people they are trying to reach, but still, many do not heed the call. A contemporary facet of this gift may be the amazing ability some have to learn languages easily, which can be used very powerfully to teach God's word. This also points to the necessity for the Divine Liturgy to be brought to people in their own language.

14:22. Therefore, tongues are for a sign, not to those who believe but to unbelievers; but prophesying is not for unbelievers but for those who believe. The gift of tongues (Corinthian Glossolalia) is a tool useful for reaching unbelievers, through astonishment with the power of God. A non-believer who prides himself on being too rational to believe in a supreme Creator could have his complacency shattered by an experience of being seized by a manifestation of a force beyond himself—a phenomenon he must then either explain away or deal with. True believers are beyond the need for this gift and are benefited more by prophecy.

14:23–25. Therefore if the whole church comes together in one place, and all speak with tongues, and there come in those who are uninformed or unbelievers, will they not say that you are out of your mind? But if all

prophesy, and an unbeliever or an uninformed person comes in, he is convinced by all, he is judged by all. And thus the secrets of his heart are revealed; and so, falling down on his face, he will worship God and report that God is truly among you. When actually witnessing someone speaking in tongues, onlookers may think they observe madness, as when some thought the Apostles were drunk on the day of Pentecost (Acts 2:13). But when witnessing God's prophets teaching, counseling, and comforting His people, those who look on may recognize truth and be brought to repentance. Prophecy then is more valuable, both for edification and as a sign of God's presence.

14:26–32. How is it then, brethren? Whenever you come together, each of you has a psalm, has a teaching, has a tongue, has a revelation, has an interpretation. Let all things be done for edification. If anyone speaks in a tongue, let there be two or at the most three, each in turn, and let one interpret. But if there is no interpreter, let him keep silent in church, and let him speak to himself and to God. Let two or three prophets speak, and let the others judge. But if anything is revealed to another who sits by, let the first keep silent. For you can all prophesy one by one, that all may learn and all may be encouraged. And the spirits of the prophets are subject to the prophets. All gifts should be used for the building-up of the Church in a peaceful manner, not for the aggrandizement of individuals. The gift of tongues is at most very rare today because there is no longer a need for it (1 Cor. 13:8), but if someone has this gift, s/he should exercise it in private, unless an interpreter is present. Prophecies that are offered must be judged as to whether they are from God or demonic (1 Cor. 12:10, 1 Jn. 4:1). Those present are to judge, using the criteria of Scripture and the writings of the Fathers of the Church, which clarify its true meaning. There should be truth and order in the Church, not chaos.

The very early Church, in the time of the Apostles, had not yet established a definite structure of worship; that structure was evolving as Christ's message was being more fully understood. This, remember, was after Jesus had ascended, leaving His followers in the hands of the Holy Spirit, Who came to them at Pentecost. The New Testament, which we have to guide us, was of course not yet in existence. The gifts that the Holy Spirit provided at that unique time filled the void until a definite form of worship evolved from those experiences and was etched in the hearts and minds of believers, to be passed on to succeeding generations through practice as well as in writing.

John Chrysostom, author of the Divine Liturgy most often celebrated during the Church year, lamented the loss of the supernatural atmosphere in the very early Church, evidence that by his time these gifts had waned:

> For in truth the Church was a heaven then, the Spirit governing all things, and moving each one of the rulers and making him inspired. But now we retain only the symbols of those gifts. For now also we speak two or three, and in turn, and when one is silent, another begins. But these are only signs and memorials of those things. Wherefore when we begin to speak, the people respond "with thy Spirit," indicating that of old they thus used to speak, not of their own wisdom, but moved by the Spirit. But not so now.[8]

14:33. For God is not the author of confusion but of peace, as in all the churches of the saints. Worship should be peaceful and orderly:

> For the Church is no barber's or perfumer's shop, nor any other merchant's warehouse in the marketplace, but a place of angels, a place of archangels, a palace of God, Heaven itself. As therefore if one had parted the heaven and had brought you in, though you would see your father or your brother, you would not venture to speak; so neither here ought one to utter any other sounds but those which are spiritual. For, in truth, the things in this place are also a heaven.
>
> CHRYSOSTOM[9]

14:34. Let your women keep silent in the churches, for they are not permitted to speak; but they are to be submissive, as the law also says. This verse is another call to proper respect in church, which is not a place for idle chatter, apparently a problem among the women in Corinth:

> For if to them that have the gifts it is not permitted to speak inconsiderately, nor when they will, and this, though they be moved by the Spirit, much less to those women who prate idly and to no purpose.
>
> CHRYSOSTOM[10]

That women are "to be submissive" is another reference to the God-given hierarchal inter-dependence of woman upon man, man upon Christ, and Christ upon God (see text and this study of 1 Cor. 11:3).

14:35. And if they want to learn something, let them ask their own husbands at home; for it is shameful for women to speak in church. If the women are talking in church to ask questions, they should ask them of their husbands at home. It is part of God's divine plan that the husband be the spiritual head of the home (Eph. 5:22–24) and give his family proper spiritual instruction. However, if the husband does not fulfill this duty, these roles must be reversed:

> Men must often assume the place of women, and women the place of men, when sin ruptures the normal conditions of human life. No less a "purist" than *John Chrysostom* orders men to follow their wives when they are wiser and better: "I would commit you to your own wives, that they may instruct you. It is true, according to Paul's law, you ought to be teachers. But since the order is reversed by sin ... let us even take this way. ... For the war against the devil and his powers is common to them (women) and the men, and in no respect does the delicacy of their nature become an impediment in such conflicts, for not by bodily constitution, but by mental choice, are these struggles decided. Wherefore in many cases women have actually been more forward in the contest than men and have set up more brilliant trophies."[11]

Thus it seems that, given circumstances in the world and in the Church today, even the "purist" Chrysostom would approve of (spirit-filled, well-informed) women teaching in the Church.

14:36–40. Or did the word of God come originally from you? Or was it you only that it reached? If anyone thinks himself to be a prophet or spiritual, let him acknowledge that the things which I write to you are the commandments of the Lord. But if anyone is ignorant, let him be ignorant. Therefore, brethren, desire earnestly to prophesy, and do not forbid to speak with tongues. Let all things be done decently and in order. Paul summarizes his message and reminds the Corinthians, with irony, of his authority to approach them on these matters. It was he who first brought them the word of

God, as he did to other communities (and to us through his writings)—all of whom are expected to live by the same truths.

FOOD FOR THOUGHT COMMENTS

(a). What is the "Wedding Garment"? How can it be acquired? Can it be purchased? Stolen? (See Mt. 22:12, Col. 3:1–17, 2 Peter 1:1–11.) The Wedding Garment (Mt. 22:1–14) is the "putting on" of Christ through Baptism (Gal. 3:27), followed by a life of attempting to become Christ-like (Jn. 14:21) to show love and faith. Thus it cannot be purchased, nor can anyone steal it from another. Each of us can acquire it only through love and obedience; or we can give it away—through sin.

> This garment is seen in the heart, not on the body.
> AUGUSTINE[12]

(b). Why is bringing family, friends, and enemies to God an indicator of love? If we truly love someone, we want the best for them. The "best" is, of course, eternal life with God in His Kingdom.

(c). Christian Pentecost (Acts 2:2–4) occurred on the day commemorating the Hebrew Pentecost of old (Lev. 23:15–22; Acts 2:1). Was this a coincidence? Of what was it an indication? It was not a coincidence that Christian Pentecost occurred on the day commemorating the Hebrew Pentecost of old. The truths of the New Testament were always prefigured by events of the Old. In this case, the Hebrew Pentecost prefigured (pointed to) the Christian Pentecost:

<u>Hebrew Passover</u>:
>   God's people saved by the blood of a lamb
>   (Ex. 12): physical liberation (see this study for 1 Cor. 5:7–8).

<u>Hebrew Pentecost</u>: (50 days after Hebrew Passover),
>   (Lev. 23:5, 15–16; Deut. 9–10).
>   Also called Feast of Weeks or Feast of Harvest
>   (Ex. 34:22; 23:16).

>   Celebrated gifts from God:
>   > Ten Commandments God gave to Moses (Ex. 20):
>   (Law of God written in stone).

>   > the end of the seven-week harvesting period:
>   grain God gave to Israelites from the "promised" land.

<u>Christian Passover</u>: ("Pascha" in Greek, "Easter" in the West)
>   Christ as the new Passover:
>   God's people saved by Blood of the perfect Lamb of God,
>   Christ, the last living sacrifice (John 1:29): spiritual
>   liberation.

<u>Christian Pentecost</u>: (50 days after the Resurrection of Christ),
>   on the day the Jews celebrated Hebrew Pentecost (Acts 2:1–
>   4).

>   Celebrated gifts from God:
>   > gift of tongues/descent of the Holy Spirit:
>   power to teach the Gospel
>   (Law of God written in heart of believer).

>   > harvest: 3000 souls brought to believe in Christ as
>   Savior (Acts 2:41).

CHAPTER FIFTEEN

Defeat of the Last Enemy

One of the false teachings being disseminated in Corinth was that there is no physical resurrection of the dead. Paul takes great pains to refute this heresy.

15:1–2. Moreover, brethren, I declare to you the gospel which I preached to you, which also you received and in which you stand, by which also you are saved, if you hold fast that word which I preached to you—unless you believed in vain. The good news of the Gospel is that those who believe it and live accordingly will be saved from eternal separation from God.

15:3–7. For I delivered to you first of all that which I also received: that Christ died for our sins according to the Scriptures, and that He was buried, and that He rose again the third day according to the Scriptures, and that He was seen by Cephas, then by the twelve. After that He was seen by over five hundred brethren at once, of whom the greater part remain to the present, but some have fallen asleep. After that He was seen by James, then by all the apostles. The basis for our salvation is not what we do but what Christ did. The fact that He was seen alive after He was crucified (as verified by the historical record of eye-witnesses) is proof that He rose from the dead, thus conquering death for us. To those who say that He did not really die but merely passed out, to be revived by the coolness of the tomb in which He was laid, there is the evidence of the blood and water which gushed from His body when the soldier pierced His side with a sword (John 19:34–35), a separation which takes place only after death.

15:8. Then last of all He was seen by me also, as by one born out of due time. Paul saw Christ also—but later than all the others (after the Ascension: Acts 9:1–9). The Greek text for the phrase "one born out of due time" uses the word *ektroma,* or "abortion." This could be a reference to "the sudden intervention by which he was torn from opposition to become an apostle."[1] Or perhaps it is "rather an expression of modesty than anything else."[2]

15:9–10. For I am the least of the apostles, who am not worthy to be called an apostle, because I persecuted the Church of God. But by the grace of God I am what I am, and His grace toward me was not in vain; but I labored more abundantly than they all, yet not I, but the grace of God which was with me. Paul feels unworthy of his calling because of the time in his life when he had zealously persecuted Christians (Acts 26:9–11, Gal. 1:13). But after He was visited by Christ on the road to Damascus, he was transformed into an even more zealous Apostle of the Gospel (Gal. 1:15-16). In cooperation with the divine grace that enabled him, Paul worked very hard out of gratitude and love for that which God had done for him.

> FOOD FOR THOUGHT: (a). The Apostle Peter denied Jesus three times (Mt. 26:31–35,69–75) and Paul zealously persecuted Christians (Acts 8:1–3), yet they went on to become leaders in the Church. How can this be?

15:11. Therefore, whether it was I or they, so we preach and so you believed. Though not one of the original Twelve, Paul is considered equal with them.

> Paul's authority as an apostle is proved by the writings of Luke (Acts 22:6–10, 26:12–18, 9:10–16),

his constant companion and fellow traveler.

IRENAEUS[3]

15:12–16. Now if Christ is preached that He has been raised from the dead, how do some among you say that there is no resurrection of the dead? But if there is no resurrection of the dead, then Christ is not risen. And if Christ is not risen, then our preaching is empty and your faith is also empty. Yes, and we are found false witnesses of God, because we have testified of God that He raised up Christ, whom He did not raise up—if in fact the dead do not rise. For if the dead do not rise, then Christ is not risen. The Corinthians were still under the influence of pagan thought, which held that the soul is immortal but spent eternity without a body. Thus they considered physical resurrection to be impossible. This was in direct opposition to the Gospel taught by Paul and the other Apostles: that Christ was raised bodily from the dead—concrete proof that there is life after death—and that there will be a general bodily resurrection of all mankind, some to eternal enjoyment of the blessings of God and some to "the everlasting fire prepared for the devil and his angels" (Mt. 25:41). If Christ did not rise from the dead, Paul and the Apostles are guilty of spreading falsehoods.

> **FOOD FOR THOUGHT:** (b). It seems that mankind has always instinctively known—or hoped—that there is some type of life after death. What in the human experience would contribute to this conclusion?

15:17. And if Christ is not risen, your faith is futile; you are still in your sins! God's plan, as revealed to mankind through prophecy, called for the Messiah to take on flesh, and then allowed Him to be put to death, to share the consequences of sin fully with man. Christ fulfilled this mission. But because He had not sinned, death could not hold Him. Thus He conquered death once and for all. If He did not rise from the dead, there is no hope for any of us, for we cannot achieve salvation on our own, as the Law of the Old Testament demonstrated dramatically (see this study for 1 Cor. 5:2).

15:18. Then also those who have fallen asleep in Christ have perished. If Christ did not rise from the dead, there is no hope beyond the grave for anyone who put his faith in Christ as the promised Messiah.

15:19. If in this life only we have hope in Christ, we are of all men the most pitiable. If Christians believe in Christ with the hope of blessings in this life only, they are to be pitied, for trying to live the life of Christ brings with it struggle and persecution of one sort or another. Without the hope of eternal life with God, we might as well eat, drink, and be merry, taking advantage of fleeting joys where we may (no matter of what sort they might be), for life is short. This seems to be the frame of mind of those who think that the main reason for life is the pursuit of pleasure.

15:20. But now Christ is risen from the dead, and has become the firstfruits of those who have fallen asleep. Christ was the first to be resurrected from the dead to die no more. Others, like Lazarus (Jn. 11:43) and the son of the widow of Nain (Lk. 7:11–15), were resurrected only temporarily, and only to die again. Those who put their faith in Christ will rise from the dead to live forever joyously, as He did.

15:21–22. For since by man came death, by Man also came the resurrection of the dead. For as in Adam all die, even so in Christ all shall be made alive. After Adam (the first man) disobeyed God, he and Eve were cast out of

Paradise into the world where the Devil and his demons were already in residence (Rev. 12:7–9, Lk. 10:18). Since all mankind descends from Adam and Eve, everyone given life enters that world, where it is easy to sin and difficult to pursue righteousness, and where everyone (except those alive at the Second Coming of Christ) must die. It is therefore necessary, and fitting, that through Man (Christ—called, theologically, the Second Man), the opportunity for eternal life with full access to all of God's goodness was returned to mankind.

15:23. But each one in his own order: Christ the firstfruits, afterward those who are Christ's at His coming. No one knows when Christ will return to earth for the second (and final) time (Mt. 25:13). When He does, the dead will be resurrected. The first to rise will be those who belong to Christ. Some theologians indicate that "each in his own order" refers to a believer's relationship to God, with the closest to Him in this life being resurrected first, etc.

15:24–25. Then comes the end, when He delivers the kingdom to God the Father, when He puts an end to all rule and all authority and power. For He must reign till He has put all enemies under His feet. Christ will reign as Head of the Church until all His enemies are made subject to Him, as prophesied (Ps. 110:1, Mt. 22:44). Then Jesus will turn Himself and His Kingdom (all His followers) over to God, ending any other rule and authority over man:

> ... to wit, the devil and the bands of demons (many as there are), and the multitudes of unbelievers, and the tyranny of death, and all evils.
>
> CHRYSOSTOM[4]

15:26. The last enemy that will be destroyed is death. The *souls* of believers are delivered from death at Baptism[5] (subject to judgment of their ensuing life), but they are deprived of their *bodies* through death. At the Second Coming of Christ, they will be resurrected with new bodies. Thus, the last enemy will have been eliminated. Those who belong to the Kingdom of God will experience it fully: body and soul.

> The bodies heretofore held [by the Devil] will be snatched away from him.
>
> CHRYSOSTOM[6]

15:27–28. For "He has put all things under His feet." But when He says "all things are put under Him," it is evident that He who put all things under Him is excepted. Now when all things are made subject to Him, then the Son Himself will also be subject to Him who put all things under Him, that God may be all in all. Everything came from God, so everything will return to His domain.

15:29. Otherwise, what will they do who are baptized for the dead, if the dead do not rise at all? Why then are they baptized for the dead? Christian Baptism is a symbol of death to sin (water: a symbol of cleansing; total immersion: a symbol of death; the bringing out of the water: resurrection to new life in Christ). If this Sacrament is participated in with faith, either on the part of the baptized, if they have reached the age of reason, or on the part of the parents and/or godparents in the case of infants, it is with the hope of resurrection from death, as promised by God (Romans 6:4–9), and as prefigured by Christ's Resurrection. If there is no resurrection from death, why participate in Baptism?

It was a heresy in the second century among the Marcionites and the Montanists to baptize, by proxy, those who had died without having been baptized—a complete misinterpretation of Paul's words:

I know indeed that I shall excite much laughter; nevertheless ... I will mention it that you may the more completely avoid this disease: when any Catechumen departs among them, having concealed the living man under the couch of the dead, they approach the corpse and talk with him, asking if he wishes to receive baptism; then when he makes no answer, he that is concealed underneath says in his stead that of course he should wish to be baptized; and so they baptize him instead of the departed, like men jesting upon the stage. So great power has the devil over the souls of careless sinners. Then being called to account, they allege that even the Apostle [Paul] said: "They who are baptized for the dead." See their extreme ridiculousness. Should we answer these things? I think not; unless it is necessary to discourse with mad men of what they in their frenzy utter. But so that none of the more exceedingly simple folk may be led captive, we must respond. If this was Paul's meaning, why did God threaten him that is not baptized? For henceforth, it is impossible that any should not be baptized, and any fault would no longer be with the dead but with the living. But to whom did He speak: *Unless you eat My flesh, and drink My blood, you have no life in you?* (Jn. 6:53). To the living, or to the dead? And again, *Unless a man be born again of water and of the Spirit, he cannot see the Kingdom of God* (Jn. 3:5). For if this be permitted, and there be no need of the mind of the receiver nor of his assent while he lives, what hinders both Greeks (pagans) and Jews thus to become believers, other men after their decease doing these things in their stead?

CHRYSOSTOM[7]

Mormons (Church of Jesus Christ of Latter-day Saints) continue this heresy. Their vast genealogical library was devised to allow their followers to trace their ancestors, for the purpose of baptizing them by proxy.

190

15:30–32. And why do we stand in jeopardy every hour? I affirm, by the boasting in you which I have in Christ Jesus our Lord, I die daily. If, in the manner of men, I have fought with beasts at Ephesus, what advantage is it to me? If the dead do not rise, Let us eat and drink, for tomorrow we die! If there is no resurrection from death, why did Paul and the other Apostles constantly put their lives at risk? Would they willingly go to early graves if there is nothing beyond this life?

15:33–34. Do not be deceived: Evil company corrupts good habits. Awake to righteousness, and do not sin; for some do not have the knowledge of God. I speak this to your shame. Christians should not associate with those who believe and teach that there is no resurrection from the dead, lest their faith in resurrection be weakened. He who believes this falsehood will act accordingly, neglecting to prepare for that which lies beyond this life.

15:35–36. But someone will say, "How are the dead raised up? And with what body do they come?" Foolish one, what you sow is not made alive unless it dies. Death and resurrection are affirmed in nature. The cycle of plant life demonstrates the fact that death is necessary to perpetuate life (Jn. 12:24). Seeds from plants that have died are cast into the earth to bloom again. Who can reproduce the miracle of the growth of a great tree from a tiny seed? Where in the seed can we see the wood? ... the bark? ... the green leaves? ... the rich fruit?

15:37–38. And what you sow, you do not sow that body that shall be, but mere grain—perhaps wheat or some other grain. But God gives it a body as He pleases, and to each seed its own body. The Corinthians thought

Christians believed that the bodies of the dead would be resuscitated. But Paul declares that from dying wheat, new wheat grows—not resuscitated old wheat. If a kernel of corn is planted, it dies, and from it new corn grows—not resuscitated old corn.

15:39-41. All flesh is not the same flesh, but there is one kind of flesh of men, another flesh of animals, another of fish, and another of birds. There are also celestial bodies and terrestrial bodies; but the glory of the celestial is one, and the glory of the terrestrial is another. There is one glory of the sun, another glory of the moon, and another glory of the stars; for one star differs from another star in glory. Just as each of God's creations (earthly and heavenly) has its own special body, each of those who enter the fullness of God's Kingdom will have a body reflecting their relationship with Him (which begins during life on earth). Those away from God's presence (II Thess. 1:9) will receive a body that reflects their degree of estrangement from God.

> What do we learn from this? That though they be in God's kingdom, all shall not enjoy the same reward; and though all sinners be in Hell, all shall not endure the same punishment.
>
> CHRYSOSTOM[8]

Gregory of Nyssa wrote that at the Resurrection, each person will receive "a distinctive mark" revealing attributes of virtue or evil.[9] Each person's appearance will reveal what he is. Basil agrees that sins affect "the external appearance of the soul" and "devastate its natural beauty." Thus the separation by Christ (Mt. 25:32) of the sheep (righteous) from the goats (sinners) will be easy.

15:42–43. So also is the resurrection of the dead. The body is sown in corruption, it is raised in incorruption. It is sown in dishonor, it is raised in glory. It is sown in weakness, it is raised in power. Just as new life grows from the seed of a plant after it dies, so it is with human beings. When the human body is buried, it has been corrupted through sin and the decaying process that takes place through disease, injury, and/or age, culminating in death, which brings further decay. At the Resurrection, the body and the soul of the person of God who is raised to eternal life will be incorruptible, unchangeable (unable to sin or decay in any way)—glorious and powerful.

15:44–45. It is sown a natural body, it is raised a spiritual body. There is a natural body, and there is a spiritual body. And so it is written, The first man Adam became a living being. The last Adam became a life-giving spirit. Life on earth takes place in a "natural" body like that of Adam, who brought death into the world with his disobedience. When we die, this natural body is buried. Our life in the Kingdom of Heaven will take place in a "spiritual" body, like the resurrected body of Jesus Christ, Who is called the "last Adam" in the sense that He undid the harm brought about by Adam's disobedience. (For a description of the spiritual body of God's Kingdom, see this study and "Food For Thought Comments" of 2 Cor. 5:1–2.)

> FOOD FOR THOUGHT: (d). Why does verse 44 imply such a complete distinction between the natural and the spiritual body? Is it not possible to be spiritual in this life?

15:46. However, the spiritual is not first, but the natural, and afterward the spiritual. Just as God's most superior creation was His last (man), so too, the more superior spiritual body follows the inferior physical body.

15:47. The first man was of the earth, made of dust; the second Man is the Lord from heaven. God created the first *type* of man (Adam), a human being, from the dust of the earth (Gen. 2:7). The second type of Man (Christ) was not created. He was sent from Heaven, and took on flesh (John 1:14) through the Theotokos, making Him both human and divine.

15:48–49. As was the man of dust, so also are those who are made of dust; and as is the heavenly Man, so also are those who are heavenly. And as we have borne the image of the man of dust, we shall also bear the image of the heavenly Man. Because of his disobedience, Adam was condemned to return physically to the dust from which he came. Because we are descended from Adam and Eve and have, therefore, inherited the consequences (not the guilt)[10] of their original sin, we live in a world where temptation abounds and the flesh is weak (Mt. 26:41). Thus we have all sinned, and all (except those alive at the Second Coming of Christ) will die. Jesus Christ came to earth to give all mankind the opportunity to rise above the sinfulness of the world and to be "saved" from that condemnation by being "born again" spiritually "of water and the spirit" (Jn. 3:3–6), through the Sacraments of Baptism and Chrismation. We can thereby become a part of the Body of Christ and receive the gift of the Holy Spirit, to be part of the "heavenly," able to grow in holiness in imitation of Christ as an outgrowth of love for Him and in preparation for joining Him fully one day. We may have to pass through death, but death will not hold us, as it did not hold Christ.

> There are four forms of wisdom: first, moral judgment, or the knowledge of what should and should not be done, combined with watchfulness of the intellect; second, self-restraint, whereby our moral

purpose is safeguarded and kept free from all acts, thoughts and words that do not accord with God; third, courage, or strength and endurance in sufferings, trials and temptations encountered on the spiritual path; and fourth, justice, which consists of maintaining a proper balance between the first three. These four general virtues arise from the three powers of the soul in the following manner: from the intelligence, or intellect, come moral judgment and justice, or discrimination [discernment]; from the desiring power comes self-restraint; and from the incensive power comes courage.

Each virtue lies between two unnatural passions. Moral judgment lies between craftiness and thoughtlessness; self-restraint, between obduracy and licentiousness; courage, between overbearingness and cowardice; justice between over-frugality and greed. The Four virtues constitute an image of the Heavenly man, while the eight unnatural passions constitute an image of the earthly man.

PETER OF DAMASKOS[11]

Rather than *"we shall also bear,"* which would refer to the resurrected body that the righteous will receive, Chrysostom wrote that the correct translation of the original Greek text of 15:49 is *"let us also bear* the image of the Heavenly Man."[12] This means that, as we have sinned, after the example of Adam, let us with fervor participate in righteousness, after the example of Christ.

15:50. Now this I say, brethren, that flesh and blood cannot inherit the kingdom of God; nor does corruption inherit incorruption. Flesh and blood are elements of the natural body, which needs food to sustain it and is subject to sickness, injury, decay, and death. This type of body cannot be a part of the Kingdom of Heaven, where nothing corruptible can exist.   A body that is corruptible cannot inherit incorruptibility.

15:51–54. Behold, I tell you a mystery: We shall not all sleep, but we shall all be changed ... in a moment, in the twinkling of an eye, at the last trumpet.   For the trumpet will sound, and the dead will be raised incorruptible, and we shall be changed.   For this corruptible must put on incorruption, and this mortal must put on immortality.   So when this corruptible has put on incorruption, and this mortal has put on immortality, then shall be brought to pass the saying that is written: "Death is swallowed up in victory." Some will be, and so will remain, alive at the Second Coming of Christ.   At the sound of God's trumpet (I Thess. 4:13–18), the dead will rise, and everyone will be changed from corruptible (capable of sin and decay) and mortal (capable of death), to incorruptible and immortal.   Then the final enemy (death of the body) will have been conquered, in fulfillment of prophecy (Isaiah 25:8).

15:55. O Death, where is your sting? O Hades, where is your victory? These wondrous words were quoted by John Chrysostom, Archbishop of Constantinople (+407), in his Resurrection sermon, which is read at the Paschal Liturgy in every Orthodox Church each year.

Death no longer has the sting it had before Christ died to atone for our sins and was resurrected to show us that there is life after death:

Before the Crucifixion and Resurrection of Christ, the price for entering the Kingdom was being perfect according to the Mosaic Law of the Old Testament.   This precluded anyone (except Enoch and Elijah, who were perfect, not in the sense

196

that Christ was, but in relation to what had been revealed to them in their time in history [Gen. 5:24 and 2 Kings 2:11]) from escaping the clutches of Hades upon their death. The victory of Hades then was every human being, body and soul.

After Christ's Resurrection, Hades lost the souls of believers but *retained* the victory of their bodies. At the general Resurrection, the Devil will lose this final round.

15:56–57. The sting of death is sin, and the strength of sin is the law. But thanks are to God, Who gives us the victory through our Lord Jesus Christ. The Old Testament Law condemned sinners. It gave sin power over man because it showed him he would have to be absolutely perfect to earn salvation (Jas. 2:10). Since this is impossible in this world in which Satan has power, man needed to be rescued from this damning dilemma. So God sent His Son to do for us what we cannot do for ourselves.

Death has lost its sting of permanence for those who are guilt-free through Christ (by being a part of Him). We owe thanks, praise, and worship to God, Who through His Son provided this victory for us.

> Jesus Christ is now the true mediator between God and men, granting us through faith and the Holy Spirit a share in Himself. To share in the life of the Heavenly Man we are called to be faithful to Him, become like Him in virtue. This cannot be accomplished without repentance, the recognition of sins, and the confession which a merciful God has provided for us. Thus we may be reconciled to Him and recover the boldness which Adam had with his Creator, and speak to him as "friend to friend" and see Him clearly.
> SYMEON THE NEW THEOLOGIAN[13]

15:58. Therefore, my beloved brethren, be steadfast, immovable, always abounding in the work of the Lord, knowing that your labor is not in vain in the Lord. All who continue the up-hill climb to live Christ-like lives will reap the fruit of their struggle.

> And these things I say, neither to grieve you nor to throw you into despair, but lest nourished by vain and cold hopes, and placing confidence in this person or that, we should neglect our own proper goodness. For if we be slothful, there will be neither righteous man nor prophet nor apostle nor anyone to stand by us. But if we have been earnest, having in sufficiency the plea which comes from each man's own works, we shall obtain the good things that are laid up for them that love God to which may we all attain.
>
> CHRYSOSTOM[14]

No matter how difficult life on earth may be—or how much we may suffer in the pursuit of the Christ-like life—confidence in the certainty of Resurrection sustains us.

FOOD FOR THOUGHT COMMENTS

(a). The Apostle Peter denied Jesus three times (Mt. 26:31–35,69–75) and Paul persecuted Christians (Acts 8:1–3); yet they went on to become leaders in the Church. How can this be? Jesus came into the world to save sinners. Part of the Gospel He brought was that anyone who comes to Him with a truly repentant heart can be forgiven and given a chance to make a new start through the authority He gave the Apostles to loose and to bind sins (Jn. 20:22–23). This authority has been passed on in the Church since that time by apostolic succession, giving those who have sinned the opportunity to partake of the Sacrament of Repentance (Confession). Those who have sinned greatly and then experienced this forgiveness through Christ often become very zealous and devoted servants of our Lord because they recognize and are humbled by and grateful for God's abundant mercy. Peter and Paul are powerful examples of this phenomenon. Peter's denial of Christ was no less serious than Judas' betrayal, but Peter repented, so was forgiven, making him an important example for all Christians. John 21:15–17 points to the fact that Jesus gave Peter a chance to repent for each of the three times he had denied Christ. Paul's zealous persecution of Christians before he was confronted by Christ serves as an example of the fact that forgiveness is available to everyone.

(b). It seems that mankind has always instinctively known—or hoped—that there is some type of life after death. What in the human experience would contribute to this conclusion? God has provided many hints in nature to lead man to the great truth of resurrection:

There are daily proofs, such as the cycle of daylight and darkness, day into night and into day again.

Also, the cycle of wakefulness and sleep. We sleep, we awaken—a prefiguration of death and resurrection. Sleep is a blessing, necessary for a healthy, vibrant life. When we are tired, we enter sleep gratefully. If we live a long, full, and productive life, contributing to those around us, knowing life's purpose (which is to find God [Acts 17:26–27] and become one with Him), and have prepared for the eternal Kingdom, we will approach death peacefully. This is one of the things for which we pray at each Divine Liturgy: "a Christian end to our life, painless, blameless, peaceful, and of good defense before the fearful Judgment Seat of Christ."[15]

When death comes early in life, it is not easy to accept. It's like going to sleep too early—giving up much of the day. But still there is Resurrection! Those who understand this die peacefully and those they leave behind are comforted with the hope that they can some day be together with their loved ones again. For these, death has lost its sting. This is why Christians, though they lament the death of loved ones, do not mourn in the same way as do those who do not have the hope of resurrection.

It is good to talk about death (but not to dwell on it) to try to understand why it is a part of life. If we do not, we build up a type of fear that prevents us from really living. It is said that some of the saints kept skeletons in their closets for this very reason. Any discussion of death, however, would be incomplete without also coming to an understanding of the truth of resurrection.

There are annual proofs: Summer fades into autumn, which rolls into winter, which bursts into spring again. Spring corresponds to man's youth, summer his prime, autumn the harvest years when he can enjoy the fruit of his labor. Winter, which corresponds to old age, can be marked by decline—but can also be rich, when used to look back on a life of meaning and to look forward with great expectation to resurrection and union with God. The seeming death of nature in winter is followed by resurrection in spring. It is fitting that Pascha be in spring—all part of God's perfect plan!

God has also implanted in man the desire to live forever, as another hint of resurrection:

> Just as, the body being mortal, its senses also have mortal things as their objects, so, since the soul contemplates and beholds immortal things, it follows that it is immortal and lives forever. For ideas and

> thoughts about immortality never desert the soul, but abide in it, and are as it were the fuel in it which ensures its immortality. This then is why the soul has the capacity for beholding God, and is its own way thereto, receiving not from without but from herself the knowledge and apprehension of the Word of God.
>
> ATHANASIUS[16]

Everything in nature points to termination followed by renewal. At the end of its life cycle, a caterpillar spins a chrysalis, which looks to the naked eye like dead matter. But when the time is right, a magnificent butterfly emerges from the remains. When, in turn, the butterfly dies, it may be eaten by a bird, which may eventually be eaten by a larger creature, and on and on in the biological chain, ultimately to return to the soil, fertilizing it to produce new life. Nothing in nature really dies but is just recycled (and no one in any laboratory has ever created a living cell—all must come from pre-existing cells). Shall then man, created by and made in the image of God, when he dies, perish and crumble to nothing?

Upon death, the body is planted in the earth like a seed. At the Second Coming of Christ, from this seed a new body will rise to join the soul, which, since death, has been experiencing a foretaste of its eternal condition (much as those who dream during episodes of sleep may have many active experiences, though their bodies remain immobile upon their beds). This will be "the restoration of our nature to its original condition."[17] And so those whose lives on earth have shown faith in and love for God will be with Him forever, body and soul.

Through the story about the Rich Man and Lazarus, Christ teaches that "when a human being, whether sinner or righteous, dies, his soul is taken to a spiritual realm, where, according to the kind of life one has lived, one experiences pain or joy (Lk. 16:22–25)."[18] The souls of both the righteous

Lazarus and the unrighteous rich man are described as "continuing to exist after death in a conscious state, capable of feeling, thinking, and remembering."

> In the first life, of which God Himself became the Creator, there was presumably neither old age, nor infancy, nor the sufferings caused by the many kinds of diseases, nor any other type of bodily misery; for it is not likely that God created such things. Human nature was a divine sort of thing, before humanity started on the course of evil. All these things attacked us when evil entered our life. Therefore the life without evil will not need to be subject to the conditions which have happened because of evil. ...
>
> If a man wearing a ragged tunic should be denuded of his garment, he would no longer see on himself the ugliness of what was discarded. Likewise, when we have put off that dead and ugly garment which was made for us from irrational skins [mortality] ... we throw off every part of our irrational skin along with the removal of the garment. These are the things which we have received from the irrational skin: sexual intercourse, conception, childbearing, dirt, lactation, nourishment, evacuation, gradual growth to maturity, the prime of life, old age, disease, and death. If we will not be wearing that skin, how shall we preserve the conditions which come from it.
>
> GREGORY OF NYSSA[19]

(d). Why does verse 44 imply such a complete distinction between the natural and the spiritual body? Is it not possible to be spiritual in this life? We can be spiritual in this life because of the indwelling of the Holy Spirit, received through the Sacrament of Chrismation. The level of spirituality we attain, however, depends upon the extent to which we cooperate with God's grace by trying to avoid sin and practice holiness. After the Resurrection, there will be no more sin and decay to hamper our spiritual growth—which will continue eternally, for perfection is not static (see this study of 1 Cor. 2:10–13).

CHAPTER SIXTEEN

Closing Concerns

In concluding this letter, in which he has advised the Christians of Corinth about many doctrinal and moral matters, Paul turns to practical concerns and to bringing the Corinthians up-to-date on news within the Church as a whole.

16:1. Now concerning the collection for the saints, as I have given orders to the churches of Galatia, so you must do also. As an expression of the love described in Chapter 13, the Corinthians are to help provide for the poverty-stricken Christians in Jerusalem (Acts 11:27–30; Rom. 15:26). To encourage a spirit of togetherness and emulation, Paul tells them that he has instructed the Galatians to do likewise. The Church of today is likewise charged with the responsibility of being concerned with the well-being of the worldwide Church.

16:2. On the first day of the week let each one of you lay something aside, storing up as he may prosper, that there be no collections when I come. They are to set something aside each Sunday, the Lord's Day, for the purpose of helping others. The noting of Sunday suggests that already this day was the focal point for Christian worship (see Acts 20:7; note the long sermon). The Sabbath (Saturday) is still a holy day but as a day of preparation for Sunday, the day of the Resurrection of Christ.

> In the new dispensation of grace ... this "holy" and "chosen day" (Lev. 23:35) is called "the Lord's day" (Rev. 1:10), because on it the more lordly and masterful events in Christ's life took place: the Annunciation, the Nativity, the Resurrection; and on this day the general resurrection of the dead will also

take place. For it was on this day that God created the visible light, says John of Damaskos, and it will also be the day of Christ's Second Coming. Thus it will last for limitless ages: it is both day one and the eighth day, as being outside the other seven ages that have days and nights in them.

PETER OF DAMASKOS[1]

John Chrysostom extols the blessings of the Lord's Day and asserts that such a day is perfect for giving to help others:

Call to mind ... what you attained to on this day: how all the unutterable blessings and that which is the root and the beginning of our life took place on this day. But not in this regard only is the season convenient for a zealous benevolence, but also because it has rest and immunity from toils: the souls when released from labors becoming readier and more apt to show pity. Moreover, the communicating also on that day in Mysteries so tremendous and immortal instills great zealousness.[2]

16:3–4. And when I come, whomever you approve by your letters I will send to bear your gift to Jerusalem. But if it is fitting that I go also, they will go with me. The Corinthians are to choose someone to take their contributions to Jerusalem. This is a precaution designed to avoid any hint of indiscretion with regard to Paul's use of the money collected (see 2 Cor. 8:19–21).

> **FOOD FOR THOUGHT:** (a). Why is it important for Christians to avoid any hint of indiscretion as they pursue their various ministries and walks of life?

16:5–8. Now I will come to you when I pass through Macedonia (for I am passing through Macedonia). And it

may be that I will remain, or even spend the winter with you, that you may send me on my journey, wherever I go. For I do not wish to see you now on the way; but I hope to stay a while with you, if the Lord permits. But I will tarry in Ephesus until Pentecost. With the phrase "if the Lord permits" (or, as we say, "God willing"), Paul reveals that although he has plans for the near future, he is always mindful that God may have other plans for him and that His will prevails.

16:9. For a great and effective door has opened to me, and there are many adversaries. He plans to stay in Ephesus a little while because he has found an opportunity to be very effective in his ministry there. Progress however, is slow-going because of great opposition to his teaching of the Gospel.

> FOOD FOR THOUGHT: (b). Why do those who do God's work always encounter difficulties and delays? How are we to react to this opposition?

16:10–12. And if Timothy comes, see that he may be with you without fear; for he does the work of the Lord, as I also do. Therefore let no one despise him. But send him on his journey in peace, that he may come to me; for I am waiting for him with the brethren. Now concerning our brother Apollos, I strongly urged him to come to you with the brethren, but he was quite unwilling to come at this time; however, he will come when he has a convenient time. Paul brings them up-to-date on the status of his fellow workers, a touching reminder that he is a part of a group of disciples working together as a team.

16:13–14. Watch, stand fast in the faith, be brave, be strong. Let all that you do be done with love. Paul's final words of wisdom: resist the tendency toward spiritual slumber and wavering intensity, fervent one moment, lukewarm or cold the next; have courage to speak out and to forge ahead with God's work; stay the course when difficulties arise. All of God's work, whether teaching, admonishing, administering, learning, or laboring, must be done in a spirit of love for God and all His creations—else the effort is useless.

16:15–16. I urge you, brethren—you know the household of Stephanas, that it is the first fruits of Achaia, and that they have devoted themselves to the ministry of the saints—that you also submit to such, and to everyone who works and labors with us. The household of Stephanas was the first to be converted in Achaia (1:16), a province that included Corinth and Athens. The members of this family thereafter devoted themselves to the building up of the Church. Paul advises the Corinthians to follow the example and the instruction of this family and others like them.

> **FOOD FOR THOUGHT:** (c).To what practice of the Orthodox way of life do these verses correspond?

16:17-18. I am glad about the coming of Stephanas, Fortunatus, and Achaicus, for what was lacking on your part they supplied. For they refreshed my spirit and yours. Therefore acknowledge such men. These men were the ones who visited Paul while he was in Ephesus, informing him of the problems in Corinth, supplementing what he had heard from other sources. They then carried his response (this epistle) back with them. Paul is pleased and encouraged by their willingness to take a long difficult journey for the good of the Church, as are the people of Corinth.

16:19. The churches of Asia greet you. Aquila and Priscilla greet you heartily in the Lord, with the church

that is in their house. Paul extends greetings to the Corinthians from the other churches in the area, and from Aquila and Priscilla, a courageous Christian couple (Acts 18:2–3, Rom. 16:3–5), knowledgeable in the word of God (Acts 18:26). This is a further effort to emphasize the unity that should exist between all Christians (1 Cor. 1:2).

16:20. All the brethren greet you. Greet one another with a holy kiss. Christians have always greeted one another with this "holy kiss" on the cheek, in recognition of each other as members of the Body of Christ (Rom. 16:16, 1 Pet. 5:14, 1 Thess. 5:26). When exchanged sincerely, this acknowledgment of oneness in Christ can serve to dissolve tensions and dissension.

> **FOOD FOR THOUGHT:** (d). It was a custom among the early Christians to exchange this "holy kiss" of love and peace during the Divine Liturgy, before the Confession of Faith. What is the symbolism of this custom?

16:21. The salutation with my own hand—Paul. Paul normally dictated his letters, adding his signature and a final word to assure authenticity (see 2 Thess. 3:17).

16:22. If anyone does not love the Lord Jesus Christ, let him be accursed. O Lord, come! He who does not love Christ (and does not live a life that affirms this love) will be cursed to spend eternity separated from God. This will be a result not of God casting him away but rather of cutting himself off from the love of God:

> The person who has opted for the path of evil, and actually commits evil, should blame only himself, for no one can force him to commit it, since God created him with free will. Hence he will merit God's praise

when he chooses the path of goodness; for he does so
not from any necessity of his nature, as is the case
with animals and inanimate things that participate
passively in goodness, but as befits a being that God
has honored with the gift of intelligence. We
ourselves deliberately and willfully choose to do evil,
being coached in it by its discoverer. God, who is good
beyond goodness, does not force us, lest being forced
and still disobeying we should be even more culpable.
Nor does He take from us the freedom that in His
goodness He has bestowed upon us.

PETER OF DAMASKOS[3]

In the original text, the Hebrew words *maran atha* are used,
meaning: "Our Lord is come," the Messiah has arrived,
according to Chrysostom; "our Lord cometh," implying imminence of the Second Coming of Christ; or "O Lord, come!" (a plea
that He come again soon) according to others.

In any case, Paul's words convey the glory of the Incarnation of
Christ: He became man to give man a way back to the
Kingdom. How can anyone reject this opportunity—or live an
unchanged life of indifference to it?

**16:23–24. The grace of our Lord Jesus Christ be with you.
My love be with you all in Christ Jesus. Amen**. Paul
began this epistle with his wish that they be blessed with grace
(1:3). He ends with the same thought, and sends his love to all.
His having to chastise and correct them does not diminish his
love for them as his spiritual children. On the contrary,
because he loves them, he continues to be concerned for their
spiritual well-being.

> **FOOD FOR THOUGHT:** (e). True love includes
> concern for the spiritual as well as the physical
> well-being of our loved ones. Whom does God say

we should love?   What then is our most important obligation to them?

FOOD FOR THOUGHT COMMENTS

(a). Why is it important for Christians to avoid any hint of indiscretion as they pursue their various ministries and walks of life? Because those looking on who do not have strong faith can become disheartened and turn away from the Church if it appears that those closely involved with it are not honest and sincere. It must also be said that there are many who look for the chance to discredit the Church and those in it as an excuse for their living apart from it.

(b). Why do those who do God's work always encounter difficulties and delays? How are we to react to this opposition? The Devil does all he can to deter those who try to live a Christ-like life. Read Rev. 12:12–17, with the following symbolism:

woman: The Theotokos (Mother of God)/The Church
(see Gen. 3:15, Jn. 19:26).

child: Jesus Christ / the Gospel.

two wings of great eagle: the Old and New
 Testaments / prayer and fasting (which strengthened Jesus when the Devil tried to tempt Him [Mt. 4:1–11]).

serpent spewed water out of his mouth: Satan spread heresies to water down Christ's teachings and divide the Church.

210

earth helped the Woman: the Martyrs, Saints, Church Fathers, and leaders of the Ecumenical Councils preserved the Truth with their lives and with their work.

The angel of lights, Lucifer (now called the Devil, Satan), was cast out of Heaven for trying to overthrow God (Rev. 12:7–9). He and his cohorts can never be a part of the Kingdom (12:8), so they want to cause as many as possible to suffer with them (12:12). Satan tried to destroy the Church with heresies (12:15), but the truth was preserved by the decisions of the Ecumenical councils and the writings of the Fathers of the Church, which explain and protect the true interpretations of scripture (12:16). As a last resort, the Devil does all in his power to thwart those who try to live their faith in God and His Son (12:17).

We should, therefore, not be surprised when we find doing God's work slow-going and difficult. We should never, however, give up—but rather "press toward the goal" (Phil. 3:14). If we do our part, God will do His. He will never desert us (Phil. 4:7, 13).

(c). To what practice of the Orthodox way of life do verses 15–16 correspond? The Orthodox way of life includes learning about and trying to emulate the lives of the Saints—in that they sought always to emulate Christ. Having examples of others who have gone before us helps us to continue the struggle (Phil. 3:17).

(d). It was a custom among the early Christians to exchange this "holy kiss" of love and peace during the Divine Liturgy, before the Confession of Faith. What is the symbolism of this custom? To receive the Body and Blood of Christ is to become one with Him. All who participate in this Mystery, therefore, are united through Him. The holy kiss of love and peace during the Divine Liturgy symbolizes this oneness and accord that should exist literally as well as figuratively among members of the Church.

In the early Church, "the greatest pains were taken to see that this ... did not degenerate into a formality ... the *Didache* (insisted) on the necessity of reconciling any fellow Christians who might be at variance with each other before they could attend the Eucharist together," or it was considered that their "sacrifice [was] defiled." It was the duty of the Bishop and presbyters to mediate in all such disputes between members of their own church, and regular sessions were held for this purpose by what was virtually a Christian Sanhedrin of elders (presbyters) under the Christian high priest (the Bishop). The Syrian *Didascalia of the Apostles* orders them to "Let your judgments be held on the second day of the week, that if perchance anyone should contest the sentence of your words, you may have space until the Sabbath to compose the matter, and may make peace between them on Sunday."[4]

(e). True love includes concern for the spiritual as well as the physical well-being of our loved ones. Whom does God say we should love? What then is our most important obligation to them? If we want long, healthy, happy lives for our loved ones on earth, we should even more want for them eternal life with God in His Kingdom. This means we must try to help them learn about God and what He expects of His people.

God calls us to love our neighbor (those with whom we come in contact in our lives [Mk. 12:31]), which includes those who might be considered our enemies (Mt. 5:44). This means we

212

should be concerned for their spiritual well-being also—the real test of love.

Amen.

The Second Letter of Paul
to the Corinthians

CHAPTER ONE

Comfort in the Midst of Tribulation

Paul's epistles to the Corinthians served the early Church as a guide to the Christian life. They play the same role for contemporary readers. The first epistle covers basics such as the need for love, fellowship, and unity in Christ in the Church; God's plan for our salvation through the Cross; Christian morality; male and female roles; the gifts of the Holy Spirit; the importance of order in worship; the Mystery of the Eucharist and our participation in it; and the promised resurrection of the dead. This second epistle delves more deeply into spiritual matters such as growth in holiness, the role suffering plays in the Christian life, the need for almsgiving and prayer, the power of repentance and forgiveness, that which happens after death, the types of bodies the righteous and the unrighteous will have after the Resurrection, and the conditions of life in Heaven. In this letter, Paul also bares his heart and soul. He has experienced the extremes of emotion, from the deep despair of unrelenting persecution and isolation to the ecstasy of being in the presence of God. His long, personal association with the Christians of Corinth allows him to share his disappointments and fears as well as his joys.

1:1. Paul, an apostle of Jesus Christ by the will of God, and Timothy our brother, to the Church of God which is at Corinth, with all the saints who are in all Achaia: Paul begins this epistle in a way that is common for him, by alluding to having literally been called by God to be an Apostle (Acts 9:1–22). This fact is especially important in this instance because there are those in Corinth who question his authority to teach the Gospel of Jesus Christ. Timothy, his spiritual son and co-worker, had visited the Corinthians as promised to reinforce Paul's work with them (1 Cor. 4:17) and is now back in Macedonia with Paul.

Achaia was a Roman province covering that part of ancient Greece that was south of Thessaly and Macedonia; Corinth was its capital. However, all of Greece was often designated broadly as Achaia. Paul's *First Epistle to the Corinthians* contained truths that they specifically needed to be reminded of or to have clarified. In this *Second Epistle*, he addresses not only the Christians in Corinth but also those in all Achaia, because he felt that they too were in need of counsel. His reference to a broader audience than the direct recipients of this letter indicates his awareness that these writings would be shared.

1:2. Grace to you and peace from God our Father and the Lord Jesus Christ. To receive *grace* is to partake of the energies of God (a bit of the power of the Creator) for the purpose of sanctification. We were created for fellowship with God (Acts 17:26–28). God is Holy, so to fulfill our potential we must become holy. But we cannot do so solely by our own efforts, only with God's grace. *Peace from God* is the inner state of contentment experienced by those who address their "reason for being" by cooperating with grace to make growth in holiness, in Christ's image, the focal point of their lives. If there is no grace in our lives, there can be no peace.

> Peace is serenity of mind, tranquility of soul, simplicity of heart, the bond of love, the fellowship of charity. It takes away enmities, restrains wars, holds back anger, treads down pride, loves the humble, calms those who quarrel, reconciles those who are enemies and is pleasing and acceptable to all. It seeks nothing that belongs to another; regards nothing as its own. It teaches a love that has never learned to

hate. It knows not how to be lifted above itself. It knows not how to be puffed up.

He who acquires this peace should hold fast to it. He who has broken it should strive to restore it. He who has lost it should seek earnestly to find it again. For whoever is found without this peace is rejected by the Father, disinherited by the Son and becomes a stranger to the Holy Spirit. ... He who is deliberately at enmity with another Christian cannot have the friendship of Christ.

AUGUSTINE[1]

FOOD FOR THOUGHT: (a). To whom does God grant grace? Do we play a role in this matter, or are we subject to His whim as to whom He will give this gift and to whom He will not? (b). In the events of life, does God first give the grace that enables righteous action, or does He wait for righteous action first, then grant grace to strengthen our efforts?

1:3–4. Blessed be the God and Father of our Lord Jesus Christ, the Father of mercies and God of all comfort, Who comforts us in all our tribulation, that we may be able to comfort those who are in any trouble, with the comfort with which we ourselves are comforted by God. Jesus Christ brought the world the good news of life after death in God's eternal Kingdom for those who love Him. He was persecuted, scourged, and then crucified because the world did not want to hear His message. Now, about a quarter of a century later, Paul is following a similar path. He expresses his adoration of God, Who comforts him during these times of tribulation. With the understanding that "all things work together for good to those who love God" (Rom. 8:28), Paul affirms from experience that those who, during very difficult times, have felt the comfort that only God can provide can in turn help bring that comfort to others.

> **FOOD FOR THOUGHT:** (c). Why did the world not want to hear the message that Jesus brought? Why does the world still not want to listen? (d). Why does a loving God allow troubled times to enter the lives of His people?

1:5. For as the sufferings of Christ abound in us, so our consolation also abounds through Christ. Because Paul imitates Christ in his willingness to suffer in order that God's work may be done, he receives divine comfort. No amount of suffering is beyond the realm of this consolation. In the midst of agony, he who keeps his focus on God feels enveloped by His warm Presence. This gift cushions the harsh jolts of life and at the same time transforms the sufferer, rendering him able to endure the unendurable. With this gift, Stephen withstood, even joyfully, the blows of the stones cast at him by those who opposed the Gospel (Acts 7:55–60). Just as there would have been no Resurrection without the Cross, this type of comfort comes only as the companion of righteous suffering.

> Nothing can be harder to bear than bodily pain; nevertheless, because of this joy in God, what even to hear of is intolerable becomes both tolerable and longed for; and if you take the martyr from the cross or the gridiron barely still breathing, you will find a treasure of joy within him that words cannot describe.
> CHRYSOSTOM[2]

1:6. Now if we are afflicted, it is for your consolation and salvation, which is effective for enduring the same sufferings which we also suffer. Or if we are comforted, it is for your consolation and salvation. The Gospel is especially powerful when its teachers are not only willing to endure the tribulation their work inevitably brings, which proves their faith in its message of salvation, but when they also seem to possess deep inner joy in spite of troubled times. Those witnessing this demonstrated faith, love, and power are consoled, strengthened, and encouraged to believe and live by God's word—so the cycle continues.

The subject of suffering stirs deep emotions. No one relishes the agony of physical or emotional pain. It is natural, alas human, to want to avoid situations with that potential. It is supernatural—touching upon the divine—to willingly endure voluntary suffering like persecution or deprivation in order that God's purposes be served, or to endure involuntary suffering like severe illness or loss without turning away from God. Dealing with the troubled times of life can leave us bitter or better—the choice is ours.

1:7. And our hope for you is steadfast because we know that as you are partakers of the sufferings, so also you will partake of the consolation. Paul hopes that all Christians will emulate his example and not shy away from the difficulties that living by and teaching the Gospel bring. His desire is not that we suffer but that we partake of the fruit that comes from willingness to endure suffering when necessary, in order that Christ's work be done (see Rom. 8:16–18 and Chapter 12 of this study).

> For no one who is self-indulgent has fellowship with Christ ... nor anyone lax, lazy, indifferent or loose in behavior and morals. He who is in affliction and temptation and who is journeying on the narrow way is near to Him ... so do not grieve when you are in affliction, considering with Whom you have fellowship, how you are purified by trials, and how great is your gain. ... Neither afflictions nor

conspiracies, nor any other thing has power to grieve
the right-minded soul.

CHRYSOSTOM[3]

1:8. For we do not want you to be ignorant, brethren, of our trouble which came to us in Asia: that we were burdened beyond measure, above strength, so that we despaired even of life. In the course of his ministry in Ephesus, Paul faced many adversaries (1 Cor. 16:8–9) and his life had been in great danger (Acts 19:21–30).

1:9. Yes, we had the sentence of death in ourselves, that we should not trust in ourselves but in God Who raises the dead ... God allowed Paul to face the ever-present danger of death so he would learn that some things were beyond his control. Only when we have exhausted all of the world's means of dealing with a serious problem can we begin to understand that ultimately we can rely only on God for those things in life that really matter. When such events seem to be leading to a certain inevitable conclusion, then suddenly, after fervent prayer, they take a favorable turn against all odds—God's existence and power are demonstrated.

> When enemies devise mischief, God allows it to come
> even to the trial and then works miracles, as in the
> case of the furnace and the lions (Dan. 3:25).

CHRYSOSTOM[4]

1:10. Who delivered us from so great a death, and does deliver us; in Whom we trust that He will still deliver us ... In Ephesus, God shielded Paul from death by the hands of his enemies. He is confident that this deliverance will continue through future trials, so he can continue his work.

When facing adversity, we should first turn to God in prayer and in Scripture, seeking His guidance, assistance, and strength. If we then take the actions that seem best under the circumstances and trust God by leaving the rest to Him, that which will surface, endure, and triumph is our love for God and His for us (Mt. 3:12)—no matter the outcome of the immediate situation.

God is in control. He has ultimate power over everything, including death. He created man to live forever. Thus, a form of life—of the soul—continues beyond the death of the body. In accordance with His divine plan, at the Second Coming of Christ, all who died believing in Him as Messiah will rise from their graves, with new bodies, and will inherit an eternal life of blessedness (I Thess. 4:13–18). God constantly reassures us of this truth with signs of resurrection all around us: the new life of spring that follows the deadness of winter in the cycle of the seasons, the daily routine of activity followed by sleep then reawakening, and the various crises of life.

> When God lifts up again a man who is despaired of ... He demonstrates a resurrection, snatching out of the very jaws of death him who had fallen into them: so in the case of those restored either out of grievous sickness or insupportable trials, it is natural to say, "We have seen a resurrection of the dead."
>
> CHRYSOSTOM[5]

FOOD FOR THOUGHT: (e). What tests of faith are we likely to face in the times in which we live?

1:11. you also helping together in prayer for us, that thanks may be given by many persons on our behalf for the gift granted to us through many ... While clearly attributing his deliverance from danger to God's mercy (vs. 10), Paul emphasizes that this mercy is granted in response to prayer, private and corporate.

We can pray in our own home; but it is not possible to pray there as in church, where the number is large and where prayer is offered up with one accord. When you pray alone your prayers are not heard in the same way as when you pray with your brethren. In the church there is something greater; the prayers are of one mind and one voice; there is the bond of charity and the prayer of the priests. It is for this reason the priests are there, so that joining their more efficacious prayers to those less strong of the people, they may ascend together with them to Heaven. For if the prayer of the Church helped Peter and delivered him from prison [Acts 12:5], how can you ignore its power.

CHRYSOSTOM[6]

Jesus' actions often illustrated the fact that God responds to prayer. He mercifully healed the daughter of the woman of Canaan after "she came and worshiped Him," saying, "Lord, help me" (Mt. 15:21–28); and He responded to the centurion's plea to "speak the word only," and his servant was healed from a distance (Mt. 8:5–13).

Paul also reminds us to remember to thank God—even if His answer to our prayers differs from our desires. These occasions present opportunities to show our trust in Him.

FOOD FOR THOUGHT: (f). We know that God, in His omniscience, knows even the number of hairs on the heads of His people (Mt. 10:30) and does not need us to keep Him informed of situations on earth. Why then is there such biblical emphasis on prayer for one another, which is echoed in the Divine Liturgy and in the life of the Church? Does God always answer prayer? Are our prayers for others always of assistance to them? (g). Do our prayers for those who are experiencing difficulties eliminate the need to offer practical physical or emotional assistance?

Chrysostom points out that if we expect God's mercy in our lives in answer to prayer, we must be "worthy." As an example, he cites the Ninevites, who were saved when "they turned from their evil way" (Jonah 3:10). No one is ever worthy in the sense that they are deserving of God's mercy, for "all have sinned, and fall short of the glory of God" (Rom. 3:23). Rather, worthiness is the state of grace of those who continually repent and acknowledge their dependence on Christ as Savior. Sincere repentance includes effort to change, so the worthy are those who try always to live in obedience to Christ, and who, when they inevitably fall short of this goal, rise to try again. Those who make this struggle a way of life demonstrate true faith in and love for God—the criteria for salvation.

> For our prayers to be heard by God, they must first come from one who is worthy of receiving. Secondly, they should be made in accordance with the laws of God. Thirdly, they should be unceasing. Fourthly, it is required of us that we pray with earnestness and not in a worldly manner. Fifthly, that we join with Him in bringing them about by asking only for what is fitting and expedient for us.
>
> CHRYSOSTOM[7]

As we mature spiritually, our prayers will change. The things of the world will seem less urgent. We will spend more time in praise, thanksgiving, and worship, and our petitions will reflect the desire that God's will be done.

> Seek from God our King the things that are worthy of Him and ... do not cease praying till you receive them. ... If a month goes by, or a year, or three years, or

four, or many, do not give up praying till you receive what you ask for; but ask on in faith, and at the same time be steadfast in doing good. It often will happen that someone strives earnestly for chastity in his youth. Then pleasure begins to undermine his resolution, desires awaken his nature, he grows weak in prayer, wine overcomes his youth, modesty perishes, and he becomes another man. So we change because we have not stood firm against our passions with high courage of soul. It behooves us, therefore, to resist all things, yet we must also cry out to God, that He may bring us aid.

BASIL[8]

If God does not seem to respond to our prayers, we should reflect upon our life, our spiritual condition, and those things we ask of Him. As we pray for guidance we may begin to understand that there is a reason He does not grant particular petitions. Paul prayed that he be freed from his *thorn in the flesh* only until he realized that this affliction made his ministry more effective (2 Cor. 12:7–10).

1:12. For our boasting is this: the testimony of our conscience that we conducted ourselves in the world in simplicity and godly sincerity, not with fleshly wisdom but by the grace of God, and more abundantly toward you. Paul's life is dedicated to doing God's work. He finds comfort in the fact that the suffering he has been experiencing was not caused by any wrongdoing on his part. The consolation referred to in 2 Cor. 1:3–7 is the divine comfort given to those whose lives demonstrate faith, whereas this verse points to the human comfort of a clear conscience. A wonderful sense of well-being is enjoyed by those who can look back on life and see that God had been at work in their helplessness if they also know that they tried, aided by His grace, to follow His will.

Seeing that Paul had said *God comforted us,* and *God delivered us,* and had ascribed all to His mercies and their prayers, lest he should thus make the hearer negligent, presuming on God's mercy only and the prayers of others, he shows that he had contributed a great deal himself ... from the purity of his life.

CHRYSOSTOM[9]

1:13–14. For we are not writing any other things to you than what you read or understand. Now I trust you will understand, even to the end (as also you have understood us in part), that we are your boast, as you also are ours, in the day of the Lord Jesus. Paul teaches only the word of God as he received it. Those who accept his message of salvation through Christ—and try to live by it—will be part of God's Kingdom because of their faith. The student is grateful to the teacher for introducing him to the Gospel. In turn, the teacher rejoices over those who, by responding favorably, became the fruit of his faith.

1:15–17. And in this confidence I intended to come to you before, that you might have a second benefit—to pass by way of you to Macedonia, to come again from Macedonia to you, and be helped by you on my way to Judea. Therefore, when I was planning this, did I do it lightly? Or the things I plan, do I plan according to the flesh, that with me there should be Yes, Yes, and No, No? Because of the spiritual bond between them, Paul was anxious to spend more time with the Corinthians. Thus he had intended to stop by on his way to Macedonia as well as after leaving Macedonia on his way to Judea (1 Cor. 16:5). Due to changing conditions, however, he did not follow through with his original plan. Is he therefore fickle as his detractors claim? Does he say one thing but then do that which suits his fancy when the time comes to keep his word?

1:18–20. But as God is faithful, our word to you was not Yes and No. For the Son of God, Jesus Christ, Who was preached among you by us—by me, Silvanus, and Timothy—was not Yes and No, but in Him was Yes. For all the promises of God in Him are Yes, and in Him Amen, to the glory of God through us. Paul's change of itinerary casts no reflection on God's promises, which are steadfast. Man has limited knowledge; he must continually reassess situations in life in order to try to make the right decisions. God sees the whole picture; His word to us remains forever true and valid.

1:21–22. Now He Who establishes us with you in Christ and has anointed us is God, Who also has sealed us and given us the Spirit in our hearts as a deposit. The Holy Trinity is at work in every true believer. According to God's divine plan, His beloved "man" becomes a part of the Body of Christ (the Church) through Baptism and remains so through a life of faith. Thus all true Christians are united *in Christ*. Through the anointing of Chrismation, we receive the gift of the Holy Spirit. The consecrated myrrh used in this Sacrament indelibly inscribes the "seal," the mark of authenticity borne by those who thus receive this indwelling Presence, which brings grace, peace (2 Cor. 1:2), and guidance to those who submit themselves to God's will. The Holy Spirit acts through both of these Sacraments, evoking confidence and joy in believers, thus providing a *deposit* (Greek: arravon): a glimpse of that which awaits in the fullness of the Kingdom. Thus the joys of the Kingdom begin in this life, when we come to the realization of the existence and love of God, and grow to the degree that faith and love prevail within us.

> Being the light of the divinity, grace cannot remain hidden or unnoticed; acting in man, changing his nature, entering into a more and more intimate union with him, the divine energies become increasingly

perceptible, revealing to man the face of the living God, "the Kingdom of God present with power" (Mk. 9:1). This divine experience, says Palamas, is given to each according to his measure and can be more or less profound, depending on the worthiness of those who experience it. The full vision of the divinity having become perceptible in the uncreated light, in its deifying grace, is "the mystery of the eighth day"; it belongs to the future age. However, those who are worthy of it attain the sight of "the Kingdom of God come with power" in this life, as the three Apostles saw it on Mount Tabor.[10]

FOOD FOR THOUGHT: (h). Ever since the Holy Spirit descended upon the Apostles in the upper room in Jerusalem, giving them power to preach the Gospel of Jesus Christ to all nations (Acts 2), man has had access to His indwelling presence. But what was the role of the Holy Spirit in Old Testament times? Did He offer any assistance to man during that age? (i). Why did Jesus say He had to leave so the Holy Spirit could come (Jn. 16:7)? Were Jesus and the Comforter unable to be in the world at the same time?

1:23. Moreover I call God as witness against my soul, that to spare you I came no more to Corinth. Those who cooperate with the indwelling presence of the Holy Spirit also grow in discernment. When Timothy returned to Paul after spending time with the Corinthians to help them understand what the Gospel required of them (1 Cor. 4:17), he reported that there was still turmoil in the church there. At that point Paul had not yet returned to Corinth because of the delays and difficulties he had encountered in his ministry. After Timothy's report, however, Paul felt guided by the Holy Spirit to further delay his return until they had time to correct their ways, so he would not have to be harsh with them upon his arrival. He had given counsel. His next step was to draw back to allow the Holy Spirit to work in their hearts. In much the same way, after giving guidance, a concerned parent or teacher might at times delay further confrontation with his charges to allow them, of their own free will, to live up to what is expected of them. There are times to be aggressive and times to stand back a little to allow slow but willing growth rather than demand begrudging compliance.

> The mind is a wonderful thing, and therein we possess that which is in the image of the Creator. ... But the mind has two faculties: the one evil, that of the demons which draws us on to their own apostasy; and the divine and the good, which brings us to the likeness of God. When, therefore, the mind remains alone and unaided, it contemplates small things, commensurate with itself. When it yields to those who deceive it, it nullifies its proper judgment and is concerned with monstrous fancies. Then it considers wood to be no longer wood, but a god; then it looks on gold no longer as money, but as an object of worship. If, on the other hand, it assents to its diviner part and accepts the boons of the Spirit, then, so far as its nature admits, it becomes perceptive of the divine ... the mind which is impregnated with the Godhead of the Spirit is capable of viewing great objects; it beholds the divine beauty, though only so far as grace imparts and its nature receives. ... If the mind has been injured by devils it will be guilty of idolatry or will be perverted to some other form of impiety. But if it has yielded to the aid of the Spirit, it will have understanding of the truth and will know God.
>
> BASIL[11]

1:24. Not that we have dominion over your faith, but are fellow workers for your joy; for by faith you stand. Paul cannot force their compliance to his guidance. As a teacher of the Gospel, he can only try to make them aware of the wonders of God's Kingdom and to awaken their desire to partake of them. Salvation comes through faith in Christ, which no one can impose on another. With the gift of free will, each of us responds to that which we learn about God. That response forms a relationship between Him and us. At the Second Coming of Christ, that relationship will be the basis for the manner in which we will spend eternity.

> For faith and godliness are allied to each other ... he who believes in Him is godly, and he who is godly, believes more.
>
> ATHANASIUS[12]

FOOD FOR THOUGHT COMMENTS

(a). To whom does God grant grace? Do we play a role in this matter, or are we subject to His whim as to whom He will give this gift and to whom He will not? God desires that everyone be saved. Thus His grace is available to all. But He insists upon honoring our free will, the gift that enables growth in holiness in His image (which includes His freedom of will), so does not force His will or His grace on us.

> God placed Adam in Paradise ... endowing him with free will, that good might be his of his own free choice, as it is His Who sowed the seeds of it. Adam was to tend the immortal trees; the divine purposes, the lesser ones as well as the greater ones; naked and unashamed, living a life of perfect simplicity, without clothing and without shelter; for it was fitting that the one who was first made should be like this. And He laid on him a law; as material on which to exercise his free will. This law was a commandment, decreeing the trees he might make use of, and the one he might not. And this was the tree of knowledge; not because

it was from the beginning evil, or that it was forbidden out of envy ... but good if partaken of in due time. To me this tree was contemplation, as I understand contemplation, safe only for those to attempt who have arrived at a more perfect manner of life, not good for the more simple souls, not for those yet strong in earthly appetites; just as solid food is not suited to those of tender age, who have need rather of milk.

GREGORY OF NAZIANZUS[13]

Salvation is a synergistic process involving God and man. God offers grace toward salvation. Those who are receptive to this gift avail themselves of its power to the extent that they open themselves to it and use it (to try to live a life of obedience as proof or demonstration of faith and love).

Jesus, the Sun of Justice, has arisen. The rays of this spiritual Sun spread out in all directions; and one indeed receives less grace, and another more; not that grace so gives itself, it is our own disposition that supplies the measure. For as the sun is one which gives light to the whole universe, and its ray is one, and its splendor, yet it does not shine with equal light upon all the world. Here is wondrous and abundant sunshine, here there is less. This house has little sunlight, this has it more abundantly; not because the sun gives more to this house and less to that but according to the windows which were opened to it by those who build the houses it has more room to enter and pours in accordingly. And since our thoughts and purposes are the windows of our soul, when you open wide your heart you receive a larger more generous, divine favor; when you narrow your soul, you can but receive a less abundant grace. Open wide and lay bare your heart and soul to God, that His splendor may enter into you.

CHRYSOSTOM[14]

We need God's help, however, in all good things—even to begin to open ourselves to His grace. He is able to give this assistance without interfering with our free will because He has foreknowledge. He guides toward salvation (thus it can be said, "predestines," in a cooperative not an arbitrary sense) those whom He foreknows will love Him (Rom. 8:29). In a similar manner, a parent will often know how each of his children will react in a given situation, though he does not cause or dictate their response. The parent's knowledge of his children is imperfect and incomplete, but still it can enable him to guide each child in the way most likely to bear fruit. God's foreknowledge of each of us is perfect and complete. It allows Him to assist us in ways that are powerful but that do not intrude upon our freedom. If, for instance, God foreknows that someone's heart will be softened toward Him if given a chance (Jer. 1:5), He may place determining influences in that person's path at the crucial moment. This explains why often, in the midst of situations seemingly devoid of the presence of God, there may arise a person with an ardent love for Him.

> When a miracle occurs, may it cause you joy. ... God has put His finger there, sometimes to reward, sometimes to punish, sometimes to encourage His faithful people and sometimes to lead sinners into the way of salvation.[15]

There are those, however, who believe that God grants saving grace to and consequnetly saves only those whom He preselects arbitrarily, with no personal input from man. The Orthodox Church considers this a heresy. According to this theory of arbitrary predestination, all mankind is rightfully damned because of the sin of Adam and Eve, but God redeems and grants grace and salvation to whom He wills, the "elect," and man can do nothing toward his election. If this were so, it would mean that God also wills that some are predestined to sin and damnation. Would a merciful, just, and loving God condemn all mankind except those whom He chooses arbitrarily, with no consideration of the mind, heart, and actions of each person? If Jesus is the Savior of all mankind (1 Jn. 4:14), how can anyone be automatically excluded from God's mercy through no personal fault of his own? If God predestines some to Heaven and the rest to Hell, why did Paul write that we must "all appear before the judgment seat of Christ" (2 Cor. 5:10)?

God made man a free agent from the beginning, possessing his own power, even as he does his own soul, to obey the behests of God voluntarily, and not by compulsion of God. For there is no coercion with God, but a good will towards us is present with Him continually. Therefore, He gives good counsel to all. And in man, as well as in angels, He placed the power of choice, so that those who yielded obedience might justly possess what is good, given indeed by God, but preserved by themselves. On the other hand, they who have not obeyed shall, with justice, receive punishment: for God kindly bestowed on them what was good; but they themselves did not diligently keep it, nor deem it something precious, but poured contempt upon His super-eminent goodness. Rejecting therefore the good, and spewing it out, they shall all deservedly incur the just judgment of God ...

If some had been made bad by nature, and others good, the latter would not be deserving of praise for being good, nor would the former be reprehensible. ... But because man is possessed of free will from the beginning, and God is possessed of free will, in Whose likeness man was created, advice is always given to him to keep fast the good, which is done by obedience to God.

IRENAEUS[16]

False teachings on this subject emerged in various forms throughout the history of Christianity but are found most pervasively in the Protestant Reformation teachings of John Calvin's "salvation by *grace alone*." This heresy is said to have its roots in the debate between Augustine, of the fifth century, and his contemporary, the British monk Pelagius.[17] Pelagius taught that the human will takes the determining initiative in the matter of salvation: that man is self-sufficient, with ability to use his free will (unassisted) to choose not to sin. Augustine protested that this concept grossly understated God's role. In refuting it, however, he went to the other extreme, overstating the role God chooses to play. Though Augustine affirmed that God gave man free will, he did not believe that God's grace, when directed upon man, could be resisted. So, he surmised, God must not desire that all be saved; if He did, according to Augustine, certainly they would be. Thus, in his zeal to insure proper appreciation of the divine role in the salvation of man, Augustine diminished the place of man's free will. Also, his stance did not take into account the awesome mystery that God, the Omnipotent, is willing to share power with mere man, and that He never overrides man's will. Augustine apparently thought this would assign weakness to God. It actually shows His strength. God remains in control, even though, for His own purposes, He allows limited power to man (and even to the Devil). As Paul wrote, "the weakness of God is stronger than men" (1 Cor. 1:25).

> Personal beings constitute the peak of creation, since they can become God by free choice and grace. With them, the divine omnipotence raises up a radical "intervention," an integral newness: God creates beings who like Him can—let us recall the Divine Council of Genesis—decide and choose. But these beings can decide against God: is this not for Him the risk of destroying His creation? This risk, it is necessary to reply, must, paradoxically, register its

presence at the very height of omnipotence. Creation, truly to "innovate," creates "the other," that is to say, a personal being capable of refusing Him Who created him. The peak of all-powerfulness is thus received as a powerlessness of God, as a divine risk. The person is the highest creation of God only because God gives it the possibility of love, therefore of refusal. God risks the eternal ruin of His highest creation precisely that it may be the highest. The paradox is irreducible: in his very greatness, which is to be able to become God, man is fallible; but without fallibility there would be no greatness. That is why, confirm the Fathers, man must undergo a test ... so as to gain awareness of his freedom, of the free love that God awaits from him.[18]

God allowed theological contention such as this question of predestination in the early Church so His truths would surface from the ensuing debate (1 Cor. 11:19). Pelagianism was condemned in 431 by the Third Ecumenical Council in Ephesus.[19] Augustine's teachings were tempered with the balance that has always been taught in the Orthodox Church— a wondrous cooperation of divine grace and human freedom.

Those referred to as God's "elect" or "chosen" are those who use their free will first to come to an understanding and acknowledgement that a divine Creator exists and then to fulfill the purpose for which they were given life: union with Him. Along every step of the way, however, man can do nothing without God's grace. God elects to grant grace to, and thus to save, those who seek and open their hearts to Him (Acts 17:27). He compels no one.

(b). In the events of life, does God first grant grace, which enables righteous action and spiritual growth, or does He wait for righteous action first, then grant grace to strengthen our efforts? Being omniscient, God knows not

236

only the actions but also the mind and heart of man. He reaches out to us in many ways, as through the wonders of creation, and in every instance foreknows who will opt to follow the divine will rather than his own. He does not force His will upon us, however, because He wants us to choose freely to follow Him. At the very moment we lean toward God, even in thought, we open ourselves to divine grace, which strengthens us to the degree we allow. This divine power enables right action.

> The grace of God is not able to visit those who flee salvation. Nor is human virtue of such power as to be adequate of itself to raise up to authentic life those souls who are untouched by grace. ... But when righteousness of works and the grace of the Spirit come together at the same time in the same soul, together they are able to fill it with blessed life.
>
> GREGORY OF NYSSA[20]

Thus for short-term actions it is often harder to make a decision to act in accordance with God's will than it is to follow through with the subsequent action required. As the choice to act rightly is made (not before and not after), suddenly, through the grace of God, our vision is clearer, the burden seems lighter, and though the task may not be easy, God helps us keep our resolve. For long-term actions, the follow-through can be more difficult than the decision, but grace remains as strength and support as long as we choose to follow God's lead.

> The Lord's help is always there. Lest our free will should bring us to utter ruin, He is there, a hand stretched out to rescue and strengthen us when He sees us stumbling.
>
> CASSIAN[21]

(c). Why did the world not want to hear the message that

Jesus brought? Why does it still not want to listen? The Gospel requires that we live according to God's will rather than our own. When Christ came to bring the good news of the Way to the Kingdom of Heaven, most Jews rejected Him because (being under Roman rule) they were looking for a Messiah who would free them from subjugation to others and create for them a kingdom on earth. Most pagans rejected Him because they did not want to exchange their many indulgent "gods" for a God Who demanded major changes in their lifestyles. In the modern world, many do not want to hear the Gospel for similar reasons: society continues to lean toward self-will and instant gratification of desires. This accounts for the fact that "many are called, but few chosen" (Mt. 20:16).

> The body has eyes to see creation ... and recognize the Creator; ears to listen to the divine oracles and the laws of God; and hands both to perform works of necessity and to raise to God in prayer; yet the soul, departing from contemplation of what is good ... wanders away and moves toward evil. ... Instead of beholding creation, she turns the eye to lusts, showing that she has this power too; and thinking that by the mere fact of moving she is maintaining her own dignity and is committing no sin in doing as she pleases. She does not know that she is made not merely to move, but to move in the right direction.
>
> ATHANASIUS[22]

(d). Why does a loving God allow troubled times to enter the lives of His people? God allows (does not cause) His people to pass through the difficult times that life in our fallen world entails to test and strengthen their faith and love and to keep them on the right path. Many important lessons can be learned through adversity. He who turns to God in times of tribulation learns to persevere. Perseverance produces character; and character, hope (Rom. 5:3–4), which comes ultimately only from the truth of Resurrection.

> The cold, ice, snow, frost, and violent winds ... which plants withstand during the winter and summer, being exposed to the chill and heat ... are the miseries without which nothing on earth can ever grow, being unable to reach fruition. ... These are the various difficulties which befall us, which every person who meditates on bearing the future fruit to be brought to the Spiritual Vinedresser must necessarily undergo with thanksgiving. For example, if one has mercy and protects the developing vegetation from miseries by building a wall around them and covering them with a roof so that they might withstand all the terrible seasonal weather conditions against them—and even takes special care of them by trimming and cleaning them—they will not bear fruit. Instead one must allow the plants to undergo all of this. For after the winter's unpleasantness, when springtime comes and blossoms, and leaf-bearing appears, together with that beautiful renewal of budding, the unripe fruit which then grows according to its little contact with the jutting rays of the sun ripens, produces and gives back pleasant food ready for harvesting. In the same way, a human being who does not endure courageously the unpleasant burdens of life will never produce fruit worthy of the divine winepress and eternal harvest, not even if he possesses all other virtues.
>
> GREGORY PALAMAS[23]

Also, if life contained no hardships to endure or obstacles to overcome—if everything we dealt with day-to-day was without care—we would forget the purpose for life.

> We are afflicted in this life by the supremely good purpose of God, so that we may not love the way more than the end of our journey. For this present life is but a way by which we travel towards our heavenly

home. And because of this we are, in the inscrutable wisdom of God, wearied by frequent disquiet, so that we may not come to love the way more than our home. For there are travelers who, when on their way, see some smiling field, and while they delight in its beauty, they slow their steps and turn aside from the straight path they had begun. The Lord therefore has made the way of this world hard for His Elect in their journey to Him, so that none of them may take his rest in this life, enjoying the beauty of the way, but may speedily hasten towards Him rather than linger by the way; or lest, delighting in the way, they come to forget they once longed for their heavenly home.

GREGORY THE GREAT[24]

Yes, we should take time to "stop and smell the roses" when the opportunity presents itself. Brief respites refresh us physically and spiritually and give us strength to continue. Jesus often withdrew from the crowds for precisely these reasons (Lk. 6:12; 8:22) but then got right back to the work He had been given to do.

"Hear me when I call, O God of my righteousness! You have relieved me when I was in distress; Have mercy on me, and hear my prayer" (Ps. 4:1). Notice that the psalmist did not say "you have prevented me from falling into distress." God is certainly able to make our path through life free of care. He does not choose to do so, however, because that would not be to our best advantage. He does promise that we can count on Him to hear our prayers and to help us carry the particular cross life brings to us (Mt. 10:38). (For more on this topic, see 2 Cor. 12:7–10.)

It is not the hanging on a cross only that makes a Martyr, for were this so, then Job was excluded from this crown. He neither stood at bar, nor heard Judge's voice, nor looked on executioner, nor while hanging on tree aloft had his sides mangled; yet he suffered worse than many martyrs. More sharply than any stroke did the tale of those successive messengers strike and goad him on every side; and keener the gnawings of the worms which devoured him in every part than a thousand executioners.

Against what martyr may he not worthily be compared? Surely against ten thousand. For in every kind of suffering he both wrestled and was crowned; in goods, and children, and person, and wife, and friends, and enemies and servants (for these too spit in his face), in hunger and visions and pains and noisomeness. And if any ask, "how can we bear these sufferings nobly?" ... by one word of thanksgiving you shall gain more than all you have lost. For if at the tidings of our loss we be not troubled, but say, "Blessed be God," we have found far more abundant riches.

CHRYSOSTOM[25]

The purpose for life is to choose whether we want to spend eternity with God in His Kingdom or away from Him, aware of but unable to benefit from His blessings. We cannot avoid making this decision. Whether consciously or subconsciously, we make our choice and spend our lives demonstrating it, walking, day by day, toward our eternal condition. If we choose to be with God, we must actively live that choice through a concerted attempt at obedience to the way of life He asks of His people, despite any adversity life may bring—the true test. The person who lives in this manner is guided and empowered by the Holy Spirit to the degree he allows, thereby producing, accordingly, the fruit of holiness, a state of being necessary for life in the Kingdom, where all is holy. Since nothing in life remains static, those who make the opposite choice or who neglect to make a choice—which amounts to the same thing (Mt. 12:30)—continue to grow away from God. They set the eternal stage for themselves.

> According to St. Maximus, freedom of choice is already a flaw, a limitation of true freedom: perfect nature has no need of choice, for it knows what is good in a natural way. Its freedom is based on this knowledge. Our freedom of will reveals the imperfection of fallen human nature, the loss of God's likeness. Since this nature is obscured by sin, it does not know its true good and is directed constantly to what is "anti-nature." Thus the human person is always confronted by the necessity of choice. It gropes its way forward. This vacillation in the ascent to what is good is known as "freedom of will." The person, called to union with God, to perfect assimilation through grace of his nature with divine nature, is bound to a mutilated nature, crippled by sin, ravaged by contradictory desires. Knowing and willing according to this imperfect nature, the person is, in practice, blind and weak. It no longer knows how to choose and too often yields to the impulses of a nature which has become the slave of sin. In this way, what was made in us in God's image is drawn down into the abyss, although it still retains its freedom of choice and its ability to return to God.[26]

(e). What tests of faith are we likely to face in the times in which we live? A Christian faces many tests of faith during his lifetime. Decisions must continually be made on such issues as friends, career, spouse, moral and ethical questions, and the like. Our ultimate decisions will indicate whether we are guided by faith in and love for God and His Son or by other factors. Whatever comes first in our hearts is "god" to us. The telling factor is whether we recognize the Creator as our Master and put obedience to Him first in our lives, or whether something else, such as money, fame, power, position,

242

pleasure, or acquisitions dominate and, therefore, take His rightful place. Nothing—not even family—should take precedence over God. If we put Him first and act accordingly, everything else will be in proper perspective (Mt. 6:33). To attend to the reasonable needs of our family is to do God's work. If we have concern for our own soul and the souls of others but fail to try to nurture spiritually those who are closest to us, we are "worse than unbelievers" (1 Tim. 5:8). But when our primary allegiance is to God, His grace makes us capable of ever more meaningful relationships with our loved ones. There will always be many demands upon the limited time, talent, and resources we have at our disposal. Discernment must be used to establish priorities. The effort we expend to learn and to live by the precepts of God's divine plan, rather than fall to the temptation to make our own rules with regard to contemporary issues, sexual conduct, achieving success, etc., will bear much fruit in our lives.

> We ask not to have sound judgment and virtuous deportment for one day only, or for two or three, but through the whole tenor and period of our life; and as the foundation of all good things, to seek not our own, but *the things which are of Christ Jesus* (Phil. 2:21). How might this be? (For besides prayer, it is necessary that we contribute also our own endeavors.) We must be occupied in His law *day and night* [Josh. 1:8, Ps. 1:1–2, Acts 26:7, Rev. 7:15].
>
> I blush for those who are scarcely seen in Church once a year. For what excuse can they have who are bidden not simply *day and night* to commune with the law, but "to be occupied in it," that is, to be forever holding converse with it, and yet scarcely do so for the smallest fraction of their life?
>
> CHRYSOSTOM[27]

Serious illness and death are always tests of faith. When faced with them, those who want to be in God's Kingdom must resist the human tendency to become bitter and turn away from Him. Rather, it is important that during those times we pray for strength and guidance. When facing illness, we should pray for healing and for direction in seeking proper medical care; but if healing does not come, we should ultimately accept His will not to intervene as we ask and pray for strength to deal with the difficulties confronting us. In this instance, the fruit of prayer is acceptance and trust. We do not have to like a situation to accept it—and to accept a situation we do not like or understand is trust. If we do this, we are never alone in our difficulties—God is with us.

> It will happen even to steadfast courageous minds to be shaken by the fear of death. It is for this reason that some came to Christ praying: *Lord, increase our faith* (Lk. 17:5). He who continues to offend through weakness of faith falls short of the fullness of faith. For as gold is tested in fire, so is faith by temptation. But the mind of man is weak and needs help from above so that he may with courage face the dangers of the way. And this our Savior teaches when He says: *Without me you can do nothing* (Jn. 15:5). And the most wise Paul confesses: *I can do all things in Him who strengthens me* (Phil. 4:13).
>
> CYRIL OF ALEXANDRIA[28]

(f). We know that God, in His omniscience, knows even the number of hairs on the heads of His people (Mt. 10:30) and does not need us to keep Him informed of situations on earth. Why then is there such Biblical emphasis on prayer for one another, which is echoed in the Divine Liturgy and in the life of the Church? Does God always answer prayer? Are our prayers for others always of assistance to them? The emphasis on praying for one another in Scripture and in the Church is not to keep God informed but to remind us to talk to Him regularly and to encourage us to be concerned about and to love one another (Jn. 13:35, Jas. 5:16). It is only by growing in this love and fellowship that we can begin to understand God's love for us and grow in love for Him.

Prayer is an important and powerful way to help in any situation. When someone is experiencing any difficulty, we can offer the comfort of a promise to pray for them—but then we must be sure to do so.

> The laws of the Church command prayer be made, not only for those in the Church but also those still outside. ... For when the Deacon says, "Let us pray earnestly for the catechumens," he encourages the faithful to pray for them; although they are not yet of the Body of Christ, they have not yet partaken of the Mysteries and are still divided from the spiritual flock.
>
> CHRYSOSTOM[29]

> We do it also because we desire to remain longer in His presence, attentively addressing yet more words to Him, giving thanks to Him, acknowledging the many blessings we have received from Him, for as long as we can.
>
> PETER OF DAMASKOS[30]

God always hears the sincere and fervent prayers of the righteous (Jas. 5:16). He also responds to them—though not always in the way expected or desired. His ultimate concern is for our spiritual welfare and salvation, whereas, too often our primary concerns are ease and pleasure in the world. Consequently, His guidance may not correspond with the direction in which our will leads.

Because God does not force His will on anyone, for the most

part our prayers for others will bear fruit only if they are not blocking God out of their lives.

> What does this mean? Does prayer not help? It helps, and exceedingly, but only when we cooperate with it.

> But someone will say, "What need have I of the prayers of others, since I please God?" What are you saying? Paul did not say, "What need have I of prayers?" Peter did not say, "Why do I need prayers?" though those who prayed for him were not worthy of him, certainly they were not his equals. Yet you say: "What need have I of prayers?" You need them for this reason: because you think that you have no need of them.
>
> CHRYSOSTOM[31]

> Prayer is not made perfect by uttering syllables ... but in the purpose of the soul and in the just actions of a lifetime.
>
> BASIL[32]

(g). Do our prayers for those who are experiencing difficulties in their lives eliminate the need to offer physical or emotional assistance? Prayer should be our immediate and continual response to the difficult circumstances of life for those around us. In addition to our private and corporate prayers as part of the Church, however, God also expects us to be His co-workers in helping to meet the practical physical and emotional needs of those who are under duress. We can accomplish this by literally being the hands, feet, mouth, and heart of Christ in doing what we can to help (1 Cor. 3:9; 12:12,27–28). When there is a need, we can hold a frightened hand, shovel a driveway, drop off groceries, scrub a floor, contribute financially, or do whatever is helpful. By doing so, we are being the Body of Christ. In trying to be of assistance, it is important to remember that each situation is different, so we must pray for and use discernment. Sometimes it is best just to be around to show love and support and, when the opportunity presents itself, to bolster confidence in God's assurances that He loves us all and will come to the aid of those who turn to Him in distress. At other times it may be best to stand back and wait for signs of when or how we may be helpful.

(h). Ever since the Holy Spirit descended upon the Apostles in the upper room in Jerusalem, giving them power to preach the Gospel to all nations (Acts 2), man has had access to His indwelling presence. But what was the role of the Holy Spirit in Old Testament times? Did He offer any assistance to man during that age? The Holy Spirit did not dwell within man until the day of Pentecost, after Jesus Christ ascended to His Father. The man of God of the Old Testament was not, however, completely denied the powerful presence of the Comforter. Since the time of Pentecost, God works within willing man; before then, He worked on man from the outside.

> The Old Testament did not know the intimate sanctification by grace, yet it knew saintliness, for grace, from outside, aroused it in the soul as an effect. The man who submitted to God in faith and lived in all righteousness could become the instrument of His will. As is proved by the vocation of prophets, it is not a question of agreement between two wills but of lordly utilization of the human will by that of God: the Spirit of God swoops upon the seer; God takes possession of man by imposing Himself from outside on his person. God, invisible, speaks: His servant listens.[33]

(i). Why did Jesus say He had to leave so the Holy Spirit could come? Were Jesus and the Comforter unable to be

in the world at the same time? Jesus and the Holy Spirit can indeed be present in the world at the same time. In fact, the three persons of the Holy Trinity are never totally separated.

> God ... the Cause, the Maker, the Perfecter, that is, the Father, the Son and the Holy Spirit ... are not so separate from each other that they are divided in nature; and neither are they so confined in their nature as to be restricted to one Person.
> GREGORY OF NAZIANZUS[34]

Referring to the Holy Trinity, Jesus said: "If anyone loves me, he will keep My word, and My Father will love him, and *We* will come to him and make *Our* home with him" (Jn. 14:23). Speaking of the Holy Spirit, Jesus said: "you know Him, for He dwells with you and will be in you" (Jn. 14:17).

> From this we understand that God the Trinity dwells all together in the sanctified as in a temple.
> AUGUSTINE[35]

> In every operation the Spirit is closely joined with, and inseparable from, the Father and the Son. God works the differences of operations and the Lord the diversities of administrations, but all the while the Holy Spirit is present too of His own will, dispensing distribution of the gifts according to each recipient's worth.
> BASIL[36]

These truths are evident in the life of the Church (Orthopraxia). We wish each other God's presence when we say, "God be with you." We partake of the Body and Blood of Christ, and thus become one with Jesus continually, through Eucharist. We receive the indwelling of the Holy Spirit through the Sacrament of Chrismation and continual prayer.

Why then did Christ say that He had to depart so the Holy Spirit could come to be with man (Jn. 16:7)?

> It appears to me that the disciples were taken up with the human figure of the Lord Christ, and, as men, were held by their human love for Him as a man. He began now to wish them to have rather a divine love and so change them from unspiritual men to spiritual: which a man does not become without the gift of the Holy Spirit. Therefore, this is what He says: I shall send you a gift whereby you will become spiritual men; namely, the gift of the Holy Spirit. But you cannot become spiritual men unless you cease to be unspiritual. You will cease to be unspiritual if this human form is taken from before your eyes.
>
> AUGUSTINE[37]

Jesus Christ promised to be with His people always (Jn. 6:56, Mt. 28:20) and is, via the Church through Eucharist. He left them bodily, however, to turn their attention to the Holy Spirit so they could begin to understand spiritual growth in holiness.

CHAPTER TWO

On Being the Fragrance of Christ to God

Because of his deep affection for the Christians of Corinth, Paul had not yet returned to visit them as he had promised. In this chapter he explains this decision and addresses the claims of his detractors who were using his prolonged absence as an opportunity to claim that he was a false apostle.

2:1–2. But I determined this within myself, that I would not come again to you in sorrow. For if I make you sorrowful, then who is he who makes me glad but the one who is made sorrowful by me? If Paul had returned to visit the Corinthian Christians while the sinfulness he had written about in First Corinthians was still taking place, he would not have been able to hide his disappointment. His demeanor would have caused them sorrow. He loved them and wanted to be with them, but not under those circumstances.

2:3. And I wrote this very thing to you, lest, when I came, I should have sorrow over those from whom I ought to have joy, having confidence in you all that my joy is the joy of you all. He wrote in First Corinthians that their conduct would determine how he would next come to them: "with a rod, or in love and a spirit of gentleness" (1 Cor. 4:21). He wanted to arrive joyfully, so they could share his joy.

2:4. For out of much affliction and anguish of heart I wrote to you, with many tears, not that you should be grieved, but that you might know the love which I have so abundantly for you. He had written in a stern tone, admonishing them for their misconceptions and wrongdoings because he loved them and wanted the best for them: salvation.

Yet his harshness had given him much pain, the type a parent feels when he must reprimand his children or punish their disobedience in order to keep them on the right path.

> A father whose ... son is afflicted with gangrene, being compelled to use the knife and cautery, is pained on both accounts, that his son is diseased, and that he is compelled to use the knife on him.
>
> CHRYSOSTOM[1]

2:5. But if anyone has caused grief, he has not grieved me, but all of you to some extent—not to be too severe. The sinfulness in Corinth is not a personal affront to Paul but a matter that brings sorrow to the whole Church (see 1 Cor. 12:26).

> **FOOD FOR THOUGHT:** (a). How can one person's sinfulness bring sorrow to the whole Church?

2:6–8. This punishment which was inflicted by the majority is sufficient for such a man, so that, on the contrary, you ought rather to forgive and comfort him, lest perhaps such a one be swallowed up with too much sorrow. Therefore I urge you to reaffirm your love to him. The man referred to had been involved in a sexual relationship with his stepmother (1 Cor. 5:1). The action Paul insisted upon at the time was excommunication, hoping this would spark the offender's desire to return to the fellowship of the Church, thus encouraging him to repent and put an end to his sinful behavior. Apparently this spiritual discipline produced the desired results. The man involved must have shown repentance, because Paul is now urging that they show love by taking the next step, which is to forgive him, welcoming him back into their fellowship. Some of the Corinthians balked at this, prompting Paul's concern that the man involved will become discouraged—and be lost permanently.

If one lets go him that has been scourged and heals him not, he has done nothing.

CHRYSOSTOM[2]

FOOD FOR THOUGHT: (b). How might a person be lost to the Church and to God's Kingdom through *too much sorrow*?

2:9. For to this end I also wrote, that I might put you to the test, whether you are obedient in all things. Paul's hope is that as they responded to the disciplinary action required initially, they would now respond to the offender's repentance with forgiveness.

> Obedience to the stern measure of excommunication might seem to have stemmed from envy and malice, but subsequent forgiveness shows the obedience to be pure and whether they are prone to loving kindness … not because he is worthy, not because he has shown sufficient penitence, but because he is weak.
>
> CHRYSOSTOM[3]

In forgiving the excommunicated man and receiving him again into fellowship, the Corinthians would be demonstrating their faith and love. The penitent's faith and love are demonstrated by his repentance and desire to be reinstated, signifying his understanding of himself as a weak human being: unable to save himself and dependent upon the mercy and the grace of God through the saving actions of Jesus Christ. This is the proper work of the Church.

> The Church is … a court of justice, a hospital, a school of philosophy, a nursery of the soul, a training course for that race which leads to Heaven … and a spiritual

bath which wipes away not filth of body but stains of
soul, by its many methods of repentance.

CHRYSOSTOM[4]

Excommunication was a tool used often in the early Church to
safeguard the true teachings of Christ until they could be
preserved by written dogma. The Sacrament of Confession and
the authority to prescribe spiritual penance came to be
understood in time as the vehicle by which the priest can lead
his flock away from sin (Jn. 20:23). The value of this instance
of excommunication in Corinth is that it shows the zeal with
which Paul taught the need for Christians to live in a Christ-
like manner.

**2:10–11. Now whom you forgive anything, I also forgive.
For if indeed I have forgiven anything, I have forgiven
that one for your sakes in the presence of Christ, lest
Satan should take advantage of us; for we are not
ignorant of his devices.** Just as sin affects the whole
Church, so do the appropriate corrective actions and
subsequent forgiveness or lack thereof. True repentance
should be responded to with the forgiveness that Christ taught,
else the Body of Christ will be divided and Satan will win souls:
those of the unforgiven, if they then stray from Christ, and the
souls of those who refuse to forgive, through disobedience and
hardness of heart. Those who withhold forgiveness from
someone who has truly repented have no right to expect
Christ's forgiveness for their sins (Mk. 11:26).

> **FOOD FOR THOUGHT:** (c). What is true
> repentance? Must one continue forever in
> despair about past sins?

**2:12–13. Furthermore, when I came to Troas to preach
Christ's Gospel, and a door was opened to me by the
Lord, I had no rest in my spirit because I did not find**

Titus my brother; but taking my leave of them, I departed for Macedonia. When Paul decided against returning to Corinth, he asked Titus to go instead and then to meet him in Troas to advise him on the progress the Corinthians were making in responding to the first epistle. When Paul arrived in Troas, however, he did not find Titus waiting for him. As there was no means of instant communication to inquire about his whereabouts, Paul became anxious. Though there had been work for him to do in Troas, he left for Macedonia, hoping to find Titus there.

FOOD FOR THOUGHT: (d). Even Paul experienced moments of despondency during trying times. What can we learn from his example (verse 2:14) in coping with difficulties in our lives?

2:14. Now thanks be to God Who always leads us in triumph in Christ, and through us diffuses the fragrance of His knowledge in every place. Paul had been in a poor state of mind. As a teacher of the Gospel, he had been enduring continual persecution. Although he longed to be in Corinth, he considered it the wrong time to return. In addition, he had been without the comfort and support of Titus when he needed it. In this verse, however, he joyously thanks God, Who not only brought him through this distressed state but in spite of it continued to use him as an instrument through which the glorious truths about Jesus Christ were dispersed wherever he went.

> We are Royal censers, breathing wherever we go of
> the heavenly ointment and the spiritual sweet savor.
> CHRYSOSTOM[5]

From the time God first began to point fallen man to the road to salvation, the burning of incense has symbolized self-denying obedience. God commanded that it burn perpetually in the Temple (Ex. 30:7–8). The constant, smoldering fragrance was a reminder of the sacrifices required by the Mosaic Law—the Old Testament Written Covenant between God and man. This created a "sweet aroma to the Lord" (Lev. 2:2) because it indicated man's love for Him. But the process was frustrating because its futility was obvious. The Law had to be followed exactly—legalistically. Each time a person disobeyed any part of it, he was required to bring the prescribed atonement to the Temple. But he would inevitably disobey again, so found himself under continual bondage. Pointing to the need for divine intervention, the Psalmist groaned in desperation, begging that his prayers rising to God be likened to incense (Ps. 141:2): that the intent of his heart be acknowledged and judged, rather than his incessant, external, legalistic attempts to follow the Law. Revelations 5:8 and 8:3–4 confirm that, in response to that yearning, God sent His Son to usher in the new covenant. The blood Christ shed willingly for the redemption of mankind put an end to the sacrifices required under the Law. According to the terms of the new covenant, the prayers of all the saints rise before God with a sweet savor. "Saints" are those who attempt to live their lives in a manner that matches their prayers: trying to be Christ-like in all things to show love and faith that Christ is the promised Messiah but freed from the necessity to *achieve, on their own,* absolute perfection to *earn* salvation.

> The odors of incense signify the fragrant sacrifice of
> the faithful which they offer by an undefiled life. ...
> The vials are thoughts from which come the fragrance
> of good deeds and pure prayer.
> ANDREW OF CAESAREA[6]

Malachi prophesied that the day would come when incense would be offered to God by Gentiles everywhere (Mal. 1:11). In fulfillment of that prophecy, incense is a companion to prayer in the Orthodox Church. The lingering fragrance is a reminder that, under the Blood Covenant of the New Testament, God's criterion for salvation is a life made sweet by faith in and love for Christ. God gave the Mosaic Law to the nation of Israel as a step toward learning obedience and as an indication of what it would mean to be perfect and holy like Christ, Who "has loved us and given Himself for us, an offering and a sacrifice to God for a sweet-smelling aroma" (Eph. 5:2).

> When our soul's own intrinsic qualities and fruits—prayer, love, faith, vigilance, fasting and the other expressions of the virtues—mingle and commune in the fellowship of the spirit, they effuse a rich perfume, like burning incense.
>
> MAKARIOS OF EGYPT[7]

2:15. For we are to God the fragrance of Christ among those who are being saved and among those who are perishing. The Gospel of Jesus Christ sets forth the terms by which all mankind may be saved from the everlasting torment of being far from God. Christ's life on earth, bringing this Gospel to mankind, created an aroma that pleased God. Those who continue Christ's work emit the same sweet scent, discernible to God, whether the message they bring is accepted or rejected.

It is sobering to consider that, if those who teach the good news of salvation through Jesus are *the fragrance of Christ* to God, then those who defy the Gospel or ignore it (which, in effect, are the same thing [Mt. 12:30]), must bear the odor of Satan.

> When the fear of God is not present with strictness, the soul is dead. ... It is not dissolved into corruption by ashes and dust, but into things of fouler odor than these: into drunkenness and anger and covetousness, into improper loves and unseasonable desires. If you want to know exactly how foul an odor it has, give me

a soul that is pure, and then you will see clearly how foul the odor of this filthy and impure one. ... For so long as we are in contact habitually with a foul odor, we are not sensitive to it.

CHRYSOSTOM[8]

FOOD FOR THOUGHT: (e). It is good to ponder what type of aroma our life emits to God.

2:16. To the one we are the aroma of death to death, and to the other the aroma of life to life. And who is sufficient for these things? The Gospel is the same to all, but because of free will, each person receives it differently. Some hear and take it gladly into their hearts, choosing to take the road through life that leads to salvation. Others ignore or reject it. To the one who accepts it, the Gospel carries the sweet aroma of eternal life. To the one who rejects it, its aroma is made caustic by the eternal death it brings—separation from God. No one, on his own, can attempt the task of teaching the Gospel, knowing the awesome consequences it brings to those who hear and reject it.

FOOD FOR THOUGHT: (f). How then were Paul, the Apostles, and others through the ages able to accomplish this task?

2:17. For we are not, as so many, peddling the word of God; but as of sincerity, but as from God, we speak in the sight of God in Christ. In spite of the claims of his detractors, Paul's mission is to teach the truth that Christ brought to the world, not to bring glory or material profit to himself—as is the case with many false teachers (2 Pet. 2:1). The great apostolic mission of the Church is to continue this work. Accordingly, each person who considers himself a Christian is called upon to learn the fullness of Christ's teachings, to live by them, and to pass them on to others. By permission of God, the Devil has power and dominion in this world, as he will until Christ returns in glory. No area of life on earth is beyond Satan's reach. Wherever God's work is being done, Satan tries especially hard to spread divisiveness (Rev. 12:17).

> Evil originates ... in the spiritual sin of the angel. And the attitude of Lucifer reveals to us the root of every sin: pride as revolt against God. He who was first called to deification by grace wished to be God by himself. The root of sin is thus the thirst for self-deification, the hatred of grace. Remaining dependent on God in his very being, since his being was created by God, the spirit in revolt consequently acquires a hatred of being, a frenzy to destroy, a thirst for an impossible nothingness. As only the earthly world remains open to him, he tries here to destroy the divine plan, and having failed to annihilate creation, to disfigure it. The drama that began in Heaven continues on earth, as the faithful angels close the gates of Heaven unyieldingly to the fallen angels.[9]

It is not surprising, therefore, that throughout its history the Church has been plagued by those who have misused the Gospel for personal gain and glory on earth, rather than to bring people to Christ. Those who sincerely desire to teach God's word or to do His work, in any capacity, must be careful that they do not fall into Satan's trap in this regard. To the extent that we are rewarded by the world for this work, we can expect no reward in Heaven (Mt. 6:1–4). This serves to encourage spiritual growth and the realization that what matters most is not what the world thinks of us but our relationship with God and what He knows about us.

FOOD FOR THOUGHT COMMENTS

(a). How can one person's sinfulness bring sorrow to the whole Church? Those who are Baptized in the name of the Holy Trinity are united as the Body of Christ. It is because of this fact that His redemptive acts made salvation possible for everyone. This also means, however, that one person's unrepentant sinfulness brings sorrow to the whole Church. Sin sets up a barrier between the sinner and God. This barrier blocks the flow of grace and causes spiritual pain, anguish, and the potential of spiritual death, just as blocking the flow of blood through the body would cause serious physical problems.

> What a responsibility the Church has, to be Christ's Body, showing Him to those who are unable or unwilling to see Him in providence, or in creation! Through the Word of God lived out in the Body of Christ they can come to the Father and themselves be made again "in the likeness of God."
>
> ATHANASIUS[10]

(b). How might a person be lost to the Church and to God's Kingdom through *too much sorrow*? If a person was given the impression that his sinfulness could never be forgiven, he could lose hope:

> ... and either do as Judas did, or live more sinfully. For if he should shrink from enduring the anguish of lengthened censure and perhaps fall into despair, he will either come to hang himself or fall into greater crimes. One ought then to take steps beforehand, lest the sore become too hard to deal with; and lest what we have done well we lose by lack of moderation.
>
> CHRYSOSTOM[11]

(c). What is true repentance?   Must we continue in

despair forever about past sins? To sin is to fall short of the mark with regard to a Christ-like way of life. True repentance is recognition of sin, followed by sorrow that one has offended God and an attempt to change in outlook and actions to preclude further sin.

> Let us not be easy-minded afterwards, but when we transgress, afflict our minds and not merely give vent to words. For I know many who say indeed that they regret their sins but do nothing to change. They fast and wear rough garments, but are more eager for money than hucksters; fall more to anger than do wild beasts; and take more pleasure in reproach than others do in praise. These things are not repentance, these things are the semblance and shadow only of repentance, not repentance itself.
>
> CHRYSOSTOM[12]

When appropriate, the penitent should make amends with those offended, then partake of the Sacrament of Confession to draw upon the grace of forgiveness Christ entrusted to the Apostles, thus to priests of the Church ordained through apostolic succession (Jn. 20:22–23). If absolution is given, the penitent should feel cleansed and reconciled with God, confident of His mercy. To continue in despair over confessed sins at this point is to doubt God's love, which could lead to loss of faith and *unmeasured sorrow.*

> The Devil can cause destruction even under the show of piety. He can destroy not only by leading into sin, but even by the opposite: the unmeasured sorrow following repentance for it. Then he uses not only his weapons against us but our own too. For he is not content with striking down by sin, but even by repentance he does this, unless we are vigilant. To take by sin is his proper work; by repentance, however, is our weapon. When even through

repentance he is able to cause destruction, think how disgraceful the defeat, how he will laugh at and call us weak and pitiful, if he is able to subdue us with our own weapons.

CHRYSOSTOM[13]

We should remember our past transgressions to the extent that they remind us of our vulnerability to sin and to avoid slipping into a prideful feeling of self-righteousness, but we should not let sincerely repented and confessed sins bog us down. Sin prevents us from acting in love freely, which is our God-given potential. To be loosed from the bonds of sin is to be truly joyful, free to be what God wants us to be—holy.

(d). Think about the fact that even Paul experienced moments of despondency. What can we learn from his example (verse 2:14) in coping during difficult times in our lives? When Paul experienced difficult times, he sought comfort, consolation, and advice from those who understood his mission. Ultimately though, he relied on God in all things. When he was able to lose himself in his work, he was revitalized, finding strength and courage to continue. Each Christian can find similar comfort from the never-ending Source, for each of us, in some way, is meant to be a teacher of the Gospel to those around us, most importantly through example. No matter what our circumstances might be, as long as we have the gift of life, we can show God we love Him and want to be with Him forever. We do this by trying to follow the road to Him ourselves and by trying to bring others to it. When we put everything in this perspective, we realize that every difficulty in life is temporary and every hurdle surmountable.

(e). It is good to ponder what type of aroma our life emits to God. Just as we leave a distinctive scent in our wake when we wear perfume, and our personality creates a certain atmosphere around us, our spiritual life—or lack of it—creates an aroma discernible to God and to those who are spiritually attuned. Wherever we go, whatever we do, our actions and demeanor should create a *sweet aroma to the Lord.* Those who visit our homes should be able to tell by what they see, what they hear, and what we do that we are Christians.

> We must therefore offer ourselves as an offering to God, and in all things be found pleasing to our Maker, with an upright heart, with sincere faith, well grounded in hope, fervent in charity, offering Him the first-fruits of His own creation. This Pure Oblation the Church alone offers to the Creator, offering it to Him from His own creation, with giving of thanks.
>
> IRENAEUS[14]

(f). If no one can teach the Gospel on his/her own, how were Paul, the Apostles, and others like them through the ages able to accomplish this task? Only through the grace of God can anyone teach the Gospel (see 1 Cor. 15:10). Thus all who desire to pass on the transforming truths about Christ—whether an ordinary traveler on the road through life or a priest in the pulpit—all need to pray for divine assistance.

> Were the Apostles not men such as you? Did they not dwell among men? Did they not have the same interests as you? Did they not do the same things? Perhaps you think they were angels? That they came down from Heaven? No! "But," you will say, "they worked miracles!" It was not because of their miracles that they were remarkable. How long must we speak of miracles to cover up our own laziness? Look at the lives of the Saints. They shone forth, but not because of their miracles. For many who even cast out devils are not honored because they did evil and for this were punished. What then you may ask was it that made them great? Their rejection of wealth, contempt of vainglory, and their turning away from the things of this world. Because had they been

wanting in this regard, or had they indulged their passions, then even had they raised thousands from death to life they would have been not merely worthless but would have been considered frauds. Behold then that it is their life which shines forth in every way and draws down on them the grace of the Spirit.

CHRYSOSTOM[15]

An effort to bring a person to knowledge and understanding of salvation through Christ will bear most fruit if it is approached not as an intellectual exercise but as a spiritual pursuit that involves both body and soul. This requires the use of spiritual tools such as prayer, fasting, and the Sacraments, as well as the tools of knowledge.

Let us return to the word which has been handed down to us from the beginning, watchful in prayer (1 Pet. 4:7) and persevering in fasting.

POLYCARP[16]

CHAPTER THREE

The Glorious Call to Holiness

Chapter Two ended with Paul's assurances that his motives for teaching the Gospel of Jesus Christ reach beyond the earthly life, into eternity. Now he offers proof of this fact.

3:1. Do we begin again to commend ourselves? Or do we need, as some others, epistles of commendation to you or letters of commendation from you? The early Church was plagued with many adversaries. Outside were pagans (who worshipped idols) and Jews (who, for the most part, rejected Christ as the Messiah). There were also troublesome factions within the Church, which consisted of those whom Paul called "false apostles" (2 Cor. 11:13–15). Some of these false apostles tried to make themselves leaders for their own personal gain; some misunderstood the Gospel and taught heresy; others were Judaizers: Jews who believed Christ to be the Messiah but still thought it necessary to conform to the legalism of the Mosaic Law. Paul expresses concern that he may appear to be boasting when he compares his ministry with these factions in Corinth, which affect the Church adversely. His intent is not to parade his accomplishments but to make it clear that his credentials as an Apostle have been established.

3:2. You are our epistle written in our hearts, known and read by all men; ... The very presence of the Church in Corinth is Paul's commendation. That infamous pagan city was notorious for the love of pleasure and lack of morals among its people. Yet, after learning the Gospel from Paul, many there responded to it and underwent an amazing transformation to the Christian lifestyle. This fact is proof of the validity of his ministry.

3:3. you are manifestly an epistle of Christ, ministered by us, written not with ink but by the Spirit of the living God, not on tablets of stone but on tablets of flesh, that is, of the heart. He contrasts his message with that of the Jews—the Gospel with the "Law." The Ten Commandments, part of the Written Covenant of the Old Testament, were given by God to Moses on tablets of stone (Ex. 31:18). The new, final, Blood Covenant between God and man was revealed to the Corinthians by Paul but was written in the hearts of the receptive by the Holy Spirit (Jer. 31:31–33). God can use each of us as an instrument to teach the Gospel, but our work will bear fruit only with those whose hearts are open to the divine.

3:4–5. And we have such trust through Christ toward God. Not that we are sufficient of ourselves to think of anything as being from ourselves, but our sufficiency is from God ... Paul puts his trust in God's final covenant with man, which operates through the saving actions of Christ. He does all he can as his part of this pact but knows that without the grace of God he can do nothing. All who try to do God's work will succeed only if they do their best with the gifts God has given them and trust Him to do the rest.

3:6. who also made us sufficient as ministers of the new covenant, not of the letter but of the spirit; for the letter kills, but the Spirit gives life. The Written Covenant contained not only the Ten Commandments but 613 laws. God's people were required to follow each law to *the letter*—an impossibility. To break one was to be guilty of breaking them all (Jas. 2:10), with the result that not even great luminaries such as Moses, Solomon, or John the Baptist could find salvation through this covenant. Only Enoch, who lived before the giving of the Law (Gen. 5:24, Heb. 11:5), and Elijah, who lived during the time it was in force (2 Kings 2:1–11), did not have to pass through death. They were taken directly into God's presence because they pleased God. They were righteous, not in the complete, death-defeating sense that Christ was, but rather in relation to the time in which they lived.[1] Enoch and Elijah point to the certainty of eternal life for man and prefigure those who will be alive at Christ's Second Coming, so will not have to pass through death.

> But many ask where Enoch was translated, and why he was translated, and why he did not die, neither he nor Elijah, and if they are still alive, how they live and in what form. But to ask these things is superfluous. ... For the Scriptures say nothing more than is necessary. Enoch's translation took place immediately at the beginning, and thereby the human soul received a hope of the destruction of death, of the overthrow of the devil's tyranny, and that death will be no more.
>
> CHRYSOSTOM[2]

The Written Covenant was given to the people of the Hebrew nation to set them apart from others in the world as belonging to God and to give them an opportunity to show faith and love through obedience. Man's inability to follow it perfectly, as required, also illustrated the fact that no one can earn salvation on his own. Under the Law, everyone deserved death. Therefore, *the letter*—the "Law"—*kills*.

> God sought to form a mind conscious of righteousness, so that being convinced in that time of our unworthiness of attaining life through our own works, it should now, through the kindness of God, be verified to us; and having made it clear that in ourselves we were unable to enter into the kingdom of God, we might through the power of God be made able. ... For what other thing was capable of covering our sins than His righteousness? By what other one

was it possible that we, the wicked and ungodly, could be justified, than by the only Son of God? Oh sweet exchange! Oh unsearchable operation! Oh benefits surpassing all expectation! That the wickedness of many should be hid in a single righteous One, and that the righteousness of One should justify many transgressors.

MATHETES[3]

The first chapter of the Book of Genesis reveals God's original intent for man: fellowship with Him. Adam and Eve had the opportunity to pursue this potential unhampered if they would obey the one commandment He gave them. When they succumbed to Satan's voice urging them to do things his way—instant gratification of their desires—they found themselves on a path away from God, and the agony of man began. Still, God's hope for man remained the same—but now required a Savior to rescue him from his perilous downward spiral. In God's subsequent dealings with man, some responded to Him and others rejected Him, preferring false gods. Through His Oral Covenant with Abraham and His Written Covenant with Moses and the Hebrew nation, He prepared the family of David to receive the Messiah and purified special people for important roles in His plan to put man back on the road to union with his Maker.

> The history of the Old Testament is that of elections linked to successive falls. Through these God saves a "remnant," whose patient waiting purifies: through the very dialectic of disappointments, the awaiting of the triumphal Messiah becomes that of the Suffering Servant of Yahweh, the awaiting of the political liberation of a people, that of the spiritual liberation of humanity. The more God recedes, the more man's goal is universalized: until the supreme purity of the Virgin is capable of giving birth to the Savior of humanity.[4]

The old Written Covenant prefigured and was fulfilled by the new Blood Covenant. Jesus Christ fulfilled the old through obedience and ushered in the new. He allowed Himself to be put to death, though He was sinless, thus offering Himself as the Lamb of God, the last living sacrifice under the Law, which required atonement for sin (Gen. 22:8, 1 Pet. 1:18–19). Christ's death was not a price God had set for man's sin, nor was it a price Satan had a right to demand. His death was, however, engineered by Satan as part of his continuing attempt to deny to as many as possible that which he and the celestial beings who followed him in rebellion had lost for themselves (Rev. 12:7–9). God allowed the Devil this liberty because He knew that through it Satan would be caught in his own trap. In bringing to death one who did not deserve it, Satan over-stepped his bounds—he went too far.

Death could not hold Christ because He was sinless. He thus achieved victory over death. He also became the *first fruits* of the dead (1 Cor. 15:20): the first to be resurrected, never to die again. His Resurrection is assurance that there is life after death; thus it offers strength and courage to those who hope for eternal life with God for themselves and their loved ones.

> As long as sin sentenced only the guilty to death, no interference with it was possible, seeing that it had justice on its side. But when it subjected to the same punishment Him Who was innocent, guiltless and worthy of crowns of honor and hymns of praise, being convicted of injustice, it was by necessary consequence stripped of its power.
>
> CYRIL OF ALEXANDRIA[5]

Those who are a part of the mystical Body of Christ through Baptism and a life of faith also cannot be held by death. Because they share His victory, they only pass through death, to God's presence. And while they are alive they are not bound by *the letter* of the Law—literally having to be perfect according to its tenets. Rather, they are willingly bound by love to its *spirit*, which turns man to Christ and accomplishes what the Law could not: righteousness which springs from a heart softened by love and grace.

> The Law is the shadow of the Gospel and the Gospel is the image of the good things to come. For the former checks bad activities and the latter provides good actions.
>
> MAXIMUS THE CONFESSOR[6]

After Christ's Crucifixion, the terms of God's covenant with man changed radically as far as what God provides and what He requires from us. He not only sent His Son to accomplish what we cannot—objectively earn our own salvation—He also gave us a partner to help us fulfill the commitment and spiritual growth He does expect from those who desire union with Him: the indwelling Holy Spirit.

> In the Law, he that has sin is punished; under the Gospel, he that has sins comes and is Baptized and is made righteous, and being made righteous, he lives, being delivered from the death of sin. The Law, if it lay hold on a murderer, puts him to death; the Gospel, if it lay hold on a murderer, enlightens and gives him life. And why do I single out a murderer? The Law laid hold on one that gathered sticks on a Sabbath day and stoned him (Num. 15:32,36). This is the meaning of *the letter kills*. The Gospel takes hold of thousands of murderers and robbers, and Baptizing delivers them from their former vices. This is the meaning of *the Spirit gives life*.
>
> CHRYSOSTOM[7]

FOOD FOR THOUGHT: (a). What are some of the other ways in which the precepts of the Old Testament prefigured and were fulfilled by those of the New Testament? (b). Under the secular law of our land, murderers are sometimes put to death, as they were under the Mosaic Law of the Old Testament. How does this fact correlate with the Gospel, which Chrysostom writes "enlightens the murderer and gives him life"? (c). Which Orthodox icon illustrates the fact that before Christ died to redeem man from his sins there was no access to the Kingdom of Heaven? (d). How does knowledge of the Written Covenant of the Old Testament help us in our walk with Christ?

3:7–8. But if the ministry of death, written and engraved on stones, was glorious, so that the children of Israel could not look steadily at the face of Moses because of the glory of his countenance, which glory was passing away, how will the ministry of the Spirit not be more glorious? The Ten Commandments condemned man to death and separation from God because of man's sinfulness and his inability to follow them perfectly, as required. The Written Covenant brought death, not because it caused sin but because it defined sin. Yet this old covenant was glorious because it was a part of God's overall divine plan for the salvation of mankind, which He revealed to His people in stages. Therefore, when Moses came down from the mountain after having received the Commandments from God engraved on tablets of stone, "the skin of his face shone. Aaron and the people were afraid to come near him" (Ex. 34:30) because he radiated divine glory. However, the glory that shone in Moses' face would fade when he was away from God's presence, symbolizing the fact that this covenant was not permanent.

Paul's point here is that if a transient covenant was so glorious that its radiance shone on Moses' face, imagine the degree of glory that is attendant to the permanent Blood Covenant through Jesus Christ, which is written in man's hearts "by the Spirit of the living God" (2 Cor. 3:3).

> The children of Israel could not look directly at Moses' face, a mark of their great weakness and groveling spirit ... seeing that even of a glory that is to be done away, or rather is in comparison no glory at all, they were not able to be spectators.
>
> CHRYSOSTOM[8]

3:9. For if the ministry of condemnation had glory, the ministry of righteousness exceeds much more in glory. As part of the family of fallen man, we were born with a tendency toward sin. Through faith that Christ is the Messiah, our Savior according to God's divine plan, we rise above this sinful nature and are saved from the condemnation of being found guilty by the Law. As part of the Body of Christ through Baptism, we take on Christ's righteousness before God—we partake of divine nature (2 Pet. 1:4)—if, as we are able, we try to live Christ-like lives: our profession of faith. Faith, expressing itself in the attempt to be obedient, is the activator. He who demonstrates faith is aided by the Holy Spirit towards growth in holiness in the image of Christ. This is the *ministry of righteousness*, which is more glorious than the *ministry of condemnation* of the Old Testament because it leads to eternal life.

> Since then the Spirit has given us life, let us remain living and not return again to the former deadness: for *Christ dies no more; for the death that He died, He died unto sin once* (Rom. 6:9–10) and He will not have us always saved by grace: for so we would be empty of all things. Therefore, He asks us to contribute

> something also from ourselves. Let us then contribute
> and preserve to the soul its life.
>
> CHRYSOSTOM[9]

If our lives demonstrate faith as our part of the Blood Covenant with God, we walk toward eternal life with Him. The inevitable sins committed along the way (succumbed to unwittingly through weakness of flesh or immaturity of faith rather than indifference to or rejection of God) are forgiven through repentance and the Sacrament of Confession. On the other hand, if our lives do not show faith, we walk in a direction that takes us away from God eternally. Only these two options are possible. There will be no respite from the agony endured by those who cut themselves off from God through lack of faith because *Christ dies no more*: there will be no additional atoning sacrifice for those who do not recognize and respond to "the single, all encompassing and unrepeatable one that Christ offered once (Heb. 9:28)."[10]

> Groan when you have sinned, not because you are to
> be punished (for this is nothing), but because you
> have offended your Master, one so gentle, one so kind,
> one Who loves you so and longs for your salvation so
> that He gave even His Son for you. For this groan,
> and do this continually: for this is Confession.
>
> CHRYSOSTOM[11]

Each of us has one opportunity—our lifetime—to respond to God's divine plan for the salvation of mankind through Jesus Christ. The required life of attempted obedience is not easy but not impossible either because of the grace to which God has given man access.

> Our body, before Christ's coming, was an easy prey to
> the assaults of sin. For after man's fall a great swarm
> of passions entered also. And for this cause it was not
> nimble for running the race of virtue. For there was

no Spirit present to assist, nor any baptism of power to mortify (Jn. 7:39). But as some horse that answered not the rein, it ran indeed, but made frequent slips, the Law meanwhile announcing what was to be done and what not, yet not conveying to those in the race anything over and above exhortation by means of words. But when Christ had come, the effort became easier and, therefore, we had a more distant goal set us, in that the assistance given us was greater. ... Unless we stoop down very low to it, sin will not get the better of us ... for grace remitted our former sins and secures us against future ones.

CHRYSOSTOM[12]

FOOD FOR THOUGHT: (e). A person may have life in his body yet be dead spiritually. What are the signs of death of the soul? ... of life in the soul?

3:10–11. For even what was made glorious had no glory in this respect, because of the glory that excels. For if what is passing away was glorious, what remains is much more glorious. Though the old covenant had glory, by comparison with the new it had no glory at all—as the brightness of the moon is dulled by the rising of the sun.

3:12–13. Therefore, since we have such hope, we use great boldness of speech—unlike Moses, who put a veil over his face so that the children of Israel could not look steadily at the end of what was passing away. Because the glory that shone in Moses' face would fade with time after he left the presence of God, he put a veil over his face after he spoke to the people of Israel, so they would not notice and become disheartened. Paul has nothing to hide. The glory of the final Blood Covenant is not temporary—nothing will replace it. On the contrary, its glory will increase, reaching its fulfillment at the Second Coming of Christ. Therefore, he is bold in proclaiming it.

> **FOOD FOR THOUGHT:** (f). Why did Moses' face shine (Ex. 34:30), rather than the tablets upon which God had written the Ten Commandments?

3:14–15. But their minds were hardened. For until this day the same veil remains unlifted in the reading of the Old Testament, because the veil is taken away in Christ. But even to this day, when Moses is read, a veil lies on their heart. The Hebrew nation in general did not recognize Christ as the Messiah when He announced the new covenant— the fulfillment of the old. It knew the letter of the Law but did not understand the spirit which imbued it with life: the promise of the Incarnation of the Son of God, Who would release them from the bondage of the Law. It looked instead, as it still does, for a messiah to lead them to perfect conditions on earth rather than in Heaven with God. "Their minds were hardened," that is, they were not *meek* (Mt. 5:5), the Hebrew word for which means, "capable of being molded." To be one of God's people we must be willing to let Him mold us according to His image, and to try with all our might to live according to His truths. A synergistic effort between God and man is required. The minds of the unenlightened Hebrew people were hardened with self-will, so the truth could not penetrate. Therefore, to this day they continue to read only the Old Testament and to misunderstand it, with the result that there is still a veil between them and the truth.

> He said not, "the veil remains on the writing," but in the reading.
>
> CHRYSOSTOM[13]

That is, the fault lies not in what was written, but in the way it is perceived. This is an example of the fact that Scripture can be misunderstood, which is why it is important to look, for its true meaning, to the Church and the truths it has preserved through the Ecumenical Councils and the consensus of the writings of the Fathers. If we give our own interpretation to Scripture, we distort it according to our own will and deprive ourselves of that which God intends to convey.

> *... their minds were hardened.* What has this to do with the veil? It prefigured what would be. For not only did they not then perceive; but they do not even now see the Law. And the fault lies with themselves, for the hardness is that of an unimpressible and perverse judgment. ... For if the Law was brought to an end by Christ, which it was, and the Law said this by anticipation, how will they who do not receive Christ, Who has done away with the Law, see that the Law was done away? Being incapable of seeing this, it is very plain that even of the Law itself which asserted these things, they do not know the power nor the full glory[14] ... for the glory of the Law is to turn men to Christ.
>
> CHRYSOSTOM[15]

Those who recognized and accepted Jesus Christ as the Son of God and their Messiah removed the veil from their hearts and their minds.

> **FOOD FOR THOUGHT:** (g). What Biblical event symbolized this removal of the veil between God's people and the truth?

It is important to remember, however, that our roots as God's people are in Judaism; that Jesus, the Apostles, and all the first Christians were Jews; and that those of Hebrew heritage who accept Christ as their Messiah are still His "chosen people," *natural branches* called first to introduce God's truths to the world (read Romans 11). It is good, therefore, to try to share the Gospel with them and with all people of the world whenever possible, as Paul did. When he entered a town he would first go to the local synagogue to tell the Jews that the Messiah they had been waiting for had arrived. Then he would go wherever Gentiles gathered, to preach the Gospel (Acts 18:4–6).

3:16. Nevertheless when one turns to the Lord, the veil is taken away. Exodus 34:34–35 relates that when Moses returned to the presence of the Lord he removed the veil from his face, an act symbolic of the fact that when one actively turns to God, he receives understanding. Chrysostom says this verse also points to the general conversion of the nation of Israel,[16] which is one of the signs of the imminence of the Second Coming of Christ (see Rom. 11:19–32; Is. 59:20).

> *When the fullness of the Gentiles has come in ... all Israel will be saved* (Rom. 11:26), at the time of His Second Coming and the end of the world.
> CHRYSOSTOM[17]

When the Jews, as a people, hardened their hearts with regard to Christ, His Gospel was brought to those not bound by the Law. At a time known only by God, when the number of Gentiles to be saved has been reached, He will soften the hearts of the people of Israel and they will *turn to the Lord.* They will begin to comprehend the message of the Old Testament: that Jesus Christ is the promised Messiah Who came to rescue them from the futility of looking to the Law for salvation. They will remove the veil from their faces. They will turn from the letter to the spirit of the Law, and will understand.

3:17. Now the Lord is the Spirit; and where the Spirit of the Lord is, there is liberty. The Lord to Whom the children of Israel must turn is the same Lord into Whose presence Moses went to receive the Ten Commandments. But He wants them now to have a fuller understanding of Him, as a triune God. Through them God revealed the truth that there is only one God—one Creator—not many gods as the pagans thought. He gave them indications of His tripartite fullness through the Old Testament (i.e., Gen. 1:26: "Then God said, 'Let *us* make man in *our* image, according to *our* likeness';" also Gen. 18:1–3: "Abraham looked up and saw *three* men. He ran from the tent door to meet *them* and bowed himself to the earth and said, *'My Lord'.'*). In time, the Incarnation and Transfiguration revealed the person of God the Son, Who revealed the person of God the Holy Spirit (Jn. 15:26), Who, in turn, breathed life into the Church at Pentecost (Acts 2). Since then, when the Holy Spirit leads a person to Christ, he is led to God the Father (Jn. 14:6) and through this Holy Trinity receives liberty from the bondage and condemnation of the Law. He finds himself free, as Adam had been, to grow in communion with God.

3:18. But we all, with unveiled faces, beholding as in a mirror the glory of the Lord, are being transformed into the same image from glory to glory, just as by the Spirit of the Lord. Love makes man a willing slave (Rom. 6:22). With liberty from the Law and a fuller understanding of God, those who have committed their lives to Christ are able to look upon His glory and to become reflectors of it to the extent of their faith and love.

> As soon as we are baptized the soul beams even more than the sun, being cleansed by the Spirit; and not only do we behold the glory of God but from it also receive a sort of splendor. Just as if pure silver is turned toward the sun's rays, it will itself also shoot forth rays, not from its own natural property only but also from the solar luster; so also does the soul, being cleansed and made brighter than silver, receive a ray from the glory of the Spirit and send it back.
>
> CHRYSOSTOM[18]

In this present life, with the veil removed for true Christians, we can see God and His divine plan for our salvation, though still only indirectly. Because of the dazzling brilliance of the sun, the human eye cannot look directly at it without damage. When a solar eclipse occurs, the moon is positioned between the sun and the earth. During this phenomenon, much or most of the sun's brilliant light is blocked by the moon, but still the sun's rays are so powerful that we are cautioned not to look at it directly but through a mirror, which allows a view but deflects its power. In similar fashion, God and His divine plan are so glorious that we are unable to have first-hand knowledge of them but are given reflected glimpses in proportion to our zeal and spiritual maturity. As we strive to be obedient— demonstrating faith—we are transformed and continually grow in His image *from glory to glory*, that is, from one glorious state of spiritual growth in holiness and awareness of God to another, through the help of the Holy Spirit.

> When the mind of man ... is raised on high and sees the Word, and in Him also the Father of the Word, it takes pleasure in contemplating Him and gains renewal by its desire toward Him ... as Adam is described in the Holy Scriptures as having at the beginning had his mind God-ward in a freedom unembarrassed by shame and as associating with the holy ones in that contemplation of things perceived by the mind which he enjoyed in the place where he was—the place the holy Moses called in figure a Garden. So purity of soul is sufficient of itself to reflect God, as the Lord also says, *Blessed are the pure in heart, for they shall see God.*
>
> ATHANASIUS[19]

FOOD FOR THOUGHT: (h). Why are the stages of spiritual growth called "glorious"?

FOOD FOR THOUGHT COMMENTS

(a). What are some of the ways in which the precepts of the Old Testament prefigured and were fulfilled by those of the New Testament?

(1). Old Testament sacrifices were commanded by God from those guilty of breaking the Law, to teach man that sin required atonement (see Books of Exodus, Leviticus, Numbers, and Deuteronomy). They pointed to and were completed by the sacrifice of Jesus Christ, the Lamb of God, the last living sacrifice, Who gave His life to redeem mankind from sin, once and for all.

(2). The Hebrew Passover (Ex. 12:1–14) was instituted by God when He sent the angel of death, who "passed over" (and thus did not bring death to) the firstborn of the homes marked by the blood of the lamb according to divine instruction. This first Passover prefigured the New Passover (1 Cor. 5:7): the shedding of the Blood of the Lamb of God, Jesus Christ. Those marked as God's people by the Blood of Christ (through Eucharist) will not be held by death. They pass through death to eternal life with God.

(3). That which was called the "Feast of Weeks" in the Old Testament (Lev. 23:15–22) was the Hebrew Pentecost. It commemorated God's giving of the Ten Commandments to Moses and the harvest from the new land. Hebrew Pentecost prefigured Christian Pentecost (the descent of the Holy Spirit and the resultant harvest of souls brought to faith). Christian Pentecost occurred 50 days after Christ's Resurrection, on the very day the Jews were observing their Pentecost (Acts 2:1–4).

(4). The Old Testament commanded that the Sabbath (Saturday), the day upon which God rested from His work of creation, be kept holy (Gen. 2:2–3, Ex. 20:8–11). The Old Testament Sabbath prefigured the Great and Holy Sabbath when Christ rested in the Tomb following His Crucifixion. In turn, Christ's Resurrection on Sunday, the Lord's Day (Rev. 1:10), prefigures life in the Kingdom for those in-Christ. The Sabbath continues to be honored as a day of preparation for the Lord's Day (Greek: Kyriaki): the day on which Christians worship God and profess faith in Christ's Resurrection and hope for their own.

(5). Under the Oral Covenant with Abraham, circumcision was required as a sign of belonging to the one, true God (Gen. 17:10–12). It was required on the eighth day of life—the day with properties beyond this world for God's people. Circumcision pointed to and was superseded by Baptism as the sign of belonging to Christ: in submitting oneself or one's child to this Mystery obediently, faith is demonstrated (see Mt. 28:18–19; Acts 2:38–39, 15:1–29).

> It is possible for us to show how the eighth day [Sunday/the Lord's Day] possessed a certain mysterious import, which the seventh day did not possess and which was promulgated by God through these rites...
>
> The blood of that circumcision is obsolete, and we trust in the blood of salvation; there is now another covenant, and another law has gone forth from Zion. Jesus Christ circumcises all who will ... with knives of stone;[20] that they may be a righteous nation, a people keeping faith, holding to the truth, and maintaining peace.
>
> JUSTIN THE MARTYR[21]

(6). The priesthood of the Old Testament, established

through Moses' brother Aaron of the tribe of Levi, offered sacrifices in the Temple on behalf of the people to atone for sin (Ex. 28–29). This Levitical priesthood pointed to and was superseded by the high priesthood of Christ Himself after the order of Melchizedek (Gen. 14:18, Ps. 110:4, Heb. 7), which is eternal. This is the priesthood in which males in the Orthodox Church who receive a calling from God participate (Mk. 3:14–15, Mt. 28:16–20, Acts 6:2–6). The Church, comprised of the faithful, is the Body of Christ; the priest is the image of Christ, the Head of the Body. As such, the priest continually offers to God, sacramentally, the one, final blood sacrifice of Christ in redemption of the sins of mankind. The priest "can fulfill this service only because the priesthood … is not 'his' … but the one and same indivisible priesthood of Christ, which eternally lives and is eternally fulfilled in the Church, the Body of Christ."[22]

(b). Under the Law of the Old Testament, murderers were put to death, as they sometimes are under the secular law of our land. How does this fact correlate with the Gospel, which Chrysostom writes "enlightens the murderer and gives him life"? There is no easy answer to the question of capital punishment. The early Church condemned it but soon realized that, like war, it was sometimes necessary—to protect the innocent and the sanctity of life in general.

Life was created by God and belongs to God. Life is each person's opportunity to discover Jesus Christ, demonstrate faith in and love for Him (the criteria for salvation), and to grow in His image toward union with God. To take a life could be to short-circuit that process—thus the Christian ideal is to reform a criminal through love. But there are those who reject any such attempt, and there are those who may be brought to a state of repentance only by the realization that they face death. This prospect, which offers time to prepare, affords the accused the opportunity to make peace with God (a chance denied murder victims). Also, the sincerity of contrition and change is difficult for any human being or council to judge.

The sixth commandment prohibits murder (Ex. 20:13), but Mosaic Law did not strike out the death penalty (Ex. 21:12–17). Capital punishment is not murder but authorized killing, which the State has the right to enforce (Rom. 13:4). To maintain a civilized society, those guilty of disobeying the secular laws of the land must face the consequences. Christ taught that secular authority is given by God and should be obeyed (Mt. 22:21, Jn. 19:11). Coming to terms with capital punishment could encourage society to reflect on the fact that actions bring consequences—in this life and the next.

There should, however, be no rush to kill. Christian principles call for a system of law that, first and foremost, emphasizes reform and rehabilitation of the criminal. The law that deems this unattainable or inappropriate because of the heinousness of a particular crime must guard against mistakes and be fair to all. Capital punishment, therefore, should not be a part of the penal code unless it is used equitably across the board, not just against those whom society does not value and those who cannot afford an expensive defense.[23]

No one, however, is ever excluded from the power of the Gospel. Till the moment of death, anyone can call upon the mercy of God. Like the thief on the cross (Lk. 23:39–43), he who acknowledges his sin and repents, though he loses his earthly life, may, subject to Christ's judgment of the sincerity of his faith, receive forgiveness and eternal life with God.

(c). Which Orthodox icon illustrates the fact that there was no access to the Kingdom of Heaven before Christ died to redeem man from sin? The Icon of Christ's Descent into Hades, also known as the Icon of the Resurrection, depicts the truth that, before Christ's Crucifixion, no one (except Enoch and Elijah) entered Heaven (read Heb. 11). It portrays the fact that while Christ's Body lay in the Tomb, His Soul descended into Hades[24] (1 Pet. 3:18–20, 4:6; Eph. 4:9–10). On this much anticipated Day, He called forth all who, before He came to earth, tried to live righteously while waiting for Him to rescue them from the despair of being unable to earn salvation for themselves by following the Mosaic Law. At His descent they (and in the case of non-Jews, those who tried to live according to what they had been able to discover about God) were given the opportunity to accept Him as Lord. This was not a second chance, but the opportunity they had not had during their lives. Symbolizing these truths, the icon depicts Adam and Eve being taken from the throes of Hell. Also depicted as having been liberated are Kings David and Solomon, Abraham, John the Baptist, Abel, and the Prophets: Old and New Testament figures who point to Him in the icon as the Messiah they awaited. The figure shown in the blackness at the bottom symbolizes the Devil.[25] Through His Crucifixion, Christ put Satan (and death) in chains and restrained them (Rev. 20:2). That is, the power the Devil had over mankind after man's sin was death, but the sting of death was now dispelled, for though man would still have to pass through it (until the Second Coming), Christ's Resurrection proved death would not be final to those who truly believe in Him.

Christ's Descent into Hades

The Fathers, however justly they lived until the Coming of the Lord, were not brought into the Kingdom until He had descended Who would open the gates of Paradise by the intervention of His death; they murmured because they had lived justly in order that they might enter the Kingdom, and yet they suffered long delay. It was, therefore, they who had labored in the Vineyard, and it was they who murmured, whom the *abodes of Hell*, however peaceful, had received after their just lives. It was, therefore, after their murmuring, that they received the reward; they who after the long ages of Hell reached at length the joys of the Kingdom. We, however, who have come at the eleventh hour murmur not after our labor but receive our reward because coming into this world after the Coming of the Mediator, we are brought into the Kingdom almost as soon as we depart from our body; and we receive without any delay that which the ancient Fathers merited to receive after prolonged delay.

GREGORY THE GREAT[26]

The "abodes of Hell" entered by those who had tried to live righteously according to the Law while awaiting the Messiah are said to have been "peaceful," because they were the regions of Hell most divorced from the realm of Satan (sometimes referred to as "Hades"). Just as those in the Kingdom differ as to their relationship with God, those in Hell are estranged from Him on the same basis.

(d). How does knowledge of the Written Covenant of the Old Testament help us in our walk with Christ? Having knowledge of the Written Covenant of the Old Testament aids our understanding of the fullness of God's divine plan for mankind and the reason we needed a Savior. As our awareness of the magnitude of what Christ did for us grows, so will our love for and obedience to Him.

(e). A person may have life in his body, yet be dead spiritually. What are the signs of death of the soul? ... of life in the soul? Signs of death of the soul are such as we see in the rich man of the parable in Lk. 16:19–31:

> ... who ate and drank and lived in pleasure only. ... When the soul does not perform the things proper to it, is it not dead? When, for instance, it has no care for virtue, but is rapacious and transgresses the law. How can I tell that you have a soul? Because you walk? So do the irrational creatures. Because you eat and drink? So do the wild beasts. Because you stand upright on two feet? This tells me only that you are a beast in human form. ... How can I see that you have the soul of a man, when you kick like an ass, when you bear malice like the camel, when you bite like the bear, when you are ravenous like the wolf, when you steal like the fox, when you are wily as the serpent, and when you are shameless as a dog.
>
> CHRYSOSTOM[27]

Signs of life in the soul are such as we see in Lazarus, the poor man of the same parable:

> ... though wrestling with continual hunger, and not even supplied with the food that was necessary, did not speak blasphemy against God, but endured all nobly.
>
> CHRYSOSTOM[28]

(f). Why did Moses' face shine (Ex. 34:30), rather than the tablets upon which God had written the Ten Commandments? The fact that Moses' face shone when he came down from Mount Sinai, rather than the tablets upon which God had written, points to the fact that God glorifies spiritually, in this life and the next, those who bring glory to Him. God's light radiates through those who do His work. It is interesting to note that at first Moses was not aware that his face radiated glory—he became aware of it through the reactions of others.

> Through the glory of the Spirit that shone from his face in such a way that no one could look at it, Moses showed how in the resurrection of the righteous their bodies will be glorified with the glory that their souls already possess inwardly during this present life.
> MAKARIOS OF EGYPT[29]

This is seen also in such phenomena as "weeping" icons, which some have been privileged to behold. In an icon of the Theotokos that has this propensity, for instance, the focus is on her—not on the wood, paint, and canvas of these icons, which are but vehicles of revelation. Through her tears, the Theotokos is recognized as having spiritual vitality because of the life of faith she lived while on earth.

(g). What Biblical event symbolized the removal of the veil between God's people and the truth? The tearing of the veil in the Temple in Jerusalem upon the death of Christ (Mt. 27:51).

In Solomon's Temple, the Holy Place, in which a lamp of oil burned continuously (Ex. 27:20–21) and incense was offered to God daily (Ex. 30:6–7), was separated from the Most Holy Place by a veil (Ex. 26:33; 2 Chr. 3). God was present among His people in the Most Holy Place, "above the mercy seat ... between the two cherubim ... on the ark," which housed the Ten Commandments (Ex. 25:17–22). No one could enter the Most Holy Place except the High Priest. Just once a year, on the Day of Atonement, he entered the Holy of Holies to offer sacrifice to God for the sins of the people (Heb. 9:6–7). The veil symbolized the fact that because of sin man was separated from God, just as cherubim and a flaming sword were placed "at the east end of the Garden of Eden, to guard the way to the tree of life" (Gen. 3:24). Through Jesus' death, which atoned once and for all for the sins of mankind, this barrier was removed, thus the veil was *torn in two*. Man once again had access to God and to everlasting life—through His Son.

(h). Why are the stages of spiritual growth called "glorious"? The stages of spiritual growth gradually bring us closer to our Lord in this life and to eternal life in His glorious Kingdom.

> Paul's garments wrought miracles (Acts 19:11–12); Peter's very shadows were mighty (Acts 5:15) ... and those looking steadfastly at Stephen, *saw his face as the face of an angel* (Acts 6:15). But this was nothing compared to the glory flashing within. For what Moses had upon his face, these carried about with them on their souls even far more. For the glory shining on Moses' face was more obvious to the senses, but this was incorporeal. And as shooting stars reflect their brilliance upon that which is near them, so does it also happen with the faithful. Therefore, surely they with whom it is thus are set free from earth and have their dreams of the things of Heaven.
>
> CHRYSOSTOM[30]

CHAPTER FOUR

A Purifying, Deifying Process

In Chapter Three, Paul expounded upon the glory of the new Blood Covenant between God and His people. He now writes that it is the light of this glory that sustains and energizes him during the dark moments of his ministry.

4:1. Therefore, since we have this ministry, as we have received mercy, we do not lose heart. The fact that God mercifully redirected Paul when he was following the wrong path is always in his thoughts. The wonder of it sustains him in his difficult ministry.

4:2. But we have renounced the hidden things of shame, not walking in craftiness nor handling the word of God deceitfully, but by manifestation of the truth commending ourselves to every man's conscience in the sight of God. Contrary to the accusations of his detractors, Paul does not twist the Gospel to achieve his own ends. He strives to be a living example of the type of life it commands, publicly and privately, no matter what the consequences might be.

It would seem that anyone who were to ponder the wonders of life with an open mind would eventually concede that all signs point to the existence of a divine Being—the Creator of all— Who would naturally have a comprehensive plan for man, His most magnificent creation. The next logical step for the sincere seeker of truth would be to search out and try to understand all aspects of that plan and to make the decisions of life accordingly, so he would be sure to be included under its umbrella. When we contemplate God and His word, we cannot keep what we like and toss out what we do not, nor can we slant interpretations according to our own desires. To do so would indicate that we believe we can create our own truth and reveal a lack of real faith in the existence of God. This is the delusion of those who proclaim love for God yet insist they have the right to live in any manner they choose—while still fully expecting to go automatically to a mythical paradise of their dreams when they die.

> A young Abbot was counseled thus, in our own day, by a Holy man: "Today many people, wishing for an excuse not to do what God asks of them, find fault with the teaching of the Holy Church and reject correct Christian belief. Instead, they choose to believe what they wish. This is akin to a man not wishing to believe that he will die, simply because the notion does not comfort him. Not only will he fail to prepare for death, as one ought to do, but he will inevitably find himself in the snare of death. Correct belief is not based on what we wish were true but on Truth itself."[1]

4:3–4. But even if our Gospel is veiled, it is veiled to those who are perishing, whose minds the god of this age has blinded, who do not believe, lest the light of the Gospel of the glory of Christ, Who is the image of God, should shine on them. Paul has no secret agenda. He teaches the truth for all to hear. Some understand and accept it. Others reject it because the "god of this age," Satan, has blinded them to the truth. They have allowed themselves to be fooled by him and grasp at any excuse to believe there is no God, rather than give up the worldly distractions that cloud their vision. Each moment lived in rejection of or indifference to Christ is one moment closer to an eternal existence devoid of God's blessings.

FOOD FOR THOUGHT: (a). Why is Satan called the "god" of this age (Jn. 12:31, Eph. 2:2)? (b). What are the enticements of the world that can lead us away from God? (c). What assistance does the Church offer to help us stay on the road to the Kingdom?

4:5. For we do not preach ourselves, but Christ Jesus the Lord, and ourselves your servants for Jesus' sake. Paul does not teach his own philosophy, nor does he slant God's word toward that which would be convenient or comfortable for him. As expected of an Apostle, he has become a servant to those he teaches in order to pass on the truths entrusted to him (Mt. 20:26). A servant caters to the needs of those he serves. That which each person needs most, whether he realizes it or not, is salvation. Every Christian is obliged to try to bring the Gospel of Jesus Christ to the unenlightened around him. We serve best if we try to determine each person's level of understanding of God and work individually from that point.

4:6–7. For it is the God Who commanded light to shine out of darkness Who has shone in our hearts to give the light of the knowledge of the glory of God in the face of Jesus Christ. But we have this treasure in earthen vessels, that the excellence of the power may be of God and not of us. The Creator of all, Who caused light to be from nothing (Gen. 1), commissioned Paul to bring knowledge of Him, through the life of His Son, to those who have receptive hearts.

> Most people are like men walking at night wholly without light and not enjoying the slightest illumination in their souls from the divine Logos, so that they scarcely differ from the blind. They are totally caught up in material entanglements and the chains of temporal life, neither restrained by divine awe nor

performing any virtuous acts. On the other hand, those who live in the world and are illumined by the holy commandments as by the stars, and who do cleave to God with faith and awe, are not utterly shrouded in darkness and for this reason can hope to attain salvation.

MAKARIOS OF EGYPT[2]

The first man was created from the dust of the earth (Gen. 2:7). Thus Paul refers to those who teach the Gospel as earthen vessels. The vessel is ordinary and weak because it easily breaks down from injury, illness, pain, fear, and sin; but that which it carries is mighty, everlasting, and priceless. This paradox illustrates the fact that the power of the Gospel comes not from that which carries it but from God. An understanding of this truth eliminates pride in those who do God's work.

Those who teach the Gospel of Christ do so by choice and must work very hard to achieve results, but without God's help their efforts would be in vain. God has deigned to work in partnership with man (1 Cor. 3:9). Man is the tool—God provides the power.

4:8–10. We are hard pressed on every side, yet not crushed; we are perplexed, but not in despair; persecuted, but not forsaken; struck down, but not destroyed—always carrying about in the body the dying of the Lord Jesus, that the life of Jesus also may be manifested in our body. These are words to write in our hearts. At Paul's conversion the Lord had said, "I will show him how many things he must suffer for My Name's sake" (Acts 9:16). Now Paul reflects that even though every aspect of his life and ministry have been fraught with great difficulty, he is able to continue by remembering always that Christ lived and died to give man a way back to God. Those who really understand this truth carry on His work, in spite of the tribulation it may bring.

> The one who loves Christ thoroughly imitates him as much as he can. Christ did not cease to do good to men. Treated ungratefully and blasphemed, he was patient; beaten and put to death by them, He endured, not thinking ill of anyone at all. These three are the works of love of neighbor, in the absence of which a person who says he loves Christ or possesses His Kingdom deceives himself. For He says, *Not the one who says to me "Lord, Lord," will enter the Kingdom of Heaven, but the one who does the will of my Father.*
>
> MAXIMUS THE CONFESSOR[3]

Paul persevered by remaining focused on the goal (Phil. 3:14). When the travails and uncertainties of life threaten to make us veer off course, this is the only solution. With our spiritual eyes set on the glory of the Kingdom to come and with the grace of God strengthening us, we carry on. This focus may not solve all our problems, but it will prevent them from defeating us.

> When, by counsel of the serpent, Adam and Eve departed from the contemplation of God ... and from desire of Him, they grew in diverse lusts and in those of the bodily senses. Next, as is apt to happen, having formed these desires, they became habituated to them, so that they were afraid to leave them. Then the soul became subject to cowardice and fear and pleasures and thoughts of mortality. For not being willing to leave her lusts, she fears death and separation from the body.
>
> ATHANASIUS[4]

4:11–12. For we who live are always delivered to death for Jesus' sake, that the life of Jesus also may be manifested in our mortal flesh. So then death is

working in us, but life in you. The daily struggles Paul experienced in disciplining his will to conform to God's will allowed the divine presence and power to be demonstrated as it could in no other way. He willingly died to the ways of this world so his spiritual life through Christ would be visible to those who understood. As the book of Acts records, there had been continual plots to kill him. He had been beaten, stoned, put in stocks, and driven out of cities. No one would willingly suffer as he had without having beheld the wonder of God. Again and again God allowed Paul to be thrust into circumstances in which he was beyond human help. At the same time, He showered him with grace to endure and overcome so those looking on would believe. Paul's willingness to put his fate in God's hands, even if it should lead to death, was a powerful witness that brought many to salvation through the Gospel.

4:13–14. But since we have the same spirit of faith, according to what is written, "I believed and therefore I spoke," we also believe and therefore speak, knowing that He Who raised up the Lord Jesus will also raise us up with Jesus, and will present us with you. Quoting the Psalmist (Ps. 116:10), Paul expresses his compulsion to teach the Gospel in spite of danger. The truth and power of the saving message of Jesus Christ cannot be restrained. To believe requires action based on that belief. It is incongruous, impossible, to really believe that through Christ we have eternal salvation and not to speak out about it and have that fact affect our life, our decisions.

> Would you think it right if the perishable glory of worldly things were gained only after great toil and sweat by those who seek them, while to reign endlessly with Christ and to enjoy inexpressible blessings was something to be gained cheaply and

easily, and could be attained without labor and effort by anyone who wished?

MAKARIOS OF EGYPT[5]

Paul knows that death can come at any time. He does not seek it but does not let fear of it guide his actions. He carries on, doing whatever is necessary to propagate the Gospel. If death should come in the course of this life of obedience, he will face it willingly. His complete faith in the Resurrection of Christ assures him that there will be a universal Resurrection, after which all true Christians will be together *with Jesus*. This was the overriding thought always present in the minds of the early Christians.

> Do you not see them exposed to wild beasts, that they may be persuaded to deny the Lord, and yet not overcome? Do you not see that the more of them are punished, the greater becomes the number of the rest? This does not seem to be the work of man: this is the power of God; these are the evidences of His manifestation.
>
> MATHETES[6]

If we keep this same thought in our hearts and minds always, it will comfort and strengthen us and urge us to continue the life in Christ, however different that may make us from those around us. Guided by this truth, nothing can separate us from the love of God (Rom. 8:37–39).

> Grant us, O Lord, to imitate the watchfulness of those who waited for Your Resurrection, so that day and night our souls may be turned towards you.
>
> EPHRAEM THE SYRIAN[7]

4:15. For all things are for your sakes, that grace, having spread through the many, may cause thanksgiving to abound to the glory of God. Everything Paul does to teach the Gospel has as its goal the hope that as many as possible will come to know and to love Christ. Those who are thus awakened attract divine grace from God to direct them in Christ-like lives. Transformed by this process, they are exceedingly grateful to have been directed toward this glorious pursuit—the purpose for life—and give rightful glory to God for His great mercy.

4:16. Therefore we do not lose heart. Even though our outward man is perishing, yet the inward man is being renewed day by day. Suffering for the sake of the Gospel is taking its toll on Paul's body, the "outward man," but he presses on because this same suffering is causing his soul, the "inward man," to be purified, strengthened, and molded in the image of Christ. The inward man—that which endures forever—is thus renewed.

> ... by faith, by hope, by a forward will; finally, by braving hardships. For in proportion to the sufferings of the body, the soul has higher hopes and becomes brighter, like gold refined in the fire more and more.
>
> CHRYSOSTOM[8]

This verse can also be applied to the earthly process of aging. For many, growing old is very difficult. To see their hair turn white, wrinkles appear, and vigor diminish is traumatic because these things are reminders of the inevitability of death. A true Christian, however, knows that for the one who loves God, the most important aspect of life on earth is that it offers the way to the eternal Kingdom. Therefore, when the outward man shows signs of aging, he who is confident of spiritual growth of the inward man in the image of Christ does not despair; he takes comfort and joy in knowing that he walks not toward death but beyond death toward God. S/he actually improves with age: the inner person grows in holiness as the outer person declines.

Such is the beauty of the soul; even in old age it has many enamored of it, and it never fades but blooms forever. In order then that we also may gain this beauty, let us go in quest of those that have it and be enamored of them. For so shall we too be able, when we have attained this beauty, to obtain the good things eternal.

CHRYSOSTOM[9]

FOOD FOR THOUGHT: (d). What qualities in those involved in the difficulties of life cause renewed faith in those around them? What qualities create doubt and fear in others?

4:17. For our light affliction, which is but for a moment, is working for us a far more exceeding and eternal weight of glory ... Life on earth, however long it may be, is very short; but it is only a moment as compared to eternity. The difficulties we encounter while trying to live according to our faith in Christ are necessary to prove that we do indeed believe in Him and to mold us in His image. They are *light*, easy to bear, when compared to the glory of being with God eternally (Rom. 8:18).

In this life there is an equal portion of toils and reward; and often, on the contrary, the toil is endless while the fruit is little, or not even a little; but in the case of the Kingdom, the labor is little while the pleasure is great and boundless.

CHRYSOSTOM[10]

4:18. while we do not look at the things which are seen, but at the things which are not seen. For the things which are seen are temporary, but the things which are not seen are eternal. The visible elements of this world, as beautiful as they may be or as ugly as they have become, are temporary. Their overriding value is what they tell us of what is unseen. The sun rising and setting without fail to sustain life on earth reminds us that we have a Heavenly Father Who created everything visible and invisible and Who cares about His creation, providing man with everything he needs to fulfill the purpose for life. The continual corruption of that which was created "good" (Gen. 1:31) reminds us that we have choices to make in this life. These choices have consequences, temporal and eternal.

> Evil consists essentially in the choice of what is lower in preference to what is higher ... adultery instead of lawful procreation; slander, insult and perjury instead of right speaking; murder, stealing, striking fellow-men, drunkenness and insatiable gluttony instead of righteousness. All of these are sins of the soul, and there is no cause of them, they are only the rejection of better things.
>
> ATHANASIUS[11]

FOOD FOR THOUGHT COMMENTS

(a). Why is Satan called the "god" of this age (Jn. 12:31, Eph. 2:2)? Angels were created before man. One of the angels—Lucifer—was more glorious than all. He was close to God in Heaven and had much power and glory. He and all the angels also had the gift of free will. But pride and greed grew in Lucifer; he coveted God's supremacy and took issue with His divine plan for man. Gathering together other rebellious spirits, he tried to unseat God from His throne (Isa. 14:12–17), forgetting that no one can win a battle against God. Lucifer and his cohorts (one-third of the celestial beings [Rev. 12:4]) were evicted from Heaven forever and relegated to earth, where God allows them a certain amount of power in order to test, strengthen, and teach those who call themselves His people.

Lucifer became known as Satan: "the Adversary." God allowed Satan to tempt Adam and Eve as a test of their love. He allows everyone given the gift of life to be similarly tested. Dealing with temptation teaches dependence on God. Through trial and tribulation we learn that only by turning to Him in obedience do we receive grace in the form of strength to resist and endure. As with physical exercise, persistence in this struggle provides strength to prepare us for whatever life brings.

> The Devil is indeed angered when cast forth from a human body; but much more so if he sees a soul freed from sin. For this is his greatest power, the spreading of sin. Because of this Christ died, that He might break this power. ... If you destroy sin you have broken the nerves of the Devil, you have bruised his head, you have destroyed his power, you have defeated his army, you have wrought a sign greater than all miracles.
>
> CHRYSOSTOM[12]

The power that Satan has during this "age" of testing, though formidable, is vastly inferior to God's power. As the book of Job reveals dramatically, in His strength as Creator and Ruler of the universe, God allows Satan only that power which ultimately results in good: the separating of the obedient from the disobedient, the true believer from the unbeliever (Mt. 3:12).

(b). What are the enticements of the world that can lead us away from God? The very temptations the Devil set before Christ (Mt. 4:1–11) are those he uses to entice us. When Satan tempted Jesus to use His power as the Son of God to turn stones into bread, he was pointing to our tendency to put satisfaction of bodily appetites first in life, whether food, possessions, or pleasure. The lure to jump off the highest point of the temple to see if God would send angels to rescue Him points to pride, our inclination to have such exalted opinions of ourselves that we make demands upon God, as the Hebrew people did in their wanderings through the desert (Ex. 17:1–7). The temptation in which Satan tried to interest Jesus in the kingdoms of the world points to our propensity to set up our own kingdoms, governed by our own rules. This is what caused Adam and Eve to disobey God rather than grow in fellowship with Him as He desired.

> The ancient enemy tempted the first man by gluttony, when he persuaded him to eat the forbidden fruit of the tree; by vainglory when he said, *you shall be as gods* (Gen. 3:5); by avarice, when he said: *knowing good and evil.* For avarice is not solely the desire of money but also of pride of place, when dignity is sought without measure. By these means [Satan] laid low the first man; by the same means he was defeated by the Second Man [Jesus].
>
> GREGORY THE GREAT[13]

Jesus' responses did not question Satan's right to tempt Him. Rather, they illustrate the fact that God expects His people to try to resist all worldly distractions that would take their eyes from the Kingdom as their goal. Jesus was tempted by Satan as Adam and Eve were and as are we, but He remained without sin (Heb. 4:15). He overcame all temptation so He could be the example and the strength of those who turn to Him when their eyes, ears, and hearts are drawn away from God (Heb. 2:18).

> God so deals with us that while making progress towards Him we shall not forget our weakness; and that tempted we recall it, so that in our progress we

may understand what we are from divine favor, and in our temptation what we are of our own strength. And such temptation would indeed lead us wholly astray were we not protected from above. Yet it assails us, though it does not break us; it incites us, though it does not move us; it shakes us, but does not make us fall: that we may see that it is because of our own weakness we are shaken, because of divine grace we stand firm.

GREGORY THE GREAT[14]

(c). What assistance does the Church offer to help us stay on the road to the Kingdom? The Church is the Body of Christ, left on earth to continue His work of salvation. To help us win the battle against Satan, the Church offers grace through the Sacraments; the spiritual disciplines of worship, prayer, and fasting; and the fellowship of others involved in the same struggle. Christ's personal involvement in the Mysteries of the Church and with the spiritual disciplines of prayer and fasting leave a powerful legacy.

> Christ fasted that we may learn how great a good it is and how effective a shield against the Devil. ... He fasted not because He needed to, but to teach us. ... And that He might lay down the length of our Lenten fast, He fasted for forty days and forty nights. ... He did not prolong His fast beyond that of Moses and Elijah, lest His taking on of our flesh might seem a thing not to be believed.

CHRYSOSTOM[15]

(d). What qualities in those involved in the difficulties of life cause renewed faith in those around them? What qualities create doubt and fear in others? When those who suffer through no fault of their own turn to God for strength and courage and show their dependence upon Him without bitterness, they help others around them to realize that there is indeed a powerful God Who loves and helps His people. Such was the effect caused by believers in the early Church who accepted torture and often painful death rather than deny Christ. On the other hand, when those who call themselves Christians mumble and complain when things do not go their way, when they quickly allow the pressures of the world to water down their obedience to the word of God, and when they turn away from Him in anger when faced with the very difficult times of life, they convey the message that being a Christian has no special meaning—that it makes no real difference.

> When God first created the rose, it was without thorns. Since then the thorn has been added to its beauty to help us know that sorrow is very near to pleasure and to remind us of our sin, which condemned the earth to produce thorns.
>
> BASIL[16]

God has not promised His people a life free of care. He has promised to help us through troubled times if we turn to Him and trust Him (Isa. 51:12, Mt. 28:20, 2 Cor. 1:3–4). His ultimate promise is eternal life with Him in His Kingdom, if judgment shows evidence of true faith through all that life brings.

> In that hour when we shall be separated from men and from the traffic of men, be to us, O Lord, a Giver of good things, bringing joy to our sadness. When we have gone forth from this world, may we behold, O Lord, clearly and in deed the power of Your aid. Pour Your peace into our hearts, and give Your rest to all our striving, that the darkness of that night may be to us as day.
>
> EPHRAEM THE SYRIAN[17]

CHAPTER FIVE

That Which Awaits Us

In Chapter Four, Paul wrote about the breaking down of the outward man due to suffering endured for the sake of preaching the Gospel and the subsequent purification of the inward man through faith, hope, and perseverance. Now his thoughts turn to that which gives him confidence to remain joyful in the midst of this difficult process.

5:1. For we know that if our earthly house, this tent, is destroyed, we have a building from God, a house not made with hands, eternal in the Heavens. The dangers inherent in preaching the Gospel continue. Therefore, Paul's suffering goes on and the possibility of death for refusing to deny Christ or forsake His work is ever-present. Paul is confident, however, of the truth that his soul is immortal. If his earthly body ceases to function, an even better body awaits him.

Paul calls the body an "earthly house." As a tentmaker, He compares it to a tent—a temporary home for the soul to abide in while on earth. After judgment at the Second Coming of Christ, he who has demonstrated faith and prepared himself for life in God's Kingdom will receive a new imperishable body, an incorruptible house for the soul to inhabit.

> If a jeweler makes in mosaic the form of an animal,
> and the stones are scattered by time or by the man
> who made them, he may gather them together again,
> form them in the same way, and make the same form
> of an animal. Shall not God be able to collect again

the decomposed members of the flesh and make the same body as was formerly produced by Him?
JUSTIN THE MARTYR[1]

5:2. For in this we groan, earnestly desiring to be clothed with our habitation which is from Heaven ... Paul looks forward to the heavenly house his soul will dwell in eternally. This will not be an entirely different body but "the same one made incorruptible."[2]

> Be tender, I beseech you, of this body, and understand that you will be raised from the dead, to be judged with this body.
> CYRIL OF JERUSALEM[3]

> Although you may say: The remains of the flesh itself do not exist anywhere: they may have been consumed by fire, or devoured by a wild beast. Know this: whatever is consumed is contained in the bowels of the earth, and from there, at the command of God, it can be brought forth. For even you, where no fire is visible, can take flint and steel and strike fire from stone. That, therefore, which you do by effort and the skill God Himself has given you, so that you bring forth what is not visible, cannot the Divine Majesty do of His power? Believe me, God can do anything.
> CHRYSOSTOM[4]

> **FOOD FOR THOUGHT:** (a). What other indications does the Bible give that everyone will spend eternity in a body? (b). ... that the immortal body of a believer will be much like the one possessed in life on earth but different, with unique spiritual qualities?

5:3. if indeed, having been clothed, we shall not be found naked. The only thing Paul is concerned about is that at

Judgment he not be "found naked" of faith, so that the body he will receive at the Resurrection will be his eternal habitation in joy, not in agony (Mt. 25:41–46).

> Although the body is dissolved at the appointed time, because of the primeval disobedience, it is placed in the crucible of the earth, to be recast again ... to each body its own soul shall be restored ... possessing in every respect the things pertaining to it: not bodies diverse from what they had been ... but as they departed this life, in sins or in righteous actions: and such as they were, such shall they be clothed with upon resuming life; and such as they were in unbelief, such shall they be faithfully judged.
>
> IRENAEUS[5]

> Be of good cheer, but work, strive earnestly; for nothing shall be lost. Every prayer, every psalm you sing is recorded; every good deed, every fast is recorded; every marriage duly observed is recorded; continence kept for God's sake is recorded ... for you shall rise clothed with your own sins, or else with your righteous deeds.
>
> CYRIL OF JERUSALEM[6]

FOOD FOR THOUGHT: (c). What will be the conditions of eternal life in God's Kingdom? (d). What will be the characteristics of the resurrected bodies of the righteous? ... the unrighteous?

5:4. For we who are in this tent groan, being burdened, not because we want to be unclothed, but further clothed, that mortality may be swallowed up by life. God created Adam and Eve to live forever and gave them one commandment to follow. After they disobeyed, He clothed them in "tunics of skin" (Gen. 3:21), the mortality that came to man as a consequence of his fall from grace.[7] Mortality is the "biological condition, subject to the necessity of death" that became "a new law of the existence of the earthly creation."[8] Life in a mortal body is burdensome, prone to many difficulties and restricted by limitations. Still, life is a great blessing. If we do not love life, why would we long to live eternally? All Christians who have even the most basic understanding of the awesome truth of salvation through Jesus Christ long not to be rid of their bodies but to be clothed again in the immortal bodies Adam and Eve enjoyed before they disobeyed.

> The transformation of the body takes place in this way: while it is mortal and corruptible, it becomes immortal and incorruptible, not after its own proper substance, but after the mighty working of the Lord, Who is able to invest the mortal with immortality, and the corruptible with incorruption.
>
> IRENAEUS[9]

After the Second Coming of Christ, believers will experience life unending and perfect, with no sickness, no sorrow, no tears, no pain, no death (Rev. 21:4). The joyful moments we experience during life on earth are tastes of the perfect joy of God's Kingdom in its fullness. Because of these bits of ecstasy, we are usually very reluctant to give up this life, wanting more and more of the "good" it has to offer. This instinctive desire to live forever is assurance from God that eternal life is a reality. The moments of suffering and despair we experience are tastes of Hell. God allows these experiences so we can make our choice. If we remember that the difficult times of life are allowed by God as a part of the process that brings His people to the surface and that strengthens and purifies them for life with Him, we help Him turn evil back to the good of His creation.

FOOD FOR THOUGHT: (e). There are those, like Jehovah's Witnesses, who believe there is no Hell (in the sense of a state or place of eternal agony). This false teaching can cause much harm and eternal suffering. How?

5:5. Now He Who has prepared us for this very thing is God, Who also has given us the Spirit as a guarantee. Eternal life in communion with God has been a part of His plan for man from the beginning. The Holy Spirit, present within from the time of our Chrismation, calls us to holiness. If we cooperate and make an effort to feed and nurture our souls as we do our bodies, we grow spiritually. As this process continues, we receive ever-increasing glimpses into the wonder and joy of the Kingdom, which begins in this present life. This has a liberating effect in our lives. Our burdens seem lighter, in spite of the corruption of the world. We become increasingly secure in knowledge of the reality of the spiritual world and begin to respond to all of creation with love.

> It might seem to men of the present day, who are ignorant of God's appointment, to be a thing incredible and impossible that any man could live eternally ... yet the ancients of the Old Testament lived to seven hundred, eight hundred and nine hundred years of age. Their bodies kept pace with the protracted length of their days and participated in life as long as God willed that they should live ... and those who were translated [Enoch and Elijah, who did not die] do live as a guarantee of the future length of days.
>
> IRENAEUS[10]

5:6. *Therefore we are always confident, knowing that while we are at home in the body we are absent from the Lord.* The early Christians faced continual persecution and the ever-present threat of death, which was often the consequence of refusing to deny their faith in Christ. Like them, Paul does not fear death. Those born again spiritually of water and the Spirit through Baptism and Chrismation (Jn. 3:3–5), followed by a life of faith, can share his confidence that to leave this life is to join Christ in His Kingdom—so there is no need for fear.

> What are we doing, we men of little faith, who grieve and rebel should one of our dear ones depart to the Lord? What are we doing, we whose pilgrimage on this earth delights us more than to be restored to the presence of Christ? In very truth, this whole life of ours is but a journey through a strange land. For as pilgrims in this world, we have here no certain dwelling; we suffer, we sweat, walking by ways that are difficult and full of peril. Treachery awaits us on every side, from spiritual enemies and from bodily ones; on every side the winding paths of error are made ready. And though beset by such dangers, not only do we wish not to be set free of them, but we even weep and mourn as lost those who have been delivered. What has God given us through His Only-begotten, if we still fear the coming of death? Why glory in being born again of water and the Holy Spirit, when we are saddened at the thought of going forth from this world?
>
> CHRYSOSTOM[11]

After their disobedience, God evicted Adam and Eve from the perfect setting they had enjoyed and placed angels at the gate so they would no longer have access to the tree of life (Gen. 3:22–23). They found themselves in the imperfect world in which we live, where the devil has reign and where they would face deterioration and death.

Death is harsh—but it is not the enemy we tend to think it is. Death saves us from having to live on interminably after quality of life is gone. If we had to face the dangers of this world, with no end to the ravages of time on our minds and bodies, at some point (through illness, age, or harm inflicted upon us) we would reach a state beyond healing. Each of us would face certain agony with no respite. Horror would ensue. God allows a glimpse of this untenable situation: all we need do is visit a long-term care facility for the very sick or very old to see that the alternative to death would be infinitely worse. Death sets limits to personal pain and suffering and prevents unending mushrooming of sin. The world would be intolerable if the evil characters of history were not contained by death.

> God, and here lies the whole mystery of the "tunics of skin," introduces a certain order at the very heart of disorder to avoid a total disintegration by evil. His beneficent will organizes and preserves the universe; His punishment is pedagogy: better that man dies, that is to say, be excluded from the tree of life, than that his monstrous condition be made eternal. His finitude itself would make repentance well up within him.[12]

In His wisdom, God also allows (does not cause) the conditions that sometimes bring illness and death to the young as well as the old. This fact discourages carelessness and indifference and reminds us to be vigilant about the state of our souls, whatever our age. Because of fallen human nature, if each of us were guaranteed a certain number of years of life, it is probable that the majority would spend the greater number of them not worrying about God and what He expects of us, thinking that there is plenty of time. Toward the end of those promised years, however, instead of then turning our attention to God, we would probably be too far from knowledge of Him to even consider Him, much less know how to find Him. The habits of a lifetime are not easily changed. The Christ-like life we are called to guides us in building virtuous habits (ascesis).

The curse of death has never been a judgment of God. It was the punishment of a loving Father, not the obtuse anger of a tyrant. Its character was educative and restorative. It prevented the perpetuation of an estranged life, the apathetic induction into an anti-natural condition. It not only put a limit to the decomposition of our nature, but, by the anguish of finitude, helped man to become alive to his condition and turn to God. Similarly, the unjust will of Satan cannot function except through the just permission of God. Satan's choice was not only limited by the divine will but also used by it, as we see in the case of Job.[13]

Before Christ's death on the Cross, however, death also meant separation from God. Man was unable to overcome the effects of sin on his own. Christ's mission was to overthrow all of them, including death, and to make possible again the union of man with God.

> The mere fact of incarnation overcomes the first obstacle to this union: the separation of the two natures, that of man and that of God. Two other obstacles then remain, linked to the fallen condition of man: sin and death. The work of Christ is to vanquish them, to banish their necessity from the terrestrial cosmos. Not to overcome them without redress, for that would be to violate the very liberty that created them. But to make death harmless and sin curable by submission of God Himself to death and Hell. Thus the death of Christ removes, from between man and God, the obstacle of sin; and His Resurrection takes from death its "sting."[14]

The fact that true Christians do not fear death does not mean, however, that we should seek premature death in any way. Life is precious and belongs to God. Only He knows His intent for each person's time on earth.

No one has the right to raise his hand against himself, or slay himself against the will of God, his Creator, or drive the soul from the dwelling place of the body. But when he is called, and when his neighbor is called, let him go cheerful and rejoicing, and let him rejoice with those who are going. For this is the sum total of Christian belief: to look for our true life after death; at the end of life, to look for its return.

CHRYSOSTOM[15]

FOOD FOR THOUGHT: (f). Christ taught the early Christians to live with the constant thought that He might return at any moment (Mt. 24:36, 25:13; Lk. 21:34–36; 1 Thess. 5:1–2). Why? (g). What happens to the soul after death?

5:7. For we walk by faith, not by sight. Though we are united with Christ through Eucharist and can know Him through the truths of the Gospel and the grace of the Holy Spirit, we do not see Him bodily as did those who lived when He walked on earth. To try to live by God's word daily, without having seen Christ, is a demonstration of faith, which He acknowledged when He said, "Blessed are they who have not seen, yet have believed" (Jn. 20:29).

5:8–9. We are confident, yes, well pleased rather to be absent from the body and to be present with the Lord. Therefore we make it our aim, whether present or absent, to be well pleasing to Him. Life on earth is precious, but those who have true faith know that to be with the Lord in His Kingdom is infinitely better. The important thing, therefore, is to live in a manner that is *well pleasing* to God, so as to be ready for death, whenever it comes.

FOOD FOR THOUGHT: (h). How can we live in a way that pleases God?

5:10. For we must all appear before the judgment seat of Christ, that each one may receive the things done in the body, according to what he has done, whether good or bad. Some are attracted to the Kingdom because of God's promise of its unequaled joy and love. The attention of others, however, is gained only through the more powerful fear of suffering. In his desire to lead all to salvation, Paul gives the full picture: each of us will face judgment at the feet of Christ and will spend eternity in circumstances determined by whether or not our lives as a whole demonstrated faith. This fact does not call for a legalistic following of rules. Rather, it calls for a continuous attempt at Theosis: growth in those works that are the facets of a Christ-like life (Eph. 2:10) that demonstrate and solidify faith and bring others to Him (Jas. 2:14–26).

Most Protestant denominations teach what is called salvation by "faith alone": the belief that those who profess faith in Christ are automatically "saved," with no qualifying works or actions required. According to this theory, those who pronounce themselves saved because of their acknowledgement of Christ as Savior are guaranteed entrance to Heaven. Scripture that points to judgment is considered to refer only to the unsaved or as a determination of placement in the Kingdom, with levels assigned according to the good or bad one has done. But this verse states that *all* must face judgment, and 2 Cor. 5:11 implies fear. Is there to be punishment in Heaven? Isn't being in God's presence, at any level, a state of glory? The Psalmist wrote: "I would rather be a doorkeeper in the house of my God than dwell in the tents of wickedness" (Ps. 84:10).

The doctrine of salvation by faith alone began as opposition to the emphasis on legalistic-type works (in the sense of earning points) that developed in the Western Church, culminating in the 16th century with the selling of indulgences, which implied that one could buy (or work) one's way to the Kingdom. Martin Luther was a Roman Catholic Priest who protested this aberration, but he went too far in the other direction, insisting that only faith in Christ is necessary for salvation, with no requirement for works of any type. His concerns were justified, but his theology constituted a break in the crucial connection between professed faith and the essential elements of a Christ-like life. The teaching of the early Church (preserved in the East, in Orthodoxy) is that faith is indeed the single criteria for salvation, but faith must be proved by one's life (2 Cor. 13:5) and will be judged by God.

Those who espouse the concept of salvation by faith alone hold that a person who believes in Christ will automatically lead a Christ-like life. Luther taught that this will happen naturally, "as a cow gives milk." In the sincere, thoughtful person, this can indeed happen. The problem is that it gives the misleading impression of a guaranteed conclusion. A person who really has zealous faith will probably seek the truth, attempt to follow it, and consequently grow in holiness through the grace of God. The crucial factor, however, is that conscious personal effort is required and is part of God's plan not to force but to work only in cooperation with man. God meets faith-demonstrating effort with His divine grace. God's grace and man's efforts, together, produce synergistic supernatural growth in Christ's image, toward the holiness that pervades in Christ's presence.

The "by faith alone" philosophy turned its adherents away from the Roman Church because its mass, hierarchical priesthood, Sacraments, etc. were considered "works" with the motivation of achieving credit towards salvation. But Luther himself soon became so distressed at the laxity of behavior in church attendance, lifestyle, etc. that his teachings began to produce in many who professed faith, that he found it necessary to impose harsh discipline. In modern days, salvation by faith alone is sometimes referred to as "instant salvation." It holds great appeal for the "lukewarm" (Rev. 3:16), who may or may not be part of a church. It allows adherents to blissfully consider themselves Christians, content that because they orally profess Christ as Savior they are headed toward Heaven, in spite of the absence of an attempt at Christ-like living. Those who have been lulled into such complacency feel that enlightened thinking has liberated them from what they consider to be the old fashioned, legalistic moral constraints of the Bible. To live in a manner unconcerned with spiritual growth and doing the work of the Lord, however, or to intentionally disobey His word shows lack of real faith. He who does only as he pleases shows faith in himself over and above anything else, including God.

For the spiritually lazy, Martin Luther's well-intentioned Protestant Reformation efforts at reform and renewal have degenerated into a simplistic catch-all theory: Jesus died for sinners, so nothing is required of us. This has contributed to the watering down of Christ's Gospel (Rev. 12:15) and helps Satan continue to do, through false teachings, that which he failed to do through persecution in the early Church (Rev. 12:13): divide the faithful and lead as many as possible away from God, like sheep to slaughter.

5:11. Knowing, therefore, the terror of the Lord, we persuade men; but we are well-known to God, and I also trust are well-known in your consciences. Paul tries to awaken everyone he meets to the fact that the aftermath of judgment is eternal: blessed life with God or the torment of being far removed from Him. This man who always zealously allowed his faith to guide his actions knows he must continue in that vein (Phil. 3:12) or face *the terror of the Lord.* He is also aware that he must be a good role model for others. This awareness of the example we set as Christians is very important. Everything we say and do—our actions, inactions and reactions—can influence, positively or negatively, those with whom we come in contact.

> He who lives a worthy life draws grace upon himself; and he who receives such grace receives that he may help others to amend their lives. ... The beauty of a good life can help others more than miracles. I mean by a good life, not simply fasting nor lying down in sackcloth and ashes but to despise riches, to have charity towards your neighbor, to give of your bread to the hungry, to control your anger, to seek not vainglory, and to turn from envy.
>
> CHRYSOSTOM[16]

5:12. For we do not commend ourselves again to you, but give you opportunity to glory on our behalf, that you may have something to answer those who glory in appearance and not in heart. Paul offers the example of his life as a guide to the type of struggle required of those whose hearts are set on God's Kingdom. This contrasts sharply with false teachers who boast about themselves and their ministries but who, in reality, are spiritually dead.

5:13. For if we are beside ourselves, it is for God; or if we are of sound mind, it is for you. Paul's exuberance leads his detractors to say that he is not of sound mind. He responds that what they have witnessed is the spiritual ecstasy that fills him because of his love for God. But whether he is in that state or in a state of sober reflection, his intent is to bring them the truth of God's promises. This brings to mind the fact that, in the jargon of the world, someone who is zealous for sports, music, or other such interests is called a fan, but someone who is enthused about God and His Kingdom is likely to be called a fanatic.

5:14–15. For the love of Christ constrains us because we judge thus: that if One died for all, then all died; and He died for all, that those who live should live no longer for themselves but for Him Who died for them and rose again. Death came through sin (Gen. 2:17). Everyone born to man after the fall inherits this consequence—and a sinful nature. Christ was born of Mary, a pious, obedient maiden who was freed of any association with Adam and Eve's disobedience when she consented to bear the Son of God in her womb. She conceived through the Holy Spirit—supranaturally—outside the natural laws of procreation and heredity. Thus Christ was born with no association with the sin of Adam and Eve. He lived a sin-free life, so did not deserve to die. Yet he willingly became the scapegoat for the sins of mankind (Lev. 16:10, 21). He passed through death, and then rose on the third day to show us there is life after death. If we try to grow in our understanding of these truths and the all-encompassing love demonstrated by them, we will develop a growing love for Christ. This love will manifest itself in a willingness to stand apart from the selfish ways of the world, in which personal goals for success and pleasure dominate. We will choose, instead, to live for Him—to continue the work He left for us.

> If there is true Christian love in a man, let him carry out the precepts of Christ. Who can describe the constraining power of love for God? Who can adequately express its majesty and beauty? No tongue can tell the heights to which love can lift us. Love binds us fast to God. Love casts a veil over sins innumerable. There are no limits to love's endurance, no end to its patience. Love is without servility, as it is without arrogance. Love knows of no divisions, promotes no discord; all the works of love are done in

perfect fellowship. It was in love that all God's chosen saints were made perfect; for without love nothing is pleasing to Him. It was in love that the Lord drew us to Himself; because of the love He bore us, our Lord Jesus Christ, at the will of God, gave His blood for us—His flesh for our flesh, His life for our lives.

CLEMENT OF ROME[17]

5:16. Therefore, from now on, we regard no one according to the flesh. Even though we have known Christ according to the flesh, yet now we know Him thus no longer. Those who realize that Christ is the promised Messiah do not consider Him as just another man who lived and died. They know Him by His position in the Kingdom, at the right hand of God, waiting for those who belong to Him. Paul writes that we should regard those around us in our lives in similar fashion: according to the degree that they reflect the image of Christ rather than the degree of worldly status they have attained. This was the attitude of Christ Himself, Who emphasized spiritual relationships above worldly when He said, "My mother and my brothers are [those] who hear the word of God and do it" (Lk. 8:21).

> Let us beg and implore of God's mercy that we may be purged of all earthly preferences for this man or that, and be found faultless in love. Though every generation from Adam to the present day has passed from the earth, yet such of them as by God's grace were perfected in love have their place now in the courts of the godly, and at the visitation of Christ's Kingdom they will be openly revealed. For it is written, *Go into your secret chambers for a very little while, till my rage and fury pass away; and then I will remember a day of gladness, and raise you out of your graves.*
>
> CLEMENT OF ROME[18]

5:17. Therefore, if anyone is in Christ, he is a new creation; old things have passed away; behold, all things have become new. The oppressive Law of the Old Testament covenant has been fulfilled by the liberating force of Christ's sacrifice. To those who belong to Christ through Baptism, nothing is as it was before.

> Behold, both a new soul (for it was cleansed), and a new body, and a new worship, and promises new, and covenant, and life, and table and dress, and all things new absolutely. For instead of the Jerusalem below we have received that mother city which is above (Gal. 4:26); and instead of a material temple have seen a spiritual temple; instead of tables of stone, fleshy ones; instead of circumcision, baptism; instead of manna, the Lord's Body; instead of water from a rock, blood from His side; instead of Moses' or Aaron's rod, the Cross; instead of the promised land, the Kingdom of Heaven; instead of a thousand priests, one High Priest; instead of a lamb without reason, a Spiritual Lamb. With these and such like things in his thought he said, a*ll things are new.* But *all* these *things are of God*, by Christ, and His free gift.
>
> CHRYSOSTOM[19]

5:18–19. Now all things are of God, Who has reconciled us to Himself through Jesus Christ and has given us the ministry of reconciliation, that is, that God was in Christ reconciling the world to Himself, not imputing their trespasses to them, and has committed to us the word of reconciliation. Through Christ, the second person of the Holy Trinity, in fulfillment of the first prophesy (see Gen. 3:15 and this study for 1 Cor. 2:6–8), God gave man the way back to union with Him—that which Adam and Eve lost for themselves and mankind when they disobeyed. This truth was given to the Apostles. All who continue their work of teaching the Gospel, whether clergy or laity, carry on Christ's ministry of reconciliation.

> Through Chrismation every member of the Church becomes a prophet and receives a share in the royal priesthood of Christ; all Christians alike, because they are Chrismated, are called to act as conscious witnesses to the Truth. *You have an anointing (chrisma) from the Holy One, and know all things* (1 Jn. 2:20).[20]

5:20–21. Therefore we are ambassadors for Christ, as though God were pleading through us: we implore you on Christ's behalf, be reconciled to God. For He made Him Who knew no sin to be sin for us, that we might become the righteousness of God in Him. An ambassador represents the leader of his country in a foreign land. He must speak the language and take part in the ways of that land but is a citizen of his own country. So too, true Christians are in the world, but not of it, "For our citizenship is in Heaven" (Phil. 3:20).

> Christians have a unique citizenship of their own. They are, of course, citizens of their own lands—loyal ones too. Yet they feel like visitors. Every foreign country is their homeland, and their homeland is like a foreign country to them.
>
> MATHETES[21]

As Christ's ambassador, Paul urgently pleads that we all come to full realization of that which our Savior has done for us. Jesus not only accepted death undeservedly on our behalf, He also endured the indignities of crucifixion, the most dreaded torture (Gal. 3:13). By humbling Himself to the utmost, Christ attained the highest glory (Phil. 2:8–11). He promises that if we acknowledge Him as Savior and try to live according to His teachings, we take part in His righteousness. As a part of Him through Baptism, Eucharist, and a life of faith, we are no

319

longer bound by the consequences of sin, and so will share His glory.

> "God made Himself man, that man might become God." These powerful words, which we find for the first time in St. Irenaeus, are again found in the writings of St. Athanasius, St. Gregory of Nazianzus, and St. Gregory of Nyssa. The Fathers and Orthodox theologians have repeated them in every century with the same emphasis, wishing to sum up in this striking sentence the very essence of Christianity: an ineffable descent of God to the ultimate limit of our fallen human condition, even unto death—a descent of God which opens to men a path of ascent, the unlimited vistas of the union of created beings with the Divinity.[22]

We find it easy to remember that God took on flesh and died to redeem us from sin, but we also easily forget the reason: that we "might become God." Consequently, too often our glorious potential remains unrealized. We can become God to the extent that we grow in union with Him, but that which man can know of God, and partake of, is not His divine essence but His "operations" or "energies."

> We know our God from His operations, but do not undertake to approach near to His essence. His operations come down to us, but His essence remains beyond our reach.
>
> BASIL[23]

God's essence is often compared to the solar disk and His energies to its rays.[24] We can see the light that emanates from the sun and feel its heat but cannot approach the source or gaze upon its brilliance directly, even from a great distance. So it is with God. We can partake of that which flows from Him but not of that which makes Him God—for He is unknowable, inaccessible. "We are created beings, called to become by grace what God is by His nature. If one could participate in the essence itself, God would no longer be Trinity, but a multitude of persons."[25]

Those who grow in holiness do so because they partake of (plug in to) the actual energies of God. We avail ourselves of those energies by disciplining our will to follow His bidding. To the extent we do so, we actually take on His qualities, as an object added to a glowing fire takes on the characteristics of fire.

> This is why the saints are the instruments of the Holy
> Spirit, having received the same energy He has.
> GREGORY PALAMAS[26]

It is through these energies of God that man is divinely activated and can actually have a direct relationship with God during his earthly life and beyond. Bishop Kallistos Ware writes: "In relation to us humans, the divine energy is in fact nothing else than the grace of God."[27] Man has access to God's grace, His energies, through the operations of each of the three persons of the Godhead.

> The Father, the Son and the Holy Spirit alike hallow,
> quicken, enlighten and comfort. No one will attribute
> a special and peculiar operation of hallowing to the
> operation of the Spirit after hearing the Savior in the
> Gospel saying to the Father about His disciples,
> "Sanctify them by your Truth" (Jn. 17:11,17). In like
> manner all other operations are equally performed, in
> all who are worthy of them, by the Father and by the
> Son and by the Holy Spirit; every grace and virtue,
> guidance, life, consolation, change into the immortal,
> the passage into freedom and all other good things
> which come down to man.
> BASIL[28]

FOOD FOR THOUGHT COMMENTS

(a). What indications does the Bible give that everyone, believers as well as non-believers, will live eternally in a body?

From the Old Testament:

> *For I know that my Redeemer lives, and He shall stand at last on the earth; and after my skin is destroyed, this I know, that **in my flesh** I shall see God* (Job 19:25–26). Job clearly foretells Christ the Redeemer ... speaking not of "my Creator," but of *my Redeemer*. ... But tell us clearly I beg you, Blessed Job, what you believe, concerning the resurrection of your own flesh ... I ask to learn the manner of this resurrection. For I believe that I shall rise again, but I desire to know of what nature shall I be? For I must know whether I shall rise again in some other subtle or perhaps ethereal body or in this body in which I die. For if I rise again in another, ethereal body, it will no longer be I who shall rise. For how can that be a true resurrection, if there cannot be a true body? Plain reason tells me that if the body is not true, then beyond doubt there shall be no true resurrection. Nor can it be rightly called a resurrection, when that does not rise which died. O Blessed Job, take from us these clouds of doubt, and as you, through the grace of the Holy Spirit, have already begun to speak to us of our hope of resurrection, make clear to us if our flesh shall truly rise again. There follows: *in my flesh I shall see God.*
>
> GREGORY THE GREAT[29]

> *Your dead shall live; Together with my dead body they shall arise. Awake and sing, you who dwell in dust;*

For your dew is like the dew of herbs, and the earth shall cast out the dead (Is. 26:19). Perhaps you fear that your dry bones cannot be clothed again in their former flesh? Do not measure the power of God by your own weakness. God, the Creator of all things, Who clothes the trees with leaves, the fields with flowers, can also, at the Resurrection, clothe your bones with their true flesh. Ezekiel the prophet on one occasion doubted this very thing, and asked by the Lord whether the dry bones he saw scattered over the plain would live again, replied: *Oh Lord God, You know* (Ez. 37:3). But after the Lord commanded him to prophesy concerning these bones, he saw the bones come together, each one to its joint, and when he had seen the dry bones bound together with sinew and interwoven with veins and covered with flesh and the skin stretched out over them he prophesied in the spirit, and the spirit of each one entered into the bodies lying there, and they rose from the dead, and directly they *stood upon their feet*. And the prophet, reassured in this way of the truth of the resurrection of the dead, wrote down the vision, that those who came after him might come to know of this wondrous happening.

CHRYSOSTOM[30]

From the New Testament:

Behold My hands and My feet, that it is I Myself. Handle Me and see, for a spirit does not have flesh and bones as you see I have (Lk. 24:39). When I was living in the city of Constantinople at the time of this Eutychius (who once said our future bodies would be impalpable and more ethereal than air), I put this testimony from the Gospel to the truth of our resurrection before him. He replied: "The Lord did this to remove all doubt of His Resurrection from the hearts of His Disciples." To this I said: "This is truly an extraordinary thing you are saying: that doubt

323

should arise in us from the same grounds which took away all doubts from the hearts of the Disciples?" If you assert that He did not possess that which He showed them, which confirmed the faith of His Disciples, then our faith is destroyed. He then went on to say that the Lord had the palpable Body He showed them. But after He had confirmed the hearts of those who touched Him, all that could be touched in the Lord was then reduced to a certain subtlety. To this I answered: "It is written that Christ, rising again from the dead, dies now no more; Death shall no more have dominion over Him" (Rom. 6:9). If, therefore, after His Resurrection anything of His Body could suffer change, contrary to the truth of what Paul has said, then after His Resurrection the Lord returned to death. And what person however foolish would say this, except one who denies the true Resurrection of His Body?

To this he objected, saying to me: "Since it is written that ... *flesh and blood cannot possess the Kingdom of God* (I Cor. 15:50), on what ground can we believe that the body shall truly rise again?" To this I replied, "In Sacred Writ flesh is spoken of in one way in regard to its nature, in another in regard to its guilt or corruption. Of flesh as nature it was written: *This now is bone of my bones, and flesh of my flesh (Gen. 2:23); and The Word was made flesh and dwelt among us* (Jn. 1:14). Of flesh as guilt it was written: *My spirit shall not remain in man forever because he is flesh* (Gen. 6:3). And the Psalmist says: *and he remembers that they are flesh: a breath that passes away and does not come again* (Ps. 78:39). And it was in this sense Paul said to the disciples: *You are not in the flesh, but in the spirit* (Rom. 8:9). It was not that the persons to whom he was writing were no longer in the body, but that they had mastered the impulses of the body's desires; and being now free through the power of the Spirit, were no longer *in the flesh*.

324

Accordingly, Paul saying that *flesh and blood cannot possess the Kingdom of God* means that flesh here stands for guilt, not for our nature. For in his next words he shows he was speaking of flesh as guilt when he adds: *Neither shall corruption possess incorruption.* Therefore flesh shall be in the glory of that Heavenly Kingdom, in its nature, but *not in the passion of lust*; and the sting of death overcome, it shall reign incorrupt forever. ... "

Going on with this question for a long time, we began to feel a great resentment towards one another. Then the Emperor, Constantine Tiberius of pious memory, received us both in private to learn of the disagreement between us. After weighing the written presentation of the case by either side, he decided that the book Eutychius had written on the Resurrection should be committed to the flames. Upon leaving, I became very ill, and the same happened to Eutychius, who died a little later. At the time of his death, as there was almost no one who followed his teaching, I dropped the prosecution of it, lest I should appear to be shooting arrows at his ashes. But while he was still alive, and while I was ill with fever, to those I knew who went to visit him he would say, holding the skin of his hand before their eyes: "I confess that in this flesh we shall all rise again." And this, they tell me, he used to deny totally.

GREGORY THE GREAT[31]

(b). What indications does the Bible give that, after the Resurrection, the immortal body of a believer will be much like that possessed in life on earth but different, with unique spiritual qualities? The references to Jesus' physical appearance after His Resurrection indicate that though those who had known Him before His death were able to recognize Him, not all did so immediately, for two reasons:

(1). they were not expecting to see Him alive again, and (2). upon Resurrection, His body was made incorruptible. So He looked similar—yet different.

<u>Mt. 28:1–10</u>: This account shows that the women recognized Jesus. Thus His post-Resurrection appearance must have been similar to His pre-Resurrection appearance.

<u>Jn. 20:11–18</u>: Mary, however, recognized Jesus only after He spoke her name, a sound familiar to her ears, indicating that there was something different about His physical appearance.

<u>Jn. 20:19</u>: When the doors were shut, Jesus came and stood in their midst. The special qualities of His resurrected body enabled Him to be present in a room without entering through a door or window.

<u>Lk. 24:13–31</u>: When two of the (70) disciples were on the road to Emmaus, Jesus drew near and began to walk with them. They did not recognize Him, however, until He blessed bread, broke it, and gave it to them, something they had seen Him do before (Mt. 14:19; 26:26). Then He *vanished from their sight,* another indication of the special qualities of His resurrected body.

The body in which we spend eternity will be a "spiritual body." Bishop Kallistos Ware wrote: "This does not mean that at the Resurrection our bodies will be somehow dematerialized; but we are to remember that matter as we know it in this fallen world, with all its inertness and opacity, does not at all correspond to matter as God intended it to be. Freed from the grossness of the fallen flesh, the resurrection body will share in the qualities of Christ's human body at the Transfiguration and after the Resurrection. But, although transformed, our resurrection body will still be in a recognizable way the same body as that which we have now: there will be continuity between the two."[32]

> After our future resurrection, our flesh shall be the same and different: the same in nature, different through glory; the same in its reality, different in its power. It shall indeed be subtle because it shall be incorruptible. It shall be palpable because it shall not lose the essence of its true nature.
>
> GREGORY THE GREAT[33]

> For it is just that in the body in which the righteous toiled or were afflicted, being proved in every way by suffering, they should receive the reward of their suffering; and that in the body in which they were slain because of their love for God, in that they should be revived again; and that in the body in which they endured servitude, in that they should reign. For God is rich in all things, and all things are His. It is fitting, therefore, that the creation itself [the body], being restored to its primeval condition, should without restraint be under the dominion of the righteous.
>
> IRENAEUS[34]

(c). What will be the conditions of eternal life in God's Kingdom? Perfection is dynamic, not static. The righteous will rise in perfect, immortal bodies and will continually grow in union with God.

> For if on earth Jesus Christ healed the sicknesses of the flesh and made the body whole, much more will He do this in the Resurrection, so that the flesh shall rise perfect and entire, with all dreaded difficulties healed.
>
> JUSTIN THE MARTYR[35]

Godliness is perfection that is never complete.
                    PHILOTHEOS OF SINAI[36]

There shall be no marrying, to beget children. For there shall be no death; nor growing up, because no one grows old. There shall be no eating, for there shall be no hunger. (The power to eat and to drink shall remain after the Resurrection, as it did with Christ, but not the need.)[37] There shall be no buying or selling, for there shall be no want. ... The Sabbath (day of rest) shall be unbroken: what the Jews celebrate for a period of time, we shall celebrate for all eternity.

There shall be ineffable rest ... for as we are born in the body to toil, we are reborn in the spirit to rest; ... Here He feeds us, there He perfects us; here He promises, there He shall give; here He foretells, there He shall show us the reality. And when we are safe and perfected, in spirit and in body, within that blessedness, the things of this world shall be no more; ...

But we shall not sleep in idleness; for sleep itself is now given to us as refreshment for the weariness of the soul. For the fragile body cannot endure the unceasing striving that agitates our mortal senses unless this fragility is renewed, through the sleep of the senses, to enable it to bear this agitation. And as the renewal to come shall be from death, so is waking now from sleep. Therefore there shall be no sleep. For where there is no death, there shall be no image of death.

All our activity shall be, "Amen" and "Alleluia". ... Do not be saddened by thinking, in earthly fashion, that if one of you were to stand every day saying, "Amen" and "Alleluia," he would soon wither away from sheer tedium, if he did not fall asleep from repetition and long for silence; and from this go on to think of that life as unpleasing and undesirable. ... We shall say "Amen" and "Alleluia," not in sounds that come and go, but with the love of our soul. ... Amen means "so be it"; alleluia, "praise God" ... because we shall, with unceasing delight, see Truth there, and contemplate it in shining clarity. Inflamed with the love of this Truth and clinging to it in sweet, chaste, and incorporeal embrace, we shall praise it and say "Alleluia." Exhorting each other to the same praise, and with most ardent charity towards one another and towards God, all who are citizens of that City shall sing, "Alleluia," as they shall say "Amen."

AUGUSTINE[38]

(d). What will be the characteristics of the resurrected bodies of the righteous? ... of the unrighteous? The resurrected bodies of both the righteous and the unrighteous will be immortal—but they will be decidedly different.

> If a man is righteous, he will receive a heavenly body, that he may be able to converse with angels; but if a man is a sinner, he shall receive an eternal body fit to endure the penalties of sins. And righteously will God assign either state, for we do nothing without the body. We blaspheme with the body, and with the mouth we pray. With the body we commit fornication, and with the body we keep chastity. With the hand we rob, and by the hand we bestow alms; and the rest in like manner. Since then the body has been our minister in all things, it shall also share with us in the future the fruits of the past.

CYRIL OF JERUSALEM[39]

> The bodies of the impious shall be unchanged; nothing shall appear to be taken from them. But their unchanged body shall be for a punishment; and this sort of consistency, if I may call it so, is a corruptible

consistency. For where there is pain there is corruption: and the former liability to pain shall not cease, pain itself shall not die. For we believe that this corruption was referred to prophetically by the term *worm*, and pain, by the word *fire*. But since this consistency shall be such that it shall neither yield to death through pain nor be changed to that incorruption in which there is no pain, for this reason was it written: *Their worm shall not die, and their fire shall not be quenched* (Is. 66:24; Mk. 9:43–48).

AUGUSTINE[40]

Well! I know what a chill comes over you on hearing these things; but what am I to do? This is God's own command, to continually tell you these truths.

CHRYSOSTOM[41]

(e). There are those, like Jehovah's Witnesses, who believe that there is no Hell (in the sense of a state or place of eternal agony). This false teaching can cause much harm and eternal suffering. How? Jehovah's Witnesses profess that, ultimately, the unrighteous will be totally annihilated. This false teaching is very attractive to many and inspires the saying: "Let us eat, drink and be merry, for tomorrow we die" (Is. 22:13). The Devil wants us to believe that there is no Hell for the same reason he would like us to believe that he does not exist. If we are unaware of his presence, we will be unaware of the traps he sets for us—the ways in which he tries to lead us away from God. Those who believe there is no Hell may choose to spend their lives following their own will instead of trying to determine and discipline themselves according to that of God, content with what they think will be a blissful future of non-existence. In either case, Satan will have attained his goal of diverting many from the Kingdom.

It will literally be a rude awakening to those who succumb to the comforts of this heresy and squander their lives with no concern for the obedience and spiritual growth God expects, to find not merciful oblivion but eternal agony: "the worm that does not die" and the "fire that is not quenched" (Mk. 9:48): an awful, never-ending, painful realization of having denied oneself blessedness and eternal joy.

(f). Christ taught the early Christians to live with the constant thought that He might return at any moment (Mt. 24:36, 25:13; Lk. 21:34–36; 1 Thess. 5:1–2). Why? For the same reason that God does not want us to know the length of our individual lives. He wants us to live in a state of readiness so we do not become negligent about our relationship with Him. Death can come upon us unexpectedly, as can Christ's Second Coming. Either event marks the end of our opportunity to demonstrate our faith and to grow in holiness in preparation for the Kingdom. Both are times of judgment. Therefore, each day of our lives we must try to grow in Christ's image so that we are always ready to meet our Lord.

(g). What happens to the soul after death? After death, the soul leaves the body and lives on because it is immortal. Partial judgment takes place. In its unending existence, the soul enters a new state in which it "pre-senses and foretastes, to a certain degree, that which it shall experience in full after the Second Coming of Christ and final judgment. The soul of the righteous foretastes and experiences the beneficences of Heaven and Paradise. ... The soul of the sinner foretastes and experiences the fearful sufferings of Hell."[42] When we sleep we experience a foreshadowing of this state of existence between death of the earthly body and the resurrected state after the Second Coming of Christ: though our body is immobile, through dreams we may participate in many experiences.

> When the body lies in bed, not moving but in death-
> like sleep, the soul keeps awake by virtue of its own

power. It transcends the natural power of the body and as though traveling away from the body while remaining in it, imagines and beholds things above the earth. Often it even holds converse with the saints and angels who are above earthly and bodily existence and approaches them in the confidence of the purity of its intelligence. Shall it not all the more, when separated from the body at the time appointed by God Who coupled them together, have its knowledge of immortality more clear? For if even when coupled with the body it lived a life outside the body, much more shall its life continue after the death of the body and live without ceasing by reason of God Who made it thus by His own Word, our Lord Jesus Christ.

ATHANASIUS[43]

The resurrection of the dead will take place at the Second Coming of Christ, when "every soul shall unite itself to the body which it possessed during its life on earth ... it will be a spiritual, not a material one. In this way we shall all appear before the tribunal of Christ."[44] After this final and complete judgment, each person will experience eternally, with both body and soul, that for which s/he has prepared. What the soul had become inwardly during life on earth will become evident outwardly in the body. We will be what we have practiced to be.

The glory that in the present life enriches the souls of the saints will cover and enfold their naked bodies at the Resurrection and will carry them to Heaven. Then with body and soul the saints will rest with God in the Kingdom forever. For God, when He created Adam, did not give him bodily wings as He gave to the birds: His purpose was to confer the wings of the Spirit on him at the Resurrection, so that he might be lifted up by them and carried wherever the Spirit desired. Such spiritual wings are given to the souls of the saints in this present life so that their understanding may be raised by them to the spiritual realm. For the world of the Christians is a different world, with different garments, different food and a different form of enjoyment. We know that when Christ comes from Heaven to resurrect all those who have died during the present age, He will divide them into two groups (Mt. 25:31–33). Those who bear His sign, which is the seal of the Holy Spirit, He will set at His right hand, saying: *My sheep, when they hear My voice, recognize Me* (Jn. 10:14). Then He will envelop their bodies with the divine glory that, through their good works and the Spirit, their souls have already received in this present life.

MAKARIOS OF EGYPT[45]

(h). How can we live in a way that pleases God? If, every time we must make an important decision, we try to determine what God asks of us and do our best to act accordingly, we will grow in the image of Christ and thus will please God.

Wear a garment of incorruption, resplendent in good works; and whatever matter you receive from God to administer as a steward, administer profitably. Have you been given riches? Dispense them well. Have you been entrusted with the word of teaching? Be a good steward thereof. Have you power to rule? Do this diligently. There are many doors of good stewardship. Only let none of us be condemned and cast out; that we may with boldness meet Christ, the everlasting King, who reigns forever.

CYRIL OF JERUSALEM[46]

If you have the fire of lust, set against it that other fire (Mt. 13:42), and this will presently be quenched and gone. If you wish to utter some harsh sounding words, think of the gnashing of teeth and the fear will be a bridle to your tongue. If you wish to plunder, hear the Judge commanding, *Bind him hand and foot, and cast him into the outer darkness* (Mt. 22:13), and you will cast out this lust also. If you are drunken, and overindulge continually, hear the rich man saying, *Send Lazarus, that with the tip of his finger he may cool this scorching tongue* (Lk. 16:24), yet not obtaining this, and you will hold yourself aloof from that distemper. If you love luxury, think of the affliction there and you will not think at all of this. If you are harsh and cruel, think of those virgins who when their lamps had gone out missed the bridal chamber (Mt. 25:12), and you will quickly become humane. Are you sluggish, and remiss? Consider him who hid the talent (Mt. 25:24–30), and you will be more vehement than fire. Are you devoured by desire of what belongs to your neighbor? Think of the worm that does not die and you will easily both put away from you this disease, and in all other things act virtuously. He has asked of us nothing irksome or oppressive. Why then do His injunctions appear irksome to us? From our laziness. If we labor diligently, even what appears intolerable will be light and easy; but if we are lazy, even things tolerable will seem difficult.

CHRYSOSTOM[47]

CHAPTER SIX

Through Whom God Works

As Chapter Five ended, Paul pleaded that his readers be reconciled to God by taking full advantage of the grace of Christ's saving work. He proceeds to warn about the perils of wasting grace.

6:1. We then, as workers together with Him, also plead with you not to receive the grace of God in vain. The grace of which Paul writes is the opportunity for salvation through Christ. He begs his readers not to waste this gift, which is available to everyone. God has offered knowledge of this grace to mankind through those who have continued Christ's work through the ages. Inspired authors of Scripture, Fathers of the Church whose writings preserve its intended meaning, priests, monks, theologians, teachers, parents, and all who have really believed the Gospel have passed on the same urgent message: use life for its ultimate purpose—to learn about God's plan for those who would like to live eternally with Him and try to live accordingly in order to demonstrate faith and be rendered righteous (Mt. 13:41–43).

> So they won't think that *reconciliation* (5:18–19) comes from merely believing in Him Who calls, he adds these words, requiring that earnestness which respects the life. ... For from *grace* we reap no benefit towards salvation if we live impurely; no, we are even harmed, having greater aggravation of our sins, if after such knowledge and such a gift we go back to our former vices.
>
> CHRYSOSTOM[1]

6:2. For He says: "In an acceptable time I have heard

you, and in the day of salvation I have helped you." Behold, now is the accepted time; behold, now is the day of salvation. Quoting Isaiah 49:8, Paul relates that God helps us to fulfill life's potential of union with Him by reaching out to each of us in *an acceptable time:* our lifetime—the time allotted to ponder and pursue salvation. We never know when this life and, therefore, this opportunity will end through death or the Second Coming of Christ, so the present day is the only one of which we can be certain. It is therefore *the day of salvation*: our chance to consciously commit or recommit our lives to Christ—tomorrow may be too late.

> **FOOD FOR THOUGHT:** (a). What regular reminders are Orthodox Christians given of the need to commit or recommit their lives to Christ continually?

6:3. We give no offense in anything, that our ministry may not be blamed. Paul does not allow himself any personal leeway. He strives to be a good example of the Christian life in all ways so those observing his way of life will have no cause to reject the Gospel on his account. This is a verse that anyone in the position of influencing others by his example would do well to memorize.

6:4–5. But in all things we commend ourselves as ministers of God: in much patience, in tribulations, in needs, in distresses, in stripes, in imprisonments, in tumults, in labors, in sleeplessness, in fastings; In carrying out the work God set before him, Paul not only patiently endures but triumphs over those external trials and tribulations his work and the enemies of the Gospel bring. Though often without adequate food and sleep, he also willingly participates in the discipline of fasting for the spiritual strength it affords, so he will be able to continue the struggle.

On a personal level regarding salvation, there is no exemption from spiritual growth and struggle for those who are God's ministers. All Christians are required to try to live the life as well as teach it to others.

> Obey those who rule over you, and be submissive, for they watch out for your souls, as those who must give account (Heb. 13:17).

> But neither he who pursues political rule nor he who pursues spiritual rule will be able to administer it unless he has first ruled himself as he ought.
> CHRYSOSTOM[2]

6:6. ... by purity, by knowledge, by long-suffering, by kindness, by the Holy Spirit, by sincere love ... These are fruits of the Holy Spirit, the gifts with which God meets man's efforts at spiritual growth (see Gal. 5:22–24). The fact that Paul possesses these gifts shows that he is a true teacher of God's word.

> Paul received grace, but he himself was the cause who by his good works and his toils attracted grace. And ... he also did not misuse the gifts of the Spirit.
> CHRYSOSTOM[3]

> **FOOD FOR THOUGHT:** (b). How can the gifts of the Spirit be misused?

6:7. by the word of truth, by the power of God, by the armor of righteousness on the right hand and on the left; The power of God is available through the Sacraments of the Church, which are vehicles of grace. Paul's effectiveness in his ministry stems from acting according to God's will, by which he clothes himself in the armor of righteousness. This advantage is accessible to all who develop, teach, and live by an understanding of the fullness of the truths preserved by the early Church (read Eph. 6:11–18).

> "But," you say, "virtue is burdensome and distasteful, while with vice, great pleasure is blended; and the one is wide and broad, but the other straight and narrow." … Suppose there were two roads, one leading to a furnace, and the other to a Paradise; and the one to the furnace was broad, while the other to Paradise, narrow. Which road would you take?
>
> CHRYSOSTOM[4]

6:8–10. by honor and dishonor, by evil report and good report; as deceivers, and yet true; as unknown, and yet well known; as dying, and behold we live; as chastened, and yet not killed; as sorrowful, yet always rejoicing; as poor, yet making many rich; as having nothing, and yet possessing all things. Paul dealt with the extremes of life, as do all who sincerely try to live and teach the fullness of the Gospel. He was honored by some, dishonored by others.

> When the teachers are held in honor, many are inspired to godliness. And besides, this is a proof of good works, and glorifies God.
>
> CHRYSOSTOM[5]

To receive *honor* is very pleasant, but it presents a particular danger to the recipient. It is difficult to accept praise humbly, in a Christ-like manner, and sincerely give all glory to God. The sin of pride can easily rear its ugly head.

> God is opposed to nothing so much as to pride. And because of this there is nothing He has not done, since the beginning, to overthrow this evil disposition. Because of it we are subject to death and live in grief

and pain; because of it we labor in sweat, in toil and in afflictions without end.

Through pride, the first man sinned because he aspired to become equal to God and so did not even keep what he already had, but fell from everything. For it is the nature of pride that not only does it add nothing to our life, it also takes from us that which we have. Humility takes nothing from us but rather adds what we do not have.

CHRYSOSTOM[6]

FOOD FOR THOUGHT: (c). What are the signs of pride?

The antidote to the spiritual danger posed by the poison of excessive honor and praise, especially to those who try to teach the Gospel, is to remember that no one can share credit for the only thing that has eternal value: God's divine plan for our salvation through Christ. It was instituted by God, executed by Christ, and empowered by the Holy Spirit. The greatest Apostles, preachers, and teachers have felt awed, humbled, and unspeakably grateful to be allowed a role in bringing knowledge and understanding of it to others. It was in this spirit that John the Baptist, whom Jesus called the greatest man to have lived, proclaimed that he was not even worthy to untie Christ's sandals (Mk. 1:7).

The true Christian walks against the winds of the world most of the time, so struggle is part of the course. Along the way there are always those who do not want to hear God's truths because they do not want to have to change their lives accordingly. Their reaction may be to try to discredit the messenger so they can feel justified in ignoring the message. Paul often faced such *dishonor.* When he did, he tried to take that also in stride, following Christ's example. Accepting dishonor when it comes is the balance to accepting honor and staves off vainglory.

> The first step in overcoming vainglory is to remain silent and to accept dishonor gladly. The middle stage is to check every act of vainglory while it is still in thought. The end—insofar as one may talk of an end to an abyss—is to be able to accept humiliation before others without actually feeling it.
>
> CLIMACUS[7]

Some have *good* things to say about Paul, and some *evil*. Some say he *deceives* those to whom he preaches, and others say his teachings are *true* to the word of God. In facing both extremes, he endeavors to respond as Christ would. To some he is *unknown*, no one important; to others he is *well-known*, and has changed many lives. Some dismiss him and the power God wielded through him because they think he is *dying*. They know he is under the constant threat of death and feel he won't be around long, yet he continues to *live* and work and bring people to God, *as chastened and yet not killed*. He is often *sorrowful* because of the ungodly conditions of the world that imperil his ministry and his life, yet he is *always rejoicing* because he knows the certainty of eternal life with God in His Kingdom for those who endure to the end (Mt. 10:22).

The Apostles were *poor* in worldly possessions yet rich spiritually and *made many rich* in that which really matters— knowledge of Christ. In addition, however, the riches of the world were available to them to partake of through those they taught. Because they were willing to trust God and spent their time and energy storing up spiritual rather than material treasures, they lived *as having nothing, yet possessing all things*. Paul experienced both extremes of human emotion: from enemies of the Gospel he received hatred and abuse, but from friends of the Gospel he received great love and generosity. Some of those friends, he wrote, would gladly pluck out their own eyes to give to him (Gal. 4:15).

> He who gives temporal aid to those who have spiritual gifts to bestow is a cooperator in spiritual giving. For since there are few who possess spiritual gifts and many who abound in temporal things, through this means they who have possessions partake in the virtues of those who are needy by relieving from their own abundance the wants of these sanctified poor.
>
> GREGORY THE GREAT[8]

> Some say that spiritual riches are spoken of here; but I would say that the carnal are too; for they were rich in these also, having, after a new kind of manner, the houses of all opened to them.
>
> CHRYSOSTOM[9]

FOOD FOR THOUGHT: (d). This brings to mind Jesus' words: "Seek first the Kingdom of God and His righteousness, and all things shall be added to you" (Mt. 6:33). How can this principle be applied to our modern lives?

6:11–12. O Corinthians! We have spoken openly to you, our heart is wide open. You are not restricted by us, but you are restricted by your own affections. The Greek text means more literally "our heart is enlarged." A heart that feels love seems to expand; it has room for more. The one who loves showers his beloved with tokens of affection. Because of the love Paul feels for the people of Corinth, his words are filled with great emotion. There is no limit to his love for them (2 Cor. 12:15), therefore, no limit to the lengths he will go to make them understand the word of God. However, they are limited in their response to the Christian life by the depth of their love for him and for God. As a person's love grows, commitment to a Christ-like life to show this love will deepen.

> He who loves the Lord has first loved his brother, for the latter is proof of the former.
>
> CLIMACUS[10]

> If you love God, you will be an imitator of His kindness.
>
> MATHETES[11]

> It is for love's sake that he who is in a state of obedience obeys what is commanded. Good works are done out of love for one's neighbor; while vigils, psalmody, and the like are done out of love for God.
>
> PETER OF DAMASKOS[12]

6:13. Now in return for the same (I speak as to children), you also be open. He asks for their love in return—that their hearts expand to include love for him and that which he is trying to teach. Since he was the first to bring the Gospel to the Corinthians, he speaks as a spiritual father to his children, who should respond to his sacrificial love for them.

6:14–15. Do not be unequally yoked together with unbelievers. For what fellowship has righteousness with lawlessness? And what communion has light with darkness? And what accord has Christ with Belial? Or what part has a believer with an unbeliever? To "yoke" is to join together. Paul does not say that we should not associate with unbelievers (1 Cor. 10:27), for then no outreach would be possible. Rather, he writes that believers should not be joined together or closely united with unbelievers, as the Mosaic Law stated that an ox should not be yoked with a donkey in plowing (Deut. 22:10) because they cannot work well together to accomplish the task at hand. In Paul's time, Christianity was new and all were converts to it, so many of the early Christians had spouses and/or other family members outside the faith.

Christians were not to leave their non-Christian spouses (1 Cor. 7:12), but an unmarried Christian was expected to refrain from marrying an unbeliever (1 Cor. 7:39), because to do so might create conflict and cause a diminishment of the believer's commitment to a Christ-like life.

The story told in Acts 16:16–18 suggests also that a Christian should not be yoked with an unbeliever in doing any form of God's work. When the evil spirit in the slave girl began to join in Paul's work by testifying as to the truth of who he was, Paul would not allow that cooperation, to prevent the evil spirit from using the association to gain people's confidence and then lead them away from God. Not all voices speaking about God are godly. Some may try to use God's word for their own purposes (2 Cor. 11:13–15).

Just as *righteousness* and *lawlessness, light* and *darkness*, and *Christ and Belial* (Hebrew for Satan) are the complete opposite of each other, a *believer* is the complete opposite of an *unbeliever* in attitudes toward life and its purpose, so the two cannot be joined with good result. This is the basis for the Church's teaching that a Christian cannot be united in matrimony with a non-Christian and that, ideally, individuals contemplating marriage should be united, not divided, in faith so as to begin their lives together on a solid foundation—suitable for creating a family and guiding all members towards God.

6:16. And what agreement has the temple of God with idols? For you are the temple of the living God. As God has said: "I will dwell in them and walk among them. I will be their God, and they shall be My people." The Spirit of God dwells in those who are Baptized and Chrismated and follow a lifestyle that demonstrates faith that Christ is Lord and Savior. They become God's temple—in which holiness pervades to the degree they allow. No one can be dedicated to both God and idols (false gods). God is "jealous" (Ex. 20:5) in that He demands our total allegiance for our own good—our salvation.

At the time Paul wrote this epistle, Corinth was a pagan city. The lives of the Corinthians revolved around idol worship. Those who became Christians were expected to make an absolute break with that type of life because worship belongs only to the Creator.

> **FOOD FOR THOUGHT:** (e). Does this verse apply in any way to the Christian life in our times? Are there pagans (idol worshippers) in our midst?

6:17–18. Therefore, "Come out from among them and be separate, says the Lord. Do not touch what is unclean, and I will receive you. I will be a Father to you, and you shall be My sons and daughters, says the Lord Almighty." Paul quotes the Old Testament (Isa. 52:11), God's word to the Hebrews to be His people, different than non-Jews who were considered unclean according to the Law. He tells the early Christians that they too must be set apart from prevalent pagan influence and activity. They are to become imitators of God, just as young children imitate their parents and thereby learn and grow.

> And do not wonder that a man may become an imitator of God. ... He who takes upon himself the burden of his neighbor; he who, in whatever way he may be superior, is ready to help another who is deficient; he who, by distributing to the needy from what he has received from God, becomes a god to those who receive these benefits: he is an imitator of God.

MATHETES[13]

God expects us to do no less. We must separate ourselves from the unclean, the ungodly in our society, as far as our thoughts and conduct. Yet at the same time we are called upon to love even our enemies, to be good examples to all, and to welcome any sincere seeker to the love of the Gospel. This delicate balance is difficult, but "with God all things are possible" (Mt. 19:26). Above all, we must allow nothing in our lives that has the possibility of coming between us and God and drawing us away from Him. If we put Him first in all we do, He will claim us as His children, entitled to dwell with Him forever.

FOOD FOR THOUGHT COMMENTS

(a). What regular reminders are Orthodox Christians given of the need to commit and recommit their lives to Christ? During the celebration of the Divine Liturgy we are prompted often to "commend ourselves and one another and our whole lives to Christ our God." These are valuable reminders of the purpose for life. They also continually offer occasions to pray for those who may need a nudge in the right direction.

(b). How can the gifts of the Spirit be misused? Gifts of the Holy Spirit are given for the purpose of bringing a person—and through him, others—to union with God. Their proper use promotes unity within the Church. Those who use these gifts to bring glory or worldly gain to themselves misuse them and cause divisions. This was the case with the Corinthian Christians in their use of the gift of tongues (see text and this study of 1 Cor. 12).

(c). What are the signs of pride? A prideful person has

distinguishing characteristics.

> First, there is loudness in the proud man's talk, bitterness in his silent moods; when he is pleased, his laughter is loud and profuse; when he is serious, he is gloomy beyond reason. There is rancor in his replies to questions, glibness in his speech; his words break out unrestrained by any seriousness of heart. Of patience he knows nothing; charity is a stranger to him; he is bold in insulting others, cowardly in bearing their insults. He does not easily render obedience except where what is commanded fits with his own wishes. He is not to be appeased when one admonishes him; he is weak in curtailing his own wishes, very stubborn when asked to yield to those of others. He is always doing his best to establish his own opinions, but never ready to bow to those of anyone else. Finally, though he is quite incapable of giving good counsel, he is always more ready to trust his own judgment than that of the elders.
>
> CASSIAN[14]

(d). How does the principle behind Jesus' words, "Seek first the Kingdom of God and His righteousness, and all things shall be added to you" (Mt. 6:33), apply to our modern lives? If we have truly committed our lives to Christ and believe that through Him we can live eternally with God, we will be guided in all that we do by Christ's teachings and His example. Every decision we make will be shaped not by what would be best in terms of success or gain in the world but rather by what He would expect of us. When this principle becomes ingrained in us, our life will have a healthy balance. It will not be easy, but the truly good things will be ours, in this life and the next.

> When you suffer anything for Christ's sake, do not merely bear it nobly, but also rejoice. When you fast,

leap for joy as if enjoying luxury; if you are insulted, react as if praised; if you spend, feel as if gaining; if you bestow on the poor, count yourselves to receive: for he that does not give in this manner will not give readily. ... In every virtue, compute not only the severity of the toils but also the sweetness of the prize ... and you will readily enter into the contest and will live the whole time in pleasure. For nothing is as apt to cause pleasure as a good conscience.

CHRYSOSTOM[15]

(e). Does verse 6:16 apply in any way to the Christian life in our times? Are there pagans (idol worshippers) in our midst? The setting is different in our day, but Paul's advice still applies. We are given life to have the opportunity to find God and grow in union with Him. Thus we were created with a space in our hearts that aches until it is filled by His presence (Acts 17:26–27). If something other than God becomes the most important element in our lives, be it career, money, power, fame, a person, or even sports or other forms of recreation, it takes God's rightful place. It becomes to us a false god—an idol—and we become idol worshippers. Idol worshippers have nothing in common with those who worship God, nor do they ever find true peace, because they misuse the gift of life. It is crucial that we place God on His throne in our hearts and lives so all other elements will take their proper place.

CHAPTER SEVEN

On Being Set Apart from the World

Chapter Six ended with a reminder that those who separate themselves from the ungodly will have fellowship with God, in a relationship of Father to sons and daughters. Now Paul issues a call to the next step—growth in holiness.

7:1. Therefore, having these promises, beloved, let us cleanse ourselves from all filthiness of the flesh and spirit, perfecting holiness in the fear of God. God's promises to those who separate themselves from the ungodly produce hope and joy. They also should awaken fear, however, because they remind us that those who do not will be heir to that which they have reserved for themselves—eternity separated from God's goodness. Therefore, it behooves us to continue our efforts to be Christ-like in all areas of our lives, "perfecting holiness" (2 Pet. 3:9–15). This necessitates being different, set apart from the world, not as elitists but to walk with and to lead others to Christ and to prepare for life in His Kingdom.

> Not only did Christ fulfill the prophecies and plant the word of truth, but also in these happenings, He gave us guidance regarding our lives, providing us with a rule of conduct for every need; teaching us by every means how to live worthily.
>
> CHRYSOSTOM[1]

FOOD FOR THOUGHT: (a).What are the attributes of holiness?

During the Divine Liturgy, before the invitation to receive the Body and Blood of Christ, we hear the words: "The Holy Things for those who are Holy." We respond: "One is Holy, One is Lord, Jesus Christ." The Eucharist that is about to be offered is itself holy and is for the holy. But the stark reality is that no one is truly holy except our Lord Jesus. How then do we dare to approach to receive Holy Communion? By the grace of God, through which we become "a holy nation, His own special people" (1 Pet. 2:9). We dare to partake of that which is reserved for the holy because we are a part of the Body of Christ through Baptism. We remain a part of Him and thus progressively partake of *His* holiness, *if*, as we are able, we continually try to become in our lives what He has already made us by grace. As long as we continue in this struggle we show our assent, our faith. By this faith we open ourselves to that which is holy, as Mary conceived Christ in her womb through the Holy Spirit the very moment she assented to the will of God (Lk. 1:38). Her assent, however, was not just verbal. She lived in obedience to that which God asked of her in all ways, as she had prior to being visited by Archangel Gabriel. Those who do not engage in this struggle shut grace out of their lives and make themselves unworthy of that which is holy. The disobedient either do not really believe, no matter what they profess with their mouth, or they "know not what they do" (Lk. 23:34).

> We partake of Holy Communion *only* because we have been made holy by Christ and in Christ; and we partake of it in order to become holy, i.e., to fulfill the gift of holiness in our life. It is when one does not realize this that one "eats and drinks unworthily"— when, in other terms, one receives Communion thinking of one's self as "worthy" through one's own, and not Christ's holiness; or when one receives it without relating it to the whole of life as its judgment, but also as the power of its transformation, as forgiveness, but also as the inescapable entrance into the "narrow path" of effort and struggle.[2]

7:2. Open your hearts to us. We have wronged no one, we have corrupted no one, we have defrauded no one. Paul introduces the element of trust. He feels he has earned a place in their hearts because of his unwavering care and concern for them. This is an important point. If we earn the love and trust of those around us through interaction with them in the day-to-day activities of life, our efforts to share the truths of the Gospel with them will bear more fruit.

7:3. I do not say this to condemn; for I have said before that you are in our hearts, to die together and to live together. Paul's admonishments are not meant as judgment of the Corinthians. His intent is not to dismiss them from his care but to redirect them, where necessary, as God redirected him, and to remain their advocate through all that life brings.

> FOOD FOR THOUGHT: (b). It would seem that to *die together* would be more difficult than to *live together*; yet the writings of the Fathers of the Church suggest that giving love and support in good times is more difficult and rare than during times of adversity. How can this be?

7:4. Great is my boldness of speech toward you, great is my boasting on your behalf. I am filled with comfort. I am exceedingly joyful in all our tribulation. The good news Paul has received regarding their spiritual progress brings him great comfort, even during times of tribulation. With the strength he receives from God, he speaks out boldly to encourage greater virtue and a closer walk with Christ.

7:5–7. For indeed, when we came to Macedonia, our flesh had no rest, but we were troubled on every side. Outside were conflicts, inside were fears. Nevertheless God, Who comforts the downcast, comforted us by the

coming of Titus, and not only by his coming but also by the consolation with which he was comforted in you, when he told us of your earnest desire, your mourning, your zeal for me, so that I rejoiced even more. When Paul left Troas and went to Macedonia from where he writes (2 Cor. 2:12–13), he was upset at not finding Titus waiting for him. He faced continual persecution for the work he was doing and was troubled by fears that it was not bearing fruit. Then, finally, Titus arrived! His arrival brought Paul comfort and joy, especially when Titus shared the encouraging news that the Christians of Corinth were responding to Paul's first epistle and the reprimands it brought with the spirit in which they were intended. They were repentant for the errors of their ways and were eager for Paul to return.

7:8–9. For even if I made you sorry with my letter, I do not regret it; though I did regret it. For I perceive that the same epistle made you sorry, though only for a while. Now I rejoice, not that you were made sorry, but that your sorrow led to repentance. For you were made sorry in a godly manner, that you might suffer loss from us in nothing. A wise parent admonishes his errant children, bringing temporary pain, in order to teach them and keep them from danger. In like manner, a spiritual father chastens when necessary to prompt repentance and correction of ways.

> To soothe that he may hurt is the way of the Devil.
> To chastise that He may bring us to greater good is
> the way of the Lord. So when things are going easily
> amid plenty, beware.
>
> CHRYSOSTOM[3]

It had saddened Paul to write his stern letter, but if he had refrained from correcting them for fear of hurting their feelings or becoming unpopular with them, he would have been guilty of allowing them to drift away from God.

FOOD FOR THOUGHT: (c). What responsibility do the faithful bear towards those who consider themselves Christians yet seem to be following a way of life contrary to that prescribed by the Gospel?

7:10. For godly sorrow produces repentance to salvation, not to be regretted; but the sorrow of the world produces death. Godly sorrow produces repentance upon realization that one has been wrong spiritually. We should not regret producing godly sorrow. The sorrow of the world, on the other hand, is worthless because it is superficial, concerned only with physical comfort and pleasure rather than spiritual growth.

> And what is worldly? If you are in sorrow for money, for reputation, for one who has departed, all these are worldly. They also work death. For he who sorrows for reputation's sake feels envy and is driven oftentimes to perish: such was the sorrow Cain felt, such Esau. By worldly sorrow he means that which is to the harm of those who sorrow. For only in respect to sins is sorrow a profitable thing. He who sorrows for loss of wealth does not repair that damage; he who sorrows for one deceased does not raise the dead to life again; he who sorrows for a sickness not only is not made well but even aggravates the disease. He who sorrows for sins, alone attains some advantage from his sorrow, for he makes his sins wane and disappear. In this case only is it potent and profitable; and worldly sorrow is even harmful. "And yet Cain," one can say, "sorrowed because he was not accepted with God." It was not for this, but because he saw his brother glorious in honor; for had he grieved because he was not in good standing with God, he would have tried to emulate and rejoice with

his brother; but, as it was, he showed that his was a worldly sorrow. But not so David, nor Peter, nor any of the righteous. They were accepted because they grieved over their own sins or those of others. And yet what is more oppressive than sorrow? Still when it is after a godly sort, it is better than the joy in the world.

CHRYSOSTOM[4]

FOOD FOR THOUGHT: (d). What is the "death" that is produced by the "sorrow of the world"?

7:11. For observe this very thing, that you sorrowed in a godly manner: What diligence it produced in you, what clearing of yourselves, what indignation, what fear, what vehement desire, what zeal, what vindication! In all things you proved yourselves to be clear in this matter. The godly sorrow aroused in the Corinthian Christians by Paul's admonitions caused them to realize the error of their ways and to set about to correct them.

FOOD FOR THOUGHT: (e). Is it possible to bring about "godly sorrow" in the modern world?

7:12. Therefore, although I wrote to you, I did not do it for the sake of him who had done the wrong, nor for the sake of him who suffered wrong, but that our care for you in the sight of God might appear to you. The immoral relationship between the man and his stepmother (1 Cor. 5:1) posed spiritual danger to the entire community. As their teacher, Paul must answer to God for his efforts to restore conditions that will allow spiritual health and growth. God's directives to His people are neither meant to restrict them unnecessarily nor to make their lives difficult. On the contrary, their purpose is to lead them to joys unending—in this life and the next.

FOOD FOR THOUGHT: (f). What does Paul's concern that he do his best "in the sight of God" to guide the Corinthians say to all Christians, especially to those who are entrusted with the care of others, like clergy, parents, and god-parents?

7:13–15. Therefore we have been comforted in your comfort. And we rejoiced exceedingly more for the joy of Titus, because his spirit has been refreshed by you all. For if in anything I have boasted to him about you, I am not ashamed. But as we spoke all things to you in truth, even so our boasting to Titus was found true. And his affections are greater for you as he remembers the obedience of you all, how with fear and trembling you received him. Paul is elated that they responded positively to his letter and to Titus as his emissary. Titus' love for the Corinthians has grown as a result of their response to him and the seriousness with which they received the guidance he brought from Paul.

> He who has faith in the Lord fears chastisement; and this fear prompts him to keep the commandments. The keeping of the commandments leads him to endure affliction; and the enduring of affliction produces hope in God. Such hope separates the intellect from all material attachment; and the person freed from such attachment possesses love for God. Whoever follows this sequence will be saved.
>
> PETER OF DAMASKOS[5]

7:16. Therefore, I rejoice that I have confidence in you in everything. Confident of their love for Christ because of their affirming actions, Paul rejoices as does any parent who sees that his charges are on the right track.

Nothing so distinguishes a leader as much as paternal affection for those he leads. Begetting alone does not constitute a father, but begetting and loving. ... Moses, for the sake of those he led, left great riches and treasures untold, *choosing to suffer affliction with the people of God* (Heb. 11:25).

CHRYSOSTOM[6]

FOOD FOR THOUGHT COMMENTS

(a). What are the attributes of holiness? Holiness is godliness (Lev. 11:44).

Holiness does not mean chastity alone but freedom from every kind of sin, for he that is pure is holy. One will become pure if he is free from fornication, covetousness, envy, pride, and vainglory. ... It is important to avoid vainglory in everything, but especially in almsgiving (since it is not almsgiving, but display and cruelty, if it is tainted with vainglory) ... in fasting, and in prayer.

CHRYSOSTOM[7]

We all accept that there is special training for philosophers, for teachers, for athletes. Equally, for those who have chosen to major in holiness, there is a special training in the word. It involves, as does any serious training, almost every detail of life: walking, eating, resting, working, every part is disciplined and every part contributes to the goal of spiritual health and beauty.

Mind you, this training (unlike some of the others) does not put people under emotional or physical strain and tension. It is not a matter of driving oneself to the limit so much as allowing the word to show us our weaknesses and moral flaws and then bringing us the Savior's own remedies, precisely gauged to meet every specific need.

CLEMENT OF ALEXANDRIA[8]

(b). It would seem that to *die together* would be more difficult than to *live together;* yet the writings of the Fathers of the Church suggest that giving love and support in good times is more difficult and rare than during times of adversity. How can this be? There are many who envy the good fortune of others, so find it difficult to rejoice when they prosper or are honored, while sympathizing with their misfortunes is easy. Envy shows lack of true love.

> Nothing more destructive springs up in the souls of men than the passion of envy, which, while it does no harm to others, is the dominant and peculiar evil of the soul that harbors it. As rust consumes iron, so does envy wholly consume the soul it dwells in. More than this, as vipers are said to be born through devouring the maternal womb, so envy devours the soul that gives it birth.
>
> BASIL[9]

(c). What responsibility do the faithful bear towards those who consider themselves Christians yet seem to be following a way of life contrary to that prescribed by the Gospel? God guides His people through His teachings, which have been passed on through the ages. The faithful try to direct their lives accordingly. Because of God's gift of free will, however, each person has the right to accept or to reject His guidance. This presupposes that all have had an opportunity to learn the fullness of His word and the obedience and spiritual growth it requires. To that end, each Christian is called upon to share its truths with those whose paths cross theirs, allowing them to make informed decisions about their lives on earth and beyond the grave. There are times when those who call themselves Christians engage in behavior or activity that is not Christ-like. In dealing with such instances, it is first of all important to remember that it is not our place to pronounce judgment upon others—judgment belongs to God.

> Let us not be overcurious about the failings of others, but take account of our own; let us remember the goodness of others, while we bear in mind our faults, and thus we shall be well pleasing to God.
> CHRYSOSTOM[10]

With that warning, however, it remains that there are times when someone might benefit spiritually from a firm nudge in the right direction—a loving gesture on the part of the one who makes such an attempt. Because we have no right to judge the person, the behavior or action in question must be our focal point.

> For example: a brother has fallen into fornication. Do not disgrace him because of his fault; but don't laugh at it either. You will do no good to whoever hears you; rather it is more likely that you will do him harm, goading him further. But if you advise him as to what he should do, you will do him a great favor: if you teach him to use speech fittingly, and guide him so that he will abuse no one, you will teach him exceedingly well, and you will have brought him grace. If you speak with him about repentance, of the love of God, of giving to the poor, all these things will heal his soul. For all this he will be grateful to you. But if you laugh at him or speak hurtfully to him, you will provoke him instead. If you show any approval of his evil doing, you will undo him and destroy him.
> CHRYSOSTOM[11]

To try to correct someone is probably one of the most difficult things we can attempt. Such an endeavor should only be undertaken with extreme caution and with prayer for discernment. It is usually best to wait for the right moment and then to lovingly do or say that which is most likely to bring repentance and healing.

> Keep in touch with them. Encourage them not to abandon their belief in the Lord's mercy towards those who repent. Assure them that if they humbly and sincerely confess their sins and turn back to God, He will receive them and give them his strength and support to change their way of life.
>
> CYPRIAN[12]

Social pressure among peers can be a very powerful influence for good or evil. The purpose of Christian correction or guidance must always be to preserve, intact, the Church and her teachings, and to try to bring the person involved into fuller fellowship with it. This must be done very carefully because harm may be done if he is lost to the Kingdom.

> Those who let us do as we like are neither good teachers nor good friends.[13]

> There is no credit in spending all your affection on the cream of your pupils. Try rather to bring the more troublesome ones to order by using gentleness. Nobody can heal every wound with the same unguent; where there are acute spasms of pain, we have to apply soothing poultices. So in all circumstances be *wise as the serpent, though always harmless as the dove* [Mt. 10:16].
>
> IGNATIUS OF ANTIOCH[14]

(d). What is the "death" that is produced by the "sorrow of the world" The death produced by worldly sorrow is not the Christian death through which one passes from this life to the fullness of the Kingdom. Rather, it is the end of any hope and joy that comes from association with the things of God.

> As you become imitators of God you will see, as you walk the earth, that there is a God Who is operative in Heaven; you will begin to focus on His mysteries; and you will know love and admiration for those who incur persecution by their refusal to deny Him. Then too, you will see through the deceitfulness and error of this world once you have found what it is to live the true life of Heaven and have learned to despise the seeming death of the body and to dread only the real death which is reserved for those condemned to the fires of eternity—fires that will torment their victims forevermore. In the knowledge of those fires, your admiration will go out to all who endure a more transient flame for righteousness sake, and you will call them blessed.
>
> MATHETES[15]

For more on the "fires of eternity," see Food For Thought Comments 2 Cor. 5 (d). and (e).

(e). Is it possible to bring about "godly sorrow" in the modern world? The modern world provides fertile ground for producing the godly sorrow that leads to repentance. As society in general strays further and further from God and the values His word teaches, the quality of life declines. Selfish concerns dominate and life seems cold, cruel, and meaningless. In such a setting, some begin to realize something is amiss, and they search for direction. If at this point they are taught or reminded about God's truths, sorrow—godly sorrow—can build in their hearts for the sad state of mankind. This can produce the fruit of repentance and subsequent renewal in the joy of life God intended. We can be helpful in this process by trying in every circumstance to share with others, in a non-judgmental way, that which God expects of His people—while at the same time acting in a loving manner toward everyone. Often the best way to do this is to be a good example, so perhaps those looking on who have strayed will realize their own lives are not following the path leading to God and will repent.

> When Christ was establishing laws for His Disciples, what did He command of them? Certainly not that they should perform wonders, that men might behold them. No. He said: *Let your light shine before men, that they may see your good works, and glorify your Father Who is in Heaven.* To Peter likewise He did not say: *If you love me work miracles*, but *Feed My sheep* (Jn. 21:17). And since on all occasions He singles him out from the rest, together with James and John, I ask why did He single them out? Because of their miracles? But all the Apostles cleansed the lepers, and raised the dead. To all alike He gave this power. Why then were these three preferred? Because of the virtue of their lives and the magnanimity of their souls. See then the need of a good life and the need of fruitful works? *You shall know them by their fruits* (Mt. 7:16).
>
> CHRYSOSTOM[16]

(f). What does Paul's concern that he do his best "in the sight of God" to guide the Corinthians say to all Christians, especially to those who are entrusted with the care of others, like clergy, parents, and godparents? All who have been entrusted with the spiritual care of others have a very serious responsibility to do all they can to teach those dependent upon them about the wonders of God and His promises; and they will answer to Him in this regard. Because everyone has free will, however, including those to whom we minister, we will not be judged by the extent to which these efforts were successful but by the care and discipline we exercised to do our best (see this study for 1 Cor. 3:12–15).

The priest, even if he disciplines his own life in a fitting manner, yet does not scrupulously have due care for both your life and the lives of those around him, shall go with the wicked into everlasting fire; and so he oftentimes, while not failing in his own conduct, will perish because of yours, if he has not done all that belonged to him to do.

CHRYSOSTOM[17]

Lay members of the Church also bear responsibility for the care and nurturing of the spiritual lives of others. As part of the Body of Christ we all belong to the *royal priesthood*, called to proclaim His praises to all who will listen (1 Pet. 2:9).

CHAPTER EIGHT

That Which is Considered Almsgiving

At the close of Chapter Seven, Paul expressed joy that the faith of the Corinthian Christians has been strengthened. He now points to the generous almsgiving of the Christians in Macedonia, from where he writes, to encourage further growth in this area of the spiritual lives of the Corinthians through emulation.

8:1–2. Moreover, brethren, we make known to you the grace of God bestowed on the churches of Macedonia: that in a great trial of affliction the abundance of their joy and their deep poverty abounded in the riches of their liberality. The Christians in Macedonia had suffered great persecution and had lost most of their worldly possessions. Yet through the grace of God that comes to those who are obedient to Him in spite of tribulation, they did not become despondent. On the contrary, they were filled with the joy of the Lord. Their love for God manifested itself in a generous offering for the poor of the church in Jerusalem, the mother church. Notice that Paul said *the riches of their liberality,* not of their gifts. The amount involved may have been small in comparison to that given by others but was abundant considering their situation.

> Just as their great affliction gave birth to great joy, their great poverty gave rise to greatness in almsgiving ... for bountifulness is determined not by the measure of what is given but by the mind of those who bestow it.
>
> CHRYSOSTOM[1]

8:3–4. For I bear witness that according to their ability,

yes, and beyond their ability, they were freely willing, imploring us with much urgency that we would receive the gift and the fellowship of the ministering to the saints. They gave willingly from the little they had and pleaded with Paul to use them and what they offered for his ministry.

> Paul mentions three reasons to praise the Macedonians: that they bear trials nobly; that they know how to pity; and that, though poor, they are generous in almsgiving.
>
> CHRYSOSTOM[2]

8:5. And this they did, not as we had hoped, but first gave themselves to the Lord and then to us by the will of God. Their response was beyond what Paul had hoped for because it was fruit of their strong commitment to Christ. They eagerly followed Paul's guidance in this and other spiritual matters because they recognized him as the one through whom God worked for their spiritual enrichment.

8:6. So we urged Titus, that as he had begun, so he would also complete this grace in you as well. Paul had urged Titus to continue his ministry to the Corinthians by giving them further guidance in almsgiving—a very important part of the Christian life.

> **FOOD FOR THOUGHT:** (a). Is all giving considered almsgiving? Does God acknowledge giving that comes from those who do not believe in Him or His Son as the Messiah but who give because they are kind or because they like the gratitude and adulation their giving brings?

8:7-8. But as you abound in everything—in faith, in speech, in knowledge, in all diligence, and in your love

for us—see that you abound in this grace also. I speak not by commandment, but I am testing the sincerity of your love by the diligence of others. Paul is not demanding that they give, nor dictating the amount. Almsgiving is a reflection of love. True love reaches outward to others.

> Whatever fruits of kindness you yield, you gather up for yourself; for the grace of good works and their reward is returned to the giver. Have you given something to a person in need? What you have given becomes yours, and is returned to you with an increase. And as the wheat that falls to the earth brings increase to the one who has thrown it there, so the bread that you give to the hungry will later bring you a great gain. Therefore, let the end of your earthly tilling be the beginning of your heavenly sowing.
>
> BASIL[3]

8:9. For you know the grace of our Lord Jesus Christ, that though He was rich, yet for your sakes He became poor, that you through His poverty might become rich. Jesus set the ultimate example of giving. He gave Himself completely, with love as the only motive. He became poor at His Incarnation when He willingly took on a form beneath His heavenly status in glory, power, and position (Phil. 2:5–8) so He could unite man with God. Through Him man has access to the riches of Heaven:

> … knowledge of godliness, cleansing away of sins, justification, sanctification, the countless good things which He bestows upon us and wants to bestow upon us.
>
> CHRYSOSTOM[4]

FOOD FOR THOUGHT: (b). Must we rid ourselves of all earthly possessions in order to be part of the Kingdom of Heaven?

8:10–11. And in this I give my advice: It is to your advantage not only to be doing what you began and were desiring to do a year ago; but now you also must complete the doing of it; that as there was a readiness to desire it, so there also may be a completion out of what you have. In his first epistle Paul told the Corinthians to begin thinking of what they would give for the work of the Church (1 Cor. 16:1–2). He now urges them to complete their collection, to act on their stated intentions.

Here Paul addresses an ever-present danger. Often, after hearing an inspiring sermon or reading a spiritually enlightening book, we are prompted to take a look at our spiritual life. We may vow to do better, to try harder, or to give more but then forget those good intentions when we get back into the routine of daily living. It is important that we guard against this lack of spiritual discipline. God honors the intentions of our heart if we are prevented from fulfilling them by circumstances beyond our control but not if they die from neglect.

> For what they hear in instructions is indeed pleasing to many people, and they set about the beginning of good works: but soon being wearied by the afflictions that come to them, they abandon the good they have begun.
>
> GREGORY THE GREAT[5]

8:12. For if there is first a willing mind, it is accepted according to what one has and not according to what he does not have. God does not expect everyone to give in equal amounts but to give gladly, according to means.

For what is much and what little God defines, not by
the measure of what is given but by the extent of the
substance of him that gives.

CHRYSOSTOM[6]

**8:13–14. For I do not mean that others should be eased
and you burdened; but by an equality, that now at this
time your abundance may supply their lack, that their
abundance also may supply your lack—that there may
be equality.** The church in Jerusalem is rich spiritually but
very poor in material effects. Paul is not asking that the
Corinthians give to the point of poverty but from their
abundance.

You are flourishing in money; they in holiness of life
and in boldness towards God. Give to them, therefore,
of the money in which you abound but they have not;
that you may receive of that boldness wherein they
are rich and you are lacking.

CHRYSOSTOM[7]

**8:15. As it is written, "He who gathered much had
nothing left over, and he who gathered little had no
lack."** Exodus 16 relates that when the Israelites were
journeying through the wilderness, after Moses led them out of
Egypt, they began to complain because they were hungry. So
the Lord said to Moses: "I will rain bread from Heaven for you.
And the people shall go out and gather a certain quota every
day, that I may test them, whether they will walk in My law or
not." They were told to gather what they needed for their
family: "one omer for each person." No matter how much
anyone gathered, they found they had neither a surplus nor a
shortage—God's way of teaching them to be satisfied that their
basic needs were met.

> ... and to persuade them never to desire to have more
> nor to grieve at having less.
>
> CHRYSOSTOM[8]

They were expected to work to the extent each was able, gathering that which God had provided. He who was able to gather an abundance could not expect to have more for himself than anyone else. Likewise, he who worked diligently but was unable to fill his quota could be assured that he and his family would not go hungry.

> **FOOD FOR THOUGHT:** (c). What is the present-day message of this verse? What is the difference between modern communistic principles and this Christian method of the sharing of resources? (d). Exodus 16:16–24 relates that God told the people to gather only what they needed daily, and to save (hoard) none till the following morning. When they disobeyed, the following morning what they had hoarded "bred worms and stank." Yet God told them that on the sixth day they could gather a double portion so they would have enough for their needs on the Sabbath, a day of rest, when work was not allowed. On the Sabbath, that which they had saved from the day before "did not stink, nor were any worms in it." Why? Are there present-day analogies of this incident?

8:16–19. But thanks be to God, Who puts the same earnest care for you into the heart of Titus. For he not only accepted the exhortation, but being more diligent, he went to you of his own accord. And we have sent with him the brother whose praise is in the Gospel throughout all the churches, and not only that but who was also chosen by the churches to travel with us with

this gift, which is administered by us to the glory of the Lord Himself and to show your ready mind ... Paul is grateful for the love and concern Titus exhibits for the Corinthians and for the zeal of his ministry to them. Though it is a long, hard journey, he has agreed to return to them in advance of Paul's visit to help them understand the merits of almsgiving as Paul requested (2 Cor. 8:6) and to help them with the practical application—the collection of the offering. The brother mentioned, who would share responsibilities with Titus, was thought by Chrysostom to be Barnabas.

8:20–23. avoiding this: that anyone should blame us in this lavish gift which is administered by us—providing honorable things, not only in the sight of the Lord, but also in the sight of men. And we have sent with them our brother, whom we have often proved diligent in many things but now much more diligent because of the great confidence which we have in you. If anyone inquires about Titus, he is my partner and fellow worker concerning you. Or if our brethren are inquired about, they are messengers of the churches, the glory of Christ. To handle the monies that are collected in Corinth, Paul is sending three trusted fellow workers. They will take this second epistle from Paul along with them to deliver to the Corinthians, and then travel with Paul to deliver the monetary offering.

Those in authority must be sure that the methods used and the individuals involved in the collection and distribution of money are above reproach, so those who are being asked to give will have no cause to doubt that their offering will be used for good purposes.

FOOD FOR THOUGHT: (e). The collection and utilization of funds is something with which every church community must be concerned. What can be learned from these verses? Is the spiritual value of our almsgiving negated if the money we give is misused?

8:24. Therefore show to them, and before the churches, the proof of your love and of our boasting on your behalf. Paul has praised the Corinthians for their spiritual growth. He has given them the example of the Christians in Macedonia, who gave beyond their means because of their love for Christ and His work, and has assured them that their money will not be misused. Now he urges them to fulfill their pledge for the church in Jerusalem as proof of their love and faith. Paul's words are very clear: our actions prove our faith.

FOOD FOR THOUGHT: (f). Why is almsgiving considered proof of love and faith?

FOOD FOR THOUGHT COMMENTS

(a). Is all giving considered almsgiving? Does God acknowledge giving that comes from those who do not believe in Him or His Son as the Messiah but who give because they are kind or because they like the gratitude and adulation their giving brings? To give alms is to give willingly and joyfully from our resources with the knowledge that all good things have their source in God and, therefore, belong to Him in the first place. Those who understand this bask in the joy that such giving brings to others and consider that ample reward.

Only giving that is motivated by belief in God and His Son as Savior is profitable toward the Kingdom of Heaven. Giving must be an outgrowth of, not instead of, a Christ-centered life. If we give without pointing to God through a life that demonstrates faith, we do only a temporary good. Lasting good comes from helping others in this life while directing attention to God, Who alone can satisfy our ultimate need: to be with Him.

To give in order to receive, in the form of either praise or returned favors, is to serve one's self, not others, and so is not almsgiving. We must strive to have what we give known only to God. If we accomplish this we will be storing up treasures in Heaven (Mt. 6:1–4, 19–20).

> It is almsgiving when it is done with willingness, when with bountifulness, when you deem yourself not to give but to receive, when done as if you were benefited, as if gaining and not losing. ... For he who shows mercy on another ought to feel joyful, not annoyed. For how is it not absurd, if while removing another's downheartedness, you yourself are downhearted? ... if you are downhearted because you have delivered another from downheartedness, you furnish an example of extreme cruelty and inhumanity. ... And why are you downhearted at all, for fear your gold will diminish? If such are your thoughts, do not give at all: if you are not quite sure that it is multiplied for you in Heaven, do not give. You seek recompense here. Why? Let your alms be alms and not bartering.
>
> CHRYSOSTOM[9]

(b). Must we rid ourselves of all earthly possessions in order to be part of the Kingdom of Heaven? As love for God and communion with Him grow, desire for the superfluous things of this world decreases, fostering greater almsgiving. This is why many Saints gave up all their worldly possessions to serve God. It is not necessary, however, to be "poor" to be part of the Kingdom of Heaven, but rather "poor in spirit" (Mt. 5:3).

> The Kingdom of Heaven shall be given to those whom humility of soul commends rather than the absence of riches. ... It cannot be doubted that this blessing of humility is more easily attained by the poor than the rich: for while meekness is the companion of those who live in poverty, pride is familiar to the rich. Yet in many among the rich, that spirit is found which uses its abundance not to increase its own inflated pride but in works of goodness and which holds as its greatest gain that which it has bestowed in relieving the misery of another's want. It is given to every kind and rank of men to share in this virtue because those who are unequal in means can be equal in good will; and it does not matter how dissimilar they are in earthly possessions, provided they are found equal in spiritual riches. Blessed therefore is that poverty which is not deluded by a longing for temporal things, which does not hunger to be made rich in the treasure of this world but desires to grow rich in heavenly things.
>
> LEO THE GREAT[10]

He who realizes that all he has belongs to God and that he actually owns nothing in this life is poor in spirit, no matter the extent of his earthly possessions. Such a person uses that which he has been entrusted with by God to do God's work, whenever and wherever possible.

> Don't despise possessions. And don't despise profits either. After all, possessions are "possessed" by us: they are our servants, not our masters. And profits are "profitable," or they should be.
>
> Wealth is at our disposal, an instrument which can be used well or foolishly. How it is used doesn't depend

on the instrument but on the person who is using it. If we use it well, it is a valuable servant—a servant which can do good things for us and for those who depend on us. If we use it badly, it is an unhelpful servant—a servant which causes us and our friends endless harm. We shouldn't blame what is blameless. Wealth in itself is neither good nor evil.

So where does the blame lie for all the evil done in the name of money and possessions? Not in the things themselves: they are harmlessly neutral. The evil is in the mind of man himself—man who by the free will and moral independence God has given him manages what he owns. Human desires express themselves through a man's possessions—desire to impress others, perhaps, or competitive instincts, which drive him always to rival his affluent neighbor. But those desires can also be noble ones, and express themselves in noble ways. Our money can feed the hungry and clothe the poor.

CLEMENT OF ALEXANDRIA[11]

When speaking to the young man who pridefully declared that he had followed God's Commandments all of his life, Jesus said: "If you want to be perfect, go, sell what you have, and give to the poor, and you will have treasure in Heaven; and come, follow Me" (Mk 10:17–22). In response, the young man walked away, "for he had great possessions" and they were very important to him. The wisdom Christ offered this young man was that he had not followed the Commandments as closely as he thought. The first is: "You shall have no other gods before Me" (Ex. 20:3). Our "god" is whatever we put first in our lives. This young man's earthly possessions had become his god— though he did not realize it.

Riches did not prevent the young man from coming to receive Baptism, and it is quite wrong to say, as some

do, that the Lord told him to dispose of his wealth so
he could be baptized.

CLIMACUS[12]

An alcoholic who tries to recover from his dependency knows
that even one drink can put him in danger of losing control
over his craving for more and more. Similarly, some people
have a need to hoard earthly possessions. Unable to keep a
healthy attitude toward them, their possessions control them,
and all their energies are directed toward increasing their
acquisitions. Jesus knew that this particular young man was
unable to maintain a spiritually healthy attitude toward what
he owned. Freeing himself from them entirely would help him
put his focus on spiritual rather than worldly treasure and
would help him conquer his pride because "he would learn to
accept the charity of others."[13]

> Why do you tremble at the thought of poverty, and
> pursue wealth so ardently? So you won't need
> anything from anyone? ... Don't you see that we are
> all in need of one another. The soldier of the artisan,
> the artisan of the merchant, the merchant of the
> farmer, the slave of the free man, the master of the
> slave, the poor man of the rich, the rich of the poor, he
> who does not work of him who gives alms? ...
>
> He who receives alms serves a very great need, a need
> greater than any. For if there were no poor, the
> greater part of our salvation would be overthrown in
> that we would not have a place to bestow our wealth.
> So that even the poor man, who appears to be more
> useless than any, is the most useful of all.
>
> CHRYSOSTOM[14]

**(c). What is the present-day message of 2 Cor. 8:15?
What is the difference between modern communistic
principles and this Christian method of the sharing of**

resources? God provides for the needs of His people, as He did with the Israelites. He counsels us to work hard so we will be in a position to provide for our own needs and those of others (Eph. 4:28). He expects us to make wise use of the gifts of life, circumstances, and ability He has given us, within the confines of obedience to the type of life He asks us to live, and to leave the rest to Him. All that we are able to accomplish in our lifetime we owe to His gifts. Those born into fortunate circumstances, with special abilities, be they intellectual, physical, or material, are what they are with no initial credit to themselves. What counts in God's eyes is what we do with that which we have been given. He who has been given more with which to work (time, talent, treasure) is expected not to hoard but to give of his excess to help those whose abilities and opportunities are fewer (Lk. 12:48).

> Whether you will it or not, you will leave the gold behind but the glory that is born of good works you carry back to the Lord, where, standing before our common Judge all the people shall call you their nourisher and their benefactor and give you those other names that signify kindness and humanity.
>
> BASIL[15]

The Gospel's principles of providing for others differ from communistic principles in that they are not intended to be enforced by a worldly authority. Rather, they find their power in the willing hearts of those touched by Christ's teachings. They encourage rather than destroy individual initiative.

> Help the afflicted. Comfort those in sorrow. You who are strong, help the weak. You who are rich, help the poor. You who stand upright, help the fallen and the crushed. You who are joyful, comfort those in sadness. You who enjoy all good fortune, help those who have met with disaster. Give something to God in thanksgiving that you are of those who can give

374

help, not of those who stand and wait for it; that you have no need to look to another's hands, but that others must look to yours. Grow rich, not only in substance but also in piety; not only in gold but also in virtue; or rather, only in virtue. Be more honored than your neighbor by showing more compassion. Be as God to the unfortunate by imitating the mercy of God.

GREGORY OF NAZIANZUS[16]

(d). Exodus 16:16–24 relates that God told the people to gather only what they needed daily, and to save (hoard) none till the following morning. When they disobeyed, the following morning what they had hoarded "bred worms and stank." Yet God told them that on the sixth day they could gather a double portion so they would have enough for their needs on the Sabbath, a day of rest, when work was not allowed. On the Sabbath, that which they had saved from the day before "did not stink, nor were any worms in it." Why? Are there present-day analogies of this incident? The message in being allowed to gather double on the sixth day in order to have enough for the seventh is that God understands our need to make reasonable provisions for ourselves if we obey His precepts along the way. When the Israelites disobeyed His instructions, the portion they hoarded became contaminated, rendering that which was given for their benefit potentially harmful to them.

God did not create evil. When He finished His creation He pronounced every element in it "good" (Gen. 1:31). The eviction of Adam and Eve from Eden and the evils of the world they subsequently found themselves in were caused by misuse of that which was good.

Modern examples of this abound. For example, God created

the grape from which man learned to make wine. Jesus' first miracle involved turning water into wine for the enjoyment of the guests at a wedding in Cana (Jn. 2). More importantly, it was a pre-figuration of the wine that became His Blood at the Mystical Supper (Mt. 26:27–28). Therefore, wine is used in the Sacrament of Eucharist, during which it becomes the Blood of Christ and is received by those who love Him, "for remission of sins and life everlasting." Yet some abuse the use of wine, and this abuse can lead to sin and destruction. The grape that God created is good, and wine made from the grape is used in the Church for the continuation of that which is good, but through improper use of wine, man can bring about evil.

Also, God instructed man to unite with woman to form a family and to multiply and fill the earth (Gen. 1:27–28, 2:21–24). Within this framework, sexual union is good, a wondrous gift from God to be enjoyed within marriage. Yet some use this gift in ways He has warned us not to—for our own well-being. The shattered lives, abuses, and diseases which often result are the consequences of misuse of one of God's most powerful gifts.

Whether in regard to sexual behavior, lifestyles, or spirituality, God's laws were given to set His people apart, to demonstrate that they are different than the rest of the world. God's laws give them a way to show obedience through guidelines that, of their own free will, they must choose to obey or disobey; they produce a better, healthier way of life on earth, with the fullness of God's Kingdom as the goal.

> You have tasted the fruit of disobedience. You have learned how bitter the food of that bitter counselor. Taste now the food of obedience, which keeps evil away; and then you will learn that it is sweet and profitable to obey God.
>
> CYRIL OF ALEXANDRIA[17]

(e). Is the spiritual value of almsgiving negated if the money we give is misused? After basic criteria are satisfied with regard to giving wisely, to those who can be trusted, those who give should not allow doubts to hamper their generosity. God honors the intentions of the giver, even if the funds are ultimately misused.

(f). Why is almsgiving considered proof of love and faith? Jesus said, "Where your treasure is, there your heart will be also" (Mt. 6:21). It is easy to see what means most to a person by the allocation of his or her time, talent, and treasure. Those who really love God give of their treasure so that His work will be done and His people cared for.

> Trials are of two kinds. Either affliction will test our souls as gold is tried in a furnace and make trial of us through patience, or the very prosperity of our lives will oftentimes, for many, be itself an occasion of trial and temptation. For it is equally difficult to keep the soul upright and undefeated in the midst of afflictions as to keep oneself from insolence and pride in prosperity.
>
> BASIL[18]

> Let us think with shame of the great benefits we have already received and the great benefits we are yet to receive. If a poor man comes to us and begs, let us receive him with much good will: comforting him, encouraging him, so that we may be treated likewise, both by God and our fellowmen (Mt. 7:12).
>
> CHRYSOSTOM[19]

CHAPTER NINE

To Encourage a Rich Harvest

Paul ended Chapter Eight by urging the Corinthians to give their offering for the Christians in Jerusalem, who were in desperate need, as a demonstration of their love for Christ. He goes on to inform them of the blessings of almsgiving.

9:1–2. Now concerning the ministering to the saints, it is superfluous for me to write to you; for I know your willingness, about which I boast of you to the Macedonians, that Achaia was ready a year ago; and your zeal has stirred up the majority. Notice Paul's wisdom. In 2 Cor. 8:1–5, he used the example of the generosity of the Christians in Macedonia, who gave willingly though they themselves were in great need, in order to encourage the Corinthians to imitate this good example. Here he confides that to encourage the generosity of the Macedonians, he had likewise boasted to them about the zeal of the Corinthian Christians.

9:3–5. Yet I have sent the brethren, lest our boasting of you should be in vain in this respect, that, as I said, you may be ready; lest if some Macedonians come with me and find you unprepared, we (not to mention you!) should be ashamed of this confident boasting. Therefore I thought it necessary to exhort the brethren to go to you ahead of time, and prepare your bountiful gift beforehand, which you had previously promised, that it may be ready as a matter of generosity and not as a grudging obligation. Paul is sending Titus and two other fellow workers ahead to be sure the Corinthians understand why their almsgiving is necessary, for themselves as well as for those in need, and that what they have promised will be ready. If he brings someone from the church in Macedonia with him, he does not want his boasting about them to seem unfounded and thereby bring embarrassment to all concerned.

> **FOOD FOR THOUGHT:** (a). By what methods did Paul encourage spiritual growth in those he taught? Which of these is most effective?

9:6. But this I say: He who sows sparingly will also reap sparingly, and he who sows bountifully will also reap bountifully. To give so God's work may be done and His people cared for is to plant seeds of faith, hope, love, courage, and joy. The more seeds we plant, the more of a harvest we can expect (Gal. 6:7–9).

> Do you not know that we live in a foreign land, as though strangers and travelers? Do you not know that it is the lot of travelers to be ejected when they think not, expect not, which is also our lot. For this reason then, whatever we have acquired, we leave here. For the Lord does not allow us to take anything with us. If we have built houses, if we have bought fields, if any other such thing, not only does He not allow us to take them and depart, but does not even credit us with the price of them. ...

> The just, although having nothing, will both dwell here amidst all men's possessions as though they were his own; and also, when he has departed to Heaven, shall see those his eternal habitations. And he shall both here suffer no discomfort ... and when he has been restored to his own country, shall receive the true riches. In order that we may gain both the things of this life and of that, let us use rightly the things we have. For so shall we be citizens of the heavens.

CHRYSOSTOM[1]

9:7. So let each one give as he purposes in his heart, not grudgingly or of necessity; for God loves a cheerful giver. Christ gave the ultimate—His life—willingly. Though few are called upon to literally follow in His footsteps all the way to the cross, those who call themselves Christians must strive to be like Him in all ways, including giving, so that His work may continue. Those who have means should give joyfully to help those who do not (read Deut. 15:7–11).

> Make a little chest for the poor at home, near the place where you stand praying. As often as you pray, first deposit your alms, and then send up your prayer. As you would not wish to pray with unwashed hands, neither do so without alms. ... If you have this little coffer you have a defense against the Devil, you give wings to your prayer, you make your house holy, having meat for the King (Mt. 25:34–36).
>
> CHRYSOSTOM[2]

9:8. And God is able to make all grace abound toward you, that you, always having all sufficiency in all things, have an abundance for every good work. As God provided seed to all living matter of His creation so that propagation is assured, He provides the means whereby His people are able to do that which He asks of them. If we plant a seed and nurture it, it will produce a harvest of its kind and a multiplicity of new seeds to continue the ever-expanding cycle. So too, if we manage to give of ourselves and our treasures without expecting any type of recognition or reward on earth, God will bless our efforts. Through His grace, all our *reasonable* needs will be met and we will have an abundance from which to help others. No one can out give God.

> I am not leading you to entire poverty, but for the present I require you to cut off superfluities and to

desire a "sufficiency" alone. ... That is superfluous which is more than we need. When we are able to live healthfully and respectably without a certain thing, then certainly that thing is superfluous.

Thus let us think also in regard of clothing and of food and of a dwelling and of all our other wants, and in everything inquire what is necessary. For what is superfluous is also useless. When you have practiced living on what is sufficient, then if you have a mind to emulate that widow (Lk. 21:2), we will lead you on to greater things than these. For you have not yet attained to the philosophy of that woman while you are anxious about what is sufficient. For she soared higher even than this; for what was to have been her support, that she cast in, all of it.

CHRYSOSTOM[3]

FOOD FOR THOUGHT: (b). What spiritual wisdom can we glean from Chrysostom's words regarding superfluous "things"?

9:9. As it is written: "He has dispersed abroad, He has given to the poor; His righteousness remains forever." Quoting Ps. 112:9, Paul reflects that when we give as a consequence of love and faith, God remembers. In the measure we give, so we receive, in this life and the next, because almsgiving is an indication of a purified heart and soul.

The merciful man is not arrayed in a vest reaching to the feet, nor does he carry about bells nor wear a crown; but he is wrapped in the robe of loving kindness ... holier than the sacred vestment and is anointed with oil, not composed of material elements but produced by the Spirit. He bears a crown of mercies, for it is said, *Who crowns you with loving-kindness and tender mercies* (Ps. 103:4). Instead of wearing a plate bearing the Name of God, He is himself like God.

CHRYSOSTOM[4]

FOOD FOR THOUGHT: (c). Is there spiritual value in giving from ill-gotten gains? (Read 1 Sam. 15:22–23).

9:10–14. Now may He who supplies seed to the sower and bread for food supply and multiply the seed you have sown and increase the fruits of your righteousness, while you are enriched in everything for all liberality, which causes thanksgiving through us to God. For the administration of this service not only supplies the needs of the saints but also is abounding through many thanksgivings to God, while through the proof of this ministry they glorify God for the obedience of your confession to the Gospel of Christ and for your liberal sharing with them and all men, and by their prayer for you, who long for you because of the exceeding grace of God in you. When those in need are ministered to by God's people, the harvest is great. Those who receive assistance are grateful that their suffering is relieved because of God's word to His people; the ministry of the teacher is shown to be effective; and the good example of those who give generously encourages love, fellowship, prayer, and spiritual growth among those looking on. All this comes together through the grace of God. Nothing good can be accomplished without grace, but grace is actuated only when man cooperates with God's will.

> When you see a poor believer, think that you behold an altar ... you honor the altar in the church because it receives Christ's Body; but he who is himself the Body of Christ, you treat with rudeness and neglect. ... When you see such a beggar you must not only refrain from insulting him, but even reverence him,

and if you see another insulting him, prevent it, repel it. ... Do you want to see the altar built by God Himself? ... The priest enters into the holy of holies. Into yet more awesome places you may enter when you offer this sacrifice, where none is present but *your Father Who sees in secret* (Mt. 6:4) ... What is the smoke, what the sweet savor of this altar? Praise and thanksgiving. And how far does it ascend? As far as unto Heaven? By no means—it passes beyond Heaven itself—and the Heaven of Heaven, and arrives at the throne of the King. For He says *your* prayers *and your alms have come up before God* (Acts 10:4).

CHRYSOSTOM[5]

9:15. Thanks be to God for His indescribable gift! The gift that words cannot describe is God's divine plan for the salvation of mankind through His Son. An important part of this plan is the method by which the physical and spiritual needs of all are met through love and sharing. He who lives the Christ-like life that is called for under this plan has access to God's grace and is blessed with all good things: the glorious riches of the Kingdom that begin in this life and extend into eternity.

God's riches are strong faith, firm hope, ardent love and good works.[6]

FOOD FOR THOUGHT COMMENTS

(a). By what methods did Paul encourage spiritual growth in those he taught? Which of these methods is most effective? Paul fostered spiritual growth in those he taught by encouraging them (2 Cor. 7:4, 7, 11, 14–16; 8:7), by pointing to the good examples of others (2 Cor. 8:1–5), by reminding them of Christ's teachings and example (2 Cor. 8:9), and by praying for them (2 Cor. 13:9).

Christ's teachings engender knowledge of and thus love for Him. For the maturing Christian, they are, therefore, powerful tools towards spiritual growth. For someone just beginning to learn about Christ, however, encouragement and good examples are probably most effective. A hardened heart is not receptive to the seeds of faith. Man learns to love only after he receives love. The sower who first softens the heart encourages a greater harvest. Prayer is a powerful tool in any circumstance.

(b). What spiritual wisdom can we glean from Chrysostom's words regarding superfluous "things"? They remind us of the principle of keeping our desires in bounds, restrained by the needs of others. To be concerned only with ourselves causes withdrawal and isolation and separates us from the rest of the Body of Christ. If we realize that we do not need the biggest, the best, or the most of everything, we will always have a surplus from which to help others and to give to God's work. If we do not grow in this direction, we will never find the occasion to give because there is always something more to gather for ourselves.

> Possessions are external things, but our desires are within us. It is quite useless to try to reform the external objects if we have not first resolved the internal motivation. We may give all our money away, but what use is that if the longing for it still burns inside us? Poor people can covet. Poor people can envy. And poor people can misuse the little money they have. Getting rid of our material possessions will do nothing, in itself, to create in us a right attitude towards them.

The real test always lies in our attitudes. We can enjoy our possessions, seeing them as God's generous gifts, and using them as much for others as for ourselves. We can possess them without allowing them to possess us.

Only then can we be quite sure that if, in God's will, we are ever deprived of them, we may accept their loss as contentedly as we did their superabundance.

CLEMENT OF ALEXANDRIA[7]

(c). Is there spiritual value in giving from ill-gotten gains? (Read 1 Sam. 15:22.) To relieve another's distress from ill-gotten gains is to give a mixed message—the end does not justify the means.

> Nothing equals the merit of almsgiving. Great is the power of this action when it flows from untarnished sources, but when it comes from sources that are defiled, it is as if a fountain were to send forth mud. When alms are given from our just gains, it is as if they flowed forth from a pure and limpid stream, one flowing from paradise, pleasant to the eye, pleasant to the touch, something cool and light given in the noonday heat. Such are alms. Beside this fountain grow, not poplars nor pines nor cypresses but trees more rare and precious: the love of God, the praise of men, glory before God, the good will of all, the wiping away of sins, great confidence in God, and small esteem for riches.
>
> CHRYSOSTOM[8]

We cannot bribe God or appease Him with token gifts. Almsgiving is a part of the Christ-like life, not a substitute for it.

CHAPTER TEN

The Struggle Against Ungodly Forces

In writing this epistle, one of Paul's primary objectives is to establish his credentials as an Apostle, in answer to his detractors who question his authority to teach the Gospel. They accuse him of being weak and ineffective when among the Corinthians but bold in his letters to them from the safety of distance.

10:1. Now I, Paul, myself am pleading with you by the meekness and gentleness of Christ—who in presence am lowly among you but being absent am bold toward you. With irony, Paul refers to the misconception of his personality held by his enemies. Though generally "meek and gentle" in imitation of Christ, which his enemies perceive as weakness, he is also, like Christ, capable of great boldness and righteous anger when confronted with false teachings or sinful conduct (Mk. 11:15–17). The Hebrew word for *meek* actually means "capable of being molded." The original Greek word for *gentleness* means, more precisely, "forbearance." To be meek and gentle in the context of Scripture, then, means to be willing to let God mold us in His image, according to His will, and to have self-control and patience under adverse conditions. Those who succeed in this are strong, not weak.

> **FOOD FOR THOUGHT:** (a). Does being meek and gentle like Christ necessitate allowing oneself to be manipulated or to be intimidated into watering down expressions of faith so as not to offend? What is the proper Christian attitude toward non-believers?

10:2–3. But I beg you that when I am present I may not be bold with that confidence by which I intend to be bold against some who think of us as if we walked according to the flesh. For though we walk in the flesh, we do not war according to the flesh. True Christians are like everyone else in that they live in the world and are subject to the consequences of fallen human nature. But those who love God are also spiritual beings. They continually engage in spiritual warfare against those forces that want to prevent them from fulfilling their potential of union with God. Paul hopes he will not have to contend spiritually with the disobedient in the church in Corinth when he arrives.

> With all our strength let us hold fast to Christ, for there are always those who struggle to deprive our soul of His presence; and let us take care lest Jesus withdraws because of the evil thoughts that crowd our soul (Jn. 5:13). Yet we will not manage to hold Him without great effort on the soul's part. Let us study His life in the flesh, so that in our own life we may be humble. Let us absorb His sufferings, so that by emulating Him we may endure our afflictions patiently. Let us savor His ineffable incarnation and His work of salvation on our behalf, so that from the sweet taste in our soul we may know that the Lord is bountiful (Ps. 34:8). Also, and above all, let us unhesitatingly trust in Him and in what He says; and let us daily wait on His providence toward us. And whatever form it takes, let us accept it gratefully, gladly and eagerly, so that we may learn to look only to God, Who governs all things in accordance with the divine principles of His wisdom. If we do all these things, we are not far from God.
>
> PHILOTHEOS OF SINAI[1]

10:4. For the weapons of our warfare are not carnal but mighty in God for pulling down strongholds ... Satan uses individuals, institutions, and philosophies to help him achieve his goal of leading people away from God. In doing so, he creates strongholds that are difficult to stand against. But God has provided those who love Him with truth, righteousness, peace, and the Cross of Christ as protection against Satan's attacks. The disciplines of prayer (which includes fasting), watchfulness, and perseverance strengthen us from within. When we use these spiritual weapons to help us live a Christ-like life, we deliver a mighty blow to the Devil's ambitions, against which he cannot stand (see Eph. 6:10–18).

A modern example of the battle the true Christian engages in is provided by the success Satan has achieved in so distorting society's moral sense that a large segment of the world's population has no understanding or acceptance of the absolute truths revealed to man by God. His universal standard of right and wrong is not widely recognized—everything is relative. Sin is rationalized away. The sinner is absolved from personal responsibility, always able to find someone or something to blame. Real heroes are few, and the more outrageously and irresponsibly one behaves, the more attention s/he attracts. The general public has a startling fascination with athletes and movie idols, who seem to set society's standards. The only way a Christian can stay on the road to God in this environment is to fortify himself with scriptural truths and spiritual disciplines.

> The baptized Christian must struggle with his whole
> free will so that in true cooperation with God he will
> be able to reach a condition of unity with God. This
> journey is called the Christian life.[2]

Carnal weapons are those things in life that Satan tries to make seem of most importance:

Wealth, glory, power, fluency, cleverness, circum-
ventions, flatteries, hypocrisies, whatsoever else is
similar to these.

CHRYSOSTOM[3]

Many individuals use most of the precious moments of their
lives trying solely to amass these carnal weapons, though they
are useless in that which, in the end, is the only thing that
really matters: the spiritual struggle to stay on the road
leading us closer to God. Sometimes individuals (clergy and
laity) become a part of the Church for the wrong reasons:
political and social connections membership may offer or the
worldly power or prestige a position in the Church may bring.
This is contrary to the message of the Gospel but should
surprise no one because it has always been thus. Of the twelve
Apostles Jesus chose, one was motivated primarily by financial
considerations (Jn. 12:6).

> **FOOD FOR THOUGHT:** (b). With His
> foreknowledge, Jesus knew Judas would betray
> Him. Yet He chose him as an Apostle. Why?
> (c). Should offenders of the Gospel be routed from
> the Church?

**10:5. casting down arguments and every high thing that
exalts itself against the knowledge of God, bringing
every thought into captivity to the obedience of Christ
...** Through the power of the spiritual weapons God gives His
people, every intellectual argument, social force, or act of the
will against Him can be shattered and brought under
subjection to Christ. With these weapons at his command,
Paul brought many to the Kingdom and subdued many who
were its enemies (read Acts 19:11–12, 17–20).

**10:6. and being ready to punish all disobedience when
your obedience is fulfilled.** Paul has delayed his return to

Corinth to give the faithful there a chance to show their love by separating themselves from the false apostles who cause disruption in the Church. Upon his return, he intends to deal with the disobedient to restore harmony.

10:7. Do you look at things according to the outward appearance? If anyone is convinced in himself that he is Christ's, let him again consider this in himself, that just as he is Christ's, even so we are Christ's. True Christians develop spiritual gifts as fruit of their struggle to grow in holiness. One of these gifts is the ability to discern right from wrong, good from bad. Those who have this gift are not deceived by outward appearances, so would not be fooled by Paul's detractors who speak against him. They would recognize him as a man of God (Heb. 5:12–14, 1 Cor. 2:14).

> **FOOD FOR THOUGHT:** (d). How does one acquire the gift of discernment? Of what assistance is this gift in the Christian life?

10:8–11. For even if I should boast somewhat more about our authority, which the Lord gave us for edification and not for your destruction, I shall not be ashamed— lest I seem to terrify you by letters. "For his letters," they say, "are weighty and powerful, but his bodily presence is weak, and his speech contemptible." Let such a person consider this, that what we are in word by letters when we are absent, such we will also be in deed when we are present. Paul refrains from expounding upon the power and authority God has given him because he does not want to give credence to his detractors' claims that he tries to intimidate them with his letters. Those who accuse him of being weak and ineffective in person will find that he is as bold and powerful as his letters when necessary.

10:12–13. For we dare not class ourselves or compare ourselves with those who commend themselves. But they, measuring themselves by themselves, and comparing themselves among themselves, are not wise. But we will not boast beyond limit, but will keep to the limits God has apportioned us, to reach even to you. Paul was chosen by God to bring His word to certain areas, one of which is Corinth (Acts 18:1–11). He, therefore, compares himself with the Apostles, chosen by God for the specific task of bringing Christ's Gospel to the world (Mt. 28:19)—not with those who create their own agenda, with their own rules, and then boast about themselves without basis and authority. When Paul stresses his power and authority, he does so not in a boastful, dictatorial manner, but to put himself in a position from which he can carry out his mission. To shrink from that position in the name of modesty or humility would be to make him impotent, unable to fulfill his responsibilities.

This verse also speaks well to the variable morality of society. Many extol the virtue of "values," but unless those values are grounded in God's truths, they mean something different to each person.

10:14–16. For we are not extending ourselves beyond our sphere (thus not reaching you), for it was to you that we came with the Gospel of Christ; not boasting of things beyond measure, that is, in other men's labors, but having hope, that as your faith is increased, we shall be greatly enlarged by you in our sphere, to preach the Gospel in the regions beyond you, and not to boast in another man's sphere of accomplishment. Paul hopes his efforts in Corinth will bear fruit so that God will expand his mission to teach into other areas to which the Gospel has not yet been brought.

10:17. But "He who glories, let him glory in the Lord." Those who try to do the work of the Lord must not boast about what "they" have done, only what the Lord has done—sometimes through them.

> **FOOD FOR THOUGHT:** (e). Is it possible for God to work through modern man as He did through Paul?

10:18. For not he who commends himself is approved, but whom the Lord commends. God alone is Judge, through His Son. He will determine whose life showed faith through love and obedience to His truth, and whose did not. We are judges of ourselves to the extent that the degree of harshness with which we judge others will be the standard that God uses to judge us (Mt. 7:1–2). What we say or think about ourselves is not what matters, but what God knows about us.

> **FOOD FOR THOUGHT:** (f). There are those who believe that each person should seek "his own" truth. What does this verse say to them?

FOOD FOR THOUGHT COMMENTS

(a). Does being meek and gentle like Christ necessitate allowing oneself to be manipulated or intimidated into watering down expressions of one's faith so as not to offend? What is the proper Christian attitude toward non-believers? To be meek and gentle like Christ requires that we not return evil for evil, no matter how reviled or provoked. However, we need not and should not be without strength of conviction. The Christian model is to pray for guidance, to try continually to grow in grace and in knowledge and to be bold in following through with what God expects of us.

> What should we do about those around us who are not believers? Certainly we should pray for them, not just occasionally or as a matter of routine but all the time, in the hope that they may have a change of heart and so find their way to God.
>
> But we should also give them every opportunity to learn the truth of Christ from us, not so much, perhaps, by preaching it to them in so many words, but by the way we behave toward them. Our attitude should reflect the attitude of Christ.
>
> So when they are hostile, meet them with gentleness. When they make angry accusations, respond with calm words. When they abuse you, pray for them. At the same time, don't compromise your beliefs or water them down to make them acceptable. It is possible to stand firm against violence and error while remaining perfectly calm and gentle. Don't be trapped into playing their game.
>
> Show them that we regard them as our brothers, children of the same Creator and simply want them to become also our brothers in Christ, sons of the same Father. Our attitude should be that of the Lord. If we imitate Him, we won't go wrong.
>
> IGNATIUS OF ANTIOCH[4]

(b). With His foreknowledge, Jesus knew that Judas would betray Him. Yet He chose Judas as an Apostle. Why? With the gift of free will that has been endowed to man from the beginning, each of us either tries to fulfill the purpose for which we were given life (to seek God and live in a way that will lead to union with Him—Acts 17:26–27), or he rejects or ignores God (there is no middle ground—Mt. 12:30, Rev. 3:16).

God knows the outcome of our life, not because He wills the results, but because He is omniscient and has foreknowledge. He allows each of us to live our life (to act out what He foreknows) so that on Judgment Day we will all realize that we had a chance for eternal blessedness and that His judgment is fair. Jesus chose Judas as an Apostle to illustrate this truth, though He knew the consequences for Himself.

As the parable of the wheat and the tares illustrates (Mt. 13:24–30), the word of God is brought to everyone so they can hear it and desire the Kingdom of Heaven. Some choose instead a kingdom on earth, as did Judas. They are the "tares" (weeds, useless or harmful growth): those who allow the enemy to sow lies in their hearts. Wherever there is "wheat" (those who attempt to grow in holiness), Satan works hard to uproot it (Rev. 12:17). God allows this because He wants the consequences of the gift of free will to take their course in each person's life in order that the gift be complete, and because many lessons are taught in this way.

> Do you think, Brothers, that the tares do not reach to high seats? Do you think they are all down among you, and none above? That we may not be such! ... But I tell you, in the high seats there are good wheat and there are tares; as among the people there are good wheat and there are tares. Let the good be patient with the wicked; let those who do evil change their ways and become as the good. Let us all, if possible, come unto God. May we all, through His mercy, escape the wickedness of this world. Let us seek good days, for we are in the midst of days that are evil: but in these wicked days let us not blaspheme, that we may reach unto the good days.
> AUGUSTINE[5]

(c). Should offenders of the Gospel be routed from the Church? If it seems to us that someone in the Church is there for the wrong reasons, we must first remember that not everything is necessarily what it appears to be:

> We have to deal with an adversary who is a great liar. ... Yet we can rejoice that we have a Judge Whom our accuser cannot deceive. Had we a man as a judge, our enemy could invent for him as he willed; for there is no one more clever at inventing than the Devil. Even now it is he who invents all the false accusations made against the saints. Since his accusations avail nothing with God, he scatters them among men ... he knows the evil he can work with them, unless the vigilance of faith resists him. And it is for this he circulates evil about the good: that the weak may then think they are not any good and so let themselves be carried away by their own evil desires and become corrupted, saying to themselves: Who is there that keeps a commandment of God? Or who observes chastity? And when a man believes that no one does, he himself becomes this "no one." It is in this way that the Devil works.
>
> AUGUSTINE[6]

Secondly, it is important to keep in mind that the Church is the best place for the spiritually unawakened or wavering to be—where perhaps the Holy Spirit can soften their hearts and bring about repentance. Whenever possible, actions and behavior should be evaluated against the precepts of Scripture and dealt with lovingly but firmly (see Chapter Seven, Food for Thought Comment (c).), but we should not judge the person—that is God's province (see 1 Cor. 4:3–5).

> We are anxious that, if it were possible, nothing evil should remain among the good. But it was said to us: *Let both grow until the harvest.* Why? Because you are prone to error.[7]

Hear what He says: *Let both grow together until the harvest, and at the time of harvest I will say to the reapers, first gather the tares and bind them in bundles to burn them: but gather the wheat into my barn.* Why hasten then, zealous servants, He says? Do you see that the tares stand in the midst of the good growth, and you wish to uproot the bad? Remain quiet; it is not yet the time of harvest. Let it come, and let it reveal to you the true wheat. Why need you be angry? Why are you impatient that the bad should not be mixed with the good? They may be among you in the field, but in My barn they shall not be with you.

AUGUSTINE[8]

(d). How does one acquire the gift of discernment? Of what assistance is this gift in the Christian life? God gives His spiritual gifts to those who indicate, by word and by deed, that they want them, so if we seek wisdom, we should ask for it (Jas. 1:5). At the same time, we should study Scripture for the guidance it contains, as the *fair-minded* Jews did when confronted with Paul's teaching that Jesus was the Messiah Whom they had been taught to await (Acts 17:11). The other important tool to which we have access is the writings of the Fathers of the Church, which preserve the original understanding of God's word to His people. Just as practice makes perfect with any skill, it is important to apply all acquired spiritual knowledge and understanding to the problems and circumstances of life day by day—for we continue to learn and grow when we actually try to live the Christian life.

> For him who possesses it, discrimination [discernment] is a light illuminating the right moment, the proposed action, the form it takes, strength, knowledge, maturity, capacity, weakness, resolution, aptitude, degree of contrition, inner state, ignorance, physical strength and temperament, health and misery, behavior, position, occupation,

upbringing, faith, disposition, purpose, way of life, degree of fearlessness, skill, natural intelligence, diligence, vigilance, sluggishness, and so on. ... It reveals the nature of things, their use, quantity and variety, as well as the divine purpose and meaning in each word or passage of Holy Scripture ... and the significance of the interpretation given by the Fathers.[9]

Discrimination is born of humility. On its possessor it confers spiritual insight, as both Moses and St. John Climacus[10] say: such a man foresees the hidden designs of the enemy and foils them before they are put into operation. ... Discrimination is characterized by an unerring recognition of what is good and what is not, and the knowledge of the will of God in all that one does.[11]

He who lacks discrimination cannot achieve anything; while the person who possesses it is a guide to the blind and a light to those in darkness (Rom. 2:19). We should refer everything to such a person and accept whatever he says, even if because of our inexperience we do not see its import as well as we would like. Indeed, he who has discrimination is to be recognized in particular from the fact that he is able to communicate the sense of what he says even to those who do not want to know it.

PETER OF DAMASKOS[12]

Among beginners, discernment is real self-knowledge; among those midway along the road to perfection, it is a spiritual capacity to distinguish unfailingly between what is truly good and what in nature is opposed to the good; among the perfect, it is a knowledge resulting from divine illumination, which with its lamp can light up what is dark in others. To put the matter generally, discernment is—and is recognized to be—a solid understanding of the will of God in all times, in all places, in all things; and it is found only among those who are pure in heart, in body and in speech.

CLIMACUS[13]

(e). Is it possible for God to work through modern man as He did through Paul? In every age, God has worked through those who love Him. Abraham, Isaac, Jacob, Moses, Noah, Job, Daniel, the Holy Prophets, the Apostles, Martyrs, Saints (ancient and modern, known and unknown), and ordinary people of every description have been instruments of His will. He can and will work through each of us if we ask Him to, allow Him to, and try at the same time to grow in obedience to His word. This is why, although the patristic age is generally considered to include those important Christian writers from the end of the first to the end of the eighth centuries A.D., it never really ends. Each age has the potential to produce a "Father" (or "Mother") of the Church.[14]

(f). There are those who believe that each person should "seek his own truth." What does 2 Corinthians 10:18 say to them? God is the only source of eternal Truth, defined as that which comprises His divine plan for man. While each person has been given free will to respond to God in his/her own way—or even to reject Him—it remains that ultimately everything will be judged against the standard God has set. Self-created "truths" have no real power, except to confuse, distract, and lead the misguided away from the unalterable, unchanging divine word. Satan, the deceiver of the world, was the first to go his own way (Rev. 12:7–9), but he has many followers. They help him to accomplish his goal of depriving as many as possible of the joys of the Kingdom (union with God), which, for the true believer, begins in this life.

There are also those who claim that the seeker should look inside himself for the solutions to life's problems. But he who does will find what has been absorbed into his being during his lifetime—which may be true or it may be false. That which is not based on God can lead to self-worship: idolization of self via one's own thoughts and ideas.

Christianity calls us to look to our Creator for the answers to the questions of life. We cannot know Truth on our own, only in communion with Him. If those who love God plant His precepts in the hearts and minds of those they can influence, they will be giving them access to His Truth, His values, His light, His power. To find the precepts of Truth, it is logical to look to that which has been preserved, protected, and taught by the historic early Church before heresies divided the Body of Christ. This is the treasure Orthodoxy offers.

CHAPTER ELEVEN

Safeguarding the Inheritance

One of the dangers to the Christians in Corinth, who are still infants spiritually, is that they will be led astray by the teachings of false apostles. Paul, therefore, continues his efforts to strengthen his relationship with them. He hopes to remain a positive influence in their lives.

11:1. Oh, that you would bear with me in a little folly—and indeed you do bear with me. In the awkward position of having to defend his authority as an Apostle, Paul finds it distasteful to seem to be boasting about himself.

11:2. For I am jealous for you with godly jealousy. For I have betrothed you to one husband, that I may present you as a chaste virgin to Christ. Exodus 20:5 relates that God is "jealous." But He covets what is best for the object of His affections rather than for Himself. He wants each of us in His Kingdom—not in Satan's. Paul feels the same type of jealousy toward the Corinthian Christians. Following the Old Testament pattern that refers to Israel as the bride of God (Is. 54:5), Paul refers to the Church as the Bride of Christ. He has promised the church in Corinth to Christ and intends to present her pure and undefiled by false teachings.

11:3. But I fear, lest somehow, as the serpent deceived Eve by his craftiness, so your minds may be corrupted from the simplicity that is in Christ. Satan persuaded Eve to follow his lead rather than God's instructions. The false apostles are trying to persuade the Corinthians that what they teach is superior to the Gospel of Jesus Christ. Paul hopes to prevent a replay of the ancient tragedy that has occurred again and again throughout the ages. Each time someone is led away from the simple truth of salvation through Christ, the Devil rejoices.

> What therefore must we do? We must wholly deny him all belief; stop up our ears against him, and regard this seducer with hate. And the more he promises the more must we avoid him. This he did with Eve. For when he had filled her with false promises, it was then he utterly ruined her and brought unending misery upon her. He is an unpitying enemy, and he has set himself implacably to war against us. We do not seek our own salvation as eagerly as he seeks our ruin. Let us turn away from him, and not in word only but in deed. And let us do none of the things that give him pleasure. In this way all we do shall be pleasing to God.
>
> CHRYSOSTOM[1]

11:4–5. For if he who comes preaches another Jesus whom we have not preached, or if you receive a different spirit which you have not received, or a different Gospel which you have not accepted, you may well put up with it. For I consider that I am not at all inferior to the most eminent apostles. If someone were to give them a better understanding of Jesus and His Gospel than what they received from Paul, they would do well to listen. But he taught them nothing less than they would have received from Peter, James, or John, who were considered the most eminent Apostles. When Paul's authority to teach is questioned, he numbers himself with the chief Apostles so that his ministry retains the power it must and does have from God.

11:6. Even though I am untrained in speech, yet I am not in knowledge. But we have been thoroughly made manifest among you in all things. Paul was not a dazzling orator and did not pretend to be, but he was highly qualified to teach the Gospel. It had been revealed to him by Christ Himself (Gal. 1:12), and the Corinthians had seen ample evidence of Christ working through him to recognize the legitimacy of his ministry.

11:7–9. Did I commit sin in abasing myself that you might be exalted, because I preached the Gospel of God to you free of charge? I robbed other churches, taking wages from them to minister to you. And when I was present with you, and in need, I was a burden to no one, for what was lacking to me the brethren who came from Macedonia supplied. And in everything I kept myself from being burdensome to you, and so I will keep myself. Though he had the right as an Apostle to be paid for the work he did (1 Cor. 9:1–14), he refused any compensation from the Corinthian church. He lived simply, so that his trade of tentmaking (Acts 18:3) provided for his meager needs. The Christians in Macedonia supplied what he lacked, a fact he refers to as robbery because they supported him while he ministered to the Corinthians. His practice of refusing remuneration from those to whom he was currently ministering allowed him freedom to correct and chasten his flock when necessary.

11:10–12. As the truth of Christ is in me, no one shall stop me from this boasting in the regions of Achaia. Why? Because I do not love you? God knows! But what I do, I will also continue to do, that I may cut off the opportunity from those who desire an opportunity to be regarded just as we are in the things of which they boast. Paul plans to continue his style of ministry to give no one reason to doubt his motives, and to thwart the pseudo-apostles who try to use the Corinthians for financial gain. He preaches and teaches to bring people to Christ, not for worldly advantage.

11:13–15. For such are false apostles, deceitful workers, transforming themselves into apostles of Christ. And no wonder! For Satan himself transforms himself into an angel of light. Therefore it is no great thing if his ministers also transform themselves into ministers of righteousness, whose end will be according to their works. Those who continuously try to demean Paul's authority call themselves apostles. They expect to be paid for their work and claim that fact as a sign of the validity of their ministry. According to their rationale, Paul accepted no compensation because even he did not think his ministry was of value. He writes that these deceivers pretend outwardly to be virtuous in order to mislead, winning followers and then leading them astray.

Satan traditionally works in this manner. He does not appear to his victims in horns and a tail as cartoonists depict but transforms himself into something that appears righteous in order to gain souls through trickery. His ministers do likewise. Therefore, we must always be on guard.

> Deceitful workers pull up what has been planted. They wear the mask of truth because they are well aware that otherwise they would not be well received.
> CHRYSOSTOM[2]

FOOD FOR THOUGHT: (a). Why does God allow Satan and his workers to practice such deceit?

11:16–21. I say again, let no one think me a fool. If otherwise, at least receive me as a fool, that I also may boast a little. What I speak, I speak not according to the Lord, but as it were, foolishly, in this confidence of boasting. Seeing that many boast according to the flesh, I also will boast. For you put up with fools gladly, since

you yourselves are wise! For you put up with it if one brings you into bondage, if one devours you, if one takes from you, if one exalts himself, if one strikes you on the face. To our shame, I say that we were too weak for that! But in whatever anyone is bold—I speak foolishly—I am bold also. The false apostles Paul alludes to at this point are Judaizers. They claim to have superior authority and are trying to lead the Corinthians back into the bondage of the Mosaic Law in order to have control over their lives. Paul had not tried to dominate those he taught. He writes, with irony, that he is "too weak for that." The Christians of Corinth were being taken advantage of, financially and otherwise. The question of integrity with regard to financial matters is important for the following reason:

> Nothing exasperates God so much as embezzlement and extortion. Why? Because it is very easy to abstain from this sin. This sin springs not from natural desire that perturbs the mind, but from willful negligence ... The passion of desire was implanted in our nature for the procreation of children, and anger for the succor of the injured, but love of money serves no purpose. So if you are made captive by it, you will suffer the vilest punishment.
>
> CHRYSOSTOM[3]

To steal, cheat, or in any way make the acquisition of money or material goods our primary goal in life is to make money our god. Therefore, the love of money is called the "root of all kinds of evil" (1 Tim. 6:10). If we allow a false god to take control of our lives, we open ourselves to unending misery.

> Let us make a comparison and see which is the more imperious, the desire of money or of beauty; for that which shall be found to have struck down great men is the more difficult to master. Let us see then what

great man the desire of money ever got possession of. Not one; only of exceedingly pitiful and abject persons, Gehazi, Ahab, Judas, the priests of the Jews: but the desire for beauty overcame even the great prophet David.

CHRYSOSTOM[4]

FOOD FOR THOUGHT: (b). Since sexual desire is inate and hard to resist, should sexual sins be taken lightly? (c). If love of money is easier to control, why do so many succumb to it?

11:22. Are they Hebrews? So am I. Are they Israelites? So am I. Are they the seed of Abraham? So am I. Paul's detractors assert that they have superior lineage, but there is nothing lacking in his background. Not only is he is of Hebrew heritage as they are, but also an "Israelite," the title reserved for those Jews dedicated to God. Under the Blood Covenant, that title now belongs to those who recognize Christ as the awaited Messiah (Rom. 9:6–8). The "seed of Abraham" are those who belong to Christ (Gal. 3:29), not those who happen to be Jews by accident of birth.

> If we, because of our faith in Christ, are deemed children of Abraham, the Jews, therefore, because of their violation of the promise have ceased to be His seed. In that fearful day when men shall be judged, good parents shall avail nothing to wicked children, as the prophet Ezekiel says (Ez. 14:14). And good children will avail nothing to evil parents; rather will the goodness of their children increase the guilt of the parents (Lk. 11:19).
>
> GREGORY THE GREAT[5]

11:23. Are they ministers of Christ?—I speak as a fool—I am more: in labors more abundant, in stripes above measure, in prisons more frequently, in deaths often.

Paul had battle scars to prove his Apostleship. He had endured all types of affliction and faced danger of imminent death many times. He could have avoided all of this had he forsaken his mission—but he pressed on.

11:24. From the Jews five times I received forty stripes minus one. Under Mosaic Law, he who was to be punished could be sentenced to no more than forty lashes with a whip so as not to humiliate him (Deut. 25:3). It was traditional, therefore, for the judge to impose one less than forty when passing sentence to insure that in his zeal the administrator would not inadvertently deliver more than forty. Paul had received thirty-nine lashes five times from his fellow Jews.

11:25. Three times I was beaten with rods; once I was stoned; three times I was shipwrecked; a night and a day I have been in the deep; ... One of the methods of punishment the Roman government employed for non-citizens was to beat them with rods. Though he was a Roman citizen, and supposedly protected from that treatment, Paul had endured it three times. He had also been stoned (Acts 14:19), the method of punishment traditionally practiced by Jews. In addition, in the course of the long, perilous journeys he undertook to preach the Gospel, he had been shipwrecked three times, once spending a night and a day drifting bodily in the sea.

11:26–27. in journeys often, in perils of waters, in perils of robbers, in perils of my own countrymen, in perils of the Gentiles, in perils in the city, in perils in the wilderness, in perils in the sea, in perils among false brethren; in weariness and toil, in sleeplessness often, in hunger and thirst, in fastings often, in cold and nakedness. He had the self-discipline and perseverance necessary to do that which was required of him, in spite of personal peril. His missionary journeys were treacherous, without adequate food, clothing, and shelter, and he faced the wrath of both Jews and Gentiles. In addition, he fasted regularly for the spiritual strength it provided. Sensing vulnerability—as he had when Christ was hungry (Mt. 4:2–3)—the Devil bombarded Paul with trials and tribulations.

> Some involved labor, others sorrow, others fear, others pain, others care, others shame, others all these at once; yet he was victorious in all. And as if a single soldier, having the whole world fighting against him, should move through the ranks of his enemies and suffer no harm, so did Paul, showing himself alone among barbarians, among Greeks, on every land, on every sea, abide unconquered. And as a spark that changes into fire the things it touches, so did this man, setting upon all, make things change over to the truth.
>
> CHRYSOSTOM[6]

If we bear Satan's darts nobly, without giving up the struggle, the strength of the weapon is turned against that ancient enemy.

> This is the brilliant victory, this is the Church's trophy, thus is the Devil overthrown, when we suffer injury. For when we suffer, he is taken captive; and himself suffers harm, when he would with joy inflict it on us. This is what happened in Paul's case; the more Satan plied him with perils, the more he was defeated.
>
> CHRYSOSTOM[7]

11:28. Besides the other things, what comes upon me daily: my deep concern for all the churches. Paul had started on the road to Damascus as a persecutor and had become the persecuted. In addition to the physical and emotional ordeals he endured, He carried the weighty burden of concern for the spiritual condition of the new Christians in the areas to which he had brought the Gospel. Those who sometimes feel weighed down by worry about the spiritual condition of their own families, friends, or communities can perhaps begin to understand the immensity of the responsibility Paul felt.

11:29. Who is weak, and I am not weak? Who is made to stumble, and I do not burn with indignation? He feels the pains of his spiritual children. When some show weakness, he himself feels weak. When some are led astray, he is outraged.

11:30. If I must boast, I will boast in the things which concern my infirmity. He allows himself to boast only about those things some may consider signs of weakness: his personal involvement with his spiritual children and the suffering he has endured.

11:31. The God and Father of our Lord Jesus Christ, who is blessed forever, knows that I am not lying. He rests his case with his acknowledgement that, in the final analysis, God will judge who is speaking and living the Truth and who is not. This is the ultimate consolation for those who have done their best and are content to leave their fate in God's hands.

11:32–33. In Damascus the governor, under Aretas the king, was guarding the city of the Damascenes with a garrison, desiring to apprehend me; but I was let down in a basket through a window in the wall, and escaped from his hands. Paul reminisces about an event that occurred soon after his conversion (Acts 9:23–25), perhaps as an example of the human frailties he had to struggle with daily, in spite of having been chosen by God to do His work. When on his way to Damascus to continue his persecution of

Christians—thinking he was doing God's will—he had experienced the very dramatic supernatural intervention of Christ, Who showed him the error of his ways. But later he fled that city and the enemies of the Gospel in a very human, even undignified manner. Those two events seem to have set the pattern for a ministry that brought him both extremes: the agony of every type of hardship imaginable and the blessed joy of being in the presence of God.

> **FOOD FOR THOUGHT:** (d). We have addressed the fact that trying to live the Christ-like life God expects of His people will inevitably bring some degree of suffering. But the suffering Paul endured was especially extensive—why?

FOOD FOR THOUGHT COMMENTS

(a). Why does God allow Satan and his followers to practice deceit? God allows Satan to use his wiles against man as part of the sorting process necessary to single out those who belong to His Kingdom. It is not that God needs to know who they are, *they* need to know who they are—and to be molded in His image. However, He also arms His people with knowledge of His word and all the tools of the Church. He advises that they examine every person and situation in the light of that knowledge to see "whether they are of God" (1 Jn. 4:1) and that they pray for guidance and discernment to avoid error. Those who follow this pattern will not be deceived.

(b). Since sexual desire is innate and hard to resist, should sexual sins be taken lightly? Scripture clearly indicates that sexual misconduct among Christians is not to be taken lightly. David's sinful conduct with Bathsheba "displeased the Lord" (2 Sam. 11:27). Paul reacted rigorously against the man in Corinth who was involved in a sexual relationship with his stepmother (1 Cor. 5:1) and against all sexual immorality in general (1 Cor. 6:9). Sexual desire was given to man by God to create loving, nurturing families. This beautiful gift should not be misused.

> I say that the desire for beauty is more difficult to master than the love of money, not as extending forgiveness to those who are conquered by lust, but rather, as preparing them to be watchful.
>
> CHRYSOSTOM[8]

God created man in His image, with the ability to control passions and channel them in the right direction, unlike animals.

> God did not abolish all desire, only that which is unlawful, for He said: *let every man have his own wife, and let each woman have her own husband* (1 Cor. 7:2).
>
> CHRYSOSTOM[9]

(c). If love of money is easier to control than sexual desire, why do so many succumb to it? Many are brought down by the love of money because they do not understand its dangers.

> They stand not so much on their guard against it as against promiscuity and fornication; for if they had thought it equally dangerous, they would not, perhaps, have been made its captives.
>
> CHRYSOSTOM[10]

Also, money buys the things of the world. Though they are ultimately meaningless, these things nevertheless hold much appeal for those whom Satan has managed to distract from the

410

elements of life that have lasting value.

(d). We have addressed the fact that trying to live the Christ-like life God expects of His people will inevitably bring some degree of suffering. But that which Paul endured was especially extensive—why? Paul had a pivotal, difficult mission to fulfill in bringing the Gospel to the Gentiles. He possessed total love for God and dedication to Christ, factors which qualified him for his task but which also made him vulnerable to intensive attacks by Satan, who wanted to curtail his mission.

> The higher anyone ascends in virtue, the harder will this world bear down on him; for the more the love of the heart turns from this present life, the more the opposition of the world mounts up. Hence it is that those who strive after and do that which is good struggle under a burden of afflictions. For though they have turned away from earthly things, they are harassed with increasing tribulations. But, according to the word of the Lord, they shall bring forth fruit in patience, and after their time of tribulation they shall be received into rest above because they have borne their cross in patience.
>
> GREGORY THE GREAT[11]

Paul picked up the cross he had been given to bear and followed Christ on the road to martyrdom (Mk. 8:34). His struggles bore much fruit.

> He endured *shipwreck* so he might stop the shipwreck of the world; *a day and a night he passed in the deep*, so he might draw the world up from the depths of error; he was *in weariness* that he might refresh the weary; he endured smiting that he might heal those who had been smitten by the devil; he passed his time in prisons that he might lead forth to

the light those who were sitting in prison and in darkness; he was *in deaths often* so he might deliver from grievous deaths; *five times he received forty stripes save one* that he might free those inflicted by the scourge of the devil; he was *beaten with rods* that he might bring them under *the rod and the staff* of Christ (Ps. 23:4); he *was stoned*, that he might deliver them from the senseless stones; he was *in the wilderness*, that he might take them out of the wilderness; *in journeying*, to stop their wanderings and open the way that leads to Heaven; he was *in perils in the cities*, so he might show the city which is above; *in hunger and thirst*, to deliver from a more grievous hunger; *in nakedness*, to clothe their unseemliness with the robe of Christ; set upon by the mob, to extricate them from the besetment of fiends; he burned, that he might quench the burning darts of the devil: *through a window was let down from the wall*, to send up from below those that lay prostrate upon the ground. ... What all the saints together have suffered in so many bodies, he himself endured in one.

CHRYSOSTOM[12]

Paul's life stands as a reminder of the power of setting a good example. If we patiently endure the hurdles Satan puts in our path and keep our eyes on God and His Kingdom, we demonstrate faith. God blesses our efforts with His grace, and we become stronger. Those witnessing this phenomenon are strengthened in their faith also. In this way, the tribulations Satan hoped would turn us away from God in bitterness and frustration can actually bring all involved closer to Him and turn evil to good. Though we may never find the answers to all our questions in this life, we may be sure that God is in control and will never abandon us.

Some [paths to the Lord] lead over hills and mountains, and others lead down a slope. To this He says: *Every valley shall be filled, and every mountain*

412

shall be brought low. Some of the paths are uneven, here they rise up, there they drop down; and they also are dangerous. To this He adds: *And the crooked shall be made straight and the rough ways plain.* This is accomplished spiritually, through the power of the Savior. Before, the way of evangelical belief and living was difficult because worldly pleasures bore heavily on the minds of all men. But God, made man, *has condemned sin in the flesh* (Rom. 8:3), and all things have become straight, unimpeded and easy to this end; nor will hill or valley now stand in the way of those who wish to go forward.

CYRIL OF ALEXANDRIA[13]

CHAPTER TWELVE

What the Unenlightened Cannot See

Paul has shared many insights into the power and glory of God. Now he expounds upon the mysteries of that which surrounds the Creator—His Kingdom.

12:1. It is doubtless not profitable for me to boast. I will come to visions and revelations of the Lord: Paul is about to relate a supernatural experience that he would normally not share with anyone because of the dangers of falling to the sin of pride. He does so now only to a limited degree, to establish, without a doubt, his authority as an Apostle.

12:2–3. I know a man in Christ who fourteen years ago— whether in the body I do not know, or whether out of the body I do not know, God knows—such a one was caught up to the third Heaven. And I know such a man—whether in the body or out of the body I do not know, God knows ... He begins as though speaking about someone else. But he would not worry about seeming to boast unless referring to himself.

Around A.D. 41, after his escape from Damascus but before he began his missionary journeys, Paul was transported to the "third Heaven," a Jewish expression for the immediate presence of God. During this experience God revealed great mysteries to him, but even he did not know whether he was in his body or out of it at the time.

> Such a person does not see by sense perception, but his vision is as clear as or clearer than that by which sight perceives sensibilia. He sees by going out of himself, for through the mysterious sweetness of his

414

vision he is ravished beyond all objects and all objective thought, and even beyond himself.

GREGORY PALAMAS[1]

God gave Paul this experience because he was chosen for his ministry after Christ had ascended, and so had not been taught by Him in person.

> ... that he might not seem to be inferior to the rest of the Apostles. For since they had companied with Christ, but Paul had not: He therefore caught him up unto glory also.
>
> CHRYSOSTOM[2]

12:4. how he was caught up into Paradise and heard inexpressible words, which it is not lawful for a man to utter. Paul speaks of having heard that which he could not reveal, as John was not allowed to write what the seven thunders had uttered (Rev. 10:4). As Jesus told Nicodemus (Jn. 3:12), God does not reveal His mysteries to the worldly man because they are beyond his comprehension.

> These mysteries cannot be fully known (or, rather, experienced) except by the saints—by those who live in perfect union with God, transformed by grace and belonging rather to the future life than to our earthly life.[3]

12:5–6. Of such a one I will boast; yet of myself I will not boast, except in my infirmities. For though I might desire to boast, I will not be a fool; for I will speak the truth. But I forbear, lest anyone should think of me above what he sees me to be or hears from me. Because he had this experience by "going out of himself," by being taken "beyond himself," Paul could refer to it as having happened to someone else. He resists the temptation to embellish facts to bring glory to himself, relating only what is necessary to establish his right to try to guide the Corinthian Christians. He wants to lead them to worship God, not him.

12:7. And lest I should be exalted above measure by the abundance of the revelations, a thorn in the flesh was given to me, a messenger of Satan to buffet me, lest I be exalted above measure. The visions and revelations Paul experienced gave him spiritual wisdom and power. But the difficulties that God allowed Satan to bring to his life would remind him and all who would learn of his life and work that he was a human being, as dependent upon God as everyone else.

> Affliction rends pride away and prunes out all listlessness and exercises unto patience: it reveals the meanness of human things and leads unto much philosophy. For all the passions give way before it: anger, envy, emulation, lust, rule, desires of riches, of beauty, boastfulness, pride, anger and the whole remaining swarm of these distempers. ...
>
> For thus has God led all the saints through affliction and distress, at once doing them service and assuring that mankind will not entertain a higher opinion of them than they deserve. For thus it was that idolatries gained ground at first; men being held in admiration beyond what they deserve.
>
> CHRYSOSTOM[4]

As we learn in the Old Testament Book of Job, the Devil cannot touch God's people without permission from Him. God will not let us be tempted beyond what we are able to endure (1 Cor. 10:13).

> It is noteworthy that Satan does not claim for himself the power to strike, he who never fails to proclaim his presumption against the Author of all things. The

416

Devil knows that by himself he is able to do nothing, for he does not even exist by himself as a spirit. It must be known that the will of Satan is always evil, but his power is never unrighteous: for his will comes from himself, but his power from God. That which he wills to do in his malice, God in His righteousness allows him to accomplish. We must not fear him who can do nothing without permission. That Power alone is to be feared Who, by allowing the Enemy to be unleashed, makes his unrighteous will serve for the execution of righteous judgments.

GREGORY THE GREAT[5]

Modern theologians contend that Paul's "thorn in the flesh" was a physical malady, perhaps an affliction of the eyes that caused unsightly scaling and made looking at him unpleasant. This could account for his large handwriting (Gal. 6:11) and shed light on his comment that his followers were willing to pluck out their own eyes if they could give them to him (Gal. 4:13–15). An ancient theory is that Paul's problem was debilitating headaches, perhaps brought on by some type of chronic fever that attacked him repeatedly. However, Chrysostom and most of the Greek Fathers, as well as some eminent scholars of later ages, assert that this thorn was his vulnerability to his enemies: those who tried to thwart his work and had him beaten, imprisoned, and living under the constant threat of death.

12:8–9. Concerning this thing I pleaded with the Lord three times that it might depart from me. And He said to me, "My grace is sufficient for you, for My strength is made perfect in weakness." Therefore most gladly I will rather boast in my infirmities, that the power of Christ may rest upon me. When it is evident that a person has been able to do much in terms of God's work in spite of personal difficulties and shortcomings, it is clear that divine power was involved. Paul pleaded for God to deliver him from his torment but was told that his "thorn" would remain with him, so it would be clear that his accomplishments could have been achieved only with divine assistance.

When Paul was in prison, he converted his captors (Acts 16:23–33). Time and again he overcame his persecutors (2 Cor. 1:9–10, 11:23–33). He repeatedly found himself in precarious situations over which, through the grace of God, he prevailed. Although his personal suffering was intense, he knew it was a small price to pay for the power of God that was working through him.

> Knowing then these things, let us not fear to suffer evil but to do evil.
>
> CHRYSOSTOM[6]

FOOD FOR THOUGHT: (a). In what way are these verses important to all Christians?

12:10. Therefore I take pleasure in infirmities, in reproaches, in needs, in persecutions, in distresses, for Christ's sake. For when I am weak, then I am strong. He takes pleasure in his awareness of those areas in which he is vulnerable because he has learned that when he has done all he can do in any situation, God steps in.

> And so it was too in the Old Testament; by their trials the righteous flourished. So it was with the three children, with Daniel, with Moses, and with Joseph; they all shone and were counted worthy of great crowns. For when the soul is afflicted for God's sake, it also is purified. It receives greater assistance from God because it needs more help and is worthy of more grace. Becoming philosophic, it reaps a rich harvest of good things even before the reward which is promised to it by God.
>
> CHRYSOSTOM[7]

FOOD FOR THOUGHT: (b). Since righteous suffering can bring purification, strength, wisdom, and other blessings to Christians, should we intentionally seek to suffer?

12:11–13. I have become a fool in boasting; you have compelled me. For I ought to have been commended by you; for in nothing was I behind the most eminent Apostles, though I am nothing. Truly the signs of an apostle were accomplished among you with all perseverance, in signs and wonders and mighty deeds. For what is it in which you were inferior to other churches, except that I myself was not burdensome to you? Forgive me this wrong! Paul regrets that he has been forced to defend himself and his authority. The Corinthians had witnessed many miracles that God had performed among them through him, and they were well aware of the fact that he asked for nothing for himself but their love and trust. They had benefited from his ministry and should be quick to praise him.

12:14. Now for the third time I am ready to come to you. And I will not be burdensome to you; for I do not seek yours, but you. For the children ought not to lay up for the parents but the parents for the children. He is planning to return to them soon. As in the past, he will expect nothing from them for himself. As their spiritual father, he seeks only their souls for God's Kingdom. This should be the primary goal of every parent and godparent for their charges.

12:15. And I will very gladly spend and be spent for your souls; though the more abundantly I love you, the less I am loved. He will gladly give not only what he has but also of his very being out of love for them; but the more he extends himself for them, the more they seem to take him for granted. They do not reciprocate his love by defending him to his enemies.

The lack of love among Christians that this type of behavior demonstrates is very detrimental in the Church. Chrysostom wrote that under such conditions:

> I behold the mass of the Church prostrate, as though it were a corpse. And as in a body newly dead, one may see eyes and hands and feet and neck and head and yet no one limb performing its proper function; so, truly, here also, all who are here are of the faithful, but their faith is not active; for we have quenched its warmth and made the body of Christ a corpse. Now if this sounds awful when said, it is much more awful when it appears in actions. For we have indeed the name of brothers but do the deeds of foes; and while all are called members, we are divided against each other like wild beasts. I have said this not from a desire to parade our condition but to shame you and make you desist. Such and such a man goes into a house; honor is paid to him; you ought to give God thanks because your member is honored and God is glorified; but you do the contrary: you speak evil of him to the man that honored him, so that you trip up the heels of both and besides, disgrace yourself. And why, wretched and miserable one? Have you heard your brother praised, either among men or women? Add to his praises, for so you shall praise yourself also. But if you overthrow the praise, first you have spoken evil of yourself, having so acquired an ill character, and you have raised him the higher. When you hear one praised, become a partner in what is said; if not in your life and virtue, yet still in rejoicing over his excellencies. Do you see what disgrace we are the causes of to ourselves? How we destroy and

rend the flock? Let us at length be members (of one another), let us become one body.

CHRYSOSTOM[8]

12:16–19. But be that as it may, I did not burden you. Nevertheless, being crafty, I caught you with guile! Did I take advantage of you by any of those whom I sent to you? I urged Titus, and sent our brother with him. Did Titus take advantage of you? Did we not walk in the same spirit? Did we not walk in the same steps? Again, do you think that we excuse ourselves to you? We speak before God in Christ. But we do all things, beloved, for your edification. Paul received no earthly benefit for himself for his work with the Corinthians. Neither did he arrange to be compensated through those he sent to continue the work. Their purpose was to bring the light of the Gospel to the Corinthians—nothing else. The money they have collected is for the church in Jerusalem, not for him.

12:20–21. For I fear lest, when I come, I shall not find you such as I wish, and that I shall be found by you such as you do not wish; lest there be contentions, jealousies, outbursts of wrath, selfish ambitions, backbitings, whisperings, conceits, tumults; and lest, when I come again, my God will humble me among you, and I shall mourn for many who have sinned before and have not repented of the uncleanness, fornication, and licentiousness which they have practiced. Paul's fear is that his desire to present the church in Corinth to Christ unblemished will not be realized—that he will find it defiled by sin.

> It is not enough to read and to study the sacred Scriptures, we must fulfill them also. To me it seems that if anyone is involved in contentions and in quarrels, his prayers are not acceptable, his

supplications are not answered, his gift rises not upwards from the earth; and neither does the giving of alms avail him for the forgiveness of his sins. And wheresoever there is no peace and tranquility, the door is left open to the Evil One.

APHRAATES[9]

Paul's hope is that he will find that the Corinthian Christians have repented, so he can guide them to the glories of continued spiritual growth.

To repent means both to lament the sins we have committed and to refrain from the sins we lament. For the one who grieves over some sins yet continues to commit others either does not know how to repent or but pretends to repent.

GREGORY THE GREAT[10]

FOOD FOR THOUGHT COMMENTS

(a). What does 2 Cor. 12:8–9 say to all Christians? There has never been, nor will there ever be, a person who has not had some difficulty to deal with in life. Thus the fact that the exact nature of Paul's affliction is a matter of conjecture is an advantage. Shrouded in mystery, it stands as a source of strength for everyone, for no one can say that it was less difficult than what s/he has had to endure. When, in spite of physical infirmities or difficult situations in our lives, we "press toward the goal" of trying to become Christ-like (Phil. 3:14), we demonstrate the power and glory of God and His divine plan. It is easy to say we love God when all is well in our lives and in the lives of those we love. Adversities test our faith. Satan refused to believe Job's faith in God was real while he had family, friends, wealth, and health (Job 1:7–12, 2:1–6). When God allowed Satan to take everything from Job, including

422

finally his health, to test his faith and love and still he remained steadfast, everything was restored to him twice-over (Job 42:1–10).

> If then you are a disciple, travel the straight and narrow way, and be neither disgusted nor discouraged. For even if you are not afflicted in one way, you must inevitably be afflicted in another. For the envious man, the lover of money, he that burns for a harlot, the vainglorious and everyone who follows what is evil endures many disheartenings and afflictions and is not less afflicted than the true Christian. ... Since then whether we follow this way of life or that, we will be afflicted: why not choose the way which along with affliction brings crowns innumerable?
>
> CHRYSOSTOM[11]

(b). Since righteous suffering can bring purification, strength, wisdom, and other blessings to Christians, should we intentionally seek to suffer? When the early Christians began to realize that there were blessings inherent in righteous suffering, some began to go out of their way to put themselves in situations that would bring pain. But contrived or self-inflicted agony is useless. We do not have the right to inflict suffering upon ourselves or others, nor should we seek it as an end unto itself—it will find us soon enough. Paul's example tells us to do all we can, short of denying Christ or compromising our faith, to avoid such situations and to keep ourselves strong for the work the Lord has for us to do. However, if suffering plants itself firmly in our lives, we should pray for God's help and, while keeping our eyes on Him, do what we can to help ourselves. If we hang on and carry on, He will do the rest—He will see us through. When addressing the possibility of facing persecution, Scripture is clearly against self-surrender:

You will be hated by all for My name's sake. But he who endures to the end will be saved. But when they persecute you in this city, flee to another (Mt. 10:22–23).

Polycarp was the Bishop of Smyrna for much of the first half of the second century. When he was about 86 years of age, he was urged to pay homage to Caesar and recognize him as "Lord." To a Christian, this was to deny Christ. Polycarp refused, so was tied to a pyre and set aflame. Marcion was an eye witness to the martyrdom of this saintly man. He wrote in glowing terms about the courage and joy with which Polycarp faced death at the hands of his persecutors.

Marcion also wrote, however, about another incident that occurred when courage failed a Christian who deliberately put himself in harm's way.

> There was one man ... Quintus by name, a Phrygian recently arrived from Phrygia, whose courage failed him at the sight of the beasts. It was he who had compelled himself and some others to surrender themselves voluntarily; and after much persuasion he was induced to take the oath and offer incense.[12] (And that is the reason, brothers, why we do not approve of men offering themselves spontaneously. We are not taught anything of that kind in the Gospel.)
>
> MARCION[13]

CHAPTER THIRTEEN

With Paternal Regard

Paul's tender affection toward the Christians of Corinth has been evident throughout his two epistles to them. Like a concerned father, he has continuously admonished them about their transgressions and postponed his next visit to give them ample time to change their ways before his arrival. In this final chapter, he makes it clear that this time has run out.

13:1–2. This will be the third time I am coming to you. "By the mouth of two or three witnesses every word shall be established." I have told you before and foretell as if I were present the second time, and now being absent I write to those who have sinned before, and to all the rest, that if I come again I will not spare— When Paul returns to Corinth he will deal with those in the church who continue to live sinfully. He quotes Deut. 19:15, the Old Testament standard for establishing guilt.

13:3–4. since you seek a proof of Christ speaking in me, who is not weak toward you, but mighty in you. For though He was crucified in weakness, yet He lives by the power of God. For we also are weak in Him, but we shall live with Him by the power of God toward you. The boldness and strength they will see in him during his next visit will stem from his authority through Christ. His reluctance to display this power in the past was not due to weakness but proof of his strengths of patience and love. The human weakness he has displayed, his vulnerability to persecution from his enemies, was the same weakness that Christ endured. Christ's willingness to bear the limitations of the human body, which put Him under the physical power of His enemies, was actually a sign of His strength.

> Because the foolishness of God is wiser than men, and the weakness of God is stronger than men. (1 Cor. 1:25)

> There is no real weakness or foolishness in God. Away with the thought! For that He had it in His power not to have been crucified He showed throughout; when He cast men down prostrate, turned back the beams of the sun, withered a fig tree, blinded their eyes that came against Him and wrought ten thousand other things. What then is this which he says, *in weakness*! That even though He was crucified after enduring peril and treachery ... yet still He was not harmed.
>
> CHRYSOSTOM[1]

13:5–6. Examine yourselves as to whether you are in the faith. Prove yourselves. Do you not know yourselves, that Jesus Christ is in you?—unless indeed you are disqualified. But I trust that you will know that we are not disqualified. Paul asks that they assess their lives to see whether they really show signs of faith. We are a part of Christ through Baptism and Eucharist and remain so as long as we try to live Christ-like lives. If we do not participate in this struggle through all the situations of life, we disqualify ourselves from God's Kingdom, just as those who participate in any quest are subject to the conditions involved.

> **FOOD FOR THOUGHT:** (a). What is the message of verses 5–6 to the modern Christian?

13:7. Now I pray to God that you do no evil, not that we should appear approved, but that you should do what is honorable, though we may seem disqualified. His prayer is that they not cut themselves off from communion with God. He would rather that all his concerns seem unfounded and his threats foolish than that he find them in spiritual decay.

13:8. For we can do nothing against the truth, but for the truth. His spiritual power stems from his faith in the truths God has revealed to those who love Him. If Paul were to act outside these truths, he would find himself powerless.

> FOOD FOR THOUGHT: (b). What special power did Paul and the Apostles have in the early Church?

13:9–10. For we are glad when we are weak and you are strong. And this also we pray, that you may be made complete. Therefore, I write these things being absent, lest being present I should use sharpness, according to the authority which the Lord has given me for edification and not for destruction. If they were spiritually strong and healthy, it would be unnecessary for him to use the power that is his when he has to battle ungodliness. But he would rather be thought weak than have to take measures against them. He would rather be severe in his letters to them than in actions toward them. The authority God gave him was to build up the Church—not destroy it.

13:11. Finally, brethren, farewell. Paul has done all he can. He has taught them the fullness of the Gospel, pointed out the areas in which they have been disobedient, and outlined the present and eternal consequences if they do not change their ways. The rest is up to them. His final words are those of an affectionate father:

Become complete ... Amend your lives—make whatever changes are necessary to be in communion with God.

be of good comfort ... Take comfort from one another, from God's word and His promises, and from a clear conscience.

be of one mind and live in peace; ... Be united, not only about doctrine but in day-to-day dealings with one another and with God's creation.

> While you are on earth, regard yourself as a guest of the Host, that is, of Christ. If you are at table, He honors you thus. If you breathe the air, you breathe His air. If you bathe, you bathe in His water. If you travel, you travel around His earth. If you accumulate goods, you accumulate what is His; if you squander them, you squander what is His. If you are influential, you are so by His permission. If you are in company with others, you are with His other guests. If you are in the countryside, you are in His garden. If you are alone, He is present. If you set off anywhere, He sees you. If you do anything, He has it in mind. He is the most careful Host Whose guest you have ever been. And be, in your turn, careful towards Him. A good host merits a good guest.[2]

and the God of love and peace will be with you. To live in accordance with God's plan for man is to know unparalleled love and peace. When we are right with our Maker, we know it, we feel it. His love is sweet.

> Taste and see that the Lord is good, Blessed is the man who trusts in Him! (Ps. 34:8)

> **Food For Thought:** (c). How does Paul's paternal approach to the Corinthians follow the pattern of God's dealings with mankind?

13:12. Greet one another with a holy kiss. As in the closing of the *First Epistle to the Corinthians*, Paul refers to the holy kiss. It is a pious tradition within Orthodoxy to greet one another in this way, as the early Christians did, as a symbol of the love Christ said we should have for one another as members of the Body of Christ (Jn. 15:12).

> What is *holy*? Not hollow, not treacherous, like the kiss Judas gave to Christ. The kiss is given that it may be fuel unto love, that it may kindle the disposition, that we may so love each other, as brothers brothers, as children parents, as parents children, but even far more. For those things are implanted by nature, but these by spiritual grace. ...
>
> We are the temple of Christ; we kiss the porch and entrance of the temple when we kiss each other ... And through these gates and doors Christ both had entered into us, and does enter, whenever we commune. You who partake of the Mysteries understand what I say. For it is in no common manner that our lips are honored, when they receive the Lord's Body. It is for this reason chiefly that we here kiss. Pay attention—those who speak filthy things, who swear, and let them shudder to think what that mouth is they dishonor.
>
> CHRYSOSTOM[3]

The holy kiss found expression in the ancient celebration of the Divine Liturgy. Just before the recitation of the Creed, the Kiss of Peace was exchanged by all in attendance, signifying unity in faith. In modern times, this beautiful practice is often eliminated, except among the clergy when more than one priest co-celebrates. Some parishes have revived this meaningful practice, allowing the faithful the opportunity to turn to each other with the words: "Christ is in our midst," and the response "He is now and always shall be." The demonstration of this type of love is powerful, capable of manifesting itself even among strangers.

> We forget that in the call to "greet one another with a holy kiss" we are talking not of our personal, natural, human love, through which we cannot in fact love someone who is a "stranger," who has not yet become "something" or "somebody" for us, but of the *love of Christ*, the eternal wonder of which consists precisely in the fact that it transforms the *stranger* (and each stranger, in his depths, is an *enemy*) into a *brother*, irrespective of whether he has or does not have relevance for me and for my life; that it is the very purpose of the Church to overcome the horrible *alienation* that was introduced into the world by the Devil and proved to be its undoing. And we forget that we come to church for this love, which is always granted to us in the gathering of the brethren.[4]

13:13. All the saints greet you. This greeting from the "saints," the other Christians with Paul, is a reminder of the universal Church. All who worship in Truth and try to live accordingly are united in love through Christ. Together they make up the Body of Christ and thus are saints.

13:14. The grace of the Lord Jesus Christ, and the love of God, and the communion of the Holy Spirit be with you all. Amen. With this invocation of the Holy Trinity, Paul reaches out to all, through the ages, who read this epistle. These powerful words have come to be known as the Apostolic Benediction, with which Orthodox priests bless worshippers during the Divine Liturgy.

Paul did, finally, return to Corinth. He spent the winter there as he had hoped (1 Cor. 16:5, 6). It was during this time that he wrote his *Epistle to the Romans* (c. A.D. 57).

FOOD FOR THOUGHT COMMENTS

(a). What is the message of 2 Cor. 13:5–6 to the modern Christian? Christ does not remain with those who live in disobedience. Those who partake of Eucharist without sincerely attempting to rid themselves of the corruption of sin receive condemnation rather than blessing (1 Cor. 11:27–30). To live long, healthy, productive lives on earth we must continually assess our physical state and do what is necessary to remain in optimal condition. To live eternally with God, it is even more important that we apply this principle to our spiritual condition.

(b). What special power did Paul and the Apostles have in the early Church? They had the power that operates through God's love to teach, heal, and admonish. Occasionally they were vehicles through which consequences of sin took physical effect immediately, as with Ananias and Sapphira (Acts 5:1–10) and Elymas (Acts 13:6–11). These actions were aimed at teaching those involved, and those looking on, that disobedience to God carries consequences (see Acts 5:11 and 13:12). Paul and the Apostles also had the spiritual powers that Priests of today have to forgive sin or not (Jn. 20:23), and to grant or to deny access to the Sacraments of the Church (1 Cor. 5:3–5).

(c). How does Paul's paternal approach to the Corinthians follow the pattern of God's dealings with mankind? A good father makes sure his children know they are loved and also what he expects of them for their own good, and he gives them every opportunity to grow in that direction. He assists them along the way, as Paul helped the Corinthians, but then follows through with stated consequences if his instructions are not heeded, in order to prevent their falling into harm. This is what God has done with man. The magnificence of His Creation is proof of his love for us. The cycle of nature is proof that He has provided life beyond death. He has made His divine plan for man known through His Son and through Scripture. These writings extol the wonders of His Kingdom but also teach, explain, and warn of the consequences of indifference to or disobedience of these precepts. He allows ample time for all to learn, to repent, and to try to comply, but the allotted time will run out. At the Second Coming of Christ, which will occur at a time known by no one, judgment will take place:

> All the nations will be gathered before Him, and He will separate them one from another as a shepherd divides his sheep from the goats. And He will set the sheep on His right hand, but the goats on the left. Then the King will say to those at His right hand, *"Come, you blessed of My Father, inherit the kingdom prepared for you from the foundation of the world;"* Then He will say to those on the left hand, *"Depart from Me, you cursed, into the everlasting fire prepared for the devil and his angels "* (Mt. 25:32–34,41).

> Let us then continue to hold these doctrines in their strictness and to draw to us the love of God. For before indeed He loved us when hating Him and reconciled us who were His enemies; but henceforth He wishes to love us as loving Him. Let us then continue to love Him, so that we may also be loved by Him. For if when beloved by powerful men we are formidable to all, much more when beloved by God. And should it be needful to give wealth, or body, or even life itself for this love, let us not grudge them. It is not enough to say in words that we love, we ought to give also the proof of deeds; for neither did He show love by words only, but by deeds also. Do then also show Him by deeds and do those things which please

Him for so shall you reap the advantage. For He needs nothing that we have to bestow, and this is also special proof of a sincere love, when one Who needs nothing does all for the sake of being loved by us. *For what does the Lord God require of you, but to love Him, and that you should be ready to walk after Him (Deut. 10:12)?*

CHRYSOSTOM[5]

Amen.

Glossary

apostolic succession: The power and authority passed on, in an unbroken chain, from Christ to the Apostles, to each succeeding Bishop of the Church through the ages, via the laying on of hands. The Apostles were the archetypes of Bishops (see Acts 1:20).

ascesis: The willing struggle through life to grow spiritually, in the image of Christ, to show love and faith and to prepare for eternal life in God's Kingdom, where holiness is required.

Bishop: From the Greek "episcopos," meaning overseer. A Bishop is the highest rank of the Christian priesthood, the shepherd of the flock of a particular diocese and spiritual father of the priests in that jurisdiction. Only a Bishop can ordain deacons and priests, with the power and authority received through Apostolic Succession. The terms Metropolitan, Archbishop, and Patriarch are administrative titles held by Bishops elected to those offices of broader administrative rights and authority within the Church.

Chrismation: A Sacrament of the Church through which a person is anointed with Holy Myron (Chrism) and receives the gift of the indwelling of the Holy Spirit.

Decalogue: The Ten Commandments, also called the natural law, given by God to Moses on Mt. Sinai for the instruction of His people.

Divine Liturgy: The word liturgy (Greek: leitourgia) means "work of the people." The Divine Liturgy, then, means the divine work of the people: the worship of God. This service has its roots in the Mystical Supper, which took place on the evening before Christ's Crucifixion: He broke bread saying, "Take eat, this is My Body," and passed wine saying, "Drink from ... this My Blood" (Mt. 26:26–28). From that day on, Christians have gathered regularly to receive His Body and Blood, read Scripture, pray, and sing hymns of praise and thanksgiving. This evolved into the Divine Liturgy of today.

economia: "A timely and logically defensible deviation from a canonically established rule for the sake of bringing salvation either within or outside the Church."[1]

Eucharist: From the Greek *eucharistia*: "thanksgiving." This term refers to Holy Communion, the Body and Blood of our Lord. As Christ gave thanks to God before offering His Body and His Blood to the Apostles, this word symbolizes thanksgiving for the salvation offered by our Savior through His Crucifixion and Resurrection and for the opportunity to continually renew our union with Him through this Sacrament.

Fathers of the Church: Important ecclesiastical writers of the past whose authority on matters of belief is "widely and indisputably accepted" and who are distinguished by "orthodoxy of belief, holiness of life, the approval of the Church, and antiquity."[2] While the age of the Fathers never really ends, for the purposes of this work, the term is used generally for important Christian writers and teachers from the end of the first century to the end of the eighth. There is particular reverence, within this realm, for writers of the fourth century, especially Basil the Great, Gregory of Nazianzus, and John Chrysostom. No individual writer or teacher is considered infallible, but the faithful can be guided by the writings of the Fathers where they agree and speak with the Church as a whole.

free will: The gift from God to man and woman as part of

being created in His image, the possession of which allows the choice to become like Him. Thus this gift grants freedom to choose one's own thoughts and actions and between good and evil. God has foreknowledge and so knows what we will choose, but He does not determine that choice. The most important choice to be made in life is whether or not to be a part of His Kingdom.

***grace*:** Divine power from God, a bit of His energies, given for purposes of sanctification.

***Logos*:** Our Lord Jesus Christ (see *Word of God*).

***Melchizedek*:** The mysterious eternal priest who appears suddenly to Abraham in Gen. 14:18–20. Melchizedek was not a part of the Hebrew priesthood established with Moses' brother Aaron to offer sacrifices to God for the sins of His people, which was temporary. The Aaronic priesthood came to an end when Christ, the Lamb of God, the last living sacrifice, was crucified. With no known beginning and no known end, Melchizedek points to the eternal priesthood of Christ (Ps. 110:4), which ordained priests of the Orthodox Church carry on.

***Mysteries*:** Vehicles through which God gives of Himself, His grace. (See *Sacraments*.)

***Orthodox Church*:** The historical Body (of Christ) established by Jesus to carry on His work, unchanged and undiluted since the Apostles, through apostolic succession. This universal Church became known as "Orthodox" in time, to distinguish it from those groups which had adopted "unorthodox" teachings and practices.

***Paraclete*:** The Greek word meaning "Holy Spirit."

Priest: From the Greek *presbyter*, meaning "elder." A clergyman of the Church, ordained to carry on the eternal priesthood of Christ, after the order of Melchizedek (see entry above as well as Gen. 14:18; Ps. 110:4; Heb. 5: 5–10, 7:11–28).

Prosphora ("offering"): The loaf of bread baked according to certain specifications in a prayerful manner and brought to Church as an offering. From this offering a portion is consecrated during the Divine Liturgy, becomes the Body of Christ, and is offered to the faithful along with consecrated wine, the Blood of Christ.

repentance **(Greek: *metanoia*):** The sorrow one feels at having acted or reacted against the will of God. True repentance includes effort to change, so as not to repeat the offense.

Sacraments: More properly called Mysteries (Greek: *Mysteria*), they are outer symbols of inner grace received from God. Generally considered seven in number: Baptism, Chrismation (Confirmation), Eucharist, Repentance (Confession), Holy Orders, Holy Matrimony, and Unction (anointing of the sick). Some early Fathers of the Church mention only two, Baptism and Eucharist, but the other five were gradually recognized through the life of the Church. Some maintain that while these seven were clearly accorded the authority of Sacraments, there are other "actions in the Church which also possess a sacramental character, and which are conveniently termed *sacramentals*."[3] In this category are the blessing of water at Epiphany, the service for the burial of the dead, blessing of homes, etc.

Second Coming of Christ: The return of Jesus Christ to earth as Judge. This event, the timing of which no man knows, will mark the end of the world as we know it and the fulfillment of

God's promises. The dead will rise with transfigured bodies, and everyone will live eternally the life s/he has chosen and for which s/he has prepared.

Theosis: The spiritual process of deification, growing in union with God, through God's grace and man's willing efforts.

Theotokos: The title, meaning "God-bearer." Given to Mary, who bore in her womb Jesus Christ, the Son of God, the second person of the Holy Trinity (God, the Son).

Way, the: Those who were Christ's followers in the first days of the Church were said to be on "the Way" (to the Kingdom) (Jn. 14:6).

word of God: Holy Scripture.

Word of God: The Son, Logos of God (Jn. 1:1–4), who became man to make it possible for man to return to union with God.

Bibliography

Alexandra, Mother. *The Holy Angels.* Still River, Massachusetts: St. Bede's, 1981.

Anderson, David, trans. *Basil the Great: On the Holy Spirit.* Crestwood, New York: St. Vladimir's Seminary Press, 1997.

Averky, Archbishop. *The Apocalypse of St. John: An Orthodox Commentary.* Platina, California: Valaam Society of America, 1985.

Barrois, George. "Women and the Priestly Office according to the Scriptures." In *Women and the Priesthood,* edited by Thomas Hopko. Crestwood, New York: St. Vladimir's Seminary Press, 1983.

Berthold, George C., trans. *Maximus Confessor: Selected Writings: The Classics of Western Spirituality.* Mahwah, New Jersey: Paulist, 1985.

Cassian, John. *Institutes, Teachings on the Spiritual Life.* Willits, California: Eastern Orthodox Books.

Cavarnos, Constantine. *Immortality of the Soul.* Belmont, Massachusetts: Institute for Byzantine and Modern Greek Studies, 1993.

Chrysostomos, Archimandrite, trans. "From the Evergetinos on Passions and Perfection in Christ." In *The Ancient Fathers of the Desert.* Brookline, Massachusetts: Hellenic College Press, 1980.

440

Chryssavgis, John. *In the Heart of the Desert: The Spirituality of the Desert Fathers and Mothers.* Bloomington, Indiana: World Wisdom, 2003.

Clark, Elizabeth A. *Women in the Early Church.* Wilmington, Delaware.

Constantelos, Demetrios J. *Marriage, Sexuality and Celibacy.* Minneapolis, Light & Life Publ., 1975.

Danielou, Jean. *The Angels and their Mission, according to the Fathers of the Church.* Translated by David Heimann. Westminster, Maryland: Newman, 1988.

deCatanzaro, C.J., trans. *Symeon the New Theologian: The Discourses.* New York: Paulist Press, 1980.

Dix, Gregory. *The Shape of the Liturgy.* New York: Seabury, 1945.

Elias, Rev. Nicholas. *The Divine Liturgy Explained.* 2nd ed. Athens: Astir, 1970.

Eusebius. *The History of the Church: From Christ to Constantine.* Translated by G.A. Williamson. New York: Dorset, 1965.

Falls, Thomas B., trans. *The Fathers of the Church,* Vol. 6. Washington, DC: Catholic University, 1948.

Ferm, Vergilius, ed. *Encyclopedia of Religion.* New York: Philosophical Library, Inc., 1981.

Frangopoulos, Athanasios S. *Our Orthodox Christian Faith: A Handbood of Popular Dogmatics.* Athens: Brotherhood of Theologians, "O Sotir," 1984.

Golitzin, Alexander. *St. Symeon the New Theologian: On the Mystical Life: The Ethical Discourses.* Vol 2: "On Virtue and Christian Life." Crestwood, New York: St. Vladimir's Seminary Press, 1996.

__________, Vol. 3. "Life, Times and Theology." 1997.

Guthrie, D., J. A. Motyer, A.M. Stibbs, and D.J. Wiseman, ed. *The New Bible Commentary: Revised.* Grand Rapids: Eerdmans, 1970.

Harakas, Stanley S. *Contemporary Moral Issues Facing the Orthodox Christian.* Minneapolis: Light & Life, 1982.

Harkins, Paul W., trans. *Ancient Christian Writers, St. John Chrysostom, Baptismal Instructions.* New York: Paulist, 1963.

Hopko, Thomas, ed. *Women and the Priesthood.* Crestwood, New York: St. Vladimir's Seminary, 1983.

Kalomiros, Alexandre. "The River of Fire," Seattle: St. Nectarios Press, 1980.

Kontoglou, Photios. *Ekphrasis,* 3rd ed., Vol. I. Athens: Astir Press, 1993.

Kucharek, Casimir. *Sacramental Mysteries, A Byzantine Approach.* Allendale, New Jersey: Alleluia, 1976.

Lossky, Vladimir. *In the Image and Likeness of God.*

Crestwood, New York: St. Vladimir's Seminary Press, 1974.

_____. *Orthodox Theology: An Introduction*. Trans. Ian and Ihita Kesarcodi-Watson. Crestwood, New York: St. Vladimir's Seminary, 1978.

Luibheid, Colm, trans. *John Cassian, Conferences*. Mahwah, New Jersey: Paulist Press, 1985.

_____ and Norman Russell. *John Climacus: The Ladder of Divine Ascent*. Mahwah, New Jersey: Paulist Press, 1982.

Makrakis, Apostolos. *The Interpretation of the Entire New Testament*. Chicago: Orthodox Christian Educational Society, 1949.

Mastrantonis, Rev. George. *A New Style Catechism on the Eastern Orthodox Faith, for Adults*. St. Louis: Ologos Mission, 1969.

McKechnie, Jean L., ed. *Webster's New Twentieth Century Dictionary of the English Language*, unabridged. 2nd Ed. New York: The Publishers Guild, 1955.

Meer, Jeff. "Speaking in Tongues: Inspiration or Imitation." *Psychology Today*, Vol. 95, No. 1, June 1986.

Meyendorff, John, ed. *Gregory Palamas, The Triads*. Mahwah, New Jersey: Paulist Press, 1983.

_____. *The Orthodox Church: Its Past and Its Role in the World Today*, Crestwood, New York: St. Vladimir's Seminary Press, 1996.

Nellas, Panayiotis. *Deification in Christ, The Nature of the Human Person*. Crestwood, New York: St. Vladimir's Seminary Press, 1987.

Nicozisin, George. *Speaking in Tongues: an Orthodox Perspective*. New York: Greek Orthodox Archdiocese of North & South America, Department of Communications.

Orthodox Church in America, Dept. of Religious Education. *Women and Men in the Church*. Syosset, New York: 1980.

Palmer, G.E.H., Philip Sherrard and Kallistos Ware, ed. *The Philokalia*, Compiled by St. Nikodimos of the Holy Mountain & St. Makarios of Corinth, 3 Vol. London: Faber and Faber, 1984.

Pappas, Barbara. *Are You Saved? The Orthodox Christian Process of Salvation, 4th ed.* Westchester, Illinois: Amnos Publ, 2002.

Patrinacos, Rev. Nicon D. *A Dictionary of Greek Orthodoxy*. Pleasantville, New York: Hellenic Heritage, 1984.

Percival, Henry R., ed. *The Nicene and Post-Nicene Fathers of the Christian Church*, Second Series, Vol. XIV. "The Seven Ecumenical Councils of the Undivided Church," Grand Rapids: Eerdmans, 1988.

Quotes Databank: *http://www.quotedb.com/quotes/1905*.

Roberts, Alexander and James Donaldson, ed. "The Apostolic Fathers: Justin Martyr-Irenaeus." *The Ante-Nicene*

Fathers, Translations of the Writings of the Fathers down to A.D. 325, Vol. I. Grand Rapids: Eerdmans, 1987.

_____. "The Twelve Patriarchs, Excerpts and Epistles, The Clementina, Apocrypha, Decretals, Memoirs of Edessa and Syriac Documents, Remains of the First Ages." Vol. VIII. 1986.

Rogich, Daniel M., trans. *Saint Gregory Palamas, Treatise on the Spiritual Life.* Minneapolis: Light and Life Publishing Company, 1995.

Rohrdorf, Willy, etal. *The Eucharist of the Early Christians.* Trans. Matthew J. O'Connell. New York: Pueblo, 1978.

Rose, Fr. Seraphim. *The Place of the Blessed Augustine in the Orthodox Church.* Platina, CA: St. Herman of Alaska Brotherhood Press.

Roth, Catherine P. *St. Gregory of Nyssa: The Soul and the Resurrection.* Crestwood, New York: St. Vladimir's Seminary Press, 1993.

_____. *St. John Chrysostom: On Marriage and Family Life.* 1986.

Schaff, Philip, ed. "Homilies on the Gospel of St. Matthew," *Nicene and Post-Nicene Fathers of the Christian Church,* Vol. X, Grand Rapids: Eerdmans, 1998.

_____. "Homilies on the Acts of the Apostles and the Epistle to the Romans," Vol. XI. 1980.

_____. "Homilies on First and Second Corinthians," Vol. XII. 1983.

_____. "Homilies on Galatians, Ephesians, Philippians, Colossians, Thessalonians, Timothy, Titus, and Philemon," Vol. XIII. 1983.

_____. "Homilies on the Gospels of St. John and the Epistle to the Hebrews." Vol. XIV. 1989.

_____. and Henry Wace, ed, "St. Athanasius: Select Works and Letters," *Second Series,* Vol. IV. 1980.

_____, "St. Cyril of Jerusalem -St. Gregory Nazianzen," Second Series, Vol. VII. 1989.

_____. "St. Basil: Letters and Select Works," Vol. VIII. 1983.

Schmemann, Alexander. *The Eucharist.* Crestwood, New York: St. Vladimir's Seminary Press, 1988.

_____. *Great Lent.* Crestwood, New York: St. Vladimir's Seminary Press, 1974.

Smith, R. Payne, trans. *Commentary on the Gospel of St. Luke, by Saint Cyril of Alexandria.* United States of America: Studion Publishers, 1983.

Sophrony. *Wisdom from Mt. Athos: The Writings of Staretz Silouan.* Crestwood, New York: St. Vladimir's Seminary Press, 1995.

Staniforth, Maxwell, trans. *Early Christian Writings,* New York: Dorset Press, 1986.

Stavropoulos, Christoforos. *Partakers of Divine Nature*. Trans. Stanley Harakas. Minneapolis: Light & Life Publ, 1976.

Toal, M.F., trans & ed. *The Sunday Sermons of the Great Fathers*, Four Volumes, Chicago: Henry Regnery Co, 1957.

Vassiliadis, Nikolaos P. *The Mystery of Death*. Trans. Fr. Peter A. Chamberas. Athens: The Orthodox Brotherhood of Theologians, "The Savior," 1993.

Velimirovic, Bishop Nikolai. *The Prologue From Ochrid, Lives of the Saints and Homilies for Every Day in the Year*. Trans. Mother Maria. Four parts. Birmingham, England: Lazarica Press, 1985.

Ware, Father Kallistos. *The Orthodox Way*. Crestwood, New York: St. Vladimir's Orthodox Theological Seminary, 2001.

Ware, Timothy. *The Orthodox Church*. New York: Penguin, 1993.

Winter, David, *Faith Under Fire*, Wheaton, Illinois: Harold Shaw, 1977.

First Corinthians

PREFACE

1. Henry R. Percival, ed., "The Seven Ecumenical Councils of the Undivided Church," in *The Nicene and Post-Nicene Fathers of the Christian Church,* Second Series, Vol. XIV, pp. 453-4.

2. Some say the quoted Epistle of Barnabas was written by the Apostle, friend and companion to Paul, but modern scholars contend that the author is a layman of the early to middle second century.

3. This title—meaning disciple—was used by the anonymous author of the *Epistle to Diognetus*, who probably wrote toward the close of the apostolic age. See Alexander Roberts and James Donaldson, "Introductory Note to the Epistle of Mathetes to Diognetus," in *The Ante-Nicene Fathers, Translations of the Writings of the Fathers down to A.D. 325*, Vol. I, p. 23.

INTRODUCTION

1. Roberts and Donaldson, eds., "Apocrypha of the New Testament, Part II—The Apocryphal Acts of the Apostles, Acts of Paul and Thecla,"A.N.F., Vol. VIII, p. 487.

2. Philip Schaff, ed., "Argument," in *The Nicene and Post-Nicene Fathers of the Church*, Vol. XII, Homilies on First and Second Corinthians, p.1. Note: Lacedaemon is now known as Sparta.

CHAPTER ONE

1. John Meyendorff, *The Orthodox Church: Its Past and Its Role in the World Today*, p. 175.

2. Roberts and Donaldson, "Dialogue of Justin, Philosopher and Martyr, with Trypho, a Jew," Vol. I, p. 270.

3. Paul W. Harkins, trans., "The Third Instruction," in *Ancient Christian Writers*: St. John Chrysostom, Baptismal Instructions, p.57.

4. Schaff, "Homily V on First Corinthians," Vol. XII, p.23.

5. ibid., "Homily III," p.14.

6. Roberts and Donaldson, "Irenaeus Against Heresies," Book V, Vol. I, p.526.

7. David Winter, *Faith Under Fire*: (Day 42).

8. ibid., Day 64.

9. Archimandrite Sophrony, *Wisdom from Mount Athos: The Writings of Staretz Silouan*, p.72.

10. Schaff, "Homily X on First Thessalonians," Vol. XIII, p.367.

11. Thomas B. Falls, trans., *The Fathers of the Church*, Vol. 6, p.64-5.

12. ibid.

13. M.F. Toal, trans. & ed., *The Sunday Sermons of the Great Fathers*, Vol. Two, p.427.

14. Schaff, "Homily III," Vol. XII, p.10.

15. Winter (Day 49).

16. David Anderson, trans. *Basil the Great: On the Holy Spirit*, p.98.

17. Toal, "On the Holy Pasch," Vol. Two, p.257.

18. Vladimir Lossky, *Orthodox Theology: an Introduction*, p.114.

CHAPTER TWO

1. Schaff, "Homily VI," Vol. XII, p.30.

2. Archimandrite Christoforos Stavropoulos, *Partakers of Divine Nature*, p.29.

3. Toal, Vol. Three, p.8-10.

4. Kallistos Ware, *The Orthodox Way*, p. 137-8.

5. Stavropoulos, p.52.

6. Ware, *Way*, p.133.

7. Schaff, "Homily XLI," Vol. XII, p.252.

8. Phillip Schaff and Henry Wace, ed., "*Discourse III Against the Arians*," Vol. IV, p.407.

9. Stavropoulos, p.33.

CHAPTER THREE

1. Winter (Day 10).

2. Toal, Vol. Three, p.363.

3. *Ascetical Homilies*, XI, 10, p.131. (Ware, *Way*, p.137).

4. Alexandre Kalomiros, *The River of Fire*, Vol. XIV, Homily 84.

5. ibid.

6. Schaff, "Homily XXIII on Matthew," Vol. X, p.164.

7. G.E.H. Palmer, Philip Sherrard, Kallistos Ware. *The Philokalia: The Complete Text compiled by St. Nikodimos of the Holy Mountain and St. Makarios of Corinth.* Vol. One, p.36.

8. Schaff, "Homily I on Hebrews," First Series, Vol. XIV, p.369.

9. Kalomiros, XIV.

10. Roberts and Donaldson, "Irenaeus against Heresies, Book III," Vol. I, p.416.

11. Schaff, "Homily V on Second Thessalonians," Vol. XIII, p.396.

CHAPTER FOUR

1. Schaff, "Homily XI," Vol. XII, p.58.

2. ibid., "Homily XII," p.67.

3. Toal, Vol. Three, p.153.

4. Winter (Day 39).

CHAPTER FIVE

1. Roberts and Donaldson, "Against Heresies," Vol. I, p.479.

2. Casimir Kucharek, "The Human Use of Divine Powers," *Sacramental Mysteries: a Byzantine Approach*, p.69.

3. Toal, Vol. Two, p.225.

4. Falls, p.208.

5. George Mastrantonis, *a New Style Catechism on the Eastern Orthodox Faith, for Adults*, p.125.

6. Falls, p.208.

7. Toal, p.144.

8. Quotations Databank: http://www.quotedb.com/quotes/1905.

9. Webster's New Twentieth Century Dictionary, 2nd ed.

10. Schaff, "Homily II on Ephesians," Vol. XIII, p.57.

CHAPTER SIX

1. Schaff, "Homily XVI," Vol. XII, p.91.

2. C.J. deCatanzaro, trans., "The Discourses," *Symeon the New Theologian*, p.107.

3. Schaff, "Homily XVIII," Vol. XII, p.102.

CHAPTER SEVEN

1. Schaff, "Homily XIV on Timothy," Vol. XIII, p.454.

2. ibid., "Homily XX on Ephesians," p.143.

3. Catharine P. Roth, *St. John Chrysostom: On Marriage and Family Life,* "Homily 20 on Eph 5:22-33," p.44.

4. ibid.

5. George Nicozisin, "Abstinence in Sex Relations," *Your Marriage in the Orthodox Church,* p.44.

6. Demetrios J. Constantelos, *Marriage, Sexuality & Celibacy,* p.22-4.

7. ibid.

8. Constantelos, p.62.   See also: Mastrantonis, "Reasons for Divorce," p.141.

9. ibid.

10. Roberts & Donaldson, "Against Heresies: Book IV," p.480.

11. God wants His people to always live in a state of readiness, so does not make known the time of Christ's Second Coming. This is so because that knowledge (or knowing the time of one's own death) could cause one to think, if that time seemed far in the future, that there was no immediate necessity to take part in the spiritual struggle because he had plenty of time "for that." This, of course, could lead one too far astray to ever return to the fold—which would fulfill Satan's desires.

CHAPTER EIGHT

1 Toal, Vol. Four, p.18-19.

CHAPTER NINE

1. Eusebius, *The History of the Church from Christ to Constantine,* p.140.

2. Schaff, "Homily XXI," Vol. XII, p.21.

3. Averky, *The Apocalypse of St. John: an Orthodox Commentary,* p.198.

4. D. Guthrie, J.A. Motyer, A.M. Stibbs, D.J. Wiseman, The New Bible Commentary: Rev., p.1063.

5. ibid.

6. Alexander Golitzin, "Life, Times and Theology," St. Symeon the New Theologian: On the Mystical Life: The Ethical Discourses. Vol. 3: p.66.

7. Roberts and Donaldson, "The First Apology of Justin," Vol. I, p.165.

CHAPTER TEN

1. Roberts & Donaldson, "Against Heresies," Book IV, p.478.

2. Schaff, "Homily XXIII," Vol. XII, p.134.

3. Barbara Pappas, *Are You Saved?: The Orthodox Christian Process of Salvation*, p.33-9.

4. George C. Berthold, *Maximus Confessor: Selected Writings*, p.52.

5. Toal, Vol. Three, p.126.

6. Schaff, p.133.

7. ibid, p.135.

8. Schaff, p.133.

9. Stanley S. Harakas, *Contemporary Moral Issues Facing the Orthodox Christian*, p.26.

CHAPTER ELEVEN

1. Schaff, Homily XXVI, Vol. XII, p.150.

2 Orthodox Church in America, Dept. of Religious Education, *Women and Men in the Church*, p.44.

3. Ware, "Man, Woman and the Priesthood of Christ," *Women and the Priesthood*, ed. Thomas Hopko, p.29.

4. Apostolos Makrakis, *the Interpretation of the Entire New Testament*, Vol. Two, p.1468.

5. Schaff, "Homilies on Ephesians," Vol. XIII, p.144.

6. Elizabeth P. Clark, "On the Good of Marriage," *Women in the Early Church*, p.28.

7. Schaff, Homily XXVI, Vol. XII, p.150.

8. ibid.

9. Toal, Vol. Three, p.205.

10. Mother Alexandra, *The Holy Angels*, p.5.

11. Nicholas Elias, "Magnificat to the Mother of God," *The Divine Liturgy Explained*, p.171.

12. Alexandra.

13. Jean Danielou, *The Angels and their Mission, according to the Fathers of the Church*, p.62.

14. Schaff, p.153.

15. Makrakis, p.1469.

16. Schaff, "Homily XXVI," Vol. XII, p.152.

17. Nicon D. Patrinacos, *A Dictionary of Greek Orthodoxy,* p.356.
18. Mastrantonis, p.123-4.
19. Kucharek, *The Ancient Celebration of the Eucharist,* p.176.
20. Rohrdorf, etal, "A Eucharistic Faith," *The Eucharist of the Early Christians,* p.147.
21. Toal, Vol. Two, p.143.
22. Schaff, Homily XXVIII, Vol. XII, p.164.
23. Elias, p.195.
24. Schaff.
25. Elias, p.22.
26. Toal, p.275.
27. Mastrantonis, p.113.

CHAPTER TWELVE
1 Schaff, "Homily XXIX," Vol. XII, p.168.
2 ibid.
3 ibid, p.170.
4 ibid.
5 Makrakis, p.1479.
6 Palmer, vol. Three, p.172.

CHAPTER THIRTEEN
1. Toal, Vol. 4, p.223.
2. Colb Lubheid, trans., *John Cassian: Conferences,* p.286.
3. Schaff, "Homily XXXIV," p.190.
4. ibid., "Homily XXXIV," p.202.
5. ibid.
6. Palmer, et al, pp.53, 62.

CHAPTER FOURTEEN
1. Toal, Vol. 4, p.225.
2. George Barrois, "Women and the Priestly Office," *Women and the Priesthood,* ed. Thomas Hopko, p.48.
3. George Nicozisin, *Speaking in Tongues,* An Orthodox Perspective, p.2.
4. ibid, p.3. Note: Dionysius was the so-called Greek God of wine and fertility.
5. Schaff, Homily XXV, p.210.

6. Nicozisin, p.1.

7. Jeff Meer, "Speaking in Tongues: Inspiration or Imitation." *Psychology Today*, Vol. 95, No. 1, p.16.

8. Schaff, Homily XXXVI, p.219.

9. ibid., p.220.

10. ibid., p.222.

11. Thomas Hopko, "On the Male Character of Christian Priesthood," *Women and the Priesthood*, p.113, quoting Chrysostom's Homilies 7 & 8 on Matthew.

12. Toal, Vol. 4, p.219.

CHAPTER FIFTEEN

1. Guthrie, p.1071.

2. Chrysostom, Schaff, "Homily XXXVIII," Vol. XII, p.229.

3. Roberts and Donaldson, "Irenaeus against Heresies," Vol I, Book III, Chapter XV, p.439.

4. Schaff, "Homily XXXIX," p.238

5. Mastrantonis, p.148-152.

6. Schaff, p.240.

7. ibid., "Homily XL," p.244.

8. ibid., "Homily XLI," p.251.

9. Nikolaos P. Vassiliades, *The Mystery of Death*, 503.

10. Ware, *Way*, p.62.

11. Palmer, etal, p.100-101.

12. Schaff, "Homily XLII," p.255, fn3: "This reading is supported—by the Alexandrian and six other uncial MSS. It is found in several versions, and has the authority of Irenaeus, Origen, Basil, Tertullian, Cyprian, and other Fathers."

13. Golitzin, "The Ethical Discourses." Vol 2, p.163.

14. Schaff, p.258.

15. Elias, p.181.

16. Schaff and Wace, "Against the Heathen," Vol. IV, p.22.

17. Catharine P. Roth, *St.Gregory of Nyssa: The Soul and the Resurrection*, p.113.

18. Constantine Cavarnos, *Immortality of the Soul*, p.33.

19. Roth, p.113-114.

CHAPTER SIXTEEN

1. Palmer, etal. Vol. Three, p.80.
2. Schaff, "Homily XLIII," Vol. XII, p.259.
3. Palmer, etal., p.80.
4. Gregory Dix, *The Shape of the Liturgy*, p.105.

Second Corinthians

CHAPTER ONE

1. Toal, "What is Peace," Vol. Three, p.39.
2. Schaff, "Homily I on Second Corinthians," Vol. XII, p.275.
3. ibid., p. 274.
4. ibid., "Homily III," p. 292.
5. ibid., "Homily II," p. 279.
6. Toal, "On Prayer," Vol. Two, p. 396.
7. ibid., p. 389.
8. ibid., "That Prayer is to be Placed before all Things," p. 380.
9. Schaff, "Homily III," Vol. XII, p.286.
10. Lossky, *In the Image and Likeness of God*, p. 59.
11. Philip Schaff and Henry Wace, "Letter CCXXXIII," *NPNF*, Second Series, Vol. VIII, *St. Basil: Letters and Select Works*, p. 273.
12. ibid., "Letter XI. Easter, 339," Vol. IV, *Select Works and Letters* p. 536.
13. Toal, "On the Holy Pasch II," Vol. Two, p. 249.
14. ibid., "On the Gospel," Vol. One, p. 417.
15. Bishop Nikolai Velimirovic, *The Prologue from Ochrid, Lives of the Saints and Homilies for Every Day in the Year*, Part One, p. 332.
16. Roberts and Donaldson, "Against Heresies," Vol. I, p. 518.
17. Seraphim Rose, *The Place of the Blessed Augustine in the Orthodox Church*, pp. 9–20.
18. Vladimir Lossky, *Theology*, pp. 72–73.
19. Vergilius Ferm, *Encyclopedia of Religion*, p. 570.
20. Stavropoulos, p. 34.
21. Luibheid, "Conference Three," *Conferences*, p. 93.
22. Schaff and Wace, "Against the Heathen," Vol. IV, p. 6.

23. Daniel M. Rogich, *St. Gregory Palamas, Treatise on the Spiritual Life*, pp. 73–74.

24. Toal, "Man is Delivered by Trials: Mystical Joy," Vol. Four, p. 197.

25. Schaff, "Homily I," Vol. XII, p. 275.

26. Lossky, *Theology,* p. 129.

27. Schaff, "Homily II," Vol. XII, p. 283.

28. Toal, "On the Gospel," Vol. One, p. 325.

29. Schaff, "Homily II on Second Corinthians," Vol. XII, p. 281.

30. Palmer, Sherrard, Ware, "Spurious Knowledge," Vol. Three, p. 202.

31. Toal, "On Prayer," Vol. Two, p. 397.

32. ibid., p. 383.

33. Lossky, *Theology,* p. 85.

34. Toal, "The Holy Trinity," Vol. Three, p. 66.

35. ibid., "Exposition of the Gospel," p. 23.

36. Schaff and Wace, "On the Spirit," Vol. VIII, p. 23.

37. Toal, "The Meaning of Pentecost," Vol. Three, p. 32.

CHAPTER TWO

1. Schaff, "Homily IV," Vol. XII, p.296.

2. ibid., p.297.

3. ibid.

4. ibid., "Homily XV," p.354.

5. ibid., "Homily V," p.301.

6. Averky, *Apocalypse,* p.91.

7. Palmer, Sherrard, Ware, "Love," (97), Vol. Three, p.328.

8. Schaff, "Homily VI," Vol. XII, p.308.

9. Lossky, *Theology,* p.81–82.

10. Winter, "The Likeness of God," (Day 100).

11. Schaff, "Homily IV," Vol. XII, p.297.

12. ibid., p.299.

13. ibid., p.298.

14. Toal, "The Eucharist in Prophecy," Vol. Three, p.113.

15. ibid., "The Leaven of Holiness," Vol. One, p.353.

16. Roberts and Donaldson, "The Epistle of Polycarp," Vol. I, p.34.

CHAPTER THREE

1. Chrysostom; Toal, "The Transfiguration of Christ," Vol. Two, p.54–55.

2. Schaff, "Homily XXII on the Epistle to the Hebrews," Vol. XIV, p.467.

3. Roberts and Donaldson, "Epistle of Mathetes to Diognetus," Vol. I, p.28.

4. Lossky, *Theology*, p.86.

5. R. Payne Smith, "On the Incarnation," *Commentary on the Gospel of St. Luke*, note 1, p.52.

6. Berthold, "Chapters on Knowledge," (90), p.145.

7. Schaff, "Homily VI on Second Corinthians," Vol. XII, p.307.

8. ibid., "Homily VII," p.310–11.

9. ibid., "Homily VI," p.307.

10. Alexander Schmemann, *The Eucharist*, p.104.

11. Schaff, "Homily IV," Vol. XII, p.299.

12. ibid., "Homily XI on the Epistle to the Romans," Vol XI, p.411.

13. ibid., "Homily VII," Vol. XII, p.312.

14. ibid.

15. ibid., p.311.

16. ibid., p.312, note 4.

17. ibid., "Homily XIX on Romans," Vol. XI, p.488.

18. ibid., "Homily VII," Vol. XII, p.314.

19. Schaff and Wace, "Against the Heathen," Vol. IV, p.5.

20. Justin explains *knives of stone* as "the words preached by the Apostles of the corner-stone cut out without hands." Roberts and Donaldson, "Dialogue of Justin, Philosopher and Martyr, with Trypho, A Jew," Vol. I, p.256.

21. ibid., p.206.

22. Schmemann, p.115.

23. Harakas, "Capital Punishment" (39), Social Issues, Part IV, p.154–7.

24. Vassiliadis, *The Mystery of Death*, p.164.

25. Photios Kontoglou, *Ekphrasis*, p.180.

26. Toal, "On the Gospel," Vol. One, p.382.

27. Schaff, "Homily VI," Vol. XII, p.308.

28. ibid.

29. Palmer, Sherrard, Ware, "The Raising of the Intellect," (62), Vol. Three, p.312.

30. Schaff, "Homily VII," Vol. XII, p.314.

CHAPTER FOUR

1. Chrysostomos, *The Ancient Fathers of the Desert*, p.66.

2. Palmer, Sherrard, Ware, "The Freedom of the Intellect," (143), Vol. Three, p.350.

3. Berthold, "Four Hundred Chapters on Love" (55), p.81.

4. Schaff and Wace, "Against the Heathen," Vol. IV, p.5.

5. Palmer, Sherrard, Ware, "The Freedom of the Intellect," (149), Vol. Three, p.353.

6. Roberts and Donaldson, "The Epistle to Diognetus," Vol. I, p.27–8.

7. Toal, "Prayer for the Future Life," Vol. Four, p.347.

8. Schaff, "Homily IX on Second Corinthians," Vol. XII, p.322.

9. ibid., "Homily VII," p.317.

10. ibid., "Homily IX," p.325.

11. Schaff and Wace, "Against the Heathen," Vol. IV, p.6.

12. Toal, "The Leaven of Holiness," Vol. One, p.355.

13. ibid., "The First Sunday of Lent," Vol. Two, p.6.

14. ibid., "Man is Delivered by Trials: Mystical Joy," Vol. Four, p.198.

15. ibid., "First Sunday of Lent," Vol. Two, p.4.

16. Schaff and Wace, "The Hexaemeron," Vol. VIII, p.78.

17. Toal, "Prayer for the Future Life," Vol. Four, p.347.

CHAPTER FIVE

1. Roberts and Donaldson, "Fragments of the Lost Work of Justin on the Resurrection," Vol. I, p.297.

2. Chrysostom; Schaff, "Homily X," Vol. XII, p.327.

3. Philip Schaff and Henry Wace, "Lecture IV" (30), *NPNF*, Second Series, Vol. VII, *St. Cyril of Jerusalem, St. Gregory Nazianzen*, p.26.

4. Toal, "On the Consolation of Death, Second Sermon," Vol. Four, p.360.

5. Roberts & Donaldson, "Fragments from the Lost Writings of Irenaeus," Vol. I, p.570.

6. Schaff and Wace, "Lecture XV," (23 and 25), Vol. VII, p.111–12.

7. Panayiotis Nellas, "Garments of Skin," *Deification in Christ*, p.46–53.

8. Lossky, *Image*, p.222.

9. Roberts and Donaldson, "Against Heresies," Vol. I, p.540.

10. ibid., p.531.

11. Toal, "On the Consolation of Death, First Sermon," Vol. Four, p.318.

12. Lossky, *Theology*, p.83.

13. ibid., p.113.

14. ibid., p.92.

15. Toal, "On the Consolation of Death, First Sermon," Vol. Four, p.318.

16. ibid., "The Leaven of Holiness," Vol. One, p.354.

17. Maxwell Staniforth, "The Blessedness of Christian Love," (49), *Early Christian Writings, The Apostolic Fathers*, p.49.

18. ibid., (50), p.49.

19. Schaff, "Homily XI on Second Corinthians," Vol. XII, p.333.

20. Ware, *Church*, p.279.

21. Winter, "The Difference," (Day 5).

22. Lossky, *Image*, p.97.

23. Schaff and Wace, "Letter CCXXXIV," Vol. VIII, p.274.

24. John Meyendorff, "Essence and Energies in God," *Gregory Palamas, The Triads*, p.108.

25. Lossky, *Image*, p.56 and note 27.

26. Meyendorff, "The Uncreated Glory," p.88.

27. Ware, *Church*, p.68.

28. Schaff and Wace, "Letter CLXXXIX," Vol. VIII, p.231.

29. Toal, "The Resurrection of the Body," Vol. Four, p.123–5.

30. ibid., "On the Consolation of Death, Second Sermon," p.359.

31. ibid., "The Resurrection of the Body," p.126–7.

32. Ware, *Way*, p.136.

33. Toal, "The Resurrection of the Body," Vol. Four, p.128.

34. Roberts and Donaldson, "Against Heresies," Vol. I, p.561.

35. ibid., "On the Resurrection," Vol. I, p.295.

36. Palmer, Sherrard, Ware, "Texts on Watchfulness," (20), Vol. Three, p.24.

37. Toal, "On the Resurrection of the Dead, Second Sermon," Vol. Four, p.386.

38. ibid., p.400–2.

39. Schaff and Wace, "Lecture XVIII," (19), Vol. VII, p.139.

40. Toal, "On the Resurrection of the Dead, Second Sermon," Vol. Four, p.395.

41. Schaff, "Homily IX on First Corinthians," Vol. XII, p.49.

42. Athanasios S. Frangopoulos, "The Completion of Redemption," *Our Orthodox Christian Faith*, p.239.

43. Schaff and Wace, "Against the Heathen," (33), Vol. IV, p.21.

44. Frangopoulos, "The Completion of all Things," p.249.

45. Palmer, Sherrard, Ware, "The Raising of the Intellect," (63), Vol. Three, p.312.

46. Schaff and Wace, "Lecture XV," (26), Vol. VII, p.112.

47. Schaff, "Homily X on Second Corinthians," Vol. XII, p.330.

CHAPTER SIX

1. Schaff, "Homily XII on Second Corinthians," Vol XII, p.336.

2. ibid., "Homily XV," p.353.

3. ibid., "Homily XII," p.338.

4. ibid., "Homily XIV on First Corinthians," p.80.

5. ibid., "Homily XII on Second Corinthians," p.338.

6. Toal, "On Jesus Ascending to Jerusalem," Vol. One, p.414.

7. Colm Luibheid and Norman Russell, "Step 22," (On Vainglory), *John Climacus, The Ladder of Divine Ascent*, p.205.

8. Toal, "On the Mystical Church," Vol. One, p.94.

9. Schaff, "Homily XII," p.339.

10. Luibheid and Russell, "Step 30," (On Faith, Hope, and Love), *Ladder*, p.288.

11. Roberts and Donaldson, "Epistle to Diognetus," Vol. I, p.29.

12. Palmer, Sherrard, Ware, "Love," Vol. Three, p.254.

13. Roberts and Donaldson, "Epistle to Diognetus," Vol. I, p.29.

14. John Cassian, "Institutes," Book XII, Chap. XXIX, *Teachings on the Spiritual Life, Selected from the Writings of St. John Cassian the Roman*, p.99.

15. Schaff, "Homily XII," p.340.

CHAPTER SEVEN

1. Toal, "On the Gospel," Vol. Two, p.176.

2. Alexander Schmemann, *Great Lent, Journey to Pascha,* Appendix, p.122.

3. Toal, "On the Gospel," Vol. Two, p.22.

4. Schaff, "Homily XV," Vol. XII, p.350.

5. Palmer, Sherrard, Ware, "Treasury of Divine Knowledge," Vol. Three, p.88.

6. Schaff, "Homily XV," Vol. XII, p.352.

7. ibid., "Homily XIII," p.345.

8. Winter, "The Word, our Instructor," (Day 52).

9. Toal, "On Envy," Vol. Four, p.142.

10. Schaff, "Homily IX," Vol. XIII, p.229.

11. Toal, "The Christian Manner of Life," Vol. Three, p.239.

12. Winter, "Helping those who Have Fallen Away," (Day 50).

13. Velimirovic, Part One, p.207.

14. Staniforth, "To Polycarp," p.127.

15. ibid., "Practical Conclusions," (10), p.181.

16. Toal, "The Leaven of Holiness," Vol. One, p.354.

17. ibid., "The Authority and Dignity of the Priesthood," Vol. Two, p.274.

CHAPTER EIGHT

1. Schaff, "Homily XVI," Vol. XII, p.357.

2. ibid., p.356.

3. Toal, "I Will Pull Down My Barns," Vol. Three, p.327.

4. Schaff, "Homily XVII," p.360.

5. Toal, "Christian Moderation," Vol. One, p.400.

6. Schaff, "Homily XIX," p.371.

7. ibid., "Homily XVII," p.361.

8. ibid.

9. ibid., "Homily XVI" p.358.

10. Toal, "Steps of the Ascent to Blessedness," Vol. Four, p.480.

11. Winter, "Enjoying our Possessions," (Day 21).

12. Luibheid and Russell, "Step 2," (On Detachment), *Ladder,* p.82.

13. ibid.

14. Schaff, "Homily XVII," p.361.

15. Toal, "I Will Pull Down my Barns," Vol. Three, p.327.

16. ibid., "On the Love of the Poor," Vol. Four, p.56.

17. ibid., "Meditation on the Mystical Supper," Vol. Three, p.156.

18. ibid., "I Will Pull Down my Barns," p.325.

19. Schaff, "Homily XVII," p.362.

CHAPTER NINE

1. Schaff, "Homily XVI," p.359.

2. ibid., "Homily XLIII on First Corinthians," p.262.

3. ibid., "Homily XIX on Second Corinthians," Vol. XII, p.370.

4. ibid., "Homily XX," p.374.

5. ibid.

6. Velimirovic, Part One, p.23.

7. Winter, "Deal with the Cause First," (Day 31).

8. Toal, "The Fountain of Alms," Vol. Three, p.311.

CHAPTER TEN

1. Palmer, Sherrard, Ware, "Texts on Watchfulness," (20), Vol. Three, p.24.

2. Stavropoulos, p.49.

3. Schaff, "Homily XXI," Vol. XII, p.376.

4. Winter, "Our Attitude to Unbelievers," (Day 25).

5. Toal, "The Tares and the Wheat," Vol. One, p.339.

6. ibid., "Meditation on the Mystery of the Word Incarnate," Vol. Four, p.167.

7. ibid., Augustine on "The Tares and the Wheat," Vol. One, p.338.

8. ibid., p.337.

9. Palmer, Sherrard and Ware, "Discrimination," Vol. Three, p.152.

10. Luibheid and Russell, "Step 25," (On Humility), *Ladder*, p.218–228.

11. Palmer, Sherrard & Ware, "True Discrimination," Vol. Three, p.158.

12. ibid., "Discrimination," p.243.

13. Luibheid and Russell, "Step 26," (On Discernment), *Ladder*, p.229

14. Ware, *Church*, p.204. See also John Chryssavgis, "In the Heart of the Desert: The Spirituality of the Desert Fathers and Mothers," p.4.

CHAPTER ELEVEN
1. Toal, "First Sunday of Lent," Vol. Two, p.21.
2. Schaff, "Homily XXIV," Vol. XII, p.390.
3. ibid., "Homily XXIII," p.389.
4. ibid.
5. Toal, "On the Mystical Church," Vol. One, p.92.
6. Schaff, "Homily XXV," p.396.
7. ibid.
8. ibid., "Homily XXIII," p.389.
9. ibid.
10. ibid., p.390.
11. Toal, "Christian Moderation," Vol. One, p.401.
12. Schaff, "Homily XXV," p.397.
13. Toal, "Fourth Sunday of Advent," Vol. One, p.75.

CHAPTER TWELVE
1. Meyendorff, *Triads*, p.38.
2. Schaff, "Homily XXVI," Vol. XII, p.399.
3. Lossky, *Image*, p.50.
4. Schaff, "Homily XXVI," p.401–02.
5. Lossky, *Image*, p.217.
6. Schaff, "Homily XXVIII," p.411.
7. ibid., "Homily XXVI, p.401.
8. ibid., "Homily XXVII," p.406.
9. Toal, "Against Discord and Anger," Vol. One, p.346.
10. ibid., "The Angelic Choirs," Vol. Three, p.210.
11. Schaff, "Homily XXVI," p.402.
12. Just as the righteous of old were urged to worship pagan gods (Dan 3:15), early Christians were often given the choice of paying homage to the reigning emperor and burning incense in his honor or losing their lives through a torturous death like being fed to wild beasts.
13. Staniforth, "The Martyrdom of Polycarp," (4), p.156.

CHAPTER THIRTEEN

1. Schaff, "Homily XXIX," p.414.
2. Velimirovic, Part One, p.254.
3. Schaff, "Homily XXX," p.418.
4. Schmemann, *Eucharist*, p.139.
5. Schaff, "Homily XXX," p.419.

GLOSSARY

1. Patrinacos, p. 131.
2. ibid., 172.
3. Ware, *The Orthodox Church*, p. 276.